Cities of the Maya
in Seven Epochs,
1250 B.C. to A.D. 1903

Cities of the Maya in Seven Epochs, 1250 B.C. to A.D. 1903

Steve Glassman *and* Armando Anaya

McFarland & Company, Inc., Publishers
Jefferson, North Carolina, and London

LIBRARY OF CONGRESS CATALOGUING-IN-PUBLICATION DATA

Glassman, Steve.
Cities of the Maya in seven epochs, 1250 B.C. to A.D. 1903 /
Steve Glassman and Armando Anaya.
          p.   cm.
Includes bibliographical references and index.

ISBN 978-0-7864-4848-7
softcover : 50# alkaline paper ∞

1. Mayas — History.
2. Mayas — Urban residence — History.
3. Extinct cities — Mexico.
4. Extinct cities — Central America.
5. Mayas — Antiquities.
I. Anaya, Armando.
II. Title.
F1435.5.G53   2011   972'.6 — dc22   2011001144

BRITISH LIBRARY CATALOGUING DATA ARE AVAILABLE

© 2011 Steve Glassman and Armando Anaya. All rights reserved

*No part of this book may be reproduced or transmitted in any form
or by any means, electronic or mechanical, including photocopying
or recording, or by any information storage and retrieval system,
without permission in writing from the publisher.*

On the cover: El Castillo step pyramid at the
Chichen Itza site in Mexico (Digital Vision)

Manufactured in the United States of America

*McFarland & Company, Inc., Publishers
Box 611, Jefferson, North Carolina 28640
www.mcfarlandpub.com*

To Mary Van Buren and
Jenny Pavon Anaya

Table of Contents

Acknowledgments — ix

Preface — 1

1. The Proto-Maya Olmec Cities of San Lorenzo and La Venta, 1250–400 B.C.: If Not the Mother Culture, an Undisputed Similar Culture — 7
2. The Mirador Basin in Times Long Gone, 1000 B.C.–A.D. 150 — 29
3. Tikal, the Eternal City, Early Classic, A.D. 250–550 — 67
4. Calakmul and the Snakehead Dynasty, a Maya Superpower — 98
5. The Tale of Two Cities, Concluded, A.D. 695–869 — 121
6. Terminal Classic in the Yucatan, A.D. 800–1100 — 155
7. Mayapan, Tayasal, and Chan Santa Cruz — 186

References — 223

Index — 233

Acknowledgments

Thanks to all at both of our institutions for the help and assistance they have provided. At ERAU special thanks to Provost Richard Heist, Dean Bill Grams, and Chair Bob Oxley. In Campeche our gratitude extends to Maria del Rosario Dominguez Carrasco, Jose "Pepe" Aranda, Cessia Chuc, William J. Folan, and Lynda Florey Folan, among many others. No acknowledgment section would be complete without singling out Sally Duncan, Raphael Barousse, Kirk Briggs, and Randy Attwood, all of whom were supportive in many ways over the years. Bob Smith, Robert Sitler, Fernando Tzib, and Patricio Balona also must be mentioned. Duncan Haynes gets a special nod for editorial suggestions that were above and beyond. Most especially, a big round of thanks goes to Liz Davis, Sue Burkhart, and Ann Cash of the ILL department at the ERAU library. Without them this book could not have been written.

No acknowledgment section for a book like this would be complete without citing the amazing work by archaeologists and art historians over the past 35 or 40 years. A special thanks to Peter Mathews, Linda Schele, Michael Coe, Kent Reilly, David Freidel, Simon Martin and Nikolai Grube, Richard Diehl, Ian Graham, Stanley Guenter, Richard Hansen, William Ringle, George Bey, Merle Green, Justin Kerr, Norman Hammond, David Grove, Susan Gillespie, Joyce Marcus, Takeshi Inomata, David Stuart, William Demarest, Diane and Arlen Chase, Susan Milbrath, Barbara Leyden, Mark Brenner, David Hodell, Christopher Pool, Don and Prudence Rice, Robert Sharer and Loa Traxler, Ricardo Agurcia, Thomas Shreiner, Eric Hansen, Edward H. Mosely, and the many others whose names escape us at the moment but who have done so much to make known the fascinating culture of the ancient Maya. Also, Mat Saunders' remarkable Maya at the Playa conference — of national, even international, renown — must be acknowledged and thanked for bringing Maya archaeology to the people of Florida and the nation.

Preface

Heinrich Schliemann died in 1890. At the time he was one of the most famous people in the world. His fame rested on his excavation of the mythical site of Troy. Modern archaeologists agree he found, if not Troy, at least a city in the area where Troy was traditionally believed to be located. That city appeared to have been destroyed by conquest in the 13th century B.C., the very time and way Troy was said to have perished.

Schliemann may no longer be one of the best known personalities on the planet, but just about everyone knows about the battle of Troy. Almost everybody is also aware that someone named Homer, reputedly a blind poet, is supposed to have passed the tale on to us. Also known is that these events, the battle and the writings about them, stand in some fundamental way at the head of Western civilization. At the same time Troy was fighting for its survival, a high culture was rising in a remote part of North America. That culture would have the same historical reach, three thousand years, as Western civilization. Its first cities began to form in the steaming rain forests of lower Mexico about 1250 B.C., and as a folk culture, the milieu is still going strong today.

While Trojans were casting objects in gold and brass, Indian sculptors hewed lifelike faces with a strange African tilt in huge boulders, some as tall as nine feet. These people survived in the tropical jungles for seven hundred or more years; and the Olmec, as they are known today, produced what is regarded as either the mother culture of Middle America or a prime example of a sister culture. As the torch of Western civilization passed from the Greeks to the Romans, after the Olmec came the Maya. Just two hundred eighty miles from the Olmec capital of La Venta, the Preclassic Maya cities of Nakbe and El Mirador rose in what today is an even more inaccessible area of jungle in northern Guatemala. Here were erected some of the most gigantic buildings of all time. After the time of Christ, those cities fell to ruin. But the Classic Maya civilization rose in the same general area, just as the Roman Empire crumbled and the Christian religion quietly colonized Europe. For six centuries the Classic Maya held sway before suddenly the many cities in what is called now the southern lowlands winked out between A.D. 800 and 900. A very few cities on the periphery survived, but some on the far northern edge actually thrived in this time frame. The great site of Uxmal in the Mexican state of Yucatan produced splendid buildings that inspired Frank Lloyd Wright's Maya Revival style, examples of which many of us pass by every day.

Perhaps the largest Maya city of all time, which is today probably the best known and most visited, Chichen Itza, reached its peak at about the beginning of the second millennium — about the time the first European knights crusaded in the Holy Land. From then until the arrival of the Spanish conquerors, various cities in the Yucatan and the Guatemalan highlands kept the flame of Maya civilization burning. Even after the Conquest, Maya civilization held on deep in the wilderness of the Peten until almost 1700 — just a bit more than three-quarters of a century before Jefferson penned the Declaration of Independence. In the mid–19th century, before the American Civil War, a Maya rebellion almost drove the Mexicans out of the Yucatan. It took the Mexicans more than fifty years to subdue the last Maya city-state. By then Americans had fought the Spanish-American War and had signed a lease for Guantanamo Bay and gained control of Puerto Rico. In short, the Indian city-states of lower Mesoamerica began in a time so far back that Western civilization cannot track it, and it carried on in an unbroken stream until the century most of us were born.

The story of the Maya tradition began to be told in earnest in the 1840s. That was when John Lloyd Stephens, often called the father of Mesoamerican archaeology, and Frederick Catherwood came to the realization there was a coherent civilization spanning lower Mexico and upper Central America. They named the culture the Maya, adapting the word of the Yucatec speakers for the entire culture. At first, excepting Stephens and Catherwood, the amateur archaeologists and savants studying this civilization did a poor job of making sense of their subjects. Truth be told, even the professionals, up until after World War II, searched pretty much in darkness. But today, thanks to the breaking of the Maya hieroglyphic code in the 1970s and the application of rigorous principles of scientific archaeology, much is known about this people. Thousands of papers and hundreds of books have been written on them. So what, you may ask, is the point of this book?

Almost all good books on the Maya are written by archaeologists (or Maya art historians). They know what they are talking about. The bad news is that archaeologists, almost without exception, write for other archaeologists. So unless you are already versed in the topic, such as a graduate student of Mesoamerican (Middle American) archaeology or art history, it is virtually impossible to understand what the authors are saying. The book in your hands meets the needs of those with an interest in the Maya, but who have not yet developed a professional interest in the topic.

Thirty years ago, I (the first-named author, Steve) received an object lesson in what is meant by the term "lost world of the Maya." My friend Father Raphael Barousse, his nephew Kirk, and I had chartered a small plane in Guatemala City with the intention of flying to the famed Maya ruins of Tikal. The site lies in the heart of Guatemala's outback province, Peten. It had been a bright sunny day when we left the city, high in its mountain valley. Then clouds developed, and after a while the pilot fidgeted a bit, looked back, and said he thought we were about there. The plane slipped beneath the clouds, and below, as far as the eye could see, stretched nothing but forest canopy. Father Raphael, an old Guatemalan hand, was a bit sore about a halfhearted attempt by the charter folks to gouge him for a higher fee. He said under his breath, "This guy is lost." We flew for what seemed a very long time. Then a palpable sense of relief enveloped all as the pilot spotted a fiery red gash in the forest. It was a dirt road, or rather a mud trail. The pilot followed the trail, and after a while, sticking up through the canopy of the forest, were the distinctive A-frame roof combs of Tikal's Temples I and II and farther back Temples III and IV. I am not sure if I was more impressed by the sight of the lost city of Tikal or the vastness of that unbroken forest below.

After visiting Tikal and a number of other Maya ruins on a couple of forays into Middle America, I knew I wanted to write a book about the Maya. By profession I am a teacher of writing, and I felt that writer's urge to somehow process this material. I chose for my first entry a relatively easy topic, that of Stephens, the modern discoverer of the Maya. All the same I was plunged into the murky world of Maya history (and prehistory). I struggled for years trying to make sense of a civilization represented by an enormous number of sites spanning five states in Mexico and parts of four other countries. But geography was not the principal enemy to understanding. The Maya's enormous span in time and the sometimes muddled state of archaeology posed more serious obstacles. For the book on Stephens, I merely had to sort out the drift of modern archaeology vis-à-vis the first great Maya explorer. I puzzled all that through and published the book.

But the Stephens book was only the tip of the pyramid. I understood there was a story in the three thousand year sweep of Maya history that had not yet been plainly told. Sure, archaeologists were aware of the story. But the average person who watched the Maya specials on cable TV or who vacationed in Cancun and out of curiosity visited Chichen Itza, Coba, or Tulum, got the impression the Maya was a fly-trapped-in-amber civilization that mysteriously disappeared a thousand or so years ago. In truth, as noted above, the cities in only one area collapsed at that time, and by then the Middle American civilization had been purring along for two thousand years and would continue to chug along for another thousand.

All of this could be learned in any good Maya textbook. But textbooks tend to focus on general principles — and cover all aspects of the topic. More specialized Maya books, despite their authors' valiant attempts to do otherwise, frequently talk about the individual trees and neglect the woods. The book I conceived would tell about the forest, meaning it would give an overview without getting lost in detail. It might even neglect a few confusing elements such as a detailed description of Maya calendrics. For sure it wouldn't dip into any discussions of pottery, essential to the archaeologist but absolutely unintelligible to the ordinary reader. Naturally a topic that could not be overlooked is how the various cities met their ends. That is almost always a burning question to anyone becoming interested in the Maya, and it helps focus the attention of the reader. Because it is almost impossible to think of the physical location of Troy today without discussing Schliemann and what he did, I would recount the difficulties the archaeologists had ferreting out the secrets of their sites.

There was only one problem with this ambitious outline. By training and background, I wasn't really up to the task. So I turned to my friend, the professional archaeologist Armando Anaya. Armando was born in Mexico City, raised to a great extent in Pittsburgh, and received his graduate education, including a doctorate, in Canada, of which country he is a citizen. He currently holds the position of research archaeologist at the Autonomous University of Campeche in the state of Campeche, Mexico. Armando has vast experience as an archaeologist, spanning areas as diverse as British Columbia and Australia. His mentor, Peter Mathews, is one of the three persons widely credited with providing the final impetus for breaking the Maya hieroglyphic code.

Armando once almost gave his life for Maya archaeology. The unhappy event occurred in the hinterlands of Chiapas, Mexico. In fact, both he and Mathews were reported as dead at the hands of a band of outlaw Maya. The men had been beaten senseless and left for dead, their money and equipment stolen. Their supposed widows were flown from Canada to Mexico. Little imagination is required to conjure the women's glee on finding their husbands had survived by swimming the mighty Usumacinta at night. They hid out for days from the bandits. On returning to Canada, the Tsuu Tína Nation, a plains Indian tribe, invited Armando to a meeting. Supposedly, the meeting was about his work among them. On arrival, he was inducted into the tribe because of the great courage he showed during the crisis in Chiapas. The name of "Running Elk" was conferred on him. In short, Armando is a man that knows not only the scholarly world of ancient Mesoamerica but the true jungle as well.

Together Armando and I have devised the book in your hands. In order to provide an understanding of the complex cultures of lower Middle America, we break the three thousand year time span into seven chapters and give vignettes of the goings on in an individual area during each of those times. We will start with the Olmec (1250–400 B.C.). That chapter of the book gives a general orientation of the way the lowland peoples of the area lived. Of particular interest in that chapter is the means by which Mesoamerican monarchs based their power to rule—on shamanistic rites similar to those discussed by Carlos Castaneda in his wildly successful book, *The Teachings of Don Juan*. Knowing about the mystical nature of Mesoamerican kingship helps a lot in terms of understanding the culture. A chapter is devoted to the Preclassic megacity of El Mirador and its near neighbor Nakbe (1000 B.C. to A.D. 150, more or less), which fell not long after the time of Christ. It was discovered in the 20th century with the help of Charles Lindbergh and his pioneering efforts of remote sensing. In this chapter we discuss the Maya creation myth of the Hero Twins and show how it helped organize Maya society. In short, we learn that the myth sanctioned divine kingship. The institution of kingship directed the Maya to erect huge buildings and to develop the cultural traits admired widely today. Three chapters will center on the best-known period of the Maya, the Classic (A.D. 250–800), when the Maya reached their maximum development culturally and physically in the southern lowlands. It was in this period that the Maya left a written record of their history that scholars only learned to read in the past several decades. In these chapters we will talk about the power struggle between the megacities of Tikal and Calakmul. We will discuss the feats of some of the great kings of the period. You will learn which city-state became the ultimate winner, and we talk about the surprising upshot of that victory. We also talk about how, one by one, the various cities in the central area collapsed. After that we will take up the Maya in the Terminal Classic in the northern Yucatan (A.D. 800–1100, more or less). The two most visited great Maya sites, Uxmal and Chichen Itza, flourished in this period. We conclude with a section on the Maya in the Postclassic (A.D. 1100–1546, more or less), colonial (A.D. 1546–1821) and republican (A.D. 1821 on) periods. In the latter time, long after Mexican independence, the last Maya city-state flourished for fifty years in the Quintano Roo area of the Yucatan.

Maya names are incredibly confusing for several reasons. First there is the name itself. Waxaklahun-Ubah-K'awil, for instance, is the official moniker of the 13th king of Copan. In the days before the Maya hieroglyphs were read, he was called 18 Rabbit. Some professional Mayanists decided 18 Rabbit was not dignified enough. They called him 18 Jog. In Maya texts today you can encounter him going under any of these three names, and perhaps others as well. To take another example, the great king of Tikal, the man who recouped the city's fortunes, is variously known as Jasaw Chan, Jasau Kan, Hasaw Chan or Hasaw Kan. We call him by his name in English translation, Heavenly Standard Bearer. Similarly, we refer to 18 Rabbit as 18 Rabbit, and always use the name that has the highest "memory peg" potential. Likewise, we have dispensed with accent marks in order to keep the prose as spare and simple as possible. Measurements have been converted into the English standard commonly used in the United States (inches, feet, miles) and temperatures are given in Fahrenheit. Speaking of measurements (as well as other concepts), we follow the author of the papers cited. This on occasion leads to incongruity in the text. At one point we might say, for instance, that Structure 2 at Calakmul is 150 feet tall and another that it is 180 feet. Because of the remoteness of most Maya sites, no independent authority has yet taken readings of such things. We simply follow the author we are citing at the time. Likewise with the datings of sites; they are plastic entities and can change considerably from author to author.

Similarly, we try to use the common English word for concepts for which specialists prefer technical terms. For instance, we say "coronation" when discussing a king's taking power. The specialist would prefer using the term "accession." The specialist has good reasons for using that term, but when covering three thousand years of a civilization, the reader has a difficult enough time following the narrative without juggling a slew of technical terms. To avoid the confusion too much detail might bring, we want to give an overview. For the fine points, go to the many books and papers written by the specialists on specific areas, many of which can be found online.

Finally, a word about blood sacrifice, one of the more interesting customs of the peoples of Mesoamerica. At first blush it may seem wholly beyond the bounds of understanding, but closer attention shows parallels in Western culture. Blood sacrifice was practiced voluntarily on one's self by opening blood vessels. Stingray spines or pieces of obsidian or flint were used to prick, slice or gouge extremely sensitive areas of the body. The pain attendant to this practice produced hallucinations that transported the subject to nether realms to commune with forbears and other beings. All this was an integral part of Maya religious observances.

Blood sacrifice was also practiced involuntarily on animals, captives, and slaves whose lives were taken for religious purposes. The universe to the early Mesoamericans was interactive. They were required — as they saw it — to give blood to nourish the gods. They gave blood and suffering, and they got back the necessities of life: sun, rain, corn, general prosperity. You do not have to look far in the cultural history of the West to see similar practices. The Bible tells us of animal sacrifice, and just about everyone knows the story of Abraham. He was about to put his son Isaac to the knife as a sacrifice to God when the young man was given a reprieve. One wonders how many other sons or captives or slaves were not as lucky as Isaac. And then, of course, the central event in Christianity is the self-chosen death of the son of God to redeem the sins of humankind. This sacrifice is ritually reenacted weekly, daily even, at Christian tabernacles around the world. Also, the Christian notion of doing physical penance, such as kneeling for long stretches, seems akin to minor forms of bloodletting.

Aside from being a mysterious and fascinating

Detail from Gran Pyramid, Uxmal. Some scholars believe the Caribbean pirates adapted their trademark skull and crossbones from the Maya (courtesy INAH).

people, the Maya have given us many of the things we take for granted. Some of these everyone knows about, such as chocolate. But many of the most important have — for whatever reason — not been much discussed. What would a North American holiday or festivity be without a ball game? It seems likely that the Maya (or their Mesoamerican peers) contributed mightily to the invention of the generic game that gave the world its favorite sports. This game was much like a cross between soccer and basketball — with giant stone hoops placed vertically rather than horizontally on the walls of the court. The Spanish carried the rubber ball and the concept of a ball game to Europe, where it mixed with other traditions and returned to our shores to be reinvented in its many forms. For as central as the ball game is to the North American cultural psyche, it pales in comparison to the importance of corn in our diet and our culture. As hard as it may be to believe, we eat more corn, both proportionately and per capita, than any Maya lord ever did. Most of our corn is first fed to animals (beef, pork, chicken, dairy cattle), which then feed the North American consumer. The race of maize that allowed the Midwestern Corn Belt to thrive is amazingly closely related to the kind of corn that adapted to the tropical lowlands of the Maya area, and which is credited with the rise of that civilization.

Probably the best venue for the material you will find in this book, to date, has been the specials on cable TV. Unfortunately, they are uneven in quality and episodic. What we offer here is cut up into bite-size pieces, and the material is fairly easy to digest. On the other hand, the reader will get a full appreciation for the Maya. In some regards the Maya are vastly different from us, but in other ways they have contributed greatly to the making of the present culture in North America. We are pleased to offer a book anyone with little or no understanding of the early peoples of this continent can understand. We hope you enjoy it.

1

The Proto-Maya Olmec Cities of San Lorenzo and La Venta, 1250–400 B.C.: If Not the Mother Culture, an Undisputed Similar Culture

Mesoamerica starts just below the desert areas of northern Mexico and runs in an east southeasterly direction, to the upper reaches of Central America. It was here that the Maya, the Aztec, the Mixtec, the Totonac, and the Olmec, among other peoples, developed sophisticated cultures sharing a number of characteristics. They all erected monumental architecture, observed sophisticated calendars, played a ritually significant ball game, contrived systems of writing, and developed complicated mythologies and religions.

The Maya, who occupied the lower parts of Mesoamerica, are universally acknowledged to have taken many of these traits to the highest level. However, they borrowed freely from the other cultures of the area. For instance, the Long Count calendar, one of the Maya's crowning intellectual achievements with its starting date of mid–August 3114 B.C., was devised elsewhere but brought to fruition by the Maya. Maya writing was the only Mesoamerican system that could be used to take down human speech verbatim. Nevertheless, the basics of the system appear to have been borrowed from other peoples of Mesoamerica.

At present, the relationship of the Olmec to the Maya and other societies of Mesoamerica is hotly debated. For many years it was universally believed that Olmec was the mother culture of the Maya and others. Many scholars, such as Michael Coe of Yale University and Richard Diehl of the University of Alabama, still adhere to this position. To them, an intelligent discussion of the Maya could not start without the Olmec. A counterposition is articulated by David Grove of the University of Florida, Joyce Marcus of the University of Michigan, James Garber of Texas State University, Jaimie Awe, head archaeologist of Belize, and author Armando Anaya, among others. They believe the Olmec were just one of many sister cultures that developed at the same time in Mesoamerica. Everyone, however, agrees that the Olmec were the first to develop monumental architecture and sculpture. The Olmec also lived in a tropical lowland similar to the Maya city-states discussed in this book (although the Maya developed cities in the highlands too). All archaeologists would agree a discussion of the Olmec offers insight into cultural practices the Maya either developed

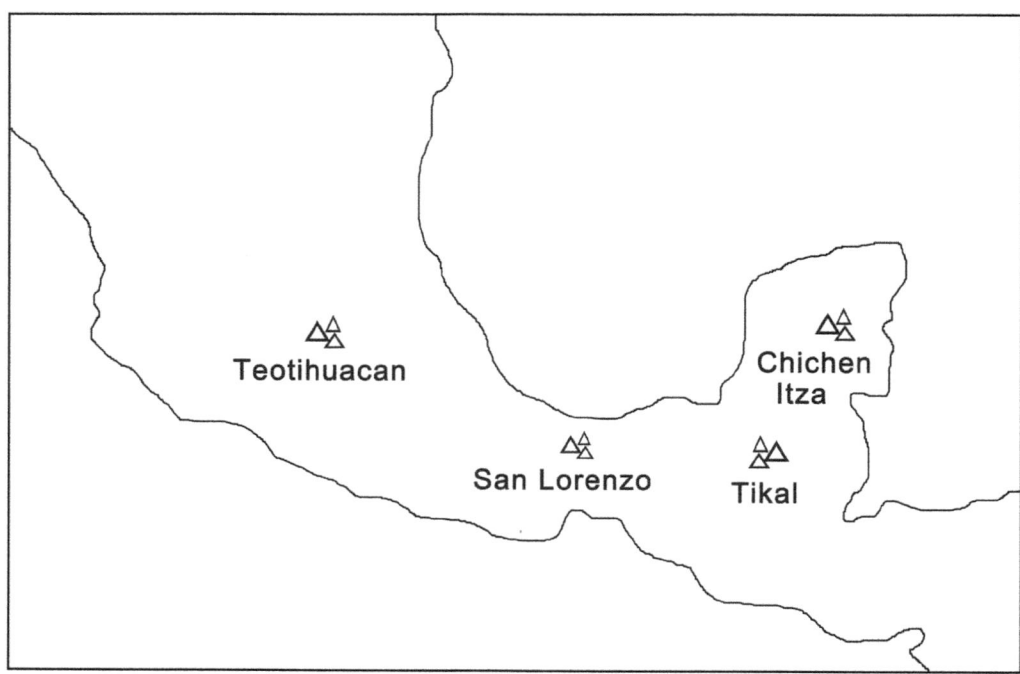

Map of Mesoamerica with representative sites, which flourished at various times during the long period of Mesoamerican high culture from at least 1250 B.C. at San Lorenzo up until the Spanish Conquest in the early 16th century of the Christian era. The last traditional Maya city-state of Tahyasal/Nojpeten (not shown) did not fall to Spanish arms until 1697.

on their own simultaneously or adopted from their neighbors. For these reasons we start our work on the Maya with a discussion of the Olmec.

Early Discovery and Exploration, the 1850s Through the 1960s

In the years before the American Civil War, a worker on Hueyapan Hacienda in the Mexican state of Veracruz found what he thought was an upside-down kettle, one of the industrial sort used to boil sugar cane sap into molasses. After receiving permission from the mayordomo, he scooped bits of mud and grass from around the dome. As he anticipated, this revealed an even larger portion of the supposed kettle. When his machete rapped the bottom, it rang hard and true, the way an iron kettle would. He dug furiously. There was no need for caution because a rusted cauldron was worthless. The campesino became more and more excited as the sides of the kettle became exposed. It was in fine shape, no hint of rust.

But the sides did not flare sharply inward as a cane kettle would have. The trench continued straight down. Appearing out of the mud was a knob where no knob would be found on a regular kettle. In due course, the knob looked like a nose, a pug nose, with a chunk taken out of it. And on the sides there were ears. And farther down a mouth. The man had found an almost perfect representation of a human head. But it was a giant's head, six feet tall from chin to top of head.

1. The Proto-Maya Olmec Cities of San Lorenzo and La Venta, 1250–400 B.C.

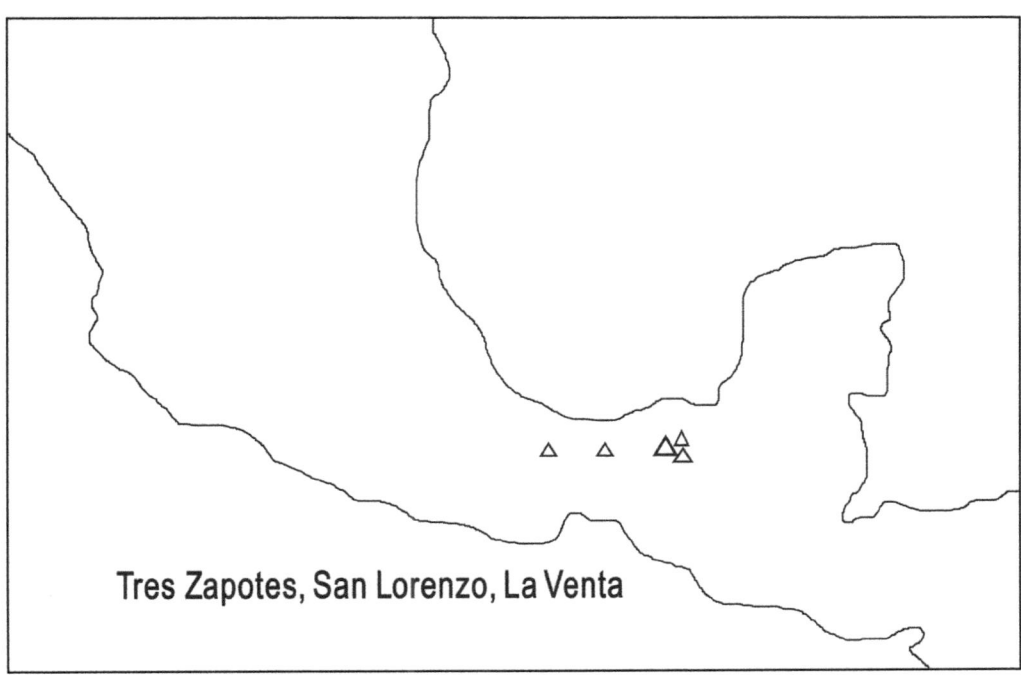

Tres Zapotes, San Lorenzo, La Venta

Three Olmec sites. San Lorenzo's dates are approximately 1250–900 B.C. and La Venta's are 900–400 B.C. Tres Zapotes (800 B.C.–A.D. 900) was the last of these sites to develop into a large center and persisted much later (Pool 2007).

What to make of this? No one had a clue. The find was fit for a 19th century Mexican Ripley's Believe It or Not. Local folk came, looked in the hole, shook their heads, and wandered away. No one had seen anything like it and could not make head nor tail of it. In due course, Mexican scholar J. M. Melgar got wind of the giant statue. On visiting the site, he wrote in a local professional bulletin that the head "measured two yards in height with corresponding proportions" (quoted in Coe 1968). He judged it to be "a work of art; it is without exaggeration a magnificent sculpture." Few modern commentators would disagree with that sentiment. He noted that the piece exhibited a flat nose and thick lips, and then he took off on a flight of fantasy, characteristic of scholars of the time, saying that "there had undoubtedly been Negroes in this country."

Over the years others visited the head, including French adventurer-Mayanist, Desiree Charnay, and the distinguished German scholar, Eduard Seler. They viewed it toward the end of the 19th or early in the 20th century, but neither they nor anyone else were able to supply a context for this astonishing find. Today, of course, these giant stone heads are among the most recognizable artifacts of New World archaeology. They have entered the popular consciousness as Olmec heads. As impressive as the colossal heads might be, art historians have noted little work was needed to produce this stupendous effect. Step one required locating a suitable boulder. Being round, it was relatively easy to roll to the site of display. Once there, minimal artistry was required to reduce it to a likeness of a human head (Drucker 1981). Strangely, neither the first head, now called the Hueyapan Head, nor any other was particularly significant in the identification or deciphering of the Olmec culture, even though another fairly large stone monument did play a large role in that process.

This monument was considerably smaller than the Hueyapan Head, standing only about four feet high. It was of a representation of a two-thirds life-size figure with a mask stacked on its head. The mask showed a surly clown mouth, almond eyes, and a divided forehead. It was these characteristics, the downturned mouth, slant eyes, and divided (or cleft) forehead that would come to be the chief marks of the Olmec culture, so far as archaeologists were concerned. The monument was discovered by the Mexican engineer Ismael Loya in 1897 while surveying San Martin Pajapan volcano, the highest peak in the Tuxtla range of mountains in Veracruz. He found the volcano to be a shade under 4,000 feet, and in the saddle between the twin points of the volcano, sat the monument. More than a quarter of a century went by before the significance of the monument as a marker of a new and important civilization was discovered. The man who tipped the world to this fact was Frans Blom.

Blom was born in 1893 in Denmark to a family of substance and sophistication. The family business assembled and sold International Harvester equipment. The family expected him to enter the firm and in due course become chief executive. The only problem was Blom's lack of interest. He took courses in the local university in art and drawing, among other things, and whiled away his time. After a hitch in the Danish navy, he headed to Mexico in 1919 where he signed on with the Eagle Oil Company. By coincidence, the company was headquartered in Minatitlan on the mighty Coatzacoalcos River. This grubby oil town was in the very heart of Olmec country; but Blom did not come to that realization at the time nor did he discover the site of San Lorenzo, now believed to be the first capital of the Olmecs, just a few miles upstream. His job was paymaster to the company's 3,000 employees. Bored with such a tame job, he asked to be sent into the field as a factotum to an exploration crew. In his spare time, he visited archaeological sites and, being fluent in English, French and German, read archaeological texts to make sense of what he saw. After three years, he obtained employment with the precursor of INAH, the powerful Mexican agency of history and archaeology. The pay was much less than that of the oil company, but finally — Blom was pushing 30 — he had found his life's work. All this led ultimately to a meeting with Sylvanus Morley.

Morley was the head of the Carnegie Institution of Washington's efforts in the Maya world. He was arguably the most important Mayanist in Mesoamerica at the time. Morley was impressed by the vast number of the sites Blom had visited, many of which were unknown to the great Mayanist. More importantly, Blom's talent as an artist and his education were both useful attributes. In time, Morley made him an offer. Blom would receive a master's degree from Harvard by studying during the fall

Hueyapan Head first described by Mexican scholar, J. M. Melgar at Tres Zapotes, Veracruz, in the mid nineteenth century. Note the slight defacement which occurred in ancient times when the power in the monument was ritually killed. On-site Museum Tres Zapotes, Veracruz (courtesy INAH).

semester when the rains prevented field work. Tuition was waived, and a stipend of a hundred dollars a month was provided for living expenses. During the dry season, Blom would toil in one of Morley's two on-going projects. The site Morley assigned him to was Uaxactun, not far from Tikal, in Guatemala's outback province of the Peten. Blom was unhappy with this choice. Access was through Belize (British Honduras), geographically close but far distant by transportation routes from the mountainous areas of Mexico he had come to love. Then fortune smiled on Blom once again.

Only one foreigner challenged Morley as the most important North American Mayanist in Mesoamerican at the time. That man was William E. Gates. Gates was widely loathed by establishment American archaeologists, but his scholarship was respected. One reason for this disdain was his outsider status. After making a fortune as a printer in his youth, he assembled the largest private collection of scholarly work on Mesoamerica in the world. Another reason was the man's cantankerousness. Gates set himself up to challenge the institutional scholars in the great universities and institutions. For instance, he finagled himself the post of head archaeologist in Guatemala. As such, he tried to block Morley's project in Uaxactun — unsuccessfully. In the States as head of a group called the Maya Society, he blackballed Morley, causing the dissolution of the organization. Now a golden opportunity was handed him to put a burr under Morley's saddle blanket. The president of Tulane University in New Orleans talked the local banana magnate, Samuel Zemurray, into making a $300,000 grant for a Mesoamerican center. Gates gifted the university the lion's share of his scholarly collection on the condition he be named head of the center. His first task was finding an assistant to undertake an expedition surveying the jungles of Mexico for archaeological ruins. He offered the job to Blom. As it happened, Morley was caught in a lurch at the time, being between grants from the Carnegie Institution of Washington. He grudgingly gave Blom leave to take the job. As a parting shot, he noted that it sometimes happened that underlings became directors of institutes.

This brought Blom, who would become one of the best known Mayanists, to the top of San Martin Pajapan volcano. He rediscovered the monument with the mask stacked atop its head. Blom's contribution to Olmec discovery seemed modest at the time. He merely noted that the stacked mask with its almond eyes, downturned mouth, and cleft forehead resembled a carved jade he'd seen in a Mexico City museum (Blom and LaFarge 1926). He presented this insight as an offhand observation, but it is clear from the details highlighted in the illustration, he understood the observation was significant. That drawing and his brief discussion of it gave rise to the now widely debated (and sometimes despised) theory that the Olmec is the mother culture of all Middle American civilizations.

His second Olmec find amounted to the largest, most important site of the culture. It was located in the neighboring state of Tabasco in an area Cortes had passed four hundred years before. In fact, the ruins had been reported by one of the first writers on Mexico, Bernal Diaz. Diaz accompanied Cortes and chronicled his exploits in his classic, *Conquest of Mexico* (as will be discussed in the last chapter of this book). He also planted seeds of an orange on the ruins of La Venta. Blom thereby proclaimed La Venta the spot at which citrus was introduced to the New World. Little did he know that in a few short years the site would be hailed as one of the first cities in North America.

He summarized the site as "a collection of huge stone monuments and at least one large pyramid. The Maya features in Stela 2, the standing figure with the diagonal ceremonial bar and the huge head-dress, are so strong that we are inclined to ascribe these ruins to the Maya culture." Blom failed to note the differences between many of the monuments at

LaVenta and the Maya. Maya art is two-dimensional and busy (compared to Olmec art). Some of the monuments at La Venta, on the other hand, were three-dimensional and bristling with tension, an unusual ingredient in primitive art. Some were the large stone heads that came to typify Olmec art to the world at large. In fairness to Blom, it should be noted that many of the La Venta monuments were two-dimensional in typical Maya fashion. And he was on an expedition looking for Maya material. At La Venta he assumed he found it.

Blom went on to visit about a hundred sites on the 1925 expedition. Back in New Orleans, he married a wealthy socialite and edged out, à la Morley's prediction, the cranky William Gates as the director of the institute at Tulane. But shortly Blom slipped into alcoholism, got the boot, and retreated to a mountaintop in the Mexican state of Chiapas (Brunhouse 1976). He named his estate Na Bolom, a play on his name and the word for jaguar, *balam,* in many of the 30 or so Mayan languages. From there he continued studying the Maya, especially the contemporary Lacandon, the only unsubdued Maya group. He died in 1963. His second wife, Gertrude, continued his work until the early 1990s. His house is still a functioning institution in the highland city of San Cristobal de las Casas concerned with Lacandon issues. His work on the discovery of the Olmec, however unwitting, stands among his greatest achievements. Here's why.

In a review of Blom's book, a German scholar noted that he, too, had had a statuette collected from a site in Mexico that resembled the monument at San Martin Pajapan (Coe 1968). Others seconded the opinion about the resemblance of small pieces to Blom's volcano-top monument. Those figurines, sometimes carved, sometimes ceramic, had been recovered from sites throughout southern and central Mexico. On the Pacific coast, similar items had been found as far south as Honduras, San Salvador, and even Costa Rica. These figures were characterized by oval eyes, thick lips, a distorted, angry-looking mouth, and a "cleft" head. The snarling mouth was believed to represent stylized fangs. Quite a few of the figures were of children or child-like beings, many of them displaying mongoloid features. Others were of jaguars in human poses.

These objects were dubbed "were-jaguars." The term is used in the same sense that the Lon Chaney film character was called a werewolf, sometimes man, sometimes wolf or wolflike. Because Blom's San Martin Pajapan monument was too heavy to have been moved far, scholars surmised the culture that produced these objects was centered near the volcano. George Vaillant, associate curator at the American Museum of Natural

This full-figured sculpture of an unknown LaVenta king shows the tension with which Olmec sculptors, working with stone tools, infused their works. On-site Museum, La Venta, Tabasco (courtesy INAH).

1. The Proto-Maya Olmec Cities of San Lorenzo and La Venta, 1250–400 B.C.

Top left: Representation of Blom's drawing of the San Martin Pajapan monument in *Tribes and Temples.* In subsequent years many figurines were found displaying the were-jaguar motif of the top mask. Illustration by John Wilton from Blom's original in *Tribes and Temples. Top right:* Reproduction of head and stacked mask of a San Martin Pajapan-like monument. Museum of Villahermosa Archaeological Park, Villahermosa, Tabasco (courtesy INAH). *Right:* Figure showing were-jaguar characteristics of triangular "jaguar" mouth and cleft head due to positioning of eyebrows. Museum of Villahermosa Archaeological Park, Villahermosa, Tabasco (courtesy INAH).

History, developed a time frame for the culture. He had excavated many such figurines in the lowest strata in the valley of Mexico. He proclaimed the culture to be of the far distant past, the millennium before Christ. As for a name, he confirmed the term Olmec because that area of the Gulf coast was known as Olman during Aztec times, 2,500 years after the "Olmec" had flourished. The name stuck.

Therefore, in the decade and a half after Blom's rediscovery of the monument atop the volcano, a school of thought developed regarding a culture in the area of Veracruz state in the far distant past. This culture's hallmark was the were-jaguar figurine with cleft head, slant eyes and snarling mouth. It was believed this culture was so admired by the other peoples of Mesoamerican that their figurines were exported to or emulated by peoples throughout the area. The time periods were known as the Early Preclassic (2000–1000 B.C.) and the Middle Preclassic (1000 B.C. to 400 B.C.). Again, it is worth noting that at this point, the middle to late 1930s, the Olmec was still just a hypothetical culture with nothing more than a name, a presumed homeland along the Gulf Coast, and the belief by some that it was possibly the cultural (and probable political) capital of all of Mesoamerica in the distant past.

Enter Matthew Stirling. Stirling grew up near Salinas, California (Pugh 1981). John Steinbeck was a family friend. Stirling was educated at the University of California, later receiving graduate degrees at George Washington University and the University of Tampa. Successful archaeologists, especially the earliest in an unexplored field, must possess numerous skill sets. The concrete ones include practical engineer, architect, art historian, and explorer. The more ethereal are abundant intuition and the ability to navigate both bureaucratic chambers and drawing rooms. Stirling clearly had an intuitive nose. That Stirling knew to schmooze is shown by his becoming director of the Bureau of American Ethnology at a relatively young age. He was also a favorite of both the National Geographic Society and the Smithsonian Institution. From the material presented so far, an archaeological foray into the lower Gulf Coast seems logical. In 1939, the view to most experts would have looked much dicier. How many would have risked the good will of two of the most important cultural forces in America on an expedition looking for a civilization scant evidence for which existed?

Or maybe Stirling was dumb like a fox. In his mind's eye he could perhaps see the stir a colossal head on a *National Geographic* cover would make. Stirling made his first dig at Hueyapan Hacienda which he named Tres Zapotes. He excavated the giant head, which until then had remained in a semi-excavated hole. His most important discovery at Tres Zapotes was the earliest fixed calendar (or Long Count) date in Middle America. The Long Count calendar was one of several cultural traits — another was writing, as noted in the preface — the Maya perfected but did not discover. The Long Count numerals were discovered on a tall stone tablet known as Stela C. Not being proficient in calendrics, Stirling broke out Sylvanus Morley's manual and puzzled out the date. "Carved on the stela in bars [indicating fives] and dots [for digits] were the numerals 15-6-16-18 with a terminal glyph 6 in front of the day sign," Marian Pugh, Sterling's wife, reported in a retrospective essay after his death. The most important number was missing. That was the cycle date. Long Count cycles can be likened to our centuries, even though they take in a time frame of about 400 years. At first it was assumed to be cycle 9 because few dates had been discovered earlier than cycle 9. That produced a date falling in the fifth century A.D. Such a date would be perfectly consistent with when the Long Count calendar was known to be used. But it was much later than the best guess at the time for the Olmec civilization, at least for those like Stirling who were Olmec partisans and who believed the culture was going strong long before Christ.

So Stirling refigured the date. He decided he had the initial "15" wrong. The monument was weathered badly, and Stirling believed a dot could be seen above the 15. That changed it to a "16" reading. This denoted the katun or twenty year period; but rather than shifting the date forward twenty years, he decided the cycle must be seven, not nine. The new date jumped back more than one complete 400 year cycle to 31 B.C. Such a date would be the earliest ever recorded for a Long Count discovered at that time. Because Stirling's date was based on hypothetical evidence, it was met with howls of derision. A decade or so later, carbon dating showed that the site of Tres Zapotes was inhabited at the period of Stirling's Long Count date. And in 1972, a farmer found the missing portion of the stela. A bar and two dots indicated the cycle was 7, just as Stirling predicted. Even today, this Long Count date remains as the second oldest discovered.

But the 31 B.C. time frame — about when Caesar marched into Rome to declare himself dictator — displeased Stirling in other ways. It was far too late given the hypothesis of an Olmec protoculture. All this convinced Stirling that Tres Zapotes was not an important Olmec capital during the culture's glory days. So he turned his attention to La Venta, the large site with Olmec heads Blom had discovered in neighboring Tabasco state. He hoped here he would find the roots of Mesoamerica.

The place had fallen on hard times since Blom's visit. Mexico had been in political turmoil since the revolution in 1910, and the Mexican countryside was sporadically plunged into anarchy by political or criminal gangs. The proprietor of the site, Don Sebastian, had twice been cleaned out by bandits. During the attacks, he had been severely wounded and two of his sons were killed (Stirling 1942). More ominous for archaeology was a tent city of Mexican geologists. They were looking for oil. And they found it. Shortly, La Venta would go from a practically unexplored wilderness to an oil boomtown complete with dance-hall floosies, a refinery, and an airstrip covering part of the ruins. But for the moment the friendly geologists supplied the expedition with a hot cooked meal now and then and useful information about the local terrain.

Stirling presented Don Sebastian, the proprietor of La Venta, a half-dozen expensive cigars. His eighty-plus-year-old host accepted the cigars, saying he never smoked but that his stout wife did. As she puffed on the stogies, ash falling onto her bare breasts, Don Sebastian warned the archaeologists that the ghosts of Moctezuma held rites on the jungle-clad site. Stirling lamented the fact that he was not lucky enough to make anthropological observations of these nocturnal rituals. Neither could he find, at first, the colossal head Blom reported.

But Stirling found plenty to keep him busy. He surveyed the pyramid Blom mentioned with a base a hundred yards square. It was an artificial clay hill an impressive hundred feet high. Just to the north of it were several enclosures walled off with basalt logs ten feet long and a foot square. Basalt is harder than granite. These "logs" had been quarried with stone tools. The nearest source of basalt was in the Tuxtla Mountains. They were fifty miles distant. In between lay equatorial-like forest and copious river crossings. Stirling was astonished. The monumental art he found was even more astonishing. One piece, now called Altar 4, featured a life-size figure in a headdress emerging from a niche in the basalt block. A perfectly sculpted hawser-like rope led to the side of the altar to another figure. Stirling proclaimed, "The sculpturing of this stone is of a very high order. The postures of the figures are easy and realistic, lacking the stiffness and conventionalization that characterize most Middle American art." Why a man should be emerging from a niche as from a cave or basement puzzled Stirling, as much else puzzled him about these mysterious people. Later archaeologists were able to piece together explanations for this and other behaviors that no doubt would have amused and perhaps astonished him. In short, we now know the man in the niche is an Olmec king returning from a psychedelic trip to the underworld. But at the time, Stirling was preoccupied with the question of the age of the ruins. Could art as sophisticated as this date at the very beginning of Mesoamerican civilization? J. Eric Thompson, among the most learned Americanist scholars, believed the Olmec civilization occurred much later during the Postclassic period at a time that would seem to match the artistic attainments of these people. Within a few years, carbon dating would show La Venta was — as Stirling suspected — a Middle Preclassic site, with a time frame of the early part of the first millennium before Christ.

Under Altar 4, positioned like necklaces, were 99 pieces of jade. This was the most modest of many caches of valuable objects Stirling's teams were to find at LaVenta. In one instance, they discovered a set of jade or serpentine (a jade-like stone) figurines. They had ritually deformed bean-like heads, shaved bald. These figurines were vaguely jaguar-like, but they also resembled the full-figured statues found at the site. Four figures were pushed forward, facing a headman. Surrounding them were small jades mimicking basalt logs. These figurines were found buried far underground. Colored layers of earth were laid on top. For some reason, this buried Christmas crib-like set had been dug down to many years after its internment. And then it was covered up once more. Stirling scratched his head at this find. What was the purpose of burying such exquisite figurines underground? What did the statuettes represent? The figurines, it was determined many decades later, represented shamans or shaman/kings conducting mysterious rites in underground chambers.

An even more startling discovery consisted of serpentine blocks set on layers of yellow and orange sand. These mosaic sculptures were found thirteen to twenty feet underground. The serpentine blocks, all told, weighed a thousand tons. They had been hauled from the

Corner view of Altar 4. Note figure rope leads onto near side of monument. La Venta Archaeological Park, Villahermosa (courtesy INAH).

mountains of central Mexico to La Venta. Then they were laid far underground. Stirling and his crew determined the pattern of the mosaic. It was a mask — in a stylized version of the were-jaguar motif the Olmec favored. Hundreds of jade or serpentine ceremonial axes were found cached above the subterranean mosaic.

Archaeologists came to understand that to the Olmec (and the Maya), all elements of the universe were alive. By stashing valuable objects, like the jade axes, with a monument, they believed they imbued the monument with a powerful life-force. Likewise, monuments could be ritually killed by removing or rearranging the cache items. Stirling, however, only had a dim recognition of these explanations as he uncovered these startling finds.

Artistically, Stirling judged Altar 2 as the best executed monument at La Venta. Like Altar 4, it shows a figure emerging from a niche. This figure carries a human infant. Four other images of infants are etched on the monument's walls. Those all bear were-jaguar faces — the infants have cleft foreheads, almond eyes, and snarling mouths. The child in the hands of the figure in the niche, however, bears the face of a normal infant. Others have theorized a chief was presenting his newborn heir. Some said the child represented the Olmec rain god. Despite the homey appearance, Stirling speculated that child sacrifice was practiced by the Olmec (Stirling 1967). More than forty years went by before this conclusion was shown accurate. Infant bones, along with wooden sculptures and cache items such as jade and rubber, were found in the peat at the bottom of El Manati spring near San Lorenzo in the 1980s (Pool 2007).

Stirling also surmised the so-called altars were actually used as thrones by rulers. The fact that a jaguar skin, the lap robe of Middle American royalty, was etched on the top of some of them led him to this idea. Because of the symbolism associated with these stone

Serpentine stone pavement in the form of a were-jaguar mask. The cleft head, slant eyes, and snarling mouth are highly stylized. This and other pavements were found buried 13–20 feet underground. La Venta Archaeological Park, Villahermosa (courtesy INAH).

blocks, later archaeologists have come to call them "sky thrones." They received this strange name because archaeologist determined the rulers depicted were embarking on hallucinatory journeys into the sky — or underworld (Reilly 1995).

Stirling took time out in the spring of 1945 to investigate a site upstream from Minatitlan on the mighty Coatzacoalcos River. It was named San Lorenzo. It lay halfway between Tres Zapotes and La Venta in the state of Veracruz. Stirling's quick survey discovered fifteen monuments, including five colossal heads. It was clear the site was not as large or as powerful as La Venta. But he found evidence that it was the first Olmec center. A full-fledged expedition did not visit San Lorenzo until the Apollo program that put a man on the moon was well under way. The year was 1966. The expedition arrived by riverboat after a five- to six-hour trip (Coe 1968). The leader of the expedition was Michael Coe. He was to become one of the world's best known archaeological writers. He also became head of the anthropology department at Yale.

Frontal view of "sky throne" Altar 4. This shaman king, wearing a harpy eagle headdress, is about to depart on a transcendental trip to other planes of cosmic reality. La Venta Archaeological Park, Villahermosa (courtesy INAH).

Coe found that San Lorenzo, like La Venta, was an island in a vast watery world. San Lorenzo, however, occupies a very high island. It rises more than a hundred fifty feet above the floodplain of the branches of the Coatzacoalcos that surrounded it during Olmec times. Lengthwise, the island runs for several miles and is a mile or more in breadth. The largest archaeological site occupies the highest ground. Stirling's first team of excavators considered the site a natural tabletop. Coe discovered it was actually a vast, artificially terraced platform about three-quarters of a mile long with wings that stretched hundreds of yards from the ridge. The plateau was built up about twenty-five feet to be level with the crest of the ridge. The highest plane appeared to have been reserved for religious or state ritual, and the lower terraces were used for residences of the ranking members of the society. On the first level below the summit, a later archaeologist found the so-called Red Palace, a large building paved with sand stained scarlet by hematite. It was fitted out with basalt stoops and drains (Diehl 2004). In an age before the backhoe and dump truck, in fact even before the wheelbarrow, millions of basketfuls of fill were required to build up the ridgeline into a flat table-like structure. The thought of all that dirt work, as it is known in modern construction parlance, boggled Coe's mind. Also boggling his mind were the returns from the radiocarbon lab. They dated occupation at the site from 1500 to 900 B.C., making the area the first known to develop into a sophisticated center in the Olmec heartland. Arguably, it is the first "city" to develop in North America along about 1250 B.C.

Most of the monuments Stirling's expedition recovered had been retrieved from ravines. Almost all of them had been horribly mutilated. The assumption was that the site had been invaded and conquered. The attackers, it was believed, razed the site, and after defacing the monuments, tumbled them into the gullies. Coe's investigation, with which he was assisted by then graduate student and later University of Alabama professor Richard Diehl, showed this assumption to be in error. The monuments had not been plundered and discarded. Rather they had been defaced and then buried with jade offerings — in straight and predictable lanes. Those found in gullies had simply been disgorged by the earth owing to the effect of gravity over the course of 3,000 years. The Olmec, therefore, believed that death was required in order to renew the universe. The view, as will be seen, was a central tenet of the Maya too. In this instance, it is shown by the ritual killing of the buried monuments. Their death was caused by defacing and burial. When notables were buried in ancient America, suitable grave goods were placed with them. Caches of valuable objects were interred with the "dead" statuary.

In place of the ritually killed monuments, new statues were then dedicated. This renewed the universe. Blood sacrifice, including human sacrifice, was practiced by the peoples of Mesoamerica for the same purpose: to renew the universe and keep it in harmony — and keep those rains falling and the corn crops growing.

The most astonishing find, however, had nothing to do with sculpture in any but the most prosaic sense. Coe's team turned up a drain system that ran 650 feet (Coe 1968). The drain "tiles" had been scratched from basalt with factory-like precision. Each segment was fitted with a basalt cover tight enough to prevent dirt from sifting into and clogging the line — for three thousand years. The lines were graded, and indeed a drain spout was discovered disgorging a fat stream of water into a ravine during the rainy season. All in all, thirty tons of basalt was worked, and the drain marked a fabulous feat of engineering, even if the purpose was unknown and of little or no utilitarian value. A similar system was also discovered at La Venta. As Coe says, "What was the system made for? We wished we knew."

In 1968, slightly more than forty years after Blom's identification of the were-jaguar motif which led to discovery of the Olmec, Coe's grant to excavate San Lorenzo ran out. He left after the last field season puzzled by much about the Olmec. Coe had shown Stirling's surmise of pillagers toppling the monuments wrong. The ritually dead monuments had been buried, and the force of gravity merely disgorged them. But Coe thought it likely San Lorenzo had indeed been sacked and destroyed at the time of its abandonment, about 900 B.C. He did not hazard a guess regarding the identity of the vandals. They could have been outside invaders. It seemed equally likely that an internal revolt did in the site during its heyday, with the revolutionaries being disaffected nobles or uprising peasants. He was, however, morally certain that the Olmec was the ur-culture of Mesoamerica; and from it other cultures, in particular the Maya, took their bearings.

The Olmec People and Lifestyle

Before taking up how San Lorenzo fell, we need to have some understanding of how it came to rise. Why of all the places in the New World was this location the one where thousands of men were coaxed into moving multi-ton stones tens of miles? Just as pertinent, why were the artisans at Olmec sites among the first to develop the talents to work stone as difficult as jade. This stone exceeds steel in hardness. The product of their work is admired even today. Coe calculated that the population of San Lorenzo probably topped out at 2,500. A later excavator of the site, Ann Cyphers, figured a population of 5,500 with another 8,000 or so in the hinterland (Cyphers 1999). The production of art in early societies, and to some extent even today, was tied to the larger political structure and the local environment. So how did the folks that produced that fabulous artwork live and come to produce that art work?

Olmec stock, along with all other native populations of the Americas, crossed the Siberian land bridge to Alaska during the last Ice Age, somewhere between 11,000 and 50,000 years ago. By about 2500 B.C., they had settled in the Olmec heartland. The houses they came to live in were square or apsidal (rectangular with rounded ends). The structures sat either at ground level or were raised slightly to avoid flash flooding during the rainy season. The roof was high pitched and thatched. The walls were made of poles set upright, sometimes daubed with a mud plaster. Aside from the main house, lean-to shelters were constructed of palm thatch for working (or socializing) under. The house lot was fenced off by a wall of plants or stakes. A "courtyard" of beaten earth connected the house to outhouses. An intensively cultivated dooryard garden and orchard were common features. The garden included many familiar vegetables such as tomatoes, squash, beans and sweet potatoes, and some that may be less familiar such as chayote and jicama.

The main corn crop was grown in lightly tended fields in the hinterland. Other crops known from later periods, such as manioc (tapioca) and cotton, may have been planted in the garden or in distant fields. The garden probably included culinary herbs and medicinal plants such as cilantro, hot peppers, and tobacco. Trees provided shade and valuable fruits such as avocado, papaya, various zapotes (fruits, such as the pumpkin-like mamey and the pear-drenched-in-light-chocolate sapodilla). Palms such as the corozo were probably allowed to grow for aesthetic reasons and in order to harvest nuts, rendered into a rich oil. Most of the protein the Olmec consumed came, it is believed, from the watery sphere; shellfish, snapper, snook, gar, catfish, and so on. The common folk appear to have eaten little red meat. Almost all mammal bones found to date have been in the garbage middens associated with mounds (and higher class homesteads). Meat animals included deer, peccary, armadillo, and the cold-blooded caiman (alligator). Domestic dog, by the number of bones recovered, seemed to have been a particular favorite, as it was in many parts of the New World.

The most important foodstuff was corn. Dried corn was soaked with lime to help dehusk and unwittingly enhance the nutritional content. The treated grains were ground on a stone metate by a mano and boiled tamale fashion. Tortillas did not come along until many centuries later.

A few such households, located in a high spot above the annual floods, would constitute a hamlet. Similar hamlets can be seen throughout lower Mexico and Central America today. With the exception of the addition of electricity, they probably function pretty similar to hamlets in rural Olman. The difference between modern villagers and the Olmec can be seen in larger villages. There a mound in Olmec days would be found on top of which a public building or the larger house of the headman was located. The subchief's residence would certainly have some significant display of wealth or rulership such as a stone monument. Towns such as Tenochtitlan (modern name; no connection to the Aztec capital), a mile or so away from San Lorenzo proper, probably consisted of more commoner residences presided over by a prince in a fairly sumptuous residential compound. Stone monuments, some of stunning artistic complexity, have been found in these outlying towns. At San Lorenzo and other Olmec centers, royalty lived in large buildings such as the red palace, mentioned above, and kept an eye on (or helped in) a monument-producing workshop near the palace.

Resources of the area included salt and shells from the Gulf, tar from the numerous oil seeps, and rubber made from the sap of Castilla elastica, the so-called Mexican rubber tree. This tree is of the mulberry-fig family. The Olmec and other peoples of Mesoamerica added the sap of the morning glory vine to turn the latex of the castilla into a durable rubber (Pool 2007). Some authors speculate that a slight bit of sulphur in the morning glory juice vulcanized the rubber. For recreation they played the Mesoamerican ball game. Certainly, the ball game was played on a serious level that had religious as well as secular overtones.

Not only did the common folk live much like modern day counterparts in Middle America, but their lifestyle probably was not much different from subsistence villagers located on waterways, with obvious regional variations, in tropical and subtropical areas around the world. None of this does anything to explain why the Olmec began constructing art works that three millennia later would be recognizable to a large portion of the world's population. Partly, the explanation has to do with the adoption of corn culture. The Olmec, thanks to their rich marine environment, could have gotten by without growing corn. The Timucuans of the St. Johns River valley in Florida did just fine consuming plump apple snails from the river in the summer and retreating to the seacoast during the "R" months to live off oysters. Their neighbors in interior Florida grew corn. The Timucuans did not need to devote any time to agriculture to live well. Early French explorers were much taken by their huge stature and leisurely lifestyle. But the Olmec began cultivating corn on the river bottoms and also in slash-and-burn upland fields. Something else grew up with the practice — a complex social and political system. This system featured an aristocracy with a ruler that commanded the respect of all in his sway. For whatever reason, that ruler was able to persuade a thousand or more of his followers to take four or more months off and hie 80,000 pound stones across the swamps. Something akin to religious fervor would be required.

And it is to religious sentiment that archaeologists attribute the motive power that transported those stones. Religious fervor also motivated the raising of the artificial plateau at San Lorenzo and that one hundred foot tall clay pyramid at La Venta.

Politics, Religion and Control of the Masses

Up to this point, Olmec culture does not seem much more distant from us than, say, the pioneer culture of our North American forebears, given the differences in climate. Both groups managed to get a living pretty much the same way based on maize horticulture supplemented by hunting and fishing. But the Olmec, and Mesoamerican cultures in general, diverge significantly when it comes to governance. This is especially true when you add the religious component to governance. And it is impossible to speak of governance in Mesoamerica without talking about religion. They went hand in glove.

Carlos Castaneda was a graduate student at UCLA when he supposedly met an elderly Yaqui Indian in Arizona or Sonora. The Yaqui, who he called Don Juan, reputedly spent his early years in central Mexico where he learned and melded the various Mexican shaman traditions. Castaneda claimed he applied to be an apprentice to Don Juan. He later wrote about these studies in a series of controversial books.

Don Juan supposedly employed three common Southwestern herbs, jimson weed, peyote and psilocybin mushrooms (Castaneda 1968/1998). Castaneda described his experiments with these drugs, supposedly under Don Juan's direction. He claimed to have undergone the symptoms reported by shamans, such as morphing into a bird and the appearance of flight. Once, after such an experience, Castaneda claimed to have woken naked in the desert. In the altered state of consciousness induced by the drugs, Castaneda was occasionally challenged by forces that seemed to be supernatural entities. He reported that Don Juan did battle with evil forces, generally in the guise of an animal familiar, while tripping in altered planes of reality.

With the breaking of the Maya hieroglyphic code, archaeologists learned for a fact something they had long suspected. That fact was that the Maya kings derived much of their power over their subjects from their supposed control of the forces of the universe by shamanistic rites (Schele and Mathews 1998). These rites included delving into trance states where as their animal familiar they were transported to otherworldly spheres. In these realms they gained information of use to the community as a whole about making war or peace, planting of crops and so on. The visions provided by these trances were depicted in Maya — though not in Olmec — art by a snake with a man emerging from its mouth called the vision serpent.

According to F. Kent Reilly of Texas State University, shamanistic activity of the sort Don Juan and the Maya and Olmec practiced is characteristic of small groups such as tribes. Common sense dictates that it would be difficult to control thousands by claims of access to special powers acquired in trance states. Historically, rulers, whether presidents or dictators, need to employ much more objective power — usually backed by a species of military force — to gain and retain leadership. But there have been instances when states were governed by institutional shamanism. Reilly cites China's Shang Dynasty (1726–1122 B.C.), Yamato Japan (circa A.D. 50–300) and Silla Dynasty Korea (A.D. 668–935). In short, according to Reilly, "Classic period [Maya] kings validated their right to royal power by publicly proclaiming their ability to perform the shamanic trance journey and transform into power animals" (Reilly 1995).

As we have seen in Castaneda's "study," shamanism is rooted in the belief that there are other planes of reality. These planes of reality are knowable through altering the mental state. The altered state is called by anthropologists "achieving ecstasy." To the rest of us, it is known as getting stoned. The altered state can be induced by various methods such as meditation, dancing, physical pain or the consumption of hallucinogens. In the trance state the practitioner often claims to be able to fly between various spheres of the universe. In most instances, the shaman believes he actually becomes his animal familiar. The creature is almost always a power animal such as an eagle or jaguar. According to Reilly, "In the other world, shamans, in the forms of their power animals, are known to have spirit battles with other shamans," much as Castaneda's Don Juan supposedly did. "Such battles can result in the death of one or both of the opponents, in which case the shaman's body also dies."

The peoples of Mesoamerica held there were three planes of the universe: sky, earth, and underworld. The three were connected by their shaman leader's ability to communicate with them in the trance state. He (or occasionally she) was considered the center of the world, the "axis mundi." The Olmec depicted the world center as a corn stalk (or as an upright alligator-like creature known as the Olmec dragon). These three planes — sky, earth and underworld — were regarded as palpable entities. Olmec rulers proclaimed that they were the lynchpin between the three planes, and represented themselves as a cornstalk or the Olmec dragon. They had the power to travel up the stalk to the thirteen planes of the celestial and down to the roots and the nine levels of the underworld. Secrets of great import were imparted to them in these journeys, mostly by the spirits of departed ancestors.

The man emerging from the niche in Altar 4 (page 18) is regarded as a king embarking on a spirit journey. The eyes and fangs on the lintel above the figure are presumed to be those of his jaguar familiar, into which he was transformed and as which he made his trip. The X between the fangs is the symbol for the sky. The figure wears a helmet that Reilly identifies as a harpy-eagle helmet; note the bird-like effigy. The harpy is the largest eagle in the New World; female birds attain the size of plump Thanksgiving turkeys, twenty pounds.

Figurine head depicting man transmogrifying into jaguar at the onset of shamanistic ecstasy. Such statuettes were common and perhaps aided in the shamanistic transformation. Illustration by John Wilton from a photograph of object in on-site museum, LaVenta, Tabasco (courtesy INAH).

Harpies pluck monkeys out of treetops. The simians are their number one food preference. Perhaps for that reason they came to be associated with human sacrifice. In this case the harpy reference indicates transcendent flight, and perhaps also refers to spilling of human blood. The rope in the shaman's hand, we remember from the photo of Altar 4 (page 16), leads to a second figure on the side panel. That personage could be a relative the shaman/chief communes with in his trance state. But there is another and probably better explanation. The figure's arm slants across his chest, the universal sign of submission in Middle American iconography. Reilly believes he is a captive about to be sacrificed. Reilly says, "Blood was a magic substance opening a portal between natural and supernatural cosmic divisions." Whether the figure on the side of the altar was dispatched or not, it is a pretty sure bet the gentleman in the niche obtained a state of ecstasy by perforating his penis with a stingray spine. Although obsidian and other substances were used for bloodletting, stingray spines were the preferred bloodletter because of their aquatic origin, water being associated with the underworld realm.

Some archaeologists believed the

Olmec shaman utilized the supposed hallucinogenic properties of the cane toad, a particularly obnoxious amphibian that has been introduced to warm areas around the world, including Florida, to control insects. Wikipedia defines the active ingredient in the psychedelic toads as "bufotenin, an alkaloid found in the skin of some species of toads and possibly in the brain of schizophrenics." The toad in question is among the largest of amphibians, and its toxic secretions can kill a dog. A later study found the abnormally high accretion of toad bones at the San Lorenzo dig site was probably caused by a topographical anomaly (Cyphers, et al. 2005). The use of bufotenin by the Olmec, therefore, is in doubt. Perforating one's private parts would probably be preferable to licking one of those vile amphibians.

Caroline Tate speculates that the were-jaguar pavements of La Venta were power symbols calculated to assist in shamanic transformation and ritual (Tate 1999). In other words, bloodletting (or taking of hallucinogens) near the pavements would enhance the ecstatic state, by dint of self-fulfilling prophesy. Those pavements, it will be remembered, consisted of tons of serpentine blocks, fashioned into stylized were-jaguar masks, buried thirteen to twenty feet underground.

A significant number of were-jaguar figurines are of acrobats turning somersaults. Peter Furst, probably the preeminent authority on New World shamanism, noted that some South American shamans are reputed to be able to flip five times forward and turn into their jaguar familiar (Furst 1967). A reverse somersault of five turns and they revert to their human form. An apprentice in one such cult reported that he witnessed his master transform into a jaguar before his eyes. He was freaked out by this vision. Furst reports the man ceased his studies with the man/jaguar forthwith.

From Shamanism to Grand Public Works and Monuments

Up to this point, the narrative has been on pretty safe ground. Most Middle American specialists would agree with the views presented here. But the political organization of the Olmec—and the Maya too—is a contentious issue. Some hold the Olmec and the Maya were chiefdoms, which indicates a weak level of political control by the headman.

Philip Drucker argued for an Olmec state as far back as the early 1980s (Drucker 1981). Drucker had been Stirling's second in command on most of his expeditions, and during the fifties became the head of the project at La Venta. After its close, he ran a cattle spread in Veracruz. As a former rodeo rider and World War II veteran, he had the wherewithal to make the operation pay (Pool 2007). In his spare time, he thought about the Olmec. Drucker began his analysis by noting that major Olmec sites such as La Venta were islands in the swamp. The carrying capacity of the land was not high enough to support the labor needed to move huge stones tens of miles across the river bottoms.

Those works included, as we have seen, erecting a clay pyramid one hundred feet tall and hauling large blocks of stone dozens of miles across the swampy bottomlands of very large rivers. Drucker noted that a study had shown a crew of approximately one thousand workmen would be needed to haul a 38-ton stone from the Tuxtla Mountains to La Venta. The stone would have been mounted on a sledge pulled on log rollers. It progressed at an average of 78.5 yards per hour. At that rate it would take about four and a half months to complete the journey to La Venta, requiring 134,000 man days of food, an incredible demand on the granaries of slash-and-burn peasants. The small land area of La Venta could not possibly provide that many extra calories. But there was land with an agricultural potential not far away. Drucker believed a high degree of central authority would have been needed to organize the society to grow and collect surplus corn. Fulltime artists and administrators would also have to be fed by the surplus yields.

Cheifdoms lay weak claim to the loyalty of their subjects. Rather than order his followers to do his bidding, a chief must ply them with argument or bribes. In particular, a chief lacks the power of coercive force, including physical punishment and death, to enforce his will. This inherent weakness was never understood by 19th-century Americans in their dealing with the Indians. Time after time treaties were made with "chiefs," often of a self-appointed variety, who were unable to talk their followers into keeping the terms. Chiefs are able to control a relatively small population. Owing to the lack of compelling force, Drucker did not believe a chiefdom could carry on tasks as complex as those performed by the Olmec.

A primitive state, Drucker continued, could control a population of 5,000 to 20,000. The populace would be spread out in a variety of situations from hamlets and villages and small towns, all controlled directly from a center such as San Lorenzo or La Venta (or Tres Zapotes, Laguna de los Cerros, or Los Limas, the other known or possible Olmec centers). Because control was direct, the outer limits of a primitive state would be one day's hard travel by foot or canoe. Drucker calculated the distance would be about 15 to 18 miles and that would mean the largest area a primitive Olmec state could effectively control would be about a thousand square miles, or the size of a standard cookie cutter county in the Midwest. However, because of the bountiful corn harvests on the river bottoms at places like San Lorenzo, an Olmec state could be as small as 300–350 square miles, a micro sized county.

The leaders would come, as hypothesized by Drucker, from a royal line, and his subordinates would be hereditary nobles. The aristocratic class probably admitted no connection whatsoever, by kin, to the commoner class. Some lower-class folk would be supported by the state in nonagricultural specialist roles such as sculptors' assistants. Drucker speculated a militia composed of commoners with aristocrat officers would defend the state against aggression. There would be no standing army.

Modern states are organized around economic production. The primitive state would yield some economic products, but these would be incidental to its larger purpose, which was entirely religious and ceremonial. The massive public works projects, including the monumental art, would be for the furtherance of religion. And religion enforced the political power of the governing class. The chief business of the Olmec city was the administration of state and religious affairs. For this reason the early Mesoamerican political seats were called regal-ritual centers.

There was no secular economy aside from procuring essential staples like salt. Taxes in the way of collecting agricultural surpluses went to support the erection of religious monuments and the elite class—and by extension to those commoners who to built or maintained the monuments. External trade was conducted for exotic objects, such as jade, used in religious observances. Craft specialization consisted of producing things, like were-jaguar statuettes, of religious value. These were acquired for their religious significance, not as overt shows of wealth. Lavish warehouses and palaces were conspicuous by their absence. Growing impersonality would be the rule regarding the interaction between the elite running the state and those they governed. Commoners would rarely come into the presence of royalty, and justice would be dispensed increasingly on an impersonal basis.

The elite class practiced head deformation as a way of separating it from the commoner class. The deformation probably resulted from binding infant's heads producing a bean-shaped pate that was later shaved or plucked bald. This ensured no social climbers jumped class boundaries. Full-time sculptors were probably mostly from this class, and they could probably be separated into those who worked large-scale stone monuments and those who crafted small-scale jade or ceramics. Trade may or may not have been carried on by a specialized order of the elite class. Trade was important for procuring ceremonial items such as jade, serpentine, cinnabar (a mercury-based drench many items, including corpses, were coated with), iron ore (used for ceremonial mirrors, a ton of which was found stashed for as yet undetermined reasons on San Lorenzo) and so on.

A complex chiefdom can have many of the features Drucker sketches for his primitive state, with one exception. That line in the dirt that cannot be crossed is coercive power. A state requires the ability to physically punish, including put to death, those who resisted the will of the ruler. Drucker believed Olmec rulers needed — though perhaps rarely used — this power to produce their great work.

What Happened to the Olmec? (1250–400 B.C., More or Less)

This brings us to the question of what happened to the Olmec. Were they victims of collapse or conquest? Early on, conquest seemed the most likely answer. Many of the first monuments, as noted above, discovered by archaeologists were found defaced or decapitated. Colossal heads usually showed minor damage, as noted by the small scarring on the Hueyapan Head, but full-figured statuary was often decapitated. The early conclusion was that invasion or revolt was responsible. After Coe found defaced monuments ceremonially buried with jade offerings, it was apparent those speculations would not do. Offerings meant that the statue had been interred with some ceremony. Later it was determined that some monuments had been recarved into other monuments. How to explain all this?

J. E. Clark believes that the Olmec believed that statuary shared the essential power of the ruler they commemorated (Clark 1997). The reasons some monuments were disfigured and others not puzzles other archaeologists. Not Clark. He believes internal power struggles among the nobility account for this discrepancy. As Winston Churchill famously said (or is supposed to have said), "Democracy is the worst form of government, except for all the rest." Democracy's best feature is its ability to transfer power. Hereditary forms of governance assume competence by its rulers in perpetuity. Clark assumes that ambitious brothers and cousins, among other members of the royalty and higher nobility, were kept happy by a share of the exotic trade goods and appointments as princes to far flung dependencies. Still, usurpation occurred now and then. When it did the monuments of those disgraced going back to a common ancestor, real or imagined, would be ceremoniously killed and buried. The common ancestor would be pointed to by the usurper to legitimize his claim. It would be left intact. This theory explains the haphazardness with which monuments appear to have been spared. And it does not rule out the occasional raid or temporary, successful invasion, which could account for some of vandalism.

San Lorenzo and most of its dependent villages passed into oblivion about 900 B.C., after maintaining a high culture for two hundred fifty or three hundred years. All that remained after the collapse on the central plateau was a medium-sized village. Of the 226 hamlets and villages that appeared to have been under San Lorenzo's sway, 54 continued to

Left: Olmec head from San Lorenzo, Veracruz (courtesy INAH). *Right:* Waiter at restaurant in southern Campeche originally from Veracruz.

be inhabited, but their population fell by more than 90 percent. Only about a thousand persons were left in what once was the mighty municipality of San Lorenzo. Ann Cyphers of the National Autonomous University of Mexico conjectures the collapse of San Lorenzo's fortunes was due to a change in the course of the Coatzacoalcos River (Cyphers 1993). San Lorenzo lost control of river traffic and with it went the political control necessary to maintain the kingdom. Did this loss occasion turmoil that forced the population to flee? So far the archaeological record is silent.

Author Armando Anaya worked Olmec sites for three field seasons under the direction of Rebecca Gonzales Lauck. He doubts Cypher's theory. He believes it is possible that San Lorenzo was abandoned and the capital moved to La Venta based on the ritual termination rite known as the "may cycle." The *may* was recorded in the katun prophecies of the books of Chilam Balam in the late Postclassic or early Colonial period. In this cycle, the seat of power moved from one regional capital to another. In the process the ritual structures were disassembled and monuments were broken in order to liberate their imbedded power. All components were ritually buried with rich offerings. It appears that similar events could have occurred at San Lorenzo. It is also possible that La Venta simply conquered San Lorenzo. Conquest could have been a feature of the may cycle, as the transfer of the power center was not necessarily a friendly act. In any case, the San Lorenzo island, probable seat of the first civilized capital in North America, lay abandoned for centuries. It was recolonized in the centuries after the birth of Christ. A small population remained from then until the Spanish conquest.

From about 900 B.C. to 400 B.C., or so, La Venta was the first city of Olman. Modern settlement studies have shown that about 400 B.C. La Venta collapsed. With it went the various villages in its outback which were politically connected to the great center. Christopher Pool of the University of Kentucky says that disease or ecological disaster may have been the cause (Pool 2007). But he thinks it more likely that an implosion of the political system was the major reason for the downfall. The ensuing vacuum, with its attendant violence and uncertainty, prompted most of the population to vote with their feet — or simply die in place thanks to warfare or pestilence.

The first site visited by scholars, Tres Zapotes, was ironically the last of the major Olmec sites to flourish. Although a significant center for centuries, it came into its own after the fall of La Venta. By then Olmec culture had been going strong for a thousand years. Just as American culture is not the same today as during the Revolutionary War, Olmec culture as practiced at Tres Zapotes differed significantly from what was seen at San Lorenzo and La Venta during their heydays. Writing and calendrics were developed or, more probably, adopted from elsewhere. As indicated earlier, the second oldest fixed (Long Count) date recorded anywhere in Mesoamerica was discovered here. It correlates to 31 B.C. in our calendar. This and other major developments at Tres Zapotes are attributed to an entirely different phase called Epi-Olmec. Like the word "epilogue," it denotes a culture past its cultural prime.

What happened to these people? Did they disappear along with the centers archaeologists now study? No, they did not. An anthropologist accompanied Frans Blom's 1925 Tulane expedition. He was Oliver LaFarge, part American Indian and part New England Brahmin and an early advocate for the Indians. Later, he penned a bestselling book about an Indian youth. He found the peoples in the Olmec regions he visited to speak the central Mexican Nahuatl language (Blom and LaFarge 1926). Melgar, the discoverer of the Hueyapan Head, was struck by the lack of physical resemblance of the local folk to the person depicted in the colossal head. Clearly the folk LaFarge and Melgar found inhabiting the ancient Olmec sites were not Olmec stock. But thanks to the partial breaking of the Epi-Olmec language found on monuments at Tres Zapotes, linguists like Terrence Kaufman and John Justeson have been able to formulate a proto-language called Mije-Sokean (Kaufman and Justeson 2008). At the time of the Conquest, speakers of this family could be found from southern Veracruz to Guatemala, but they had been penetrated by the pockets of Nahuatl (Aztec) speakers beginning in A.D. 600–900. This area takes in the entire Olmec heartland. All this offers evidence that some or all of those inhabiting the Olmec centers spoke variants of Mije-Sokean. The rulers of Tres Zapotes conversed (or at least wrote) in a Sokean language. The speakers of the various Sokean languages who live in the area of old Olman, and they are many, can be said with a fair degree of certainty, to be the true descendants of the Olmec.

2

The Mirador Basin in Times Long Gone, 1000 B.C.–A.D. 150

From the time of its completion in 1931 until the World Trade Center inched above it in the early 1970s, the Empire State Building was the tallest structure in New York. In the minds of many, it is still the world's — or at least America's — preeminent skyscraper, the tallest of the tall in the age of the tall. By any standard, the Empire State Building is impressive. If counting to the very tip of its pinnacle, originally intended as a dirigible docking port, it stands 1,454 feet, and it goes up 1,250 feet to the actual top floor of the building, the 102nd (Empire State Building 2009).

Now imagine laying the Empire State Building on its side going all 1,454 feet to the spire. In the other direction, count out the 1,250 feet up to the 102nd story. The resulting rectangle, if you'd complete the sides, would be slightly smaller than the 40-acre base of the Danta Pyramid, the largest — but hardly the only — skyscraping pyramid at El Mirador, Peten, Guatemala. Depending on the source, the peak of the Danta is claimed to stand from just over 200 feet to as much as 250 feet above the surrounding city, with most settling on about 230 feet, about 23 stories or one-fifth the height of the Empire State Building (Guenter n.d.). It was arguably the hemisphere's tallest skyscraper (some say the Pyramid of the Sun at Teotihuacan erected several centuries later is a few feet taller) until almost the turn of the 20th Century. The Danta is at least twice as tall as the first U.S. skyscraper, only ten stories high, erected in Chicago shortly after that city's famous fire in the early 1870s when Americans had mastered the elevator and other technologies that allowed the building of hollow mountains. As far as that goes, the Tigre Pyramid at El Mirador would also vastly overtop that first American skyscraper and so would the Los Monos Pyramid also facing the half-mile square main plaza at El Mirador.

The comparison between the Empire State Building and the Danta Pyramid is by no means facetious. The 85 usable stories of the Empire State building have slightly more than two million square feet of floor space. The Danta Pyramid has about 1,900,000 square feet of usable space. The Empire State Building's space, of course, is internal and is rented out to companies for humdrum office work. The Danta counted its usable space on its exterior, and it was used for purposes of state and religion. For as impressive an effect as an address in the Empire State Building must have had on business associates (and competitors), it pales in comparison to the thrill of the thousands participating in bloodletting and sacrifice rituals on the various levels of the Danta and the plaza it overlooked. The Empire State

Building cost about 40 million 1930 dollars to build. It took slightly more than a year from the original excavations until the completion of the building, and about 5,400 workers, most of them European immigrants, were employed in its construction. No one knows how long it took to construct the Danta, nor at the present time can a reasonable estimate be derived regarding the number or background of the work force; but it is highly unlikely that the Danta Pyramid was completed in less time than the Empire State Building. The cost also must have been stupendous. Not only was limestone (that could have been employed for domestic use) quarried and hauled in on the backs of thousands along with fill, but enough stucco was burned — incinerating acres of trees — to face the entire 1,900,000 feet of exposed surface. All that stucco was tinted a vivid ochre red, made from hematite ore. Imagine standing in the center of the plaza. A quarter mile to the east looms Danta Pyramid, and at the same distance to the west Tigre soars 18 stories above you. To the south is Los Monos Pyramid, almost as tall, and all are painted blood red. Add to that scene the rites practiced here. They involved thousands of costumed celebrants who notched their ears until the blood flowed and who probably danced and chanted in consonance with direction from the top of the pyramid. Times Square on New Year's Eve at the turn of the millennium would have nothing on that. All this gives an idea of the capital of the Americas at the birth of Christ.

New York City, the first city in the Americas during the 20th century, consists of five boroughs and takes in an area of about 300 square miles. Eight million people lived (and live) there. Numerous cities such as Naachtun, Nakbe, Wakna, and Tintal, aside from El Mirador, occupied the Mirador Basin in which it is estimated hundreds of thousands lived. The basin takes in about 500 square miles, not counting the 60 percent of the area covered by bajo swamps or other watery environments (Wahl 2000). In other words, the Mirador Basin is about one and a half times larger than the city limits of New York. Almost none of the eight million inhabitants of New York are currently fed by farms inside the city limits, but back in the days when its population was counted in the low hundreds of thousands, much of New York's comestibles were grown on neighboring Long Island or New Jersey. It is assumed that almost all of the residents of Mirador were supported by the agricultural output within its boundaries.

The similarities between these two great capitals, and there are many, shift to stark contrasts when water and transportation come into play. New York is situated at the mouth of the Hudson River where it joins the Atlantic Ocean. It was from the first an important seaport, and its growth was spurred by the Erie Canal. That canal connected the city to the commerce of the Great Lakes and the interior of the continent. The Mirador Basin, on the other hand, is landlocked in the very heart of the Yucatan Peninsula. The Yucatan today is shared by three countries. The northern half is Mexican and includes three states, Campeche on the west, Quintana Roo on the east — Cancun is located on the northeastern coastline of Quintana Roo — and the state of Yucatan in the central and northernmost portions. The southern half of the Yucatan is divided between Belize fronting the Caribbean on the east and the Guatemalan district of Peten in the central part. The Usumacinta River, far to the west of the Caribbean, demarcates the western boundary of the peninsula. The Mirador Basin lies dead in the middle of the Peten snuggled up against the Mexican border, in what even today is a vast forest unbroken by large streams or modern roads — or in fact anything that could be called roads at all.

Unlike New York, the basin not only lies nowhere near a flowing body of water, little year-round water can be found there. Today, the Mirador Basin resembles the New York of

Planet of the Apes, the movie where Charlton Heston finds the wrecked and abandoned Statue of Liberty. The few guards and archaeologists who more or less permanently occupy the basin sometimes have difficulty coming up with enough drinking water during the dry season. It is as untouched by the hand of man as any place in the former precincts of the Maya. The supposed reason for its "pristine" state is the forest reserve set aside by the Guatemalan government. But in truth the basin lies in a part of the world where laws are easier to make than enforce. Many other formerly protected areas are now wall to wall with flourishing pioneer farmsteads, the product of squatters, mostly highland Maya refugees of the civil war of the '80s and more recent economic pressure, practicing what amounts to slash-and-burn horticulture. The basin remains pretty much inviolate. The reason is because campesino farmers — should they find enough drinking water — cannot eke out a living on these lands that once supported the capital city of North America. The term "mysterious" is often coupled with the word "Maya." In no place do the Maya seem more mysterious than in the Mirador Basin during the Preclassic Period where they managed a flourishing civilization and a degree of self-supporting urbanism with hundreds of thousands of population in an area that today cannot sustain homesteading campesinos.

Discovery, A.D. 1929–1979

The discovery of El Mirador can be laid squarely at the feet of the best known aviator in the first half of the 20th century, Charles Lindbergh. The story of how this happened is fairly involved. Even more interestingly, Lindbergh (and the others) became known as the father of remote sensing owing to their quest for Maya ruins. What is carried on today by satellite and high-tech imaging was first conducted using the human eye and a biplane.

Shortly after Lindbergh's electrifying solo flight across the Atlantic, Juan Trippe hired the young eagle, recently dubbed "Colonel" by the U.S. Army, to make publicity appearances throughout Latin America to promote Pan American Airways. In Mexico in particular, Trippe wanted to soften the populace, in the grip of a socialist revolution and anti-gringo sentiment, to the idea of an American airline landing in their country. Abundant good fellowship was obtained among both the Mexican people and their leaders, and one of the unexpected upshots of this trip was the meeting of Lindbergh with his future biographer, erstwhile press agent and wife, Anne Morrow, the daughter of the American ambassador to Mexico. In February of 1929, he'd just finished barnstorming the Caribbean on one such trip. He flew out of Belize bound for Havana and the East Coast of the U.S. (Jose n.d.). For no reason in particular, Lindbergh veered inland over the uncharted forests of Quintana Roo. He spied a hill thirty miles from Playa del Carmen in otherwise completely flat countryside. Lindbergh was surprised, on buzzing it, to find the top was masonry construction. The hill had been built by men. Today that site is known as the Maya city of Coba, and it is visited by hundreds of thousands of Cancun–based tourists every year. But in 1929, Lindbergh missed by just three years being the first westerner in the 20th century to see the site, lost in the wilderness only a few miles back from the coast.

On his return to Washington, Lindbergh got in touch with the head of the Smithsonian, offering to put together an aerial reconnaissance of archaeological sites. The Smithsonian referred him to the Carnegie Institution of Washington. A. V. Kidder, head of Carnegie's archaeological division, enthusiastically accepted Lindbergh's offer (Kidder 1930; Ricketson and Kidder 1930). In the summer, Lindbergh, assisted by his new wife, shot aerial photographs of pueblo and Anasazi ruins out of Kidder's base at Pecos, New Mexico. Both men were so pleased with the results of this work — including the discovery of heretofore unknown ruins — that they decided to apply this new instrument — air power — to the ancient people who first gave Lindbergh the idea, the Maya. So just months later in early October of 1929, Colonel and Mrs. Lindbergh rendezvoused with Kidder and fellow archaeologist Oliver Ricketson at the Pan Am base at Belize City, ready for their second round of aerial archaeology. Clearly, Americans in the 1920s, or at least heroes like Lindbergh, were get-up-and-go sorts who allowed no moss to grow on them.

It didn't hurt any that Pan Am was interested in developing the tourist trade in the area. The company put at the expedition's disposal its refueling stations in the Caribbean and a four-seat Sikorsky S-38 biplane fitted out with pontoons and huge radial engines. Each of the Pratt and Whitney Wasp motors developed 425 horsepower and guzzled up 50 gallons of gasoline an hour. The first leg of the aerial surveys ran from Belize to the beautiful city of Merida, capital of the state of Yucatan, Mexico, a distance of about 400 miles. First, the airmen, including only one archaeologist, set off on a south southwesterly heading over the Maya Mountains. It was hoped new ruins would be found. Their intuition was correct. A huge site to be named Caracol was waiting to be discovered high in those hills. It was to be found shortly but not by the aviators. Then on they went to the lake district of central Peten. Lindbergh buzzed the great site of Tikal, the most famous Maya ruin whose many large pyramids poked through the forest canopy. The photographers snapped shots of the temples. Then they headed north a few miles to the site of Uaxactun, where Ricketson was the archaeologist in charge. He observed rather ruefully that it took him a full day by mule to cover the distance that the Skikorsky traveled in six minutes. They were flying at an altitude of 500 feet and going around 85 mph.

At this point, Lindbergh nosed more or less due north. El Mirador lies 31 air miles from Uaxactun. But its heading is to the north northwest. The first ruin they spotted lay about 60 miles from Uaxactun — in Mexico, west of the present-day city of Chetumal. And that was the last ruin and almost anything else they spied until they crossed the border of the state of Yucatan in the north central part of the peninsula. They landed in Merida at about 2:30 after having been airborne for a bit less than five and a half hours, covering 455 miles. The return and subsequent trips out of Belize City turned up no more in the way of unknown ruins. Indeed, what each day's journey produced in the two archaeologists aboard was a profound sense of relief when they returned safely to land. Beneath them, the only thing they saw for hours on end was forest. It stretched on and on. Rarely was there a lake they could set down on, if need be. Now and then a river was visible, but often even the large rivers were obscured by trees. What they didn't see were ruins.

All the same, every one of the principals involved with this expedition was convinced of the utility of aviation in the exploration of Maya territory. British archaeologists reviewing the article Kidder and Ricketson submitted guffawed at their American cousins' characteristic belief in technology. Clearly, so far as the Brits were concerned, the only way to do archaeology was the old-fashioned spade-in-the-ground method. Although perhaps a bit piqued by the expensive tools at the Americans' beck and call, the British clearly had a point, given the lack of results of the first aerial expedition. But neither Lindbergh nor the Carnegie team was daunted. Aviation was able to provide a holistic glimpse — a bird's eye view — of the Maya world that had never before been seen. To archaeologists who had traveled through deep forests on the backs of mules, they often felt they had only a worm's eye view. And though the expedition discovered little in terms of ruins, they did in fact learn a lot from

An aerial-archaeological expedition of the University Museum in the 1930s poses with their gear by their Pan Am seaplane at the Dinner Key airplane facility—now a marina—in Miami. From left to right, Dr. J.A. Mason, William Carey (co-pilot), Frank E. Ormsbee (chief pilot), Robert A. Smith, Percy Madeira, Jr., and Gregory Mason (courtesy University of Pennsylvania Museum).

the aerial reconnaissance. Aside from matters of archaeological context, they also learned the color of the vegetation changed around a site. They figured this might help in locating ruins in the future—and this modest observation gave birth to the concept of remote sensing. Lindbergh promised to help with further efforts.

Presumably his hand was behind Pan Am's lending of a Sikorsky pontoon aircraft late the following year for the University of Pennsylvania Museum expedition. This effort seemed at first blush like something that might have been dreamed up in a Hollywood boiler room.

The direction was provided by a gentleman archaeologist with the unlikely name of Percy Madeira. It was bankrolled by the New York Times and a local Philadelphia paper (Madeira 1931). The members of the team posed for a photograph in Miami, where they arrived after a two day railroad trip from Philadelphia. They were togged in neckties and blazers. Madeira had on a sedate business suit, but the others topped off their dashing flying suits with jaunty headgears, barracks caps for the pilots and a cloche-style hat for one of the gentlemen savants. They looked more like a Jazz age send-up than men about to embark on serious archaeological work. A two hour, two hundred sixty mile hop put them in Havana for the night.

On the morning of December 3, they departed Havana and refueled at Pan Am's San Julian station on the west end of Cuba. They arrived over the northeastern coast of Yucatan at 11:08 A.M. Then it was on to Pan Am's refueling stop in Cozumel (which, incidentally, served as overnight port for Maya sea canoe traders during the Terminal Classic and Postclassic periods). Before getting down to the real business of aerial archaeology, they gave Cozumel officials a short ride in the airplane, and they dutifully allowed themselves to be feted by all the local males and that portion of the women who were not married. Madeira complained that the women married young and there were few of them, that a little tequila went a long way, and that one of the members of the expedition unwittingly slept with a five-inch scorpion.

The next morning was occupied testing the aircraft. Over the sea, where a landing could be affected, they climbed to an altitude of about 1,200 feet. One engine was cut off. After a downward glide for ten miles, the plane held steady at 250 feet. All this meant they could fly on one engine and conserve gas; and should an engine burn out over the vast forested reaches, they could limp back to an airport or find a suitable body of water to set down on. With this nicety that Lindbergh doesn't seem to have bothered with out of the way, they got down to the business of aerial archaeology. Stuffing cotton in their ears to drown out the deafening roar of the giant Pratt & Whitney engines, they cruised low over the canopy. By doing so, they were able to spy shadows cast by ruins. This they discovered by flying over known ruins. They reconnoitered south along the Caribbean coastline. They saw only formerly charted cities such as Tulum and Muyil. Then they headed to the state of Yucatan, passing a few suspicious mounds and more known ruins such as Chichen Itza and Itzamal before setting down at Merida. Relying on contacts developed on earlier visits, Madeira made the acquaintance of a government forester who had ranged throughout the peninsula. Did he know of any unexplored ruins near a lake or body of water? Yes, he did, came the reply. But it lay two days (called by muleteers two *jornadas*) ride from the lake. With time the forester volunteered he could pack in the needed supplies to meet the aircraft.

When chartering expensive aircraft, time was the one luxury not even well-heeled explorers like Madeira and the University Museum could afford. The forester also said he knew of ruins as large or larger than the megacity of Chichen Itza. This piqued Madeira's attention. These ruins were located due south of Merida, almost on the Guatemalan border in the headwater drainage of the Candelaria River. No body of water big enough for the Sikorsky was anywhere near. End of Madeira's interest. So the expedition flew on to the city of Carmen on the Gulf of Mexico in Campeche state. There they headed south along the Usumacinata River where they overflew the already discovered—but even today remote—cities of Piedras Negras and Yaxchilan. (It was between these sites in 1997 that author Armando and Peter Mathews had the adventure that almost cost them their lives, as related in the preface.) But their discoveries amounted to very little. At base camp in Carmen, Madeira enquired of the opinion of gringo acquaintances. These men, both managers of huge forest concessions of northern companies, agreed with the Merida forester. The best bet for a large ruin would be the upper Candelaria region close to the Guatemalan border. As it happens, all three of these stranger opinions seem to hint at a Maya capital hiding in the bush on the Mexican side of the frontier. Today we know those ruins as Calakmul, one of the two most important Classic Maya cities. It is the one the University Museum set out to find on the morning on the fateful date of December 7. They set a heading of 120 degrees, south southeast for Belize. They left just a bit before 11:00 A.M. At first they saw the delta of the Candelaria with branches of the river snaking every which way beneath them and a few thatch huts in clearings. Then after a while there were only trees. An hour into the flight, off to the south a volcano-like cone appeared. They veered in its direction, expecting to be disappointed by finding neither an extinct volcano nor a pyramid. Twenty minutes flying time—and about thirty miles—went by before Madeira realized "the big mound turned out to be the biggest of a group of four artificial elevations.... A smaller mound rose immediately in front of and a little to the right of the big elevation and two others slightly larger than the second mound were still nearer us, one directly in line west from the big mound and the other more to the south."

Clearly, Madeira was describing the skyscrapers of the first city of the Americas at the time of Christ. The big elevation was Danta Pyramid, the one closest to him on the west was Tigre and the southernmost one Mono. He declared, "The bush covered summit of the largest mound towered far above the treetops, which here was at least a hundred feet high. At a conservative estimate, the top of the largest ruin must be one hundred fifty feet above the surrounding territory and the other three ruins are perhaps two thirds that height," which was a fair appraisal of the height of the buildings considering he was making the estimate from a moving aircraft, something few had done at the time. While circling the ruins, an eagle-eyed observer spotted other ruins seven miles to the southeast. These were Nakbe, which was also flown around and photographed. With these observations, the University Museum expedition put itself on the archaeological map. Later it was noted that these ruins had been visited a few years earlier by Enrique Shufelt and F. V. Agnew of the Shufelt Company of British Honduras. And as a matter of fact, the ruins were not only generally known but even had a name, Mirador (Lookout), given by the forest-product rangers of the interior. But the University Museum published the first account of the site.

For all that, Madeira, unlike Lindbergh and the Carnegie people, felt areo-archaeology in the Maya area was a bust. Their expedition had come equipped with an inflatable boat, shotgun, hammocks, and emergency rations. Madeira and his friends had visions of finding an impressive ruin on a lake or large river. They'd land, ferry themselves to shore, set up camp, and go about snapping Graflex plates of the monuments of a "lost city." Because they couldn't find a new one in a suitable location, they picked for their on-site examination the already known city of Yaxha on Lake Yaxha. (Interestingly, Yaxha was the name of the site in Classic times as well as today, one of the very few where the name survived over the centuries.) What they got for their efforts were many insect bites. They also made a discovery. That discovery was that even on the ground finding Maya ruins could be difficult. A part of the city, long since known, had seemingly been swallowed up by the jungle-like growth. They never did locate it.

In the thirty-two years following its discovery, El Mirador was known to have been visited just once. Archaeologists from a Carnegie Institution of Washington project to Calakmul penetrated the jungles to the site from the north (Ruppert 1943). They were able to do little more than admire the ruins and then, owing to a lack of water, moved on. It wasn't until 1962 that something approaching a real on-ground archaeological investigation was conducted. That was made by Ian Graham. Because Graham's investigations are indicative of what archaeological explorers have put up with since time immemorial, we'll go into some detail discussing his tribulations — and character.

Many of the archaeologists of the Carnegie days were of the self-styled Lost Generation; characters like Sylvanus Morley that would have fit comfortably into a Scott Fitzgerald or, perhaps better, a Hemingway novel. They were, by and large, members of America's up-and-coming ruling class, to a great extent well-heeled (either old money or second generation products of technology such as mining engineering) and Ivy League educated.

Graham, on the other hand, could be termed a British version of a Beat Generation archaeologist. He dropped out of Cambridge University to fight in World War II (Dorfman and Slayman 1997). After the war he returned to the University of Dublin and graduated with a degree in physics in 1951. He bumped from job to job. Sometimes, he worked on developing radar. At other times, he restored pictures in Britain's National Gallery. In 1958 he "by accident" visited Maya sites in Mexico. Soon he was returning to Mexico and upper Central America on an annual basis. He mounted expeditions to sites whispered about by local forest gatherers and oil explorers.

Never minding the occasional hitch-hiking of rides in oil-company helicopters, Graham's expeditions were every bit as arduous as those conducted by the classic Maya explorers of the 19th century. For instance, he related his first journey to Machaquila (between Poptun and the Pasion River in the southeastern Peten) took five days. The second visit, after Hurricane

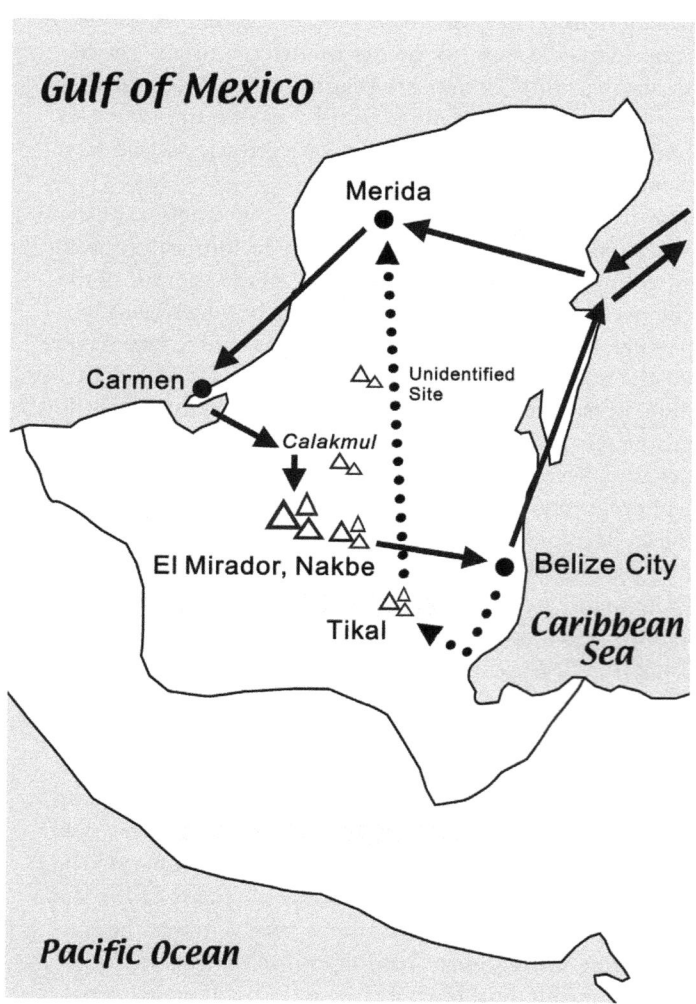

Map of early aerial exploration of Mirador Basin and vicinity. Dotted line indicates first leg of Lindbergh flight. Solid line shows University Museum flight that resulted in aerial discovery of El Mirador.

Hattie, required 27 days (Graham 1963). Wind-fallen trees blocked the crude path, and more than once his men (and mules) mutinied. The men grew sickly because they had to eat flour tortillas. So he sent one of his muchachos back for a hundred weight of corn. Then the man returned for yet another hundred fifty pounds of the grain.

The savanna-bred mules ate sparingly of the ramon (breadnut) leaves which Peten mules relished. They grew wan and then listless and finally rebellious. Their owner, one Lencho, seeing the source of his wealth wasting away before his eyes, withdrew within himself. He threatened to abandon the expedition. Graham, his money exhausted, sent a note to an oil company friend begging a hundred dollar loan. One of the workers, in a rare display of high spirits, shot a female spider monkey to capture its baby. The cub repaid them by bawling all the first night. On the second night, the squalling continued. Not a wink of sleep was gotten by anyone. Don Juan, as the men called Ian, put the monkey in a tree in hopes he would be rescued by his kind and pushed on.

When the expedition started, late May, the rains hadn't begun. Always by June the rainy season is roaring in full earnest. During the four weeks the expedition chopped and hacked and slogged toward the site, the rains poured down. Among Graham's many vexations, his supply of paperback books ran out. So he amused himself studying a Quaker Oats can in order to teach himself to translate Chinese hieroglyphics, thanks to the panels of English and Chinese instructions. Finally on the fortieth day — now they'd reached the site and were hard at work — their food was all but gone and the salt had completely run out. The men said it was time to return to civilization — well, their huts in better-roaded clearings. Much persuasion, the promise of bonuses, and a suddenly found cornhusk of salt allowed him to finish making latex casts of the many fine stelae at the site.

Is it any surprise then that a man of Graham's intrepid nature was the first to make a real reconnaissance of El Mirador? Helping guide Graham were Madeira's account and a map he discovered in the Direccion de Cartografia's offices in Guatemala City. An anonymous technician working for Royal Dutch Shell in the Netherlands in the late 1930s had meticulously plotted Mirador's buildings and sacbeob (causeways).

Graham attained Mirador after three days on a mule from Flores, the district capital (Graham 1967). He went roundabout going from waterhole to waterhole. On arrival, he set about surveying and mapping the ruins. He used British war surplus equipment and a sort of primitive dead-reckoning approach that worked quite well. It was obvious that Mirador was among the largest of Maya ceremonial centers (as the cities were known at the time by archaeologists who did not believe they were real cities). He pronounced its buildings the most massive of all Maya centers. All this was marred to some extent by the condition of the structures, "more thorough[ly] ruined than most ... not a freestanding wall, much less a vault[ed arch], remains intact." Although, he noted that "a plaster floor of extreme hardness remains at the top of Structure 706 even though exposed to the weather." He noted a characteristic architectural feature at the site. It was a triadic arrangement of structures topping most pyramids. This feature was comprised of two long thin structures parallel each other. A taller and larger structure stood at right angles. This triadic arrangement was to be known as the hallmark of the Mirador sites.

On his second trip into the Mirador Basin in the spring of 1962, he looked for Nakbe, the second site Madeira's team discovered from the air. His camp, improbably dubbed Las Camarones, "The Shrimp," lay about a mile due east of where he reckoned the ruins were located. Graham and his men thrashed around in the bush for more than two days before they found Nakbe.

Ultimately, he concluded, correctly, that most of the centers in the basin dated to the Preclassic period, the era that ends at about A.D. 250 (or 300) when the Maya began chiseling Long Count dates on their monuments. For whatever reason — his lack of formal archaeological credentials perhaps — Graham's conclusion was not taken to heart by the professionals. In the early 1960s, it was believed the best that could be said of the Preclassic lowland Maya was that they were peasant farmers. What little Maya civilization that existed was occurring in the highlands — or so it was believed at the time. The conventional wisdom had it that the Olmecs or Olmec-influenced peoples had crossed the Isthmus of Tehuantepec and colonized sites down the Pacific Coast all the way to El Salvador. From these Olmec centers, it was supposed, came the spark that ignited the contagion of Maya civilization after A.D. 250. No serious archaeologist in the early 1960s entertained the idea that a Maya megacity had developed in the southern lowlands during the Preclassic Period.

Almost twenty more years passed before the first university-sponsored archaeological expedition was mounted to the basin. The 1979 project was a joint effort of Brigham Young University and the Catholic University of America (Matheny 1980). Bruce Dahlin was the director. Among its startling conclusions was that Graham's dating of El Mirador and Nakbe was correct. The massive cities of the basin, among the largest in Middle America, reached their glory in the Late Preclassic. Both were ghost towns not long after Christ walked the earth.

The fates of the early explorers of the basin are also a study of ups and downs, rather like El Mirador itself, once the mightiest city in North America but now languishing in a wilderness. After his solo flight across the Atlantic, Lindbergh became one of the world's best known celebrities. In the late 1930s his renown was tarnished by his apparent endorsement of the Nazi experiment. His wife, Anne Morrow, spent much of the quarter century she survived the hero penning articles and books attempting to squelch that impression. Oliver Ricketson, one of the two archaeologists who flew with Lindbergh, was heir to the Carnegie fortune. He was also the first Carnegie that ever worked for the institution. Nevertheless, he resigned his post in the 1940s in semidisgrace. For the remaining few years of his life, he lost focus, being something of an embarrassment to himself and his family. He died in his late fifties. The biography of Percy Madeira, the gentleman director of the second aerial archaeological flight, on the other hand, stands in stark contrast to Ricketson. After practicing law for about twenty years, Madeira enrolled as a graduate student in archaeology in 1929, and he sponsored the aerial survey of the Yucatan in 1930. Later, he became a member and ultimately the president of the Board of Managers of the University Museum of the University of Pennsylvania. While he was president, the University Museum excavated and restored Tikal in one of the more ambitious projects of its sort in the world. Perhaps the least promising of this group was Ian Graham. His wanderlust drew him to Maya ruins on an annual basis when most would be thinking of buckling down to a long-term job and a mortgage and the other middle-class trappings. But Graham funded his own expeditions. For this, he received modest remuneration from the odd magazine article. So what happens to such people? In Graham's case, he was one of the first ever to be awarded a MacArthur Foundation's genius award (with a grant of hundreds of thousands of dollars) in 1981. He was also the founder of a project to publish a *Corpus of Maya Hieroglyphic Inscriptions,* which is based at Harvard University's Peabody Museum. Not a bad ending to a career choice that must have given his family in Britain many a restless night.

The Climate Changes and Corn Becomes King: Maya Civilization Becomes Possible, 2500–1000 B.C.

In the 1920s, a professor of tropical forestry at the University of Miami, Dr. John Gifford, claimed all American civilization was based on Indian culture (Glassman 1978). He pointed out that the Indians taught the early pioneers to grow Indian crops. In grade school we all learned that Squanto imparted the practice of placing a fish in a corn hill to the Pilgrim settlers. It was a trick that provided the fertilizer needed in the barren forest lands of the East. But Gifford also noted that the log cabins of the early settlers were based on those of the Indians. The first cash crop of the British colonies, tobacco, was of Indian origin. He speculated that our sports such as hockey (acknowledged by all) and football (not acknowledged by many) were inspired by the matches of shinny ball Indians played.

In the following pages we examine the nuts and bolts of the early lowland Maya's material culture. Much of this information, as Dr. Gifford suggested, will also help us understand North American material culture. For instance, scientists can conduct isotopic analyses to determine the diet of the ancient Maya. Frequently, it is found that the upper crust Maya ate more corn than the hoi polloi. Similar tests conducted on contemporary North American bones show our diet to be even more corn-rich than the best-fed Maya noble—and the race of corn, strangely enough, that made possible the settlement of the Maya lowlands is closely related to the dent field corn that North American material culture relies on. In short, the Maya milpa (or corn patch) in the seemingly steamy, far-off isthmus of Central America can be regarded as the cradle of the American breadbasket. To understand what grew in the steamy jungles of the Peten, we first have to understand the climate and then get to know the crops that came to grow there. Hint: the development of corn as a staple allowed the Maya to coalesce into centers with sophisticated religious observations and political structure.

Ten thousand years ago at the end of the last Ice Age, the Mirador Basin was covered by trees familiar to northerners (Leyden 1984). There were junipers, elms, oaks, and pine. The first two species were probably those that still inhabit mountainous terrain in Central America, the elm producing huge specimens that grow to 300 feet tall. Oaks and pine grow today in the Yucatan, and they are similar to the longleaf pine and live oak of the Deep South. If the vegetation seems familiar, the creatures of the basin ten thousand years ago would certainly not be. Mammoths, short-faced bears, the giant armadillo-plated glyptodon, dire wolves, and the last of the saber-tooth cats prowled about. These critters were preyed on by the first humans of the area. They produced what archaeologists call Clovis spear points, which they hafted on long poles. The first Clovis point was found near the town by that name on the New Mexico–Texas border among bones of extinct and very large bison. These brave people, making their living dispatching big game, followed a nomadic existence stretching across the Great Plains and at least as far south as Ladyville, Belize. A Clovis spearhead was found in this location eighty miles east and a bit south of the Mirador Basin. Whether the Clovis people were related to the Maya is unknown and unknowable, as aside from the spear point, they left little trace. Once the climate changed, the megafauna disappeared—and with them the Clovis way of life.

By 8,500 years ago (6500 B.C.), a lush tropical forest similar to that in the area today was growing over the bones of the megafauna. Rain to the tune of 75 inches a year began pelting the basin. Up to 90 percent of it fell in the period between May and November. The rest of the year could be bone dry. In particular, the time from April until the rains

Strangler fig. This tree in the banyan family produces small, insipid figs that are favored by howler monkeys.

begin to fall in May or early June is frequently parched. For that reason the climate is called seasonally dry tropical forest. Many of the tree species inhabiting it will drop their leaves during the driest period making the forest semi-deciduous. Nevertheless, a luxuriant growth of very large trees clothed the uplands. Tropical forests are characterized by the enormous number of species that may inhabit a given space — just as far northern forests may have only one or two species represented in acres of growth. In the basin up to eighty tree species may be found in an acre. Among the tall species most commonly encountered are the ramon or breadnut. This tree was used by the Maya for tortillas when the corn crop fails. Other characteristic species are allspice, familiar to us as an ingredient in pumpkin pie, and gumbo limbo, the so-called tourist or gringo tree because of its reddish bark that peels like a sunburned tourist. Many species of strangler figs are also commonly encountered. These trees are of the banyan family. They have many octopus-like trunks. True to their name, they produce fruits recognizable as figs. Insipid to modern human tastebuds, these figs were eaten by the ancients and are the preferred food of troops of howler monkeys. The understory yields a crop of plants familiar to us such as the parlor palm and wild coffee and shrubs related to the black pepper of table fare.

During the rainy season three to six feet of water settles in the low spots known today as *bajos* (as in low or below such as Baja California). Today these bajos are swamps inhabited by shrubby trees that refuse to grow straight up. This peculiarity is due to the fact that these low-lying areas dry out during the spring dry season (Wahl 2005). The clay hardpan contracts and then during the wet season expands pitching the trees every which way. Growing today in these swamps is the fearful black poisonwood, an arboreal cousin of poison ivy. Another characteristic species is the black olive, familiar as a hurricane-resistant landscape tree in south Florida. Various eugenia are found there; the crepe myrtle or "southern lilac" is closely related and shares the trait of many of having naked bark. The most important species is the shrubby logwood. The inconspicuous, not to say runty, logwood hardly seems the product from which fortunes could be made. But in the days before aniline dyes were synthesized by German scientists back in the 19th century, it was sought as the preferred yellow coloring. Gangs of hearty woodcutters trekked through the forest seeking it. During Maya times, it is likely that logwood did not inhabit the vast acreages it does today, pretty much unmolested. There is good reason to believe that back then these areas were shallow lakes or saw-grass marshes.

Now flash back 4,500 years ago to about 2500 B.C. when the story of the first settled human inhabitants of the Mirador basin begins. At that time, the climate abruptly changed. It became drier and the woods thinned out, and in their place came grasses and weeds of the daisy family. Most importantly, the bottom of a lake on the basin's western edge recorded a single incident of *Zea mays* corn — pollen. Corn pollen wouldn't turn up as a common component of the record for another thousand years. David Wahl, a University of California PhD student, conducted his doctoral research on the climate of the area as shown by the pollen and geological record of the lake bottom (Wahl 2005). He theorizes that the grass and weeds were the result of slash-and-burn clearing by early farmers. Were these farmers ancestors of the Maya? The archeological record is absolutely mute. With the exception of that fossilized corn pollen found several feet below Laguna Puerto Arturo, not a hint of the culture of those corn growers has ever turned up. But of all the cultivated grains, corn is the only one that absolutely cannot grow without human assistance. It is a sure bet humans were there planting corn — and altering the environment to do so.

Early Americans had no draft animals to plow their fields. To prepare a seedbed, they used a different technology: fire. With the help of chert tools, farmers would bark the trees months before the dry season. After several weeks or months the leaves would wither and die. Then using flint (a specialized type of chert) to strike a spark into kindling, the patch of woods would be fired before the rains began to fall in early summer. Then using a sharpened pole called a dibble stick, corn kernels would be inserted at the proper depth into the loam of the forest floor. The suddenly opened forest canopy invited the many weedy seeds contained in the soil to burst into competition with the corn, beans, squash, and other crops planted by the early agriculturalists. But the planted seeds had the advantage. Normally, the first crop would be heavy. The second season's yield would be reduced but adequate, then subsequent years diminishing returns would force the farmer to turn his efforts to other patches of woods.

During the drier period beginning about 2500 B.C., these slash-and-burn pockets in the forest came back not as woods but as grassy or weedy fields (Leyden 1984). Slash-and-burn (technically known as swidden) horticulture was a simple technological innovation. Its discovery occurred spontaneously in many parts of the world.

The development of the chief agriculture crop grown in the swidden fields of the Mirador Basin was anything but a simple phenomenon. In fact, even today modern agricultural scientists are by no means sure where corn came from or how it was developed. Unlike all other cultivated grains, corn does not occur in a state of nature, owing to the unusual nature of the corn cob. Most wild grains have developed distribution systems that induce dispersal of individual seeds. Anyone who has eaten a roasting ear can attest that the cob is ranked with hundreds of individual kernels. Drop that ear into the ground, water it, give it optimal warmth and light and dozens of plants struggle up, each attempting to crowd out its brethren. All are successful in that mission and none is able to reproduce — or at least not for more than a generation or two. Because of this, the corn plant cannot do what Darwin (and Freud) deemed the absolute requisite for all species, reproduce itself (Wilkes 2004).

On occasion anyone reading about the ancient Maya wonders if he should admire them for their astonishing accomplishments or castigate them for incredible myopia. The list of Maya technological shortcomings is long. They did not produce a metal-based technology nor did they domesticate beasts of burden; but then there were no animals suitable for domestication, and few ores occurred in the mostly flat limestone country of the classic Maya. Nor did they discover a use for the wheel. They knew about the wheel, but employed it only for toys. Imagine building a pyramid with a base of more than forty acres rising to a height above two hundred feet without a shovel, block and tackle, or even a wheelbarrow. But before you get too carried away with your verbal flogging of the Maya, remember that the Maya invented the zero. The Maya also developed the equivalent of the decimal system, which they used for their Long Count calendar dates. Another intellectual achievement of roughly equal importance to the modern world — especially the American world — was the development of garden-variety corn.

It is entirely possible that the Olmec food supplies did not include corn (although we are pretty sure they did because of the presence of the Maize God). Their populations of a few tens of thousand could have subsisted on marine resources and root crops (Lawler 2007). The much more numerous Maya, counted initially in the hundreds of thousands then later the millions, could not have survived without corn. They understood this and adored the grain. Images of corn decorate their temples and adorn the ritual costumes of their rulers. Isotopic analysis reveals that in many instances aristocratic Maya consumed more corn than the hoi polloi (although occasionally the elite ate more meat and the peasant class ate the corn). Bowls of fat tamales are depicted in feasting scenes on pottery. For all that, as noted earlier, studies on the skeletons of modern-day North Americans show that we consume more corn than even the plumpest, most corn-fed Maya dignitary of days gone by.

Even if a grain of sweet corn never passes one's lips, any nonvegan in North America, and increasingly the world, owes her food supply to corn. The reason is almost all animals consumed by our notoriously overindulged meat culture are fed corn. That steak or hamburger you ate last night was not fattened on a western prairie but in a feedlot eating corn. Pigs are raised in breeze-conditioned houses and fed corn. Likewise, chicken feed is corn-based, and even most of the catfish, trout, and other increasingly farm-based fish we consume live on corn pellets — a precondition for selecting a species for aquaculture is its acceptance of grain feed. Our pet canines live on corn, as the dry food is better, on balance, than supposedly meat-based canned goods, which in any case would also be corn fed. Seventy percent of America's huge corn crop goes to feeding animals. The other 30 percent is used in many other ways. High fructose corn sweetener notoriously produces the sugary taste in candy and baked products, and North America's favorite beverages whether they be soda, beer, or bourbon (or rye or white lightning and even Jameson Irish whiskey) are based on the grain. Our indebtedness to corn rests not only on consumables but also as an industrial base product. Corn can be found in many products such as paper, industrial chemicals, gasoline (the base for the ethanol additive), penicillin (the medium upon which the mold spores are grown), and on and on and on.

American corn culture centers on what used to be tall grass prairie in the humid Midwest stretching from Ohio to eastern Nebraska and Kansas and north into southern Ontario. During the growing season this area resembles the tropics with high daily maximum temperatures and abundant rainfall. For a time, the Na-Tel race of corn grown in the Mirador Basin (and the Maya Lowlands generally) was believed to be the progenitor of dent or field corn, the type grown industrially in North America. Research has shown that not to be the case, but dent corn is a close relative, and Na-Tel, for that reason, is of particular interest to geneticists.

Northern scientists have been trying to determine the origins of corn for more than a hundred years. As far back as 1893, J. W. Harshberger deduced the location of corn's genesis. He determined that corn developed in the semiarid highlands of Mesoamerica, in particular at an altitude of more than 5,000 feet with an annual rainfall of about fifteen inches (Wilkes 2004). He made these deductions by studying the productivity of early corn races. Like rice and wheat and other grains (millet, barley, sorghum, and so on), corn is a grass. Early researchers narrowed the possible parents of corn to two genera, teosinte and tripsacum. At first blush, teosinte would appear to have had the upper hand in the claim to motherhood of the most important food crop of the Americas. Some species of teosinte are dead ringers for corn. To an uninformed eye the stalk looks like a cornstalk, and the plant tassels out as corn does. Also, it produces an "ear" in the axel of leaves as corn does. But the ear (a term used by farmers to describe the fruiting head of wheat and other grains) of teosinte forms no cob. The scant fifteen or so grains per ear break free individually, and the hard kernel passes, unscathed, through the gullet of critters who consume it. Teosinte is restricted in its distribution to the western highlands of Mexico and Upper Central America.

Tripsicum species, on the other hand, can be found growing from North America to Argentina. The most prominent member of the genus in our area is called eastern gamagrass, and it was a common component of the mostly defunct tall grass prairie of the Midwest, now converted to corn belt. Gamagrass — not to be confused with grama grass, a dominant species of the short grass prairie farther west — is a clumping perennial that can grow to ten feet tall. It is the most common species in the tall grass prairie in wet areas where it out competes big bluestem and Indian grass. Its seed grains are said to have three times the protein of corn. They have been found preserved in caves in Arkansas and northeast Mexico. On occasion tripsacum has been utilized by American frontiersmen. For instance, early botanists in Florida reported cracker hunters would use tripsacum grains as a trail food when in the woods.

In the 20th century, geneticists have been puzzled as to which of these species is responsible for the paternity of corn. Superficially, teosinte looks much more like corn. Tripsacum proponents explained that inconvenient fact away by claiming teosinte was merely the product of the tripsacum-maize crossbreeding. Be that as it may, attempts to recross tripsacum with maize end in failure. Though the two species will produce a first generation hybrid, subsequent crops become sterile. The advent of technology that could count chromosomes explained this anomaly. Corn has ten base of chromosomes while tripsacum has eight. This in the minds of researchers made it impossible for tripsacum to have been the parent of corn. Then at the beginning of the 21st century, researcher Mary Eubanks showed how tripsacum could have indeed been the progenitor of maize. Her experiment did not prove tripsacum was the parent, only that it was a possibility. Therefore, the situation regarding corn's paternity was thrown into confusion again.

Garrison Wilkes of the University of Massachusetts, Boston, estimates that during the past century the conventional wisdom regarding the origin of this important crop has undergone a revolution about every twenty years. Sometimes the weight of opinion tilts toward tripsacum. But teosinte has generally been regarded as the parent. Each time an entirely different, hypothetical genetic chronology is developed. Even with all the genetic advances of the last generation, scientists still cannot sort out the complicated genetic structure of corn. Genetic researchers may be able to isolate a criminal perpetrator from the population of the planet with a micron of organic matter, but their machinery is not at present sophisticated enough to solve the riddle of corn. The best guess for the moment is that a mutation of the species of teosinte native to the Balsas River valley of highland Mexico resulted in the first maize. The Balsas valley is just south of the valley of Mexico and not far from Aculpulco. That race of teosinte is believed to have developed over the millennia into the crop that feeds the Americas.

Whether or not further research affirms the current conventional wisdom, we can thank Mesoamericans—if not exactly the Maya—for carefully selecting sports (mutations) of better ears of corn. They planted and replanted them to yield larger, more productive product. Henry Wallace was Franklin Roosevelt's vice president from 1937 to 1941. FDR dumped him, probably because of his left-wing political views. Wallace started what became Pioneer hybrid seed corn company. Pioneer is now one of the leading producers of seed grain in the world, and though Wallace had passed on by the time of Khrushchev's first visit to America, it was Wallace's Pioneer associates who invited the crusty Soviet premier to Iowa. They attempted to impress the commissar who oversaw a Ukrainian famine with American cornfields. Wallace claimed to have conducted the experiments that led to his development of hybrid corn in his backyard garden. It is entirely possible that one Native American plantsman, working alone, found that budsport in a teosinte (or tripsacum) plant, recognized its value, and, by backcrossing, improved it significantly. Or perhaps an Indian society (similar to the one Armando was inducted into as noted in the preface) devoted itself to improving crops and was responsible for the development of this singularly helpless food crop.

Material Culture of the Mirador Basin, 1000 B.C.–A.D. 150

Corn was the most important plant domesticated in Mesoamerica. Many others were also developed. A partial list would include snap beans, various dried beans, lima beans, papayas, vanilla, various tropical tree fruits, squash, hot chili peppers, sweet peppers, cacao, and cotton (among other crops) that were brought under cultivation. The Indians of Mesoamerican may not have invented the wheel, but in a significant way they invented the American way of life.

After that one lone indication of corn pollen in the Mirador basin at about 2500 B.C., 1,500 years passed until about 1000 B.C. This is the beginning of the time frame archaeologists designate as Middle Preclassic. At that time isolated hamlets and villages began appearing in the basin in the archaeological record. After a while—counting time in centuries as though it were minutes—these early farmers began erecting what are assumed to be temple mounds; and by the end of the Middle Preclassic, 300 B.C., impressive pyramids were going up more than 150 feet at Nakbe and elsewhere. Archaeologists believe the development of the Na-Tel race of corn is principally responsible for this complexity. Unlike early varieties of maize that required a semiarid, highland climate, this variety was able to thrive in the humid tropical lowlands such as the Mirador Basin. Na-Tel, which is now known to be more like popcorn than dent corn, nourished generations of lowlanders. And others impressed by the productivity of the corn and free land and perhaps absence of political or religious strife, followed Na-Tel into the Mirador Basin. Migration must have occurred because the population of the basin grew faster than natural increase can account for. (Unfortunately, at present the archaeological record is silent on where these folks came from and why they felt compelled to leave wherever their homeland was.) Calculations made by Oliver Ricketson, one of the Lindbergh archaeologists and among the first to investigate the Preclassic Maya, indicated a population density of about 270 persons per square mile, equivalent to the density of the state of New York in the 1930s (Ricketson and Ricketson 1937). He estimated about 13 million could have inhabited the Maya area at that density. More recent studies have concluded the Maya lands supported a population similar to that at present of Western Europe, confirming Ricketson's estimates. That is a lot of people for a tropical agricultural system to support.

So what farming techniques were used by the early Miradorans to fill the larders with enough corn to feed those immigrants — the same immigrants who became the sweating masses erecting pyramids, stone by stone, basketful of fill by basketful of fill? The short answer is that the archaeological record in the basin is fairly silent. But the basin was not the only place in the Maya area inhabited during the late Middle Preclassic.

Pulltrouser Swamp lies about a hundred miles northeast of Mirador in far northeastern Belize. It consists of a clover-like pattern of three connected bajos surrounded by highlands much like the basin. Back in the 1970s archaeologists working in the area, notably Dennis Puleston, noticed that something very unusual was evident in the swamp — straight lines. Lots of them. Nature abhors a straight line as much as it despises a vacuum.

At the time it was believed that the Maya employed only slash-and-burn agriculture. This view accorded with the belief that Maya cities were basically empty ceremonial centers where a few philosopher-priests lived. There from atop the pyramids they gazed at the stars and made the astronomical observations, which have astonished generations of northerners. At certain seasons of the year, the simple farmers in the countryside would gather for religious rituals — and pass surplus foods and grain to the priests. Puleston was among the archaeologists who challenged that view. He conducted some excavations on Albion Island, not far from Pulltrouser, that showed the Maya did employ intensive agriculture. Before he could investigate the mystery of Pulltrouser Swamp, he was struck by lightning while atop the Castillo at Chichen Itza, an untimely but fitting end for a Maya archeologist. The investigation of the strange parallel lines fell to B. L. Turner and Peter Harrison.

Excavation proved that the lines were indeed man-made canals (Turner and Harrison 2000). The higher ground between canals showed a vein of enriched black soil two feet deep. This soil contained not only corn pollen — and a lone carbonized corn stalk — but pottery associated with both the late Preclassic and Classic periods. There was some evidence of pollen from other crops. The Maya horticulturalists who tended these gardens occasionally scooped up the muck on the canal bottoms and enriched the seed bed with it. Detritus of water lily leaves was also found in the rich soil. This indicated that lily pads may have been used as mulch, and no doubt water lettuce and the many kinds of vegetation that can clog up waterways in the tropical Americas were piled under the corn plants for this purpose. After the fields were abandoned, rather than revert to open marsh, many of the raised fields were colonized by bajo tree species similar to those in the Mirador bajos.

The ancient site of Becan lies approximately fifty miles northeast of the Mirador Basin in the state of Campeche, Mexico. The topography is similar to the Mirador Basin with gentle rises of several hundred feet. The early inhabitants of Becan are famous for digging — early on — a moat around their city. They also turned their mole-like powers to the gentle slopes in the surrounding hinterland. They terraced them, which means they broke the natural slopes with lateral ridges. Terracing prevents topsoil from washing away in the heavy summer rains and preserves moisture. It is extremely labor intensive (Beach et al. 2002). It is not a strategy employed by slash-and-burn agriculturalists who frequently don't bother weeding their fields.

Clearly, another simple strategy that could have been employed was weeding the fields. Any husbandman going to the trouble of reducing a slope with terraces probably paid close attention to the crops growing on them, and weeding ranks among the strategies archaeologists call "intensive agriculture." Mulching could also have been used. For instance, much of the Florida central ridge is nothing more than old coastal dunes. Areas swept by fire regularly yield only pine barrens. But spots protected from fire by natural breaks in the terrain develop a carpet of mulch. Growing through those few inches of forest duff will be jungle-like hammocks of a profusion of understory shrubs and live oak trees hung with bromeliads and orchids — and all because of a few inches of leaf litter. The mulch maintains soil moisture, and it also helps make soluble minerals not otherwise available to the roots of plants. The Maya worked notoriously hard — a glimpse of their skyscraping temples proves that, but mulching field crops may have taxed even their industry. Gathering grass and forbes, packing them into the fields, and spreading them among the roots of their cornstalks would have been backbreaking. Mulching probably would not have been cost productive for field crops, but it may have been useful for a few highly productive crops.

Another strategy, which they are known to have employed, was intercropping. This strategy can provide many of the benefits of mulching without nearly as much labor. It has the added benefit of yielding two different types of vegetables to the larder. Intercropping simply means planting a row (or rows) of another crop alongside the corn. Modern experiments interspersing faba beans with corn in tropical fields has shown a 30 to 40 percent increase in both crops (Li et al. 2007). The nature of tropical soils is such that certain important elements, especially phosphorous, are not available to growing plants. Chemical analysis may show plenty of phosphorous in the ground, but it does the plants no good because their roots are blocked from absorbing it. It has long been known that intercropping beans and corn provided nitrogen, the first in importance of nutrients. Lawn fertilizer is high in nitrogen in order to promote healthy green growth. These recent experiments show the usefulness of intercropping to phosphorous absorption, the essential nutrient necessary for flower, fruit, and root production. The leaves of the beans also provide shade, keeping the ground cooler and allowing less moisture to evaporate, thus mimicking mulch to an extent.

The milpa (swidden) system traditionally intercropped corn, beans, and squash. Perhaps growing this triad, especially in combination with some sort of intensive horticulture, produced even more benefits in terms of yield, soil development and so on. By whatever means, the gardens and farms of the Mirador Basin and surrounding areas produced enough grains and vegetables to support a population large enough to erect dozens of pyramids up to twenty-five stories tall.

The archaeological record is again silent, as yet, on the animal proteins consumed by the folks in the basin. But a veritable time capsule was discovered in a residential structure at the minor middle Preclassic site of Cahal Pech in Belize. Cahal Pech is located almost on the border of Guatemala. In that regard it may be regarded as similar to the Mirador Basin, although the Belize River, which it overlooks and which shoots directly to the sea, marks a distinct difference between the sites; the basin, as noted earlier, is completely landlocked. The assemblage that archaeologists examined was found in a "chultun" inside a collapsed structure at an outlying hamlet. Chultuns were storage pits excavated into bedrock. They frequently had a bottle shape structure with a narrow neck opening to a larger and deeper cavity below. The ones outside buildings generally were cisterns which captured runoff water during wet periods. Interior chultuns functioned as storage cellars or pantries (or cisterns). The folks in the house examined by Jaimie Awe, Christine White and others were not dainty in their eating habits (Powis et al. 1999). They used their chultun as a refuse pit. The resulting midden paints an interesting picture of the diet of late Middle Preclassic folk. That the structure was more than a third of a mile from the center of this minor polity, indicates the inhabitants were not of great status. But the inhabitants could have been the principal personages of the hamlet. The chultun was ten feet by seven by about a yard deep, and it was slightly more than half full of carbonized animal and vegetable matter. The find was an archaeological cornucopia, a window into the dietary, lifestyle and trade habits of Preclassic Maya.

Analysis revealed that the home's cooking fires were fueled by pine wood. In terms of animal food, about half of the remains consisted of freshwater mollusks, notably apple and jute (pronounced hootie) snails and a local river clam. The other half of the bones consisted of just about anything that had wings, paws, claws, hooves, or fins. Turkey and currasow bones lounged in the midden alongside those of the hog-like peccary. Paca bones were prominently featured. Today, the paca, a large succulent rodent, is called gibnut in Belize and is still a favored food item. Also found were remains of armadillos and opossums (both eaten by Euroamericans in pioneer days) and smaller rodents, which probably weren't consumed by Euroamerican pioneers in normal times or at least were not admitted to. The most amazing find in the rubbish heap were heads of marine fishes. Cahal Pech lies 66 miles from the Caribbean. Many of the marine species were those moderns find delectable; grouper, snapper and hogfish. Parrotfish, prized in parts of the world but not currently in North America, were also found. Even more surprisingly, evidence pointed to the heads having been cooked on the spot, indicating that they may have been brought inland — no doubt by canoe on the Belize River — without salting or smoking. What this has to say about the sophisticated nature of trade in the Preclassic period has not been followed up on as yet — but it is enormous. Far fewer heads of freshwater catfish, locally available, were found in the pit, although many unidentifiable fish bones were also located. These bones may have been catfish.

Other studies have paid attention to the inclusion of dog meat and venison, both eaten at Cahal Pech in the Preclassic. One such study attempted to settle the question of whether deer were kept as domestic stock during the Preclassic period. A Spanish chronicler noted that deer were pen raised at time of contact. This assertion was made memorable by the claim that some Maya women suckled the domesticated whitetails. Analysis of deer bones found at a site in northern Belize showed they had foraged exclusively on browse from the woods. (Had they been fed corn or corn-fed maiden's milk the isotope signature would have been radically different.) This study also attempted to determine the status of dogs.

Were dogs considered primarily as food items? Modern Maya in the northern Yucatan report they were eaten in the past there, as they were in many parts of precontact America. Or were they raised for ritual purposes — or simply as pets and guardians of the hearth, as Maya mythology designates them? The scavenger habits of canines foiled this analysis. The assumption was that dogs fed corn would be fattened up for some particular reason such as burial companions or sacrifice or butchery and consumption. But analysis of the dogs that should have been pampered yielded unpredicted patterns, owing, it was believed, to the canines' habit of eating feces. In short, the study seemed to say dogs were sometimes eaten, sometimes sacrificed, and sometimes tolerated thanks to their usefulness around the domicile (White et al. 2001).

Vegetable remains in the Cahal Pech pit include guava, the insipid wild fig, corn, and squash. No evidence was found of species such as beans, cotton, cohune palm, and breadnut. It is believed these species slipped through testing cracks. Another species not found but definitely known to be used by preclassic Maya was manioc or tapioca, which we can only assume was used by the Olmec (Hather and Hammond 1994). Nor was evidence of cacao found, which is known to have been widely, if perhaps sparingly, used in the time period. Evidence for the early use of cacao rests on curious spouted pots — looking much like tea pots — found in northern Belize. Analysis showed residue of cacao. The early chocolate drink, which tasted bitter, was prepared in a specific way. A concoction of cacao, corn gruel and chili was poured back and forth until it frothed. The most prized part of the early chocolate drink was the sudsy, spicy froth, red in color (Hurst et al. 2002).

The human bones found at the Cahal Pech house belied the old truism that dead men don't talk. A forensic analysis of the bones interred near the house showed that, unlike the scavenging dogs, they had been nourished by substantially less corn products (or reef fish, which test the same as corn products) than folks at another hamlet in their village (Powis et al. 1999). That hamlet produced specialty crafts. Its residents may have received more corn or reef fish as remuneration. Broadly, though, the corn intake for these folks was similar to that at most other sites in the area. All this means the people of the Mirador basin probably had a high corn diet supplemented with game from the countryside. They also probably consumed fish and shellfish from the 60 percent of the surrounding wetlands, which are presumed to have contained water more or less year round in Preclassic times.

The houses of common folk, like those of the Olmec, were rectangular or apsidal and made of wood, thatch, and wattle and daub. They differed from the Olmec in situating several structures together on a raised platform. This grouping is called a plazuela by archaeologists, and it is speculated that the houses were occupied by the families of a male and his adult male children. One end of the house likely was given over to the men and their implements, tools, clothes and so on. The other belonged to the women. Because of division of work by gender, all houses were inhabited by one adult male and a female. On the basis of modern anthropological research, it is assumed that about 80 percent of these couples were married with children. The other 20 percent represented a widow with younger unmarried male relatives or an older widower and unmarried daughter and so on.

On the basis of studies conducted on Late Classic period houses, thatch structures took about 67 person days to build (Abrams 1998). And this was probably put up like a New England barn raising by many working over a period of a day or a couple of days. In short, though two people could build a structure in a month, it would take four persons fifteen days or eight people a week. Sixteen persons working and socializing together could get the job done in a long weekend. Stone houses, which were beginning to be built by those who had begun to think of themselves as aristocrats, required many more person days. In short, it took a thousand person days to erect one. Mobilization of whole hamlets or neighborhoods would probably be required to get the job done.

So what tools were used by stone age carpenters and masons? Limestone is fairly soft and easy to work when freshly exposed to the air. It was quarried by sawing (Shafer 2000). The saw was a cord run back and forth. On the other end of the spectrum, small pieces of stone or shell were worked using a burin-spall drill. This device used a piece of chert for the drill bit. The bit was attached to a stick. Rotary action was supplied by a hand-operated belt. This primitive drill could shape stone as hard as jade, but the operation took many hours and much dedication. Chert, the cutting edge on Maya tools, is a sedimentary stone. The strength in chert is supplied by silica or iron nodules. Dark chert, high in organic impurities such as clay, is sometimes called flint. All flint is chert; not all chert is flint, but the terms are sometimes used interchangeably.

Chert deposits are widely distributed through the Maya lowlands, especially near bajos. They were worked in shallow pit mines, which produced pieces or macroflakes of the raw product. A well-aimed blow to a macroflake approximately seven by ten inches would yield a sliver of stone that looked like an orange peel. This blow would also produce a sharp edge. The Maya workman hafted the resulting stone to a pole to produce an adze capable of dropping a tree or plowing ground. Anyone who has ever stopped halfway through chopping a tree to run a file over the edge of an axe will feel for the Maya woodsman. The next blow of the file-sharpened ax chops deeper and cleaner, but the Maya could not sharpen their flint. At times blazing away with a chert adze must have felt like trying to chop a tree down with a baseball bat.

As the edge broke away, the chunk of chert was reknapped to become a hatchet (called a celt by archaeologists) or a spear or arrow point. Knives were manufactured for domestic use. Obsidian, which is volcanic glass, was obtained in trade and was also used as a knifepoint. It was sharper but much more expensive than chert. Its use was probably reserved for autosacrifice, although chert was also used for bloodletting. Hammerstones and manos and metates were optimally granite or basalt from the Maya Mountains of Belize or the highlands of Guatemala or Chiapas. When limestone was used to reduce nixtamalized corn to dough, the tiny flakes of stone — over a lifetime — played havoc with the teeth as shown by the many worn-down molars in Maya graves. On average, scientists have determined chert-bladed hoes, billhooks, and axes were about one third as efficient as the steel tools their modern descendents use.

The major industrial process undertaken by the stone age Maya was lime kilning. Lime was a universally required substance. The early pyramids and some households were plastered by inches of concrete made from lime. Later the Maya became more efficient in the use of stucco, plasters, and cements made of the lime. But their continual use of the material — as we shall see — is believed to be a significant contributing factor to their demise in the Preclassic period. Even had the Maya been aware of this dilemma, it is unlikely they could have given up lime burning. They would have perished without it. It was vital to their existence.

Lime added to corn produces, ultimately, masa harina dough, the basic ingredient for tamales, tortillas, atole, and the many other food products of the corn plant. The addition of lime to corn was adopted because Mesoamerican manos and metates could not otherwise reduce the flinty kernels to a workable product. Our iron-age pioneers had no difficulty grinding corn into meal at local mills. The cornmeal was baked into hoecakes, johnnybread, and the various other synonyms for cornbread. It became the staple of the frontier homestead.

And the pioneers suffered mightily for being outlying members of the industrial revolution. Pellagra was endemic among those hearty folk.

The Maya did not suffer from pellagra because of the nixtamalization process. Two parts lime to a hundred parts corn steeped in water overnight releases niacin (Caballero-Briones 2000). Lack of niacin causes pellagra. In areas of the third world where corn has become the staple crop but nixtamalization not adopted, pellagra is still a common problem. Nixtamalization also makes calcium available and may have other health benefits allowing a broader range of B vitamin availability. But the jury is still out on these claims. Early American woodsmen, taking a page from the Indian's cookbook, prepared hominy by soaking corn in a highly alkaline lye solution derived from wood ash. This prevented pellagra but added no calcium to the diet. Lime burning, as we will see in the next section, provided more than essential trace elements in the Maya diet. It gives us a glimpse of the world view of the Maya.

Lime Burning and Religion

Eight-five percent of the population of North America believes in God and attends services at least occasionally. This statistic makes the continent the most religious industrialized area on the globe. And just about all of that small 15 percent minority who claim never to grace a place of worship with their presence are familiar with many of the stories of the Bible. In some way those folks can be considered "cultural" religionists. For that, we are pagans compared to the Maya. Religion and religious ritual permeated all phases of their life. As we will see, an enterprise as seemingly simple as the building of a lime kiln was done according to a prescribed religious manner. As for the lime kiln, so too for the edifices and cities the Maya erected. In fact, just about everything the Maya did can be related to the creation myth, a story that, unlike our Genesis, is in no way related to sexual reproduction.

For as simple as the Maya principle may sound, the working out of it is incredibly complex. The myth of the Hero Twins puzzles the northern mind. Even more perplexing is the manner in which elements from it are incorporated in the sculpture and architecture of Maya buildings and city planning. Most importantly, the creation myth underscored the right of Maya kings to rule. The rituals the Maya used their buildings for also trace back to the story of the Hero Twins.

Religious ritual even prescribed the proper way to make lime, the one industrial product the Maya could not do without. In the late 20th century, this ritual was still followed by some traditional Maya lime burners. Going along with the ritual was a body of knowledge, as recognized by R. S. Boynton in *Chemistry and Technology of Lime and Limestone* when he admitted that "in spite of incontrovertible scientific data delineating calcinations, this process remains to some extent a technique or an art that only the experienced lime burner fully comprehends.... Formally trained engineers are simply no match, at least at the outset, for the veteran lime burner" (Boynton 1980). As uncertain as the process may be in the industrial world with its carefully constructed kilns and controlled ignition sources, it is doubly true for the traditional Maya lime burner who built his kiln, like a giant shepherd's pie, out of freshly cut logs interspersed with chunks of limestone or shell.

Making lime ranks among the oldest known industrial processes. Technically, it consists of heating a calcium carbonate (limestone or mollusk shells in the Maya area) to 1,470–

1,650 degrees Fahrenheit. The process extrudes the carbon dioxide from the raw material, reducing the weight by up to 45 percent. The resulting quicklime is caustic and can be used as a treatment of sewage — a use the Maya may or may not have employed. For long-term stability and handling, quicklime requires slaking. This occurs by the addition of water. The preferred method of slaking by modern Maya is to simply allow the material to absorb humidity from the atmosphere. This may take from one to three years. The test for maturity is conducted by inserting a rod into the pile. If after a day the rod is cool to the touch, the lime is thoroughly slaked. Mixing water with slaked lime causes it to bind to aggregates such as sand and is called — depending on the ingredients and use — mortar, concrete, plaster, or stucco. When the mixture dries, it once again becomes calcium carbonate.

The traditional Yucatec term for lime, according to Thomas Shreiner who wrote his dissertation on the topic, is *sac ch'upal*. He translates the term as "pure, beautiful maiden, born of fire." Implicit in the concept of producing lime is a glimpse of the Maya worldview, death followed by resurrection. In this instance, we see the destruction of limestone by fire and rebirth as the beautiful lady of lime. That lime should be accorded such a high status fits in nicely with its place in the material culture of the Maya, yesterday and today. It is a necessary ingredient in the preparation of the most important foodstuff, corn, and the material from which Maya buildings were held together and plastered. Even the most modest wattle and daub Maya huts were often lime whitewashed. Lime was sometimes added to tobacco to produce an additional kick. To the Maya this intoxicating property reinforced the belief in lime as an elemental substance.

As a first item of business, the master lime burner draws a circle in the dirt demarcating the site of the open-pyre *trinchera* kiln. A jury-rig thatch shelter is then constructed above the circle, and the maestro might remain on the spot until the firing is complete (E. Hansen 2000). Keeping an eye on the kiln may prevent evil persons from hexing the burn. Such a person might plant a nail among the logs ruining the burn; a coffin nail is a certain pyre killer. A piece of electrical wire also can be counted on to cause trouble because copper, a metal known from the centuries just prior to the Conquest, is linked to lightning. Anyone smoking a cigar needs to be shooed away. Cigars are likened to logs, and a man puffing on a cheroot would draw the power from the logs of the kiln.

Most importantly of all, women must be banished from the site. Pregnant women are the most dangerous of all. Should one stumble into the area, a hair is sliced from her head and buried among the logs of the kiln. Then she is made to sit for a time on the chimney hole to draw the evil power back inside her. In the same vein, pregnant women have to avoid crossing a newly plastered floor for fear of cracking it; they must refrain from baking cakes because the pastries will not rise, the swelling in the belly prevents this; and snakes crossing her path may wriggle and writhe all they please but they cannot escape because the pregnant women draws away their force. These examples are just some of the folklore Eric Hansen found associated with lime burning.

Lime burners quarry stone found below the cap rock and just above the water table. This stone is moist and easy to work. The favored fuel for the lime kiln are trees that have a high moisture content. Four of the more common ones are grown sparingly in the southernmost U.S. Two are fruit trees, the so-called golden plum (also known as hog plum) and the jocote, neither of more than incidental interest as fruits to be eaten out of hand in the grove. The botan palm is a first cousin to the sabal palm, the state tree of South Carolina and Florida. The botan is a valuable species used for thatch and other things; but unlike its relative in South Carolina, it is slow growing and not prolific and a poor choice for kilning.

The most important species is the gumbo limbo, mentioned earlier as the gringo tree because of its reddish bark that peels like a sunburned tourist. The gumbo limbo is practically worthless for any use aside from wet pyre burning. But a branch poked into the soil easily strikes root. With a little care and attention, it will flourish. Modern studies of fossilized pollen found below the floor of lakes have shown that during the Preclassic and Classic era vast stretches of the uplands were tree farmed with this species. Those groves were almost certainly dedicated to the production of lime.

A lime pyre is usually eight to ten feet wide. The shape may be circular, square or irregular. The master burner alternates layers of logs with fist-sized chunks of limestone. Before firing, which generally occurs at midnight when the wind has died, nine corn cobs and nine chile peppers are dropped into the chimney hole. A handful of salt is spread over the load and a hair from the maestro's head is secreted in the pyre. The corn cobs are meant as insurance should a worker violate the rule of sexual continence during construction. The peppers will impart their fiery warmth to the flames, and the salt gives an example of whiteness the finished product should emulate. The hair from the maestro's head prevents the ill fortune that would befall the pyre should one of the workers have two cowlicks!

Alleys are meticulously riven through the pyre to allow the fire to properly draw. The alleys — in the kilns of the most traditional master burners — line up with the cardinal directions. Fragmentary evidence suggests that in days gone by wood was laid on the kiln by color coding. Gumbo limbo, with its reddish bark, was put on the east side. The yellow variety of gumbo limbo went on the south and whitish variety on the north. A dark-colored wood lay opposite the red on the west. Inserted in the chimney was a pole with a lateral, forming a cross. The cross had double meaning, part Christian that we all recognize and also as the symbolic Maya tree of life, variously interpreted as a corn stalk or a giant ceiba tree — symbolizing the axis mundi. The four directions and the cross in the centerpiece are the five cardinal points of the Maya cosmogram. Whether the superstitions surrounding the corncobs, chili pepper and salt included in the lime kiln have enduring significance, the number nine, as we will presently see, has recognizable importance. This cosmogram hearkens back thousands of years to Olmec times, as was noted in the first section of the book. The cosmogram is also central to the Maya worldview.

Red symbolized east and the rising sun; Maya depictions of the cosmogram invariably put east in the topmost position where north is located in our maps. West is shown as black, indicating not only the setting sun but also night. North, white, represents the celestial sphere and south, yellow, the underworld. (The Maya cosmogram could be likened to a clock more than a compass. North, twelve o'clock, denotes the sky more than the direction north.) The tree of life, that is the cross, pivots in the center between each pair of opposites. It is with the Maya, as the Olmec, the connector, the axis mundi which mediates between night and day, the heavenly plane (the celestial sphere indicated as twelve o'clock high or north) and Xibalba, (the underworld, six o'clock or south).

The Creation Myth and the Hero Twins

Now let's coordinate the cosmogram with the Maya creation myth. There are three protagonists in the Maya creation myth, a father and the father's Hero Twin sons. The father's twin brother is of lesser importance. The father and uncle of the Hero Twins annoyed the lords of the underworld by being noisy (Tedlock 1985). The lords challenged them to a game of the soccer-like ball game. The boys lost — as they must — and were sacrificed on the ball court by having their heads chopped off. Their bodies were buried in the playing alley. The skull of the father was tucked in a calabash tree. On spying a passing maiden, the skull was so moved by the girl, a teardrop fell. The tear landed in her palm. She became pregnant with a set of twins, who on growing up challenged the lords of the underworld to a game of ball. Having learned from the difficulties of their father and uncle, the Hero Twins tricked the gods using magic. One of twins chopped up the other and then brought him back to life. Each of the lords of the underworld begged to be shown this wonderful trick. The boys killed each of lords but refused to bring them back to life thereby achieving vengeance. Among their other exploits, they subdued with a blowgun a giant and malevolent bird known as Seven Macaw. In the fray, the elder twin's arm was severed (which, like a cartoon character, is later restored).

That in a nutshell is the "creation myth" of the Maya Hero Twins. It comes to us in its most perfect form from a manuscript called the *Popul Vuh* discovered in highland Guatemala in the 19th century. The manuscript, so far as can be determined, was originally transcribed in the Quiche Mayan language and taken down from recitation by highland Maya bards (McKillop 2004). Another school of thought holds that it is a translation of a Maya book written in the original hieroglyphs. The original transcription has been dated by scholars to about 1550 or shortly after the conquistador Alvarado reduced the highland Mam, Quiche, Kachichel and other Maya groups to submission. The preserved copy, now in a library in Chicago, was copied by an 18th-century Franciscan padre, who translated it into Spanish.

What the monk did not do is explain it. The first-named author spent years trying to figure out what the so-called creation myth of the Maya had to do with creation exactly. (The second author had the advantage of being an undergraduate in archaeology, so he could simply ask his professors to explain it.) The Christian creation myth in the Book of Genesis tells about a man and a woman. They do what they are not supposed to, euphemistically, by eating the forbidden fruit. The result is children in the form of Cain and Abel. Genesis explains the miracle of insemination and birth. It also offers the doctrine of original sin, springing from Adam and Eve's transgression. This doctrine explains the travails and difficulties the human race faces on the cruel orb.

Genesis is also credited by social historians with much more. For instance, it explains the human fascination with sex. The commodity is delightful — but forbidden and tricky, as aptly demonstrated by Eve seducing Adam and one of their sons killing the other. But the fascination with sex, strangely enough, is not constant in all societies. Rorschach blots are supposedly neutral ink spots on cards. When psychologists show them to western-world patients, a high proportion are interpreted in a sexual manner. An ink blot towering over a hunkered-down figure may be claimed to be a rapist about to ravish a cowering female. When anthropologists showed this same card to South Sea islanders, almost to a person, it was interpreted as a stronger figure attempting to steal food from a weaker one. South Seas islands, especially atolls, were frequently overcrowded. Obtaining enough to eat was a constant worry. Sex, on the other hand, was much less of a concern. The myth of Genesis has even been used to explain the rise of the United States. Supposedly, the Pilgrim fathers came to these shores seeking perfection in the way of a new Garden of Eden. Whether one credits the studies of Freud and the rise of America to the Book of Genesis, it is clear that it has been used as a mirror for dissecting and explaining Western societies.

The creation myth of the Maya also has a central place in the intellectual framework of that society. Allusions to the myth of the Hero Twins are found on carvings and paintings back to the beginning of the Late Preclassic period. Murals depicting this story have been recently unearthed at the site of San Bartolo, not far from El Mirador. The murals date to just after the birth of Christ. The meaning of the myth to the Maya may be found in Michael Coe's preface to Linda Schele and Ann Miller's *Blood of Kings.* There Coe mentioned in passing that one of his former graduate students had deduced that the story of the Hero Twins replicated the life cycle of maize (Coe 1986). According to Coe's former student Karl Taube, by then a professor at University of California, Riverside, the entering of the underworld and the resurrection of the Hero Twin mimicked the growth of corn. A grain is planted, the roots go down, the stalk shoots up, a cob fill out, and the ear is harvested — that is, decapitated from the plant the way early Maya sacrificed their victims. Birth, resurrection and death (by sacrifice) are integral to the successful culture of corn, in the view of the ancient Maya.

Corn was central to the Maya way of life. The *Popul Vuh* relates that the gods attempted to make people from various materials. Early attempts with clay and wood did not succeed. Wood produced beings that looked human but lacked souls. These folks were incapable of worshipping the gods. This accounts for the origin of monkeys. Each of these three attempts was punctuated by the destruction of the world, probably by a great flood. We are now in the fourth age, the one in which humans were created and which is believed to have begun in August 3114 B.C. Corn dough proved to be the right stuff, the material from which humans were successfully created. To the Maya, who believed their very flesh and blood hearkened back to corn, this explanation rang a bell.

The material about the Hero Twins in the *Popul Vuh* occurs in the text after the failed attempts to make intelligent creatures but before the successful creation of humans. The early Maya, therefore, interpreted the text to mean that (1) the ball game had ritual significance and (2) the gods desired blood sacrifice, like the sacrifice of both sets of twins and the lords of the underworld (Miller 2001). Without blood sacrifice, it was believed the sun could not be counted on to rise in the morning. And the rains would not fall, or they would deluge the earth in another great destructive flood. The place of sacrifice was the ball court, giving the ball game ritual significance. For their good work in taming the nine lords of the underworld, the Hero Twins were rewarded by being transformed into the two most important celestial bodies to the Maya. The younger of the two sons became the sun, the older Venus.

To return for a moment to the modern lime kiln. You may recall nine corncobs and nine chile peppers were secreted in the stack. That number refers to the nine lords of the underworld and shows how the myth of the Hero Twins has been a unifying force in Maya culture for thousands of years. And it continues to linger as one. Thomas Schreiner, the lime-burning researcher, also mentioned that the number four was important to the lime burner. The Mayan word for "four" is almost identical to the word for "sky." So four can be interpreted as having significance as sky — or heaven, the celestial sphere.

Religion and Architecture

Now let's go to the small ceremonial center of Cerros during the Preclassic period. We will see how the principal building and the ceremonies performed on it also flowed from the creation myth of the Hero Twins.

Cerros is in Belize, northeast of the Mirador Basin on a peninsula jutting into the Caribbean. During the Preclassic period, the population of Cerros, like the folks in cities in the Mirador Basin, began constructing platforms. On one such platform four huge masks were found many years later by archaeologists. A stairway coming up from ground level goes up four steps to a landing and then continues up nine steps to the top of the platform. A three-chambered temple occupies the top of the platform. Also on the top are holes in which were set, like four telephone poles, the trunks of four trees. The side of the pyramid with the masks faces south. The four trees atop the Cerros pyramid, like the traditional lime-burning kiln, are representations of the Maya cosmogram. The officiating priest during ceremonies, like the Olmec shaman of the last chapter, completes the cosmogram as the fifth point, the axis mundi, connecting east (birth) to west (death) and celestial sky (north) to the underworld (south).

The masks, Schele and Freidel tell us, are stylized visages of the Hero Twins. The lower two masks are devoted to the sun and the younger twin, who in Preclassic times was known as Yax Balam (First Jaguar). The masks on the upper register refer to Hun Ahaw, the first born of the twins, who morphed into the skies as Venus. Venus is the morning star part of the year and the evening star in other parts of the year. It also spends a fair amount of time out of sight, as though residing in the underworld. Venus was an incredibly powerful force for the Maya. During the Classic period in the time we call winter, Venus' appearance in the evening sky was a harbinger of war.

The Maya believed that when the sun went down, it took the heavens with it. Therefore, the night sky was a representation of the underworld or Xibalba (Schele and Mathews 1998). As wondrous and terrifying as the Milky Way appears to us, imagine how it must have been regarded by the Maya. One of their greatest fears was that the night cap would not morph to the day cap, that the sun would not rise. The Hero Twins story in the creation myth, they believed, clued humans to what needed to be done to properly nourish the gods. That activity consisted of blood sacrifice.

The archaeologist who unearthed this platform is one of the cleverest of our age, David Friedel from Southern Methodist University. He was assisted in interpreting his find by one of the greatest Maya epigraphers of her age, Linda Schele. Epigraphers are those who study and interpret dead languages. Long ago Schele was a simple art history professor at the University of South Alabama. One summer, she piled her husband and children into the family car and drove to the Yucatan. Like many other tourists, she became enamored of the works of the ancient Maya. Unlike most of us, her background in art history provided the wherewithal to make a modicum of sense out of what the Maya were doing. In a few short years she was invited to a round table seminar of the very best minds in the field. It was held at the incomparable Maya site of Palenque. There with renowned Yale archaeologist, Floyd Lounsberry, and graduate student Peter Mathews — and building on the discoveries of the past twenty years — she helped decipher the names and dates of the dynasty of kings of Palenque (Coe 1992). This achievement is considered a seminal breakthrough in reading the hieroglyphs of the ancient Maya. Because of her writings and her exposure on cable TV shows on the Maya, Linda's folksy ways and bluff good nature became widely known. Many of us who never met her consider her an acquaintance, even a friend. Schele was struck down in mid career, dying from cancer. But among the fine work she left behind was a rendering — with Friedel — of Structure 5C-2nd of Cerros (Schele and Freidel 1990). Schele and Friedel speculate that temples such as 5C-2nd were sites of great spectacle. All this was done to insure the rising of the sun and the ordering of the universe.

Imagine the scene. A crowd of Cerros villagers gather before 5C-2nd. At the appropriate time, an officiating personage, dressed in a white cotton tunic, parts the throng. A retinue of high officials accompany him. With appropriate dignity, the procession inches its way to the front of the building. The head official ascends the first four steps. Although today there are more than 30 Mayan languages, the rulers of almost all of the great Classical cities spoke Yucatec or Chol Mayan. As noted earlier, the word for "four" (chan or kan) in both of these languages is very similar to the word for "sky." The four steps of the stairway, therefore, represent the celestial realm. On the landing above the fourth step, the presiding official turns and pauses, showing his clean white tunic. Then with the train following, he ascends the next flight of steps, nine in number. Each step refers to one of the nine levels of the underworld. At the top the official halts and again presents himself to the crowd gathered below.

Now the procession angles to the right, the east, the direction from which the sun and Venus rise. The men proceed into the small stone temple atop the pyramid. Inside the chamber, the headman lifts his tunic, baring his loins. Using a stingray spine, he stabs his penis. Blood splatters onto strips of bark paper in a ceramic bowl held under his groin. The tunic is then dropped. The cotton fabric stains red from his oozing loins. Supported by those in his train, the now light-headed celebrant continues the procession. The procession came in the east door symbolizing the rising of the sun and Venus. Now it exits the west door, representing the setting of those heavenly bodies.

This ritual mimicked the passage of both the sun and Venus through the heavens. As noted in the preface, the ancient Maya believed the universe was interactive. Sacrifice on the part of humans was necessary to assist those heavenly bodies on their course. In short, the Maya believed blood sacrifice was essential to keep the universe in good working order. The official now presents himself between the two sets of giant stucco masks, dead in the center of the trees marking the corners of the world. He was in this guise the equivalent of the cross inserted in the chimney hole of the lime kiln — or the cornstalk axis mundi of the Olmec. He symbolized the sacred world tree (or cornstalk) in the very center of creation.

Thanks to the state of pain he found himself in, the headman was seeing visions. As noted in the Olmec chapter, archaeologists call this the state of ecstasy. The rest of us would probably find a more apt word to be "hallucinating." The Maya in the state of ecstasy communed with their ancestors. The ancestors aided them to see into the future. The ancestors proposed guiding actions to keep the ship of state on course. Rituals performed at 5C-2nd not only kept the universe functioning smoothly, they also helped guide — from the view of the participants — future actions of the political and religious leaders of the town.

The Father of the Hero Twins Is Also the Principal Bird Deity, the Maize God, and Itzamna

When the narrative wandered off into a discussion of the origin myth and showed how the Hero Twins story is exemplified in ritual, sculpture, and monumental buildings at Cerros, we were in the very heart of the landlocked Yucatan, the area now called Peten, Guatemala. It was here in the Mirador Basin that the Preclassic Maya rose to their apogee; and the first city to achieve prominence was Nakbe, seven miles from the downtown plaza at El Mirador, the two ruins the University Museum aerial expedition discovered from the chartered Pan Am biplane.

Structure 1 at Nakbe rises a lofty hundred fifty-seven feet — more than fifteen stories —

above the desolation of the ruined city. At 600 B.C., in the time frame just after Homer penned the great epic poems of *The Iliad* and *The Odyssey* and a century or so before the ancient Greeks were to enter their golden age, Nakbe could be called a bustling village. In terms of architecture, the best that could be said is that there were a few stone buildings with thatch roofs (Hansen 1992). Also, there were a few public platforms probably used for ritual purposes. But by 490 B.C., when the Athenians beat the Persians at the Battle of Marathon and ushered in their golden age, things began to change at Nakbe. Lime became a commodity in great demand as stone houses and large public buildings mushroomed up throughout the site. By 323 B.C., when Alexander the Great died and the best days of Greece were behind it, Structure 1 which looms 15 stories overhead was nearing its final stage, and the phase archaeologists call Late Pre-

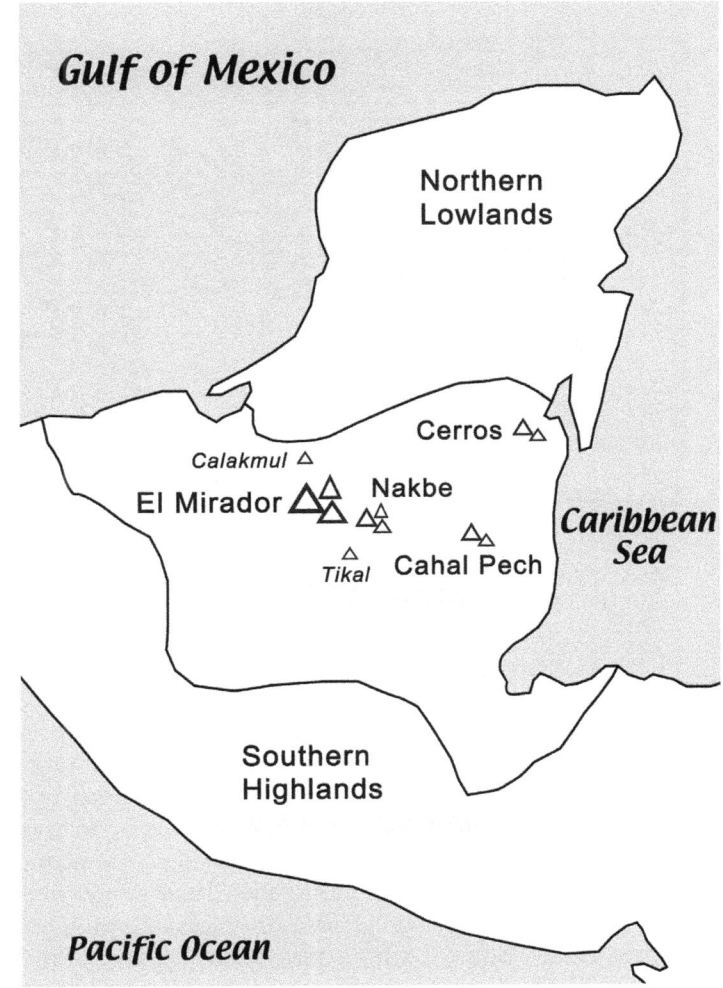

Some Preclassic sites and their relative positions to Tikal and Calakmul.

classic was beginning. Two hundred eighty miles away, in the swamps along the Gulf Coast, La Venta, the Olmec capital, had fallen to ruin. It had been gone for the best part of a hundred years, perhaps even two hundred years. No one, at present, knows what Nakbe's role, if any, in the end of that once proud, rich and cultured city was.

Standing at the northern base of the 15-story pyramid, you notice a trench opened by archaeologists. You enter it and walk to the midpoint of the base of the pyramid. You look up and see framed on the rock wall a behemoth of a mask. It is 10.5 feet tall and 12.5 feet wide. What is left of the mask is the stone armatures stucco once covered. The stucco is gone for reasons that puzzle archaeologists. Later Maya had carefully interred this mask, ritually killing it. It had not been exposed to the elements. By rights, the stucco should have survived. It did not. But the stone armatures have. They are impressive — if a bit frightening. Clearly it is a representation of a monster-like being. The mask has large eye sockets — as any mask ten by twelve feet must — with pronounced eyebrows. Those brows flame upward

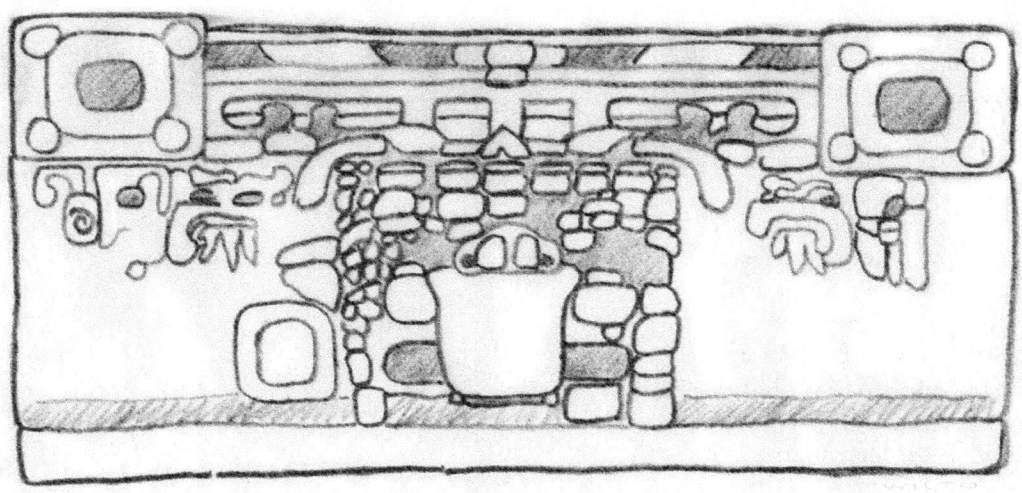

Mask of the Principal Bird Deity at the base of Structure 1, Nakbe. Illustration by John Wilton based on that of T. W. Rutledge (Hansen 1992).

much as the flame brows of Olmec art. The mouth is open and set back, a sort of maw. The most remarkable feature of the mask is the beak-like projection. It extends out and dips down from the wall. At its broadest point, it is about four feet wide. Crowning this magnificent creature is a three-pointed design similar to a three-leaf clover (Hansen 1992). Each of the leaves — in actuality a stylized depiction of a three-leaved corn shoot — are about a foot long, and this symbol is designated by archaeologists as "the jester headdress." It is called such because the jester hat-like design — sometimes wildly stylized — was depicted on the heads of Maya kings during the Classic period when it was known as the *hunal.*

According to Richard Hansen, the excavator, this grotesque mask represents the father of the Hero Twins. As will be recalled, he was one of first two brothers sacrificed by the lords of the underworld and buried on the ball court. His name is Hun Hun Ahaw. He was a supernatural of the very highest order. Among his most important role is as the Maize God. That he should be the Maize God flows naturally from the idea discovered by Karl Taube that myth of the Hero Twins is in a large part about corn, its decapitation from the stalk by picking the ear, then its burial when sown, and finally its resurrection when the stalk shoots up and ultimately bears fruit (Taube 1985, 1998). It will be remembered that the father of the twins was decapitated and buried on the ball court and that the sacred ball game, therefore, is regarded as an important ritual that assists in the nurturing of the corn. Therefore, just as the masks at the site of Cerros were dedicated to the Hero Twins, this huge mask on Structure 1 at Nakbe is a representation of the father of the Hero Twins. He was the Maize God, but he had other incarnations as well. In this instance, the depiction is of him in his guise as the Principal Bird Deity.

The mythological figure the Principal Bird Deity refers to is Seven Macaw, the bird the first-born Hero Twin dispatched with his blowgun. It was a ferocious creature who tried to set itself up as a false god by imitating the sun. How could a hostile supernatural bird be elevated to a beneficent deity? The Maya believed that one captured a foe's essence when subduing him. Maya kings in the Classic period claimed the prestige of those they captured or slew in battle. In this way, Seven Macaw went from being a malevolent spirit to being one of the chief gods of the Maya representing the father of the Hero Twins.

The father of the Hero Twins was also identified with another very important Maya deity, Itzamna, the creator god. At the time of the Conquest, 1,800 years after the mask on Structure 1 was created, Itzamna was reported by the Spanish friars as first among the Maya gods (Landa 1940). Itzamna was usually depicted as an old man. However, he was sometimes shown as a younger figure wearing priestly robes, and at yet other instances he was portrayed as patron god of writing. In other instances, Itzamna was depicted as a practitioner of the medical arts. He also appeared at times to be associated with sorcery and darkness. (And occasionally he is depicted as a horny old man!) Because of the various guises of Itzamna, the first among their gods, the great archaeologist J. Eric Thompson came to believe that the Maya were actually monotheists. Thompson himself was a devout Christian. He believed fervently in the Christian Trinity, that is God the Father, God the Son, and God the Holy Spirit, three manifestation of the one Christian God. That the Maya should have a similar, if more complicated belief, seemed natural to him. Few Maya archaeologists agreed with Thompson's conclusions regarding a monotheistic Maya religion. But almost all now recognize the rough similarity of the Christian Trinity by virtue of the various incarnations of the twin's father as the Maize God, Itzamna, and the Principal Bird Deity—as well as the trinity of the father and the two Hero Twins.

Richard Hansen not only uncovered the giant mask at the base of Structure 1, but he also determined its identity. In 1978 he finished his undergraduate degree—double major in archaeology and Spanish—at Brigham Young University. He was hired as area field director of an archaeological expedition to the Mirador Basin cosponsored by BYU and Catholic University of Washington, D.C. He has continued working in the basin under various titles ever since. In his many months in the basin, he has had much time to think about the huge mask at the base of Structure 1. He has explained its significance in a way that will impress even those who are most difficult to impress.

Hansen was well aware of how strange his claim about that grotesque mask might appear. Could it really be that a foe of the Hero Twins was in actuality their father? Much of his reasoning for this conclusion came from another bird deity sculpture that had been unearthed years before in the northern Yucatan. Unlike the mask at Nakbe, the Yucatan Principal Bird Deity was accompanied by two registers of framed images. These pictures provided essential clues to the multiple guises of the deity—and of its ultimate identity, Hun Hun Ahaw, the father of the twins. The first two frames depict a bird and apparently the glyph that refers to *ahaw*, king or ruler. The third to the sixth frames show a bat—the bird deity has shape-shifted to that other flying creature, one associated with the night. The next frame is a key one. In it is depicted a figure carrying a sack and disgorging what appears to be a corn cob. Hansen identifies this figure as Hun Hun Ahaw, the father of the Hero Twins, because of clues that hearken to the monumental game of soccer with the lords of the underworld that resulted in his decapitation and burial. (Later he was resurrected by his sons and became the Maize God.) But the explication is not yet over. Hansen goes on to identify the Principal Bird Deity with Itzamna, the creator god, as we have seen, and also the jester god, whose three-leaved headband is a feature of Maya royalty of the Classic period. All this shows the shape-changing character of the Maya pantheon, and its ability to collapse on itself. Where you thought you were perceiving a snake, you find you are indeed seeing a bird. And a bat may simply be the night version of the bird, and that bird can well be a metaphoric incarnation of the god responsible for keeping the corn, and on and on. In short, just as shaman can slip into the persona of their animal familiar, the gods shift from one guise to another.

The Greeks had Aeolus, the minor supernatural of the wind who Odysseus captured and held tight as he changed shapes until subdued and stuffed in a sack. Many or perhaps all of the Maya gods exhibit this miraculous trait and contribute to the notion of the "mysterious" Maya. To us all this seems incredibly confusing. The Maya, on the other hand, were steeped in stories about supernaturals from birth. They were the nursery yarns, TV cartoons, and Claude Van Damme action movies of their day all rolled together. The concept of shape-shifting was not only understandable to them, they actually believed beings, even human beings, were capable of such things on a daily basis. And as far as beliefs go, they also believed there were three realms of the universe. To us it may seem that only the earthly realm is truly knowable. The Maya believed just as firmly in the celestial realm and the underworld, both of which they thought were depicted in the heavens (and which most of them probably actually traveled to in hallucinogenic visions). Given all this, it should not be surprising that they referred to their myths in what seems to us a kind of short hand slang of the kind children and underworld figures might employ today. We may view a Preclassic mask of a wing and a snake, for instance, and scratch our heads; but the Maya, schooled from childhood in the myths and understanding the creative grammar of allowing the part to substitute for the whole, got it. It has taken many decades and quite a few false starts for intellectuals studying the Maya to get it.

Now let's climb the 15 stories of Structure 1. It is not an easy climb. The stairs of the north face barely show and the sides of the old building are very steep. You have to grab at bushes here and avoid falling into the occasional looter's trench there before, puffing, you achieve the top. Here you find a peculiar assemblage of three small buildings. Two are long and parallel each other. The third is taller and is centered between them at right angles. In short, they are arranged in the triadic arrangement Ian Graham reported in his first survey of the Mirador Basin. Masks adorn the larger middle building, two on the lower level and another pair placed above. They have been exposed to the elements for more than two millennia. The masks are all but destroyed. You walk around the building and see another double set of two masks. They are in the same stage of deterioration. You can only tell that once upon a time masks were affixed to the walls. We step to the back edge of the platform, as far away from the main cross building as possible. We look down. We see to our upper left a steep, tall (ten story) pyramid about sixty feet below. It is called Structure 27. It too has the crown of triadic structures on its top. The center structure had also been adorned with masks, now all but obliterated because of two thousands years of exposure to the tropical sun, wind and rain.

Immediately below, across a small open courtyard and about a hundred feet down, lies Structure 13. It is "only" six stories tall. Archaeological workers found near the smaller side buildings many sherds of domestic pottery and a mano suggesting nixamalized corn had been ground there, possibly indicating the side structures were used as residences. Edifices constructed for residential use generally incorporated a stone sleeping bench. There are no sleeping benches here, leaving archaeologists to wonder if the rooms had a dual administrative-residential use. Perhaps those living here were priests of some sort. The triad of buildings is dominated by the larger cross building, which rises 17 feet above the plaza. Thirteen steps, symbolizing the 13 celestial levels, run from the plaza to the cross structure. Its doorways, like the doorways of Structure 5C-2nd at Cerros, are offset. Presumably Structure 13 was used for ceremonies similar to those at Cerros, where, as you will recall, it is believed the officiating person became the axis mundi, the connecting rod of the three spheres of the universe. He performed blood sacrifice by perforating his private parts. All this occurred under the watchful gaze of the two Hero Twins masks in their guises of the sun and Venus. The ceremonies insured the rising of the sun daily and propitiated Venus, that most wily, treacherous and fickle of the planets. At Nakbe where the presiding deity was the father of the Hero Twins in the form of the Principal Bird Deity, the recreation of the universe was also ritually observed — by autosacrifice and ritual display of a similar kind.

Exploring El Mirador and Its Rise and Decline, 200 B.C.–A.D. 150

The Romans beat Hannibal and closed the Second Punic War at about 200 B.C. It was about that time that Nakbe's prominence in the basin began to give way to El Mirador. Nakbe is connected to El Mirador by an ancient road called a *sacbe*. There are few options for getting to El Mirador from Nakbe. One is by helicopter — if you happen to have one. More likely options are mule back or shank's mare. So let's make our way to El Mirador by foot. We can't take the sacbe the whole way because the limestone from which it was constructed has weathered into soil, and the roots of trees and shrubs have sunk into the rich layer of organic and mineral duff in most places. So we slog through the bajo. The vegetation we pass by is runty, hardly what one would expect from a near rain forest environment from watching Disney nature movies or the National Geographic Channel. You wonder how a civilization could ever have risen given these puny resources. Then you remember the Mirador Basin flourished more than two thousand years ago. Hard as it is to keep this in mind, the environment was not the same then as now. Though still humid, it was drier, more like the drier western end of the modern Midwestern corn belt. And according to Richard Hansen, the man who excavated Nakbe, this scruffy tree-lined swamp that the sacbe to El Mirador passes through today was probably a sawgrass marsh in those days. The deeper areas of the marsh were lakes or ponds, which provided snails, mussels, and fish — and during those desperate days of the late dry season, water for drinking.

Now and then we bump against the remains of the old sacbe. By modern American standards the lime produced by the Maya is graded as "poor." These grades were developed for easy, not to say superficial, analysis. That "poor" rating stems from the slight grayish look to the Maya lime, which is a result of the high organic content of the preferred limestone. The grade doesn't speak to the qualities of the material. An artist in Maitland, Florida, visited the Yucatan in the 1930s. He returned home and, inspired by the Maya, built his own pyramid using locally available commercial materials. Once when one of the authors attempted to visit this artifact, he was unable to do so. The structure was closed in order to refurbish it. In short, American concrete cannot stand up to the subtropical elements for eighty years without requiring extensive rehabilitation. You bump up against a section of the sacbe. It is about twenty feet wide and from a foot to waist high. Examining the exposed section closely, you see concrete, still in good condition, mortaring together blocks of limestone. It has stood up to the tropical elements — including the invasive roots of trees which love the moisture in the crevice between the stone blocks — for more than two thousand years.

We have now entered El Mirador. The giant Danta Pyramid towers above us. But rather than appearing as a twenty-five story building, it seems only a vegetation-covered hill. Only the front of the temple has been cleared by excavators. We cannot see it as yet, and we pay little attention to it. We are heading for the Tigre Pyramid. It is more than half a mile away, almost due west. As we go, we pass many a small promontory that hides various pyramids and platforms including ball courts, E-Groups and residential palaces. John Clark of Brigham Young University studied the layout of the "downtown" areas of Olmec, Olmec-inspired, and early Maya centers to try to determine the influence of the earlier cities, if any, on the later ones. Clark noted that a ball field, E-Group and palace situated hard by a principal pyramid were common to all. Ball courts we have discussed already in our discussion of the Hero Twins and the ball games played by them and their relatives. We'll talk about E-Groups shortly; and structures believed to be residential palaces usually are elevated on a platform and are long and relatively narrow with a number of small rooms not connected by interior passageways, often containing benches or shelves used as beds. The rooms without benches were perhaps used for ritual or administrative purposes. Those residing in "palaces" near city center naturally were believed to be upper crust nobility. Because activities other than residence occurred in this sort of building, archaeologists sometimes refer to them as "range buildings."

Clark noted that at La Venta this set of structures, the palace, ball court, and E-group, are oriented in a north-south direction around the main pyramid (Clark and Hansen 2001). The same was true of the post–Olmec sites in Chiapas. The early Maya communities, such as here at El Mirador on the other hand, are laid out on an east-west axis in consonance with the passage of the sun and the various other heavenly bodies which cross the heavens from east to west. Those who see the glass half full, such as Clark, take this as evidence of the Olmec connection to the Maya, owing to the same sorts of buildings being found in the core of all the sites, even if they are oriented differently. Those who view the Maya as an exceptional culture which grew up on its own, as his coauthor Hansen for that article, see the different orientation — east-west for Maya, north-south for Olmec, as proof of lack of influence from the earlier culture.

We ascend Tigre Pyramid. It only goes up 180 feet or so, a mere 18–20 stories and not much higher than Structure 1 at Nakbe. The pyramidal platform on top, however, is almost identical to that on the Danta Pyramid. John Clark wondered how the New World peoples could progress from egalitarian hunter-gather societies to complex civilizations capable of building a city like El Mirador in just a few thousand years. To answer this question, he studied a smaller community on the Pacific coast. Why, Clark wondered, would humans in more or less equal societies give up their status as equals? In truth, Clark notes, that even the most egalitarian society recognizes differences based on age, ability, gender. Clark believes the social distinctions in egalitarian societies — stemming from age, gender, or specialized skills — lay the groundwork for recognizing inherited social distinctions. So why would folks give up their equality? Obviously, the members of a particular society believe it to be in their best interests. Probably, they didn't, at first, even see themselves as losing status so much as obtaining a benefit.

Those whose family fortunes increase over time, that is those who gather to themselves material or labor, Clark calls accumulators. He believes the aggressive "accumulator" personality exists in all (or most) societies. Certain conditions allow these folk to establish the first generation as dominant and, finally, pass their status on to subsequent generations. These conditions require that the individual have intercourse of some kind outside of the community. In the case of the Miradorans, that probably meant control of the obsidian or salt trades. All this would make for local prestige and probably also a larger than usual share of the local agricultural wealth, which the big man's family probably used to treat the populace to feasts and such things. The prestige from these endeavors would also be used to organize locals into community works projects of obvious merit to all. That is, the big man would call everyone to the ceremonial area to do some work, after which he footed the bill for a banquet.

Subsequent generations — at all social levels — would expect leadership from the family, and naturally the family would adopt the trappings of power and devise rules to guard their position against upstarts or rival families. Rather than wrapping themselves in the flag, the big man in a preindustrial village or small city wrapped himself in religion. We know that because religion played a central role in all precapitalistic societies. The big man would, say, organize work parties to build pyramids to pay homage to the Maize God and the Hero Twins. Such works helped regulate the cosmos, the members of the society believed. They made the sun and Venus come up and the rains fall and the corn grow. Also, if the same family took the lead in these celebrations, after a while that family assumed political leadership of the area.

We stop now in front of Structure 34, a minor temple — in the usual triadic arrangement — on the Tigre platform. Here there are only two masks, one of either side of the nine stairs leading to the main structure lying at a right angle to the smaller parallel buildings. Though badly eroded, Hansen has been able to determine they represent the second-born of the Hero Twin brothers, he who is identified with the sun. The east mask shows his face half fleshed, that is the left side of his face is skull-like. This depicts the sun rising, not yet at full strength. The west mask shows the descending sun in a jaguar guise, the night jaguar. This visage must hunt souls and blood to nourish it and allow it to rise in the morrow. Most germanely to the present discussion, we see the trilobed jester god headband. Hieroglyphic texts from the Classic age tell us the jester god denoted royalty. Maya kings were seldom depicted without a jester hunal crowning his head. Here and at Nakbe and Cerros the jester motif adorns effigies of the Hero Twins or their father. Can we doubt that the persons most responsible for erecting these masks and the huge edifices they adorn was subtlety claiming a divine right to rule for himself and his family? All that largesse that went

Structure 34, El Tigre Pyramid, El Mirador. Masks are Sun Jaguar masks. The one on the east (right) is half fleshed and indicates the rising sun. The west mask depicts the younger of the Hero Twins in the guise of the night jaguar, the hunter of souls. Illustration by John Wilton based on that of T.W. Rutledge (Hansen 1992).

into those feasts for the workers and the apparently selfless effort that motivated the community to build the structures dedicated to the Hero Twins and their father paid off. The family ended up, presumably, as the rulers of Mirador. He would be the fellow in the white cotton tunic allowed to bare his loins and perforate his penis, thereby insuring the sun would rise for the good of all.

"E-Group" is the name given to an association of two buildings on an east-west axis. The eastern structure runs north and south, and often it is T-shaped with the foot of the T extending eastward. The second building is a pyramid, often of the sort called a radial pyramid with stairs going up all four sides. Assemblages of this sort came to be called E-Groups because of a curious alignment noted at Uaxactun. This alignment was believed to be astronomical. It was thought that the sun — as viewed from the west pyramid — would line up with the north wing during the summer solstice and the south at the winter one. The person who isolated this arrangement was our old friend from chapter one, Franz Blom. He did this in 1924, before his exploration of the Olmec region. The supposed astronomical significance of the Uaxactun group was shown to be in error by archaeo-astronomer Anthony Aveni of Colgate University sixty years later (Aveni 1989). In any case, Richard Hansen theorizes the E-Group morphed to the triadic arrangement of the many summary temples in the Mirador Basin. Hansen seems to suggest — but doesn't explicitly state — that the trio of supernatural heroes, the Hero Twins and their father, may also suggest the triadic relationship.

During the Preclassic period there has turned up — to date — almost no evidence of images of individual Maya kings. The two exceptions are late Preclassic images at Uaxactun — and one image on a stela (stone tablet) Hansen found at El Mirador. The glyph identifying the individual ruler at Mirador had been defaced so he remains unknown to history, unlike his Classic age cohorts, many of whose names and exploits are now known. As we chug to the top of Tigre Pyramid, we cogitate on all of the other nameless kings or chiefs who contributed over the centuries to the development of this huge city. They are just as anonymous as the peasants who they cajoled into giving up their off-farming hours to erecting this temple.

Though the mysteries of the Mirador Basin may be far from deciphered, the most pressing question for us is known with as much certainty as for any Maya age. That is, what happened to them? Looking down at your feet, you see a chert spear point. Reflexively, you pick it up without thinking — artifacts in unexcavated areas should not be moved for fear of destroying the archaeological context. Even though the damage is done, you immediately drop it and think, so that is what happened to the Miradorans. A huge battle occurred here, and they were conquered.

Indeed a huge battle did occur right on top of Tigre Pyramid. But it had nothing to do with the demise of the Preclassic Miradorans. They had passed from the scene hundreds of years before that battle. At the time, this pyramid had long been abandoned. The study of the pollen and other data disgorged by the bottom of Lago Puerto Arturo provides the answer. By about 3,400 years ago (or about 1400 B.C.), the forest began to thin out as early peasant farmers planted corn. This was shown in the lake bottom study in two ways. First, fossilized corn pollen was found. Secondly, a thin layer of "terrigenous input" was discovered. Subjecting the sample to a scientific analysis called magnetic susceptibility yielded information regarding the kind of soil found at that level. It was clay. The population at this time was so small its archaeological footprint was miniscule. But the slash-and-burn farming practices impacted the local environment.

As the years rolled on — and once again we are counting in the hundreds — the water lily population of the lake shrunk and pollen laid down by sedges increased. Water lilies are finicky about water quality. They grow poorly in turbid or highly enriched water. Sedges, on the other hand, show no such sensitivity. Sedges are grass-like plants, such as sawgrass. They are the weeds of the watery world, as useless to humans as the grasses are beneficial. They proliferated. On land weeds took over fields that had formerly been forest and which were not planted to corn. For more than a thousand years, weed, grass (corn), and sedge pollen dominated the fossil record meaning that the Mirador Basin was under cultivation. A graph charting the record would by no means be steadily ascending.

A two-century period at the end of the Middle Preclassic showed a decline in cultivation. Also, the initial terrigenous input tapered off as farmers terraced their lands and did other things, such as mulching some crops, to slow down or almost stop erosion. But as the Mirador Basin reached its apogee in building construction, sludge began draining into lowlands anew. This of course was the period when the skyscraping pyramids went up at Nakbe, El Mirador, Tintal, Wakna, and other cities. It was the time when huge amounts of lime were applied to the walls in stucco arrangements and the causeways called sacbes were laid down connecting the cities in the basin. From 300 B.C. until A.D. 100, the area flourished. Then starting about A.D. 110, there came an abrupt decline. Forest pollen began replacing weed and grass pollen as pioneer (that is weed-like woody trees such as crecopia) began edging into the cornfields. By A.D. 150, El Mirador and the surrounding cities were abandoned.

What caused this collapse? Drought, a very severe one (Wahl 2005; Wahl et al. 2006). What brought on the drought? Scientists at present can only speculate, but it is clear from the record that the climate of the Yucatan Peninsula has varied over the past several millennia. For the last thousand years it has been considerably wetter than it was during the periods of intense Maya occupation. Indeed, today the climate is similar to that shortly after the decline of the last Ice Age.

There was little the Miradorans could have done to foreshorten the drought, although they may well have resorted to additional sacrifice and such things as peoples under stress are prone to do. However, there is something they could have done prior to the drought to have aided them substantially — and that was control erosion. That very thin layer of terrigenous input over a period of centuries filled in the low-lying areas around the towns. This extremely impervious material is known today by archaeologists as "Maya clay." What had formerly been shallow lakes, became marshes and then finally wooded bajos in which water didn't stand all year, even in very wet years. The water that could have been used for irrigation and drinking was gone. And following it went the population of cities of the region. A small populace recolonized parts of the basin in the Classic period, but El Mirador, Nakbe and other cities of the basin with their skyscraping pyramids became forevermore ghost towns.

If peasant farmers learned to control erosion, what was the source of this Maya clay? When lime slakes, it draws moisture in and gives off a slight sludgy precipitate (Shreiner 1994). That precipitate, which was so small as to be all but unnoticeable, was gathered by the torrential rains of the rainy season and carried to the lowlands. Even though the Miradorans had succeeded in developing sustainable agriculture, they failed at controlling the environmental impact of all phases of their society. Gradually — and remember we are talking in the Late Preclassic a period of at least 450 years, more time than has passed from the docking of the Pilgrims at Plymouth Rock until today — the wetland lakes of the Mirador

Basin became sawgrass marshes then wooded bajos (or seasonally flooded lands). When dire times in the way of a drought brought on by the sunspot cycle or other causes struck, water resources that had sustained them in former times were not there to fall back on. Today, the Mirador Basin is as untouched by the hand of man as any place in the former precincts of the Maya. Farmers find the soil almost completely inhospitable (Hansen 1994). It lies pretty much as it did when drought forced the last of the Miradorans out in A.D. 150.

3

Tikal, the Eternal City, Early Classic, A.D. 250–550

Discovery and Early Exploration, A.D. 1848–1969

In 1840, a traveler in the highlands of Guatemala with an interest in ethnology met a parish priest with a lively intelligence and enquiring mind. The priest invited the traveler into his private study which "he always locked to prevent the women throwing things into confusion. When we entered it was of a class that beggars description. The room contained a table, chairs, and two settees, but there was not a vacant place even on the table to sit down or lay a hat upon. Every spot was encumbered with articles, of which four bottles, a cruet of mustard and another of oil, bones, cups, plates, minerals and large stones, shells, pieces of pottery, skulls, bones, cheese, books and manuscripts formed a part" (Stephens 1969). It was just the sort of parlor where one could expect to learn of dark secrets or hidden treasures.

And the traveler, who came to be known as the father of Mesoamerican archaeology, was not to be disappointed. What he hoped to find was a city still occupied by the race that built the fabulous ruins scattered across upper Central America and lower Mexico. He knew that the Spanish had laid a living Maya city to waste a little more than a century earlier. It was possible that a thriving city existed somewhere in the fastness of the jungles. The priest told him that when he was young, "with much labor he climbed to the naked summit of the sierra, from which, at a height of ten or twelve thousand feet, he looked over an immense plain extending to the Yucatan and the Gulf of Mexico, and saw at a great distance a large city spread over a great space, and with turrets white and glittering in the sun. [It was] four days on the road to Mexico. The traditional account is that no white man has ever reached the city [and] that the inhabitants speak the Maya language."

Strangely enough, the padre's account was 100 percent accurate, although only in a nominal sense. During the early 19th century a huge Maya ruin in north-central Peten had been repopulated by Yucatec-speaking Maya. The site was called Tikal, meaning the place of spirits, because the 19th-century inhabitants had been driven out by a combination of ghosts and a plague of vampire bats (Harrison 1999). Alternately, the name might mean the place of the waterhole because local transients made use of one of the reservoirs built by the Classic Maya for use during the dry season.

The official discovery of this megacity came eight years after our traveler heard the old priest's yarn — 1848. Then the governor of Guatemala's outback province of Peten, Ambrosio Tut learned from locals of magnificent buildings in the jungle. The city lay less than forty miles north of the seat of the Guatemalan government at Flores (and about the same number of miles southeast of El Mirador). An expedition was shortly mounted. The chronicler of the expedition was Col. Modesto Mendez, the commissioner of the Peten district. His account was published in Berlin, and so to him and Ambrosio Tut go the credit for the discovery of a city whose existence had been whispered for years. The name they gave the site was the one already in use. Some claim that the common name "Tikal" like "Yaxha," a site twenty miles away, may actually be a holdover from classic times. But a glyph read as "Mutal" has been deciphered by epigrapher David Stuart as that used in the Classic period. (In truth, the Maya frequently had several names for a site, one of which the emblem glyph may have referred to the dynasty as much as the place, and so it is entirely possible the term Tikal was also used.)

Though located deep in the heart of the Peten, in an area without navigable rivers or all-weather roads, Tikal from the start was recognized by scholars as an important capital of Maya civilization. An enormous number — given the fact that they had to travel for days by mule — of proto-archaeologists and adventurers visited (and sometimes plundered) the ruins. The first notable example of this type was Dr. Gustav Bernoulli. He was a Swiss national encouraged by his physicians to move to Guatemala for his health (Adam 2005). He died in his mid forties after twenty years residence. Maybe the advice was useful — or perhaps it accounted for his relatively youthful death. In any case, Bernoulli removed several carved lintels from Temples I and IV. These precious works of art, in a fine state of preservation, can be found today in a museum in Basel, Switzerland.

Alfred Maudslay, a British noble, visited the ruins in 1881–82. He packed cumbersome photographic equipment into the Peten, and he served as his own darkroom technician, mixing chemicals and developing plates in the humid tropical night. His photographs detail elements that have since eroded or gone missing. They remain one of the treasures of 19th-century Maya archaeology, of particular use to epigraphers studying ancient Maya hieroglyphs. Teobert Maler, an Austrian national, served in the employ of Harvard's Peabody Museum. In the late 19th century and early 20th century, he explored the ruins, but the years in the isolation of the jungle took their toll psychologically (Harrison 1999). Maler refused to forward some of the data he generated. After that the Peabody pretty much left the field in favor of the Carnegie Institution of Washington.

The head of the Carnegie project, Sylvanus Morley, designated Tikal as the capital of the "Old Empire" of the Maya, a theory thoroughly discredited nowadays. But he seems to have been intimidated by Tikal's magnitude. The downtown area of Tikal takes in six square miles. It was just too big. Also, Morley was working another huge site in the northern Yucatan, Chichen Itza. So he concentrated excavation activity on other sites including Uaxactun, just twelve miles north of Tikal. Two world wars intervened before a systematic study of the site was contemplated. Percy Madeira, the aerial discoverer of El Mirador, broached the idea of a massive Tikal project to the director of the University Museum of Pennsylvania in 1947. Froelich Rainey, the director of the museum, was for the idea. How could he not be? Madeira was president of the board of directors at the museum and the man who would produce the money required for the expedition. One little problem intervened.

That was global politics. Starting in the late 1940s, Guatemala came under domination of army officers with socialist tendencies who believed in such unspeakable things as land reform for the peasants and taxing the holdings of the United Fruit Company. The welcome mat was jerked out from under the proposed expedition. Those possible American agents were barred even in the outback province of Peten. The political Gordian knot was severed in one fell swoop by the CIA with the help of a single P-51 aircraft buzzing Guatemala City in 1954. The Arbenz regime fell, and the colonel turned president along with his communist wife and Czech helpers went into exile in Mexico City. Suddenly, the Tikal project was approved, and American archaeologists moved into the north-central Peten. But the project's good luck was the cause of Guatemala's enduring pain. The seeds of a guerrilla war were sown. Ultimately, it claimed the lives of tens of thousands of Maya peasants. The civil war did not end until the mid 1990s. By then many Maya were pushed from their fertile fields in the highlands to the vacant lands of the Peten.

In any case, Madeira and Raney's project was the biggest in the history of New World archaeology to that point, and perhaps ever. It started in the mid 1950s and officially ended in 1969. Madeira died in January of 1967. An enormous amount of the University Museum's resources had been diverted to the Tikal project. With his death, the support of the museum waned. The government of Guatemala, seeing the value of the project, funded it for several years. The result was the restoration of some of the temples and the beginning of a tourist industry. Altogether 113 professional archaeologists (including graduate students) participated in the project (Harrison 1999). In 1979 a Guatemalan project headed by Juan P. LaPorte continued exploring the site.

For a very short period in the late 20th century, Tikal's hold on the imagination of archaeologists — though never the public — waned when those long silent hieroglyphs began to be read. It became apparent that Tikal was not always the preeminent Classic-era Maya city. Indeed, on several occasions the city was thrashed in battle rather soundly, the center city sacked, and for a period of about a hundred thirty years, its prestige was held in check. However, by the beginning of the new millennium, as we will see in the upshot, Tikal had regained its status among scholars as arguably the first among Maya cities of the Classic period, albeit not without a blemished history or a rival claimant to the title of queen city of the Maya.

How Tikal Came to Be a Maya Powerhouse—Thanks to Geography and Economy

Today, most archaeologists would agree that Tikal was the largest in population of the Classic-era Maya cities in the southern lowlands (although several others such as its great rival, Calakmul, was almost the same size or perhaps somewhat larger). The southern lowlands is the region where the Maya reached their high point culturally, artistically, and in some sense politically. Low estimates of Tikal's population at its peak during the 8th century A.D. run at about 40,000. Some recent estimates place the population at a quarter of a million, but that includes those living in a sizeable hinterland area outside the obvious defenses of the city. Most population guesses run from just under 50,000 to somewhat more than 100,000 (Sharer and Traxler 2006). In the 4th century A.D., the population would have numbered in the few thousands.

The core area of the city, occupied by great temples and other elite constructions, took up six square miles. An additional 19 square miles, 25 square miles altogether, were occupied by buildings. Another 22 square miles — 47 square miles altogether — was passively defended by walls, moats and natural boundaries. These 22 square miles were farmed intensively.

They were the granary that the city made sure was never destroyed by enemies, and may indeed have been another of Tikal's many reasons for rising to prominence.

Tikal's architecture is among the most impressive in the Maya area. Its Temple IV is the tallest of all pre–Columbian New World structures (yes, the third pyramid for which that claim has been made in these pages, but such is the unsettled state of affairs in New World archaeology). Temples I and II, juxtaposed across the Great Plaza, must be among the most visually pleasing buildings anywhere on the planet, whether ancient or modern.

The great city of Tikal came to be established on a subcontinental divide between the great rivers of the Yucatan Peninsula. A drop of water falling on the highest point of the city would split. Half would flow east and would ultimately be gathered into the drainage system of the Belize River and tumble into the Caribbean. The other half would roll downhill to the west. After a while it would end up in the mighty Usumacinta River where it would flow north into the Gulf of Mexico. The hills making this divide are fairly impressive in a land that is to a great extent flat. The fact that there are hills and that those hills divide a watershed were of symbolic interest to the first inhabitants. The hills, which rise 160 feet above the local swamps, were no doubt considered suitable stand-ins for mountains. Mountains, along with caves and bodies of water, held supernatural and mythical significance to the Maya because of their importance in the creation myth; the mountains rose above the water allowing the development of the fourth creation. Caves and water were considered portals to the underworld.

The first inhabitants of the area migrated up the Belize River valley. They arrived about 800 B.C. (Harrison 1999). They took up residence on the edge of Bajo de Santa Fe, the huge swamp that marks the eastern boundary of the city. By this time, many areas that were to become notable Maya city-states had been inhabited for hundreds of years. Many of those areas were located on watercourses. Altar de Sacrificios and Seibal on the Pasion branch of the upper Usumacinta were going strong, as were many of the cities in Belize. The pioneer Tikalese settled on the edge of the lowland swamp, which probably at the time was a shallow lake or a sawgrass marsh with ponds of open water. Those living on the edge of the water found a ready supply of shellfish in the way of apple and jute snails. The marsh, free of trees, had another practical advantage. Shallow trails made by the Morlet's crocodile, the only indigenous species of crocodilian, could be deepened and used for canoe transport during much of the rainy season. In this way, archaeologists theorize, canoe traffic that came up the branches of the Belize River, with a few portages, could make its way all the way to the center of the peninsula. Traffic from the Usumacinta by way of the Rio San Pedro Martir branch — to the west — could reach almost as close.

In time, villages sprung up on the ridge that rises above the swamp. It runs east to west from Bajo de Santa Fe to the giant swamp (also a lake or marsh early on) on the western perimeter. These villages were established on the highest ground, indicating that defenses were a consideration. The earliest of these hamlets occupied the very highest point in Tikal, which came to be known as the North Acropolis. It was a ceremonial center of many low pyramids in which notables came to be buried. Over the centuries it came to form the northern boundary of the Great Plaza, the very heart of the city, with Temples I and II on the east and west sides of the plaza. Other villages sprang up a third of a mile away in the area known as the Lost World (Mundo Perdido), where the largest pyramid — by volume — was to be built.

At first, these pioneers were an egalitarian folk striving to get by in a subsistence way. They'd plant slash-and-burn cornfields and hunt game in the woods. The same can be said for many other Maya villages in the southern lowlands. So why did Tikal in the Classic period grow to be a supercity similar to El Mirador forty miles to the north during the Preclassic? Trade was one of the reasons, and the favorable location of Tikal allowed an especially significant trade to develop.

Given the canoe routes coming from the east and the west and overland trails from the mountains to the south converging at Tikal, the city was located at a major crossroads of the southern Yucatan Peninsula. Traders passing the crossroads would be taxed. These transit charges helped gain Tikal a toehold of economic and political power. And locals also got involved in trade. Every item that crossed the Yucatan Peninsula had to be packed — at the frequent portages or on the trails out of the mountains — on the back of a human. The early Maya were subsistence based. With their own hands or those of their family members, they produced everything they needed to live happily, more or less. Obsidian blades may have been sharper and more prized, but chert — found everywhere in the lowlands near swampy bajos — did well enough. One small exception to this rule was volcanic ash used to temper the better grade of pottery. But local, coarser tempers would do. The giant exception to the rule was salt.

The only food that supplies salt naturally is meat. Meat was the substance the Maya ate the least of. Archaeologists have discovered one brine source in the lowlands (Andrews and Mock 2000). Its waters were boiled down to produce salt. Salt could also be procured locally by burning palm fronds. The ash was leached to produce the valued mineral. The procedure was not cost effective. Therefore, most salt was imported from outside central Peten. Brine springs have been located in the highlands of Guatemala. And archaeologists have discovered saltworks in coastal Belize where the valuable mineral was produced laboriously by filtering sea water through salt-impregnated earth and boiled down to a solid state. The most efficient means of salt production was located on the north and northwest coasts of the Yucatan Peninsula. There salt pans cured the product by sun evaporation.

In Preclassic times, the village of Komchen prospered, thanks to those salt pans, and the industry continued operation in that and contiguous areas throughout the Maya period. (The industry is still going strong today!) Tikal, dead in the middle of the peninsula, stood to gain from the salt trade as most product going south, west, or east passed through its sphere. Brine-boiled salt going north from the southern highlands or west from Belize also would go through the Tikal area, but this trade was less important owing to its lesser amount. Also traded were honey, cotton cloth, and salted fish and meats. Archaeologists cannot be sure of this because these items leave no archaeological footprint. They are mentioned only obliquely in the stone records which were almost without exception dedicated to elite ritual, not the sort of thing where everyday trade products were discussed. The major long-distance trade was in elite goods. Among these elite goods were the long tail feathers of the resplendent quetzal of the cloud forest. Maya kings' headdresses required lots of quetzal feathers as a badge of office. Also, from the mountains came jade and obsidian, both of which were mainly used by elite members of the society.

The tropical lowlands yielded a number of products of interest to high-end consumers elsewhere (Foias 2002). These included skins of high-status animals such as jaguars and pumas and the feathers of brilliantly plumaged tropical birds like parrots and especially macaws. Other goods of elite interest included tropical hardwoods, various spices such as allspice, and herbal medicines. It is believed hallucinogens used for religious rites (or recreation) were a trade item. Dye products and finished dyed goods such as cotton woven into intricately patterned mantles were also in the system. And of course there was always cacao.

Cacao beans were used as money when the Spanish arrived and may have been used the same way during Classic times to purchase consumer items in open-air Maya markets. Half a bean would buy a rabbit. A hundred was the price for a slave. Eight to 10 would procure the services of a prostitute in Nicaragua (outside the Maya area) in colonial times (Steinbrenner 2006). No doubt prices were affected by supply and demand and varied widely. Cocoa was brewed, hot, frothy and red to look like the favorite substance of Mayas, blood. Anyone who drank a cup must have been painfully aware it was worth its weight, if not in gold, at least in currency. It is unlikely that many commoners consumed chocolate in any form. Shell and jade beads, salt, and cotton mantles were also used as money at the time of contact and possibly during the Classic period as well.

The economic trade in elite goods and such workaday consumables as salt would not be enough to account for the rise of a site with the political power of Tikal. So how did this city, whose residents appear to have supported themselves on a subsistence basis, develop the economic clout of a Maya superpower? Ironically, the economic engine that drove Tikal was the same that propels the world's economies today: consumerism.

The cacao seeds, jade and shell beads, and so on, obtained in trade were used in many cases to buy luxury foods for feasts that would turn a Roman emperor green with envy. Guests at these affairs were treated to dainty foods of all sorts. Naturally, there was cacao in lavishly decorated cylinder cups (stenciled with the guests' names). The main course would include a whole "pheasant" (probably a chachalaca or perhaps even a small turkey). Guests were treated to party favors such as ""five four hundred piece lots [of cacao] each, five cotton mantles of four breadths each, a string of red [shell] beads as long as one's arm, and one score of green stones" or precious painted pottery (Foias 2002). That these banquets were bouts of conspicuous consumption is shown by the heaps of pottery sherds found outside the doorways. Fine plates and pots, often painted with scenes of elite life, were smashed after use, like drinkers tossing champagne flutes against the wall. Although archaeologists have found the Maya to be meticulously tidy, these middens were allowed to build up to show the wealth of the owner of the palace where banquets were served.

Archaeologists have found that only 2 percent of pots were imported into the communities where studies were done. But 20 percent of the pottery found in such feasting middens came from a hamlet other than the one the palace was located. Some kind of exchange (if only tributary) occurred to gain those pots. Likewise, of the products known to have been exchanged as money of sorts — cacao, shell beads, cotton mantles, and jade — only half were products of the interior lowlands. Shell came from the coasts and jade from the mountains of the Motagua Valley more than a hundred fifty miles from Tikal. Cacao could only be grown in favored locations in the Peten. Those cacao beans may very well have been imported from better watered areas of Belize or coastal Guatemala.

We know of these feasts of the upper classes that drove the Classic period economy from archaeology from scenes painted on surviving pots and from accounts of the Spanish shortly after contact. To date, the record does not show similar feasts occurred among the nonelite. Archaeologists suspect that such banquets were a feature of Maya life at all social levels. Modern anthropology shows that is the case among the Maya today. Commoners, of course, would restrict their eating and drinking and gift giving substantially. But the same kind of events that occasioned feasts among the wealthy — rites of passage such as coming of age, marriage and funerals, naming of heirs, and perhaps most importantly, ancestor worship — were celebrated by all. Why should ordinary folk not celebrate in a commensurate way?

All this activity fattened the coffers of the budding Tikal state by the paying of tribute. The term we would use today is "payment of taxes." And naturally the larger the tax base in terms of population and economic activity, the larger the amount of commodities pouring into Tikal's coffers. This wherewithal could be converted to ritual use or war materiel, both of which increased the power of the city in the eyes of the Maya world. The pictures we have of tribute paying are mostly of subject lords giving up their gains, for which the Maya word "burden" was used (Foias 2002). Payment seems to have been in both "Maya money" (cacao beans, jade, shell beads) and subsistent products such as frijoles and corn. It is assumed the subsidiary lord similarly taxed the peasants in his fiefdom — or perhaps some of the product came from lands the peasants worked as a means of paying back the lord for the services he rendered. These services the lord took credit for would include living in a state that was fairly secure from attack and of which the lord claimed to be the supernaturally ordained authority. Perhaps more importantly, tribute payments also came in from conquered states. The tribute from those who lost wars was no doubt substantial. At times, it entailed enormous contributions of labor, grain, and building materials.

Warfare itself was practiced on at least four vastly different levels of intensity. Diane and Arlen Chase of the University of Central Florida have undertaken a study of the Maya glyphs for warfare (Chase and Chase 2003). These glyphs show several different levels of warfare, ranging from low-scale ritual skirmishes to something approaching total war. Here they are in the simplest English equivalent: (1) capture, (2) destruction, (3) axe, (4) star war. The first, "capture," according to legendary archaeologist Payson Sheets the excavator of the Maya Pompei of Ceren in El Salvador, does not much resemble "warfare" in the northern world's sense at all. It may involve something more akin to a raid in which a subject is captured. That person was then ritually used (generally sacrificed but perhaps tortured), and the capturers would carry on as they had scored an impressive religious and military victory. As Sheets notes, if those raided also managed to get hold of one of the raiders, both sides then boasted of a successful campaign. The supposed motivation for these raids would probably be revenge, perhaps for a similar raid against the aggressor or some simmering, long-standing feud. An "axe" event, according to Sheets was similar to a capture event, but the victim would be a notable victim. In the early days of the Maya, his capture may have been enough to gain his visage, hands bound and abject look chiseled into a stela (stone tablet).

In neither case did the event have much economic significance, although it had abundant ritual and prestige value. The "destruction" glyph denoted warfare of wider social consequence, which entailed economic losses. The "star war" evidently appeared on the scene at the end of the Early Classic period, circa A.D. 550. This was no-holds warfare in which one side attempted to assimilate much of the population and territory of the other. A star war event could be of enormous economic consequence. In the Late Classic (A.D. 550–800), Maya cities grew in wealth and inhabitants, and the winners in these star wars tussles erected impressive monuments. But no Maya city is known to have completely disappeared at the hands of a rival. As time went on, warfare among the Maya became more bitter and engaged a wider segment of society. Complete consensus can be found on almost no topic regarding the Maya, and the art of warfare is among the most hotly debated. Nevertheless, for big states, such as Tikal, it seems likely its wealth came, in a large part, from tribute payments made by unfortunate cities bested in battle.

The Kings of Tikal, A.D. 100–869

By warfare and internal and external tribute payments, the early aristocrats built up the site and population of Tikal and their own fortunes. Up until about 300 B.C., the early Tikalese (and the Maya generally) seem to have worshipped at home using domestic figurines (usually with were-jaguar features). These home services were augmented by worship in neighborhoods at fairly small public platforms. But at the beginning of the Late Preclassic (300 B.C.–A.D. 250), communities started erecting larger pyramids. As we saw in the last section, these were adorned with Hero Twins imagery, sometimes of Hun Ahaw, the elder Hero Twin, at other times of his younger brother, Yax Balam, in his guise as the day and/or night sun bearer, the hunter of human souls to nourish the sun. The father of the Twins, Hun Hun Ahaw, might also be represented in his various guises as Principal Bird Deity, Maize God, Itzamna, and so on. Some of the temples in the older sections of the city, especially the Lost World and North Acropolis, exhibit Preclassic characteristics such as triadic arrangement of temples, E-Groups, and so on.

Enormous social organization was required to build these huge pyramids. A leader with the power of a king would be needed. Many scholars, such as Linda Schele and David Freidel, believe that the institution of kingship evolved in the Peten, including Tikal and surrounding territories, at the beginning of the Late Preclassic. How else can one account for those huge buildings, they ask? The divine kings identified with the Hero Twins (Freidel and Schele 1988). But the early kings at El Mirador, Tikal and elsewhere were self-effacing, perhaps as a legacy of the village accumulator who gave away his gain for the public good. Only two Preclassic kings are known to have left monuments with their names on them. But we can assume they began to claim they were divine kings, appointed by the deity to shepherd the masses, even if they were careful not to take too much credit for themselves.

It wasn't until about A.D. 100, give or take a few decades, that a record of Tikal's first king appears. His name was Yax Ehb Shock. The term "Yax," means first (or green in the sense of verdant). "Ehb'" is step or ladder. The term "Shock" is of interest because it means "big fish." The term has special reference to that scariest of common big fish, the shark. Oddly enough, the Maya word for shark appears to have been the root for our English word. Up until the 16th or 17th centuries, sharks were called dogfish, a term still used for some species.

If Yax Ehb Shock's coronation followed the pattern used during most of the Classic period, he endured a number of initiation rites from childhood on. The first was a bloodletting at about the age of reason, six or so. Number one in line to a Maya throne was the firstborn male of the present king. But the youth had to show he was courageous in battle, and capturing a noble from a hostile town was a quasi requirement before he could become king. The coronation, as per royal investitures the world over, was rife with spectacle to entertain, impress, and frighten friend and foe alike.

In Yax Ehb Shock's case, no doubt an elaborate dais was prepared, atop which lay a scaffold with a jaguar-pelt cushion (Martin and Grube 2000). The king was seated on the jaguar-skin bolster, and a jade stone in the trilobial shape called a hunal was tied around his forehead. The emblem on the jade looked a lot like a three-leaf clover. As noted in the last section, the jade on the king's forehead was meant to represent a three-leaved corn shoot. It hearkens back to the Maize God, the father of the Hero Twins, and as such, reminds his subjects that he rules because of the sanctions of the creation myth. Also, it not so subtly keeps them focused on the belief that the health of the city-state resided in the king's ability to mediate with the gods. This was a point Maya royalty reinforced again and again. A crown of jade and shell topped off with an elaborate display of quetzal feathers was also placed on Yax Eb Shock's head. The hunal jade was infinitely more important than the jade, shell feather crown. A version of the hunal can be found on most representations of Maya kings.

Among other ceremonies at Yax Ehb Shock's investiture, there was a human sacrifice. It is possible that sacrifice might have occurred by having the new king order the prisoner bound into a ball. Yax Ehb Shock, garbed in ballplayer yoke and other paraphernalia of the Hero Twins, dribbled the prisoner down the stone steps of a temple until his backbone snapped or his skull cracked like an egg and his brains oozed out. This ceremony reminded the many onlookers, once again, of the creation myth in which Hun Hun Ahaw was sacrificed on the ball court by the lords of the underworld—in order that he might be reborn as the Maize God, all of which kept the cornfields growing.

The most important part of the coronation ceremony may or may not have occurred in public. This would be when Yax Ehb Shock undertook to commune with the other world on behalf of his new charges. Among the Olmec, these rites appear to have been conducted in underground chambers. According to Schele and Freidel, the rulers of Preclassic Cerros sheathed themselves in white tunics and secreted themselves in the small temple atop ceremonial platforms. There they conducted bloodletting rites while an assembled throng awaited to affirm that the bloodletting had indeed occurred by the bloodstain on the tunic and the bloody strips of paper caught in a ceremonial bowl. In both instances, the ruler was transported by these exertions from the plane of ordinary reality to one most moderns would designate as mystical or hallucinatory.

As we have seen, the peoples of Mesoamerica had a completely different world view from the scientific materialism characteristic of the modern age. It is a rare modern who does not believe, deep down, that facts are "stubborn." To us, a fact is an objective reality. It cannot be altered or changed except through the intercession of the natural laws of physics or other sciences. One would not have to look far into the peasant past of Western societies to find a mentality much different, one that believed in miracles and many unseen or seldom seen beings such as elves, fairies, hobgoblins, wraiths, and so on. This alternate view persists in a sort of nether, half-believed world by many who claim to be skeptical of the prevailing modern view. And as a matter of fact, serious Western philosophers often do entertain the notion that the basic matter of the world consists of ideas—as opposed to matter. To the Western "idea-ist" philosopher, facts made of ideas were still stubborn and subject to the laws of science.

But to other "idea-ists" (in the sense that the basic stuff of the universe is more similar to a mental idea than matter), ideas need not necessarily be stubborn. They are much more easily manipulated than materialistic facts. And the "laws" manipulating them may be magical. The Maya clearly believed in a world like this "idea" one, and the very fabric of the world could itself be alive and have souls. We have noted several locations to the Maya, such as caves, mountains, bodies of water, that were imbued with mystical properties. Likewise, a Maya temple was charged with a soul force, called *ch'uel,* by undergoing a ritual and the placement of a cache vessel (Brown and Garber 2003). The vessel might contain sacred ornamental images of jade or flint or exotic foodstuffs and so on (Pagliaro 2003). A human or animal might be sacrificed to seal the deal. In any case, to the Maya the basic properties of matter could be altered by ritual. In addition, as we have seen, the Maya universe consisted of many levels aside from the one experienced on a day to day basis, nine in the underworld and 13 in the celestial sphere.

Ancestors were not dead; they simply existed on a different plane. They could be consulted by a conjuring. At the séance they would divulge important information about the future. The medium used to conjure was bloodletting or use of hallucinogenic drugs or perhaps other ways. All members of Maya society attempted to consult with dead family members, and they all had their share of good spirits and evil ones on the other side to deal with. And they no doubt had their own local sorcerer and alchemists to bribe to make the world as they wanted. However, the main role of the divine kings was to manipulate the arcane arts to learn of, head off, or destroy threats to the state and his people in all spheres. Keeping the city-state secure in this mystical, occult mode was just as important as the various other duties of the king.

The dynasty that Yax Ehb Shock founded lasted, in an unbroken line of succession, for about 800 years to A.D. 869. As we will see, "dynasty" had a special meaning for the Maya, more akin to the modern idea of a government than a family dynasty. A usurper could overthrow a king, undergo the accession ritual, and claim Yax Ehb Shock as his progenitor. This happened many times. Still, by any standard, 800 years is a long time, and this long political heritage—along with her history of conquest and dominance—gives Tikal a claim for being the eternal city of the Maya.

Diagnostic Clues to the Early Classic, A.D. 250–550

The most significant development in ritual life during the Early Classic was the observation of fixed periods of time. This was done with considerable pomp. The centerpiece of the ritual was the dedication of a monolith with, as we have seen, the technical name of stela (plural stelae). Surviving stelae are usually made of stone and many are adorned with hieroglyphic texts and images of a king and a notable subdued in battle. Wood, stuccoed wood, painted and plain stone, and other media were also used. A hieroglyphic text might tell a story of the city's great accomplishments in the years since the last dedication of a monument. The most significant and common period observed was called a katun. It was a cycle of about twenty years. A "tun" was 360 days, five days short of a full calendar year. It was just one of the many measurements of time the Maya used including a vague year of 365 days, a quarter day shy of our calendar year; the Maya understood the need for correcting for a leap year, but for whatever reason, they did not make the adjustment. The sacred almanac calendar was 260 days, and so on.

As you recall from the first section of this book, Frans Blom believed La Venta was a Maya site because of the stelae he found there. Those stelae seemed to be Maya monuments. His confusion was perfectly reasonable given that the Maya took the stela form and developed it more fully than any other Mesoamerican society. The Zapotec, around present day Oaxaca, were erecting stelae as early as 500 or 600 B.C. These people also developed a script almost that early, many centuries before it is believed the Maya committed their language to writing. The Maya may not have been the people who developed the stela cult or a writing system. But during the Early Classic period they developed both concepts far beyond that of any other people in the area. Indeed, they were the only culture in the western hemisphere to produce a complete system of writing as we know it. The versions of the other cultures ranged from simple logograms (words that resembled the object denoted—bird symbol for a bird, for instance), to something that can be likened to elaborate note taking. The Maya were actually able to transcribe spoken language word for word. Their system was complex and literary. For instance, the word for lord or ruler, "ahaw," could be written at least six different ways (Martin and Grube 2000). This would be the equivalent in English of having six different acceptable spellings for the word. It stems from the fact that one spelling might be a stylized picture of a word that sounded similar, another of a couple of syllables that made up the word, and so on. Unfortunately, all classic Maya poetry and other literary texts written on their bark paper books have been lost. But these properties that would have been the poet's delight have been the decoder's bane, and the language's literary embellishment was just one of the many things that caused the Mayan hieroglyphs to be the last major language deciphered. Writing, therefore, is another characteristic marker of the Classic period.

Matthew Stirling, who we remember as the first excavator of the Olmec sites, found what was at that time the earliest Long Count date of 32 B.C. at the Epi-Olmec site of Tres Zapotes. (Only one date in the eighty years since has been found to be earlier — by only four years.) Therefore, the Long Count calendar, like the stela cult and writing, was borrowed by the Maya from other peoples of the region. It came into use in the Maya world during the Early Classic period. Marking monuments with the Long Count date is another major diagnostic for the Classic period. The Long Count has a fixed starting date in mid–August 3114 B.C., much as the calendar used in the modern world has a fixed starting date of January 1, A.D. 1, from which we can count forward and backwards. The Maya used that date to count forward and backward to events that were both historical and fictitious. Dates of a million years into the far mythical past were recorded, for instance, at Palenque and elsewhere.

The skyline of the Classic era Maya cityscape altered substantially from those of the Late Preclassic period. The triadic arrangement of temples atop pyramids characteristic of the Mirador basin disappeared at Tikal and most other sites. Also, gone at Tikal were the E-Groups. As you recall, the E-Group consists of a radial temple on the west and a long rangy eastern building. This assemblage apparently was used to mark, more or less, the solstices and equinoxes or other solar events, such as the passing directly overhead of the sun. This happened twice a year in all parts of the Maya area. The first of these passings heralded the onset of the rainy season. Predicting the arrival of the rains was of great importance to Maya farmers. At Tikal, only one E-Group has been found and that in an early phase of the Lost World complex. None was erected after the Preclassic.

Even more significant than what not was built is the main architectural innovation, the so-called corbelled arch. Maya engineers never quite figured out the principle of the keystone; true arches cannot be found among their architecture. But they did devise a means of spanning interior space without running a beam across a roof. They did this by cantilevering stones in a stair-step fashion on the longitudinal sides of a room, the weight of massive ceiling fill holding the stones in place. A flat rock of a couple of feet in width took the place of a keystone at the very top of the "corbelled vault." This arrangement, though incapable of spanning great distances, was quite stable (though less so than a true arch). Even more importantly, it was one of the features that helped produce a pleasant and characteristic look of Maya architecture. In many other ways, Maya architecture advanced in this period as the structural properties of the buildings became more stable than those of the Preclassic period, many of which Graham reported in a deplorable state of collapse when he made the first serious surveys in the 1960s.

In the micro vein, Maya material culture advanced — or at least changed — in the Classic period. Pottery began to be finished in polychrome, meaning three or more colors were evident on ceramics destined for ceremonial purposes or elite residences. Another marker of the Classic period was the development of a name glyph for a city, and only cities that

Corbelled arch at Becan, Campeche, Mexico. The corbelled arch consisted of a stair-step series of stones with a wider "capstone" held in place by the sheer weight of the overload. Though perhaps not as efficient as a true arch, the corbel produced a pleasing visage and a characteristic look of Maya architecture (courtesy INAH).

achieved a significant degree of political independence could display a glyph. By the end of the Classic period, there would be 60 to 80 cities in the Lowlands with name glyphs.

The great Olmec capital of La Venta collapsed somewhere between 500 and 400 B.C., about the time the first cities of the Mirador basin began to develop into true urban centers. David Freidel speculates that the Olmec were responsible for the political development of the lowland Maya (Freidel 2008). Olmec traders exchanged rubber for salt in the northern Yucatan, and they traded that salt for their beloved blue-green jade in the Motagua Valley. As a by-product of their trade, the Olmec counseled the Maya (by example) in the benefits of divine kingship. So the

Tikal's Emblem Glyph (courtesy INAH).

Maya began organizing into a complex society. By the beginning of the Late Preclassic, the Maya cities in the Mirador Basin could very well have attacked and defeated La Venta, according to Freidel. Thus the Olmec passed from the scene and the first great age of the Maya commenced.

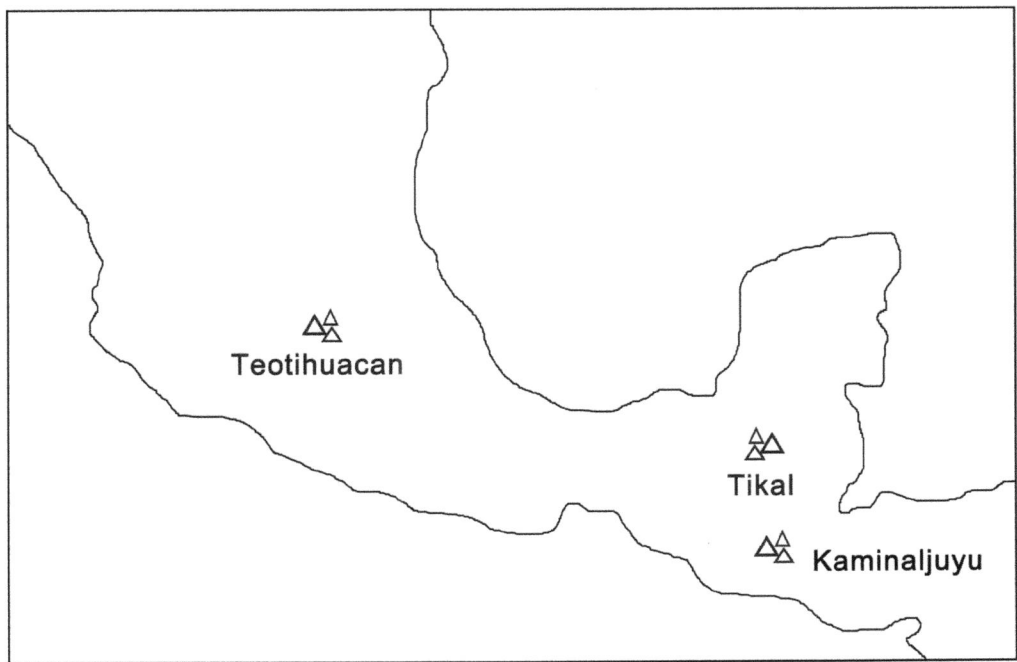

This map shows the relative distances from Teotihuacan in the Valley of Mexico to Kaminaljuyu on outskirts of modern day Guatemala City in the highlands and Tikal in its lowland Peten site.

Likewise, it is worth nothing that Yax Ehb Shock came to power a half century (more or less) before El Mirador collapsed. As we remembered from the last section, a severe and disastrous drought struck the Peten at the time of El Mirador's disappearance from the scene. El Mirador, like Tikal, was surrounded by swamp lands. But hundreds of years of erosion from agriculture and building appear to have filled the open water holes in the swamps. El Mirador's water supply was gone. The drought would have affected Tikal much less severely. Its marshes or shallow lakes may have shrunk to ponds. But the shallow lakes or marshes on each side of Tikal retained some water. The layer of Maya clay due to building and erosion, owing to Tikal's smaller population and shorter period of occupation, had not yet completely filled in its marshes. In so many ways, the situation of Tikal resembled that of El Mirador, also at a trade crossroads, but without the disadvantage of centuries of buildup and the attendant wearing down of the natural resources. Some archaeologists theorize (without hard evidence) that Tikal may even have been a subordinate to El Mirador. In any case, during a drought when El Mirador was reeling, a foreign power could easily sneak in and install a client king in an important polity in a place like Tikal, which some theorize the highland city of Kaminaljuyu did. Just as likely, a local lord with a full granary and enough water may have seized the opportunity to establish himself as a full blown king of Tikal, throwing off his allegiance to El Mirador. It would be easy to visualize an army of Tikal warriors heading north, raiding the city that for many years had lorded it over them. The Tikalese, perhaps in conjunction with other cities, may even have delivered the coupe de grace that toppled the Mirador king and drove those of his followers not enslaved out of the basin. But at present all this is speculation informed only by a vague knowledge of the situation at the time.

This brings us up to A.D. 378, a hundred years into the Early Classic age. Yax Ehb Shock has been gone for about two hundred years, and the successor on the throne is known as Great Jaguar Paw. Foreign aggression and violent collapse is about to play an important role in the history of the Maya. For many years, archaeologists understood that Teotihuacan, a great state in the Central Valley of Mexico located not far from present day Mexico City, exerted an immense effect on the culture of the Maya lowlands. However, new evidence in the way of the deciphering of hieroglyphs has shed light on how this influx of cultural ideas and traits from central Mexico occurred.

Following, we will give a dramatized view of a significant day in the life of Great Jaguar Paw. He ruled beginning at about A.D. 360, the fourteenth in line of succession from Yax Ehb Shock. We will also discuss those very regal activities of war and the ball game, and show how both relate to the myth of the Hero Twins. We will also discuss one of the more puzzling aspects of Tikal and that is its relationship to the great Central Mexican city of Teotihuacan—and how this relationship came to be. Not the least important thing this dramatized tableau does is give a picture of Maya life at the time.

Great Jaguar Paw's Day of Reckoning, January 16, 378

For Great Jaguar Paw, divine lord of Tikal, the morning in the Maya Long Count calendar of 8.17.1.4.12 11 EB 15 Mac (January 16, 378) started earlier than usual, in the predawn. He vaulted from his sleeping bench into the sandals on the floor. Wrapping his breechclout around his loins, he parted the curtain that acted as a door to his bedchamber and gazed skyward. In the cold, clear morning air, the moon shone large and bright. It formed a vee, with the two heavenly bodies shining just as bright above it, bodies we call Venus and Jupiter.

Venus, in particular, beamed and sparked, shooting rays in all directions. The astral body had been out of sight for many weeks. All this had been foretold by Jaguar Paw's court soothsayers. But one could never be sure until he saw the star burnishing bright with his own eyes. And there it was, just as predicted. Venus reappearing like this meant Hun Ahaw, the first born of the Hero Twins, would be shooting his darts to earth killing men with abandon. It was a time for caution — or an opportunity to be bold, because Hun Ahaw himself would be assisting with the death of the unwary and unfortunate. For sure, there would be death.

Somewhere in the land war was afoot, and Great Jaguar Paw knew where that was, at El Peru, forty miles to the west northwest. The site had fallen to a force claiming to be from Teotihuacan in central Mexico, more than 600 miles away. Jaguar Paw had bruited about the fact that he was all in favor of this conquest. He, after all, was a great friend of Teotihuacan, and the fact was warfare between the cities of the Peten area had been getting out of hand. A little war was fine, necessary even. It provided nobles for sacrifice and commoners for slaves. But lately the Kan Snakehead people of the north had been raiding the central Peten. Their raids had been a constant menace. Harvest in outlying areas had been impossible without armed guards. Trade had become haphazard. Something needed to be done; and officially, Jaguar Paw was pleased that his allies the Teotihuacanos were doing something.

He started to. It was full light out now, with just a little rosy tint in the east. He'd been mooning at the sky for minutes, maybe a full hour. He realized also it was seasonally cool. The temperature was in the low fifties. A great shiver coursed through Jaguar Paw's body. He doubted the shiver had much to do with the cold, but he pretended it did. He kicked into gear, striding briskly through the passageways of his palace. He barely noticed the women, dressed in rags, huddled under the thatch lean-to in the corner of a courtyard. They paused from their work. Some were grinding softened corn kernels with a rolling-pin shaped granite mano against the trough-like basalt metate. Others were processing the bean of the cacao tree into a chocolate paste that would be turned into a chile-ladened, frothy drink of bright red color. The women bowed and saluted their lord. He paid them no attention. They were serving women. They were preparing the feast that would be served after the game. Let them hunker close to the large clay pots resting on the three-stone fires for warmth and not bother him.

On a normal feast day, he'd go to them and make small talk to make sure all was going well with the preparations for the feast that would be served the elite guests at the palace after the game. Others elsewhere were preparing the tamales that would be served to the great crowd of commoners. The work of both groups of women were important. Jaguar Paw wanted the masses looking forward to a feast. And he wanted their bellies full and them happy after they had gotten it. Similarly, he had gone to lengths to make sure the aristocrats that he would entertain here in his palace would be pleased. He would serve them on fine dishes that they could take home with them. Or they were free to smash and throw over the side of the dining verandah of the palace as was customary — to show the riches of Jaguar Paw were so vast the few days labor of a peasant involved in making a bowl was insignificant. A new plate with more tamales or venison stew would be fetched by a servant and the feast continued. Each noble had a drinking cup which would be kept full of the spicy chocolate drink or honey wine. That cup was a tall, thin-walled, cylindrical vessel. Then later, as a sort of party favor, Jaguar Paw would pass out jade beads or quetzal feathers to his guests. These gifts, though not unheard of, were lavish for an after ball game feast. Jaguar Paw had let it be known what the menu and gifts would be. He wanted the leaders of the hamlets of Tikal on his side this day. He wanted to make sure they all cheered after the gifts were passed out. It would be then that he took the drinking cup of the sajal of the Lost World. He looked forward to smashing that drinking cup. He would then discard the pieces over the side of the dining verandah.

As the divine lord, he knew he had been selected by the universe to be king of Tikal. That meant all decisions he made would ultimately turn out correctly, did it not? Well, maybe ultimately. But he knew from past experience that that there were better and worse choices to be made. If his plan for the feasting didn't keep the other aristocrats in line, he could cause himself, his family and his city needless trouble.

He stamped up the limestone stairway, thirteen steps, one for each of the thirteen celestial levels. As he reached the ninth step, he cast his eye up and noticed a woman swaddled in cotton mantles. It was his Mexican wife, Lady Jade Bead. Why of all people did she stop him on the ninth step, the number of death, he wondered? He shook his head in annoyance with himself for his superstition. There were real intimations of the supernaturals, and there were old women hexes and nonsense. His worrying about seeing Lady Jade Bead when he was on the ninth step clearly was an old woman superstition, he told himself.

But why did she avert her gaze, look down and give that tooth-showing grin? A woman in love with a man for the first time might act like that, but a wife of several years? And one that he did not get on with all that well. Some other reason was behind that look. Then Great Jaguar Paw reminded himself he was doing it again. He was looking too deeply into things, tricking himself by turning shadows into substance. His marriage with her had been a marriage of convenience. He had forged trade ties with the huge metropolis of Teotihuacan in the Central Valley of Mexico, more than six hundred miles away. His caravans hauling tropical bundles of tapir hides, cotton bales, packs of macaw feathers, sacks of cacao beans, and pouches of salt to the metropolis had returned with the valuable green obsidian of central Mexico. That green obsidian was much more prized than the cheap stuff from the mountains of Guatemala just a few days away. Also, from Teotihuacan came precious art objects, pots and clay plaques, that any Maya noble or lord would kill to have ornamenting his throne room. Great Jaguar Paw distributed these to the leaders of the smaller city-states in the Peten and even as far as Belize. As a result, a steady stream of nobles poured into his city offering their fealty. Everyone said Great Jaguar Paw was the greatest since Yax Ehb Shock founded the line.

One of the prizes of this trade was Lady Jade Bead. She'd been given to him to cement the alliance between him and Teotihuacan. He didn't like her because, among other things, she did not try to please him. For instance, she did not keep herself up. She had been among the Maya for more than five years. Some things he could not blame her for, such as the shape of her head. The only truly beautiful visage, the way a Maya lord looked at things, included a flattened forehead. This was accomplished when the infant was in the cradle. A board was roped to the head above the eyes and in time the spot between the brows and hairline would be perfectly flattened. A bead was attached to the board. The child would focus on the bead and grow cross eyed. From the side, the head of a proper Maya aristocrat looked like an upended flowerpot and, if he was lucky, he'd be cross-eyed, a real mark of beauty.

It may have been too late for Lady Jade Bead to do anything about her head and her eyes, but she could wear a nosepiece and dress her hair in the Maya way. The Maya had prominent noses which they preferred to accentuate by adding an artificial piece. This made their proboscis grander. Jade Bead's nose was small and stub. Even with these deficiencies, she never attempted to procure some artificial help. The "flowerpot" shaped head was meant to resemble a cob of corn. A person's hair was the silk. Each corn silk needed to be pollinated by a grain of pollen for a kernel to grow out. Therefore, the more lavish and luxuriant the hair, which Jaguar Paw's Maya pulled up and tied like silk coming out of the ear of corn, the better. Similarly, it would be a simple matter for Jade Bead to dress her hair in the Maya way, but she wore it in the disgusting Mexican way, in a sweeping semi-circle.

And a look at her mouth was equally nauseating. She could have her teeth filed like any proper Maya, noble or commoner. Sure filing hurt. But the pain was good. Enduring it showed that you had the grit to be called an adult Maya. In addition, the filed incisor teeth symbolized the life-force and helped keep's one's spirit strong. The reason for this was that the Maya hieroglyph for "wind" resembled a capital T. To the Maya, wind, which was air in motion, symbolized the life-force, literally the breath of life. By choosing not to file her teeth, Jade Bead flew in the face of Maya standards of beauty — and beliefs. Looking at her toothy smile annoyed Jaguar Paw.

At this moment, Jaguar Paw's first wife, the queen of Tikal, appeared on the landing. She was wearing a sort of brocade shift that would be appropriate at any time of the day in any capital of the world. The woman had both taste and good sense. Seeing her husband several steps below Jade Bead, she rushed to the scene. By proper etiquette Jade Bead should scuttle away, understanding her lowly position in comparison to the queen. The queen was the first wife, his real wife. She was also a Maya and a legitimate queen. Another of the things Jaguar Paw had against Jade Bead was her parentage. After he had been married to her, he learned she was not the daughter of the emperor of Teotihuacan but a daughter of a chief of a minor north Mexican tribe, not even a city-state. Her status was not nearly high enough to be even a subsidiary wife of a man of his high rank. That she didn't fly away at the approach of the queen showed her lowly parentage and her lack of manners. Indeed, that she stood for an instant above him was unthinkable — yet there she stood still, not budging.

The queen opened her mouth to speak. Jaguar Paw admired her set of teeth. Of course, they had been properly filed. Just as importantly they were inlaid with jade and hematite. The hematite, an iron substance, was shiny and showy and useful for its own sake. The jade, however, was the most expensive and beautiful substance known to the Early Classic Maya. It freshened the breath and helped make the proper words pour out of a speaker's mouth. A scowl froze on the queen's face, and as the queen opened her mouth — set of jade-inlaid teeth or no — not a word issued forth. She had never had to scold a subordinate wife many miles from her family and friends. They all knew she was the mistress of the palace. She had to be obeyed.

Finally, after what seemed many minutes but probably was just a few seconds, the queen shot out, "Mind your manners, child."

For a moment, Jade Bead stood her ground. Then she suddenly capitulated. She squatted. Her butt plopped against her heels. Her head dropped far below the level of Jaguar Paw's. He continued up the steps. The queen too had ducked as though lowering her head below her husband's. He continued up the tenth, eleventh, twelfth, and finally ascended the landing. He signed the queen to rise. He pretended to pay no attention to Jade Bead, but he shook his head at her lack of courtly manners. Commoners squatted on their haunches. Courtiers were used to sitting on furniture and did not squat, though they might bend from the waist. Jaguar Paw was tall, five feet seven inches, a veritable giant. His people averaged about five feet. Squatting was not necessary. A simple duck of the head would do.

"Your ceremonial dress is laid out in your chamber, my lord," the queen said to Jaguar Paw.

Jaguar Paw gave the briefest nod in acknowledgment of her statement. He was at the top level of the palace. The building was essentially an artificial hill. A few small, narrow rooms had been carved out on the two stories below. Atop the hill, four rooms were added like the top story of a wedding cake. But Jaguar Paw continued going, climbing up the spiderhole-like, secret passageway to the roof of the top tier.

As he climbed his eye slid into the courtyard of his palace, the central part of what would be known many years later as the Central Acropolis. Even given his mental consternation, Jaguar Paw was charmed by the site of the complex below him. Over the hundreds of years of royal residency in this area, many buildings had been put up. Attention to architectural detail was the watchword for all of them. Courtyards were planned between buildings, all of which were at differing levels. Staircases, some as wide as the courtyard they gave onto, others simple and utilitarian-seeming, connected them. With each step Jaguar Paw went up, the view of the three-dimensional maze changed. It was like viewing an Escher print, only the scene was much more visually stimulating. Stucco masks of supernatural monsters adorned the walls here. A gaily painted mural of a battle scene took up that space there. Most surfaces were tinted a vivid red, and the paintings and masks were colored green, yellow, and red. Though it was still early and cold, courtiers darted back and forth across open spaces. Jaguar Paw's people lived the way they worshipped, out of doors with the small rooms of the temples and the commoner's thatch houses reserved for such mundane exercises as sleeping. There he saw several of his courtiers, a dwarf and his sidekick, a hunchback. Like Jaguar Paw himself, despite the cold, they wore only loincloth and sandals, and they skittered across the courtyard. The hunchback hobbled along going fast, the dwarf almost running to keep up. They were heading to the cooking lean-to, looking for something to eat. As one who was divine, Jaguar Paw preferred to associate with others of supernatural origins. The king represented the sacred corncob of the maize plant. Dwarfs and hunchbacks

Grand Plaza, Tikal. The view is from the northwest corner. The North Acropolis is in the right foreground. Temples I (left) and II (right) would not be built for 300 years. The ball court is hidden behind Temple I. The long narrow rangy building in the far distance is the Central Acropolis where Great Jaguar Paw looked out on the Great Plaza. His palace, known today as 5D-46, was in the far eastern edge of the building to the left of Temple I (courtesy INAH).

were suitable companions of god-like kings because they represented the deformed ears of corn which were common on corn stalks. In short, they were supernatural entities in human bodies.

Turning his gaze out of the palace complex, Jaguar Paw watched his city stir to life. Dead ahead he saw the small temple that several hundred years later would develop into the 150-foot high Temple I. Across the plaza, on its western end, lay the temple mound that would morph into Temple II. Catty-corner across the football-size field of grass could be seen the North Acropolis. It was a complex of more than a dozen pyramids, mostly in the form of radial temples; that is, square pyramids with stairs all four sides. Tikal architects and city planners continually remodeled these buildings, building them up and connecting them, all this leading archaeologists at a later time to give such complexes the designation "acropolises." Though not quite as pleasing to the eye as Jaguar Paw's Central Acropolis, they were by no means laid out in a monotonous, cookie-cutter fashion. They were built on many different levels. These temples were adorned with stucco texts and masks and painted stunning basic colors, mostly red like that sacred fluid, human blood. Inside these pyramids, the bodies of many of Tikal's royals had been laid in crypts, such as Jaguar Paw's own father, Hawk Skull. The saying was that the commoners were buried with dirt in the face, but nobles were laid to rest in vaulted crypts. In short, the North Acropolis was the great cemetery of Maya notables.

Jaguar Paw's father had been gone eighteen years. He'd been buried with the finest in grave goods. Many necklaces of jade lay on his breastbone. His cadaver had been drenched in reddish cinnabar, the color of the east and the rising sun, to assist in his resurrection. Lavish and intricately painted bowls filled with expensive items like cacao and rubber were included in a place of honor in the vault in which a scene depicting the celestial sphere was painted. To serve Hawk Skull six young men were sacrificed and their bodies piled along the wall of the crypt. A ball of copal shaped to resemble a head lay where Hawk Skull's skull should be.

Looking to the right in the area called the East Plaza, Jaguar Paw watched the commoners toting baskets to the open-air market. They were spreading their wares on the ground, piling a few chilies here and a basket of squash blossoms there. All this was meant to collect a few grains of salt, shell beads, or similar petty earning. On a day like this, when the very fate of the nation hung in the balance, the peasants worried about nothing more important than a chili pepper or a morsel of salt!

For no apparent reason, Jaguar Paw thought of a building to the southeast. It was on the banks of the pond used for water during the dry season. It was an outlier of Group 6, a palace acropolis much like the central acropolis where he stood. It was a funeral temple. Two men had been buried there in what to Great Jaguar Paw was a peculiar way. They were interred sitting up in altar-like mounds. And the mounds had been plastered over. This was the style of the mountain folk around Kaminaljuyu, a town much under the influence of Teotihuacanos. As a matter of fact, many of the goods in the grave also resembled those hybrid Kaminaljuyu-Teotihucan style. There were large cylinder pots with hollow women's breast-type legs. Jaguar Paw knew this because his father Hawk Skull had desecrated the temple. He destroyed the pots and scattered the sherds around the building. He also broke into the tombs and scattered the bones of the two skeletons along the floors and then burned all that could burn. He did this to destroy its power and to root out the claims of those folks to the leadership of Tikal. It was a signal that the rightful heirs to the throne of Tikal were back in charge, not the usurpers from Kaminaljuyu who claimed a bogus tie to Teotihuacan. Their claim came from associating with Teotihuacan warlords.

The Lost World clan had allied themselves with the Teotihuacano warlords operating in the highlands. They thought they could depose the rightful kings of Tikal and be inserted into the royal line of succession. The Teotihuacano land pirates, who called themselves armed traders, only used them. They put one of the second clan on the throne, all right, but he was only a figurehead. The Teotihuacanos plundered the city and its riches. The clan of the Lost World had learned its lesson, hadn't it? Well, maybe not.

Dead ahead, between the mound that would be Temple I and the palace, lay the ball court. Already, onlookers were gathering. They were commoners and nobles. They hoped to get a good spot from which to view the contest that would occur later in the day. Again, Jaguar Paw felt a thrill of disgust course through his body. Those ghouls were jockeying for a place to view the contest. The contest would leave one man dead, his head chopped off in sacrifice. His sacred blood would flow into the grass.

As he looked at the ball court, Jaguar Paw could hardly believe he was having such thoughts. They were both sacrilegious and unpatriotic. The person who was supposed to win would win. That is what ball court contests were all about, to settle such disputes. And Jaguar Paw knew he would win. He was the king of Tikal, elected by the universe, no less.

The ball court playing field was shaped like a capital "I," with the narrow grassy alley bound by a low stone wall. The head and the foot of the "I" were open areas beyond the wall, where players positioned themselves to field balls. The rubber ball could be kicked down the alley, caroming like a billiard ball from wall to wall before the player would engage it. Because playing a ball kicked down a narrow alley would be entirely too easy, the walls sloped above the narrow part of the alley. A player pushing forward anticipating an alley shot could be surprised by a ball with lots of body English going up the wall, hitting the molding and bouncing over his head into the foot of the "I." He would lose the point. At the top of the sloping walls, dead center in the alley, a stone hoop was anchored into the apron. This hoop was oriented vertically. A ball could go through it from either side, and one was situated on both sloping walls. The round hole in the middle of the hoop was fractionally larger than the ball. If a goal was scored by the ball passing through the hoop, the player making the shot automatically won the game, no matter the score.

The balls came fast and furious. Players protected themselves with wood-armored hip protectors. They also wore shin guards and chest protectors, looking much like a baseball catcher. The ball was made from rubber. The latex of the Panama rubber tree (*Castilla elastica*) was tempered using the sap of the moon vine. The moon vine had a touch of sulfur which helped to vulcanize the rubber, making it pliable. This would be especially good on a chilly morning such as this. Strips of this substance were fastened around a human skull to make a ball. The skull allowed for a hollow center and therefore lightened the ball. The ball could be as large as a modern medicine ball or smaller than a soccer ball. The rubber allowed the ball to bounce lively. The ball itself seemed hard as stone.

The entire ball court was sacred ground. Those ball matches played by the father and uncle of the Hero Twins made it so. As did the game between the Hero Twins and the lords of the underworld. A limestone marker with the visage of the Maize God, the twins' father, was buried midfield. And the stone hoops were decorated with their imagery. If a player shot a ball through the hoop — guided almost certainly by a supernatural being — the opposing player would not only lose the game but his life.

At times, the game was played for sport. But not on this day.

Jaguar Paw's sajal had challenged him to a game, and Jaguar Paw had accepted the challenge. The sajal was an underlord, the headman of the Lost World hamlet of Tikal. Yes, he was of the same hamlet and clan that had acted in collusion with the Teotihucanoes in days of old. Under ordinary circumstances a sajal would not challenge his overlord. But the circumstances of late were by no means ordinary. The raids of the Kan or Snake people had always been troublesome. They were the traditional enemies of the Tikalese. Some said they were an emigrant tribe from El Mirador who had moved north and east and who came to the Peten to raid. Over the years they had forged alliances with some of the cities close to Tikal. They used these cities to launch attacks on Tikal and its allies. It was because of them that the walls had been built from lake to lake, on both the north and south sides of the city. The moats in front of the walls were filled to the brim with water. Jaguar Paw had even ordered a new palisade of sharpened stakes erected atop the wall.

But the harassing raids continued. They rained down, not just on Tikal but on its allies and friends, such as El Peru. Then the report had come that strangers led by a "general from Teotihuacan" had invaded the city of El Peru, a mere forty miles from Tikal. Jaguar Paw supposed this "general" was simply a warlord with a small force of armed porters. It was claimed the king of El Peru had been overthrown and a puppet set up in his place—in order to insure the peace of its citizens and the Peten. That was what the proclamation put out by the warlord said. Jaguar Paw suspected this was all bluff. But in truth Jaguar Paw's agents had not been able to determine how large the warlord's force was. Nor was it able to determine the location of the army. Some advised Jaguar Paw to send all men to the fortifications to the north and south of the city. Other of his advisors told him to do nothing. He was the supernaturally ordained king. They said rash action would make the people doubt him. Jaguar Paw chose the middle course. He doubled the guard on the walls of the city, but otherwise ordered all men to leave their arms at home today. In particular, he wanted to make sure the commoners from the Lost World were not armed during the ball game.

Their lord had acted unwisely. He had smarted off to Great Jaguar Paw. He had complained about the unsettled state of affairs in the Peten. He cited the ongoing friction with the Kans of the north. And he had bragged about how much more secure the area had been during the regimes of his ancestors, backed by the armed might of the Teotihuacanoes. (He always left out that those people were a thuggish lot of road agents and thieves, always pretending that they were a state-ordained force from central Mexico.) And now another "arrival of strangers" supposedly from central Mexico roamed about in the area. The Lost World sajal was just taking advantage of the situation. And he was playing a very dangerous game.

Jaguar Paw did not believe a real force from Teotihuacan would go against him. Had he not been the man who opened trade with them? Had the Teotihucanos not given him a wife to show their appreciation? And if the Teotihuacanos were simply bandits, he was sure the loyal armies of Tikal could deal with them. The sajal of the Lost World was towing a very stupid line. He was hoping the Teotihuacanos would overthrow Jaguar Paw. Then he would offer himself as their puppet. The sajal would soon learn the foolishness of such a course of action.

The square surrounding the ball court was filling with people. Jaguar Paw, as holy lord king, could arrive when he chose. He saw no reason to heighten the tension by dragging things out. He sneaked from his hidey-hole down the stairs to his throne room. His robes were laid out, as the queen had informed him, in the small chamber to the rear where the shrine to his father was. Jaguar Paw knelt before the skull and leg bones of his father. "May the course of action you advised me be the correct one," he said.

He believed the skull answered him, "It is."

Jaguar Paw's lord-in-waiting appeared. He helped him don the royal loincloth. The apron hung down between his legs. It was ornately painted with a vertical mountain monster which hearkened back to the Olmec dragon. It was a symbol of the sacred cornstalk (or ceiba) that was the axis mundi, the link between the underworld, celestial sphere and the human world. It was Jaguar Paw's special office as king to be the link between these worlds. It was while he was in a state of ecstasy by virtue of bloodletting that his father had appeared to him and advised him to do as he was doing today.

The queen had set out Jaguar Paw's quetzal headdress. It was on a coat-rack-like stand. It was so powerful that it had a royal spirit of its own, parts of it having been recycled from the headdress of his father and his father before him. His lord of the privy chamber, the only other person allowed to touch it, reached for the headdress.

Jaguar Paw said, "No. Get me the corn-leaf headdress."

The headgear looked like the leaves around a roasting ear. The quetzal-feather headdress would have reminded viewers of his divine right to rule. But this headdress would kick them in the gut. His role as king kept the corn growing. Should anyone mess with him, they risked a famine.

"Bring me the hunal," he ordered. The lord of the chamber placed the jade token of kingship around his forehead and tied the string around his head. Jaguar Paw stood up. "Now arrange my father's skull and bones." The attending lord bowed and secured the skull and leg bones of Hawk Skull in the small of the king's back. Jaguar Paw wanted his father close to counsel him today.

Next the lord of the chamber strapped a belt around Jaguar Paw's waist. The shrunken and smoke-cured heads of enemies Jaguar Paw had slain dangled from it.

"Let us go."

He and the chamber lord made their way, slowly, stately, down the stairs of the palace. As they went others fell in behind or in front. By the time they had circled into the grass near the ball court, the retinue was substantial and consisted of men swinging ceramic censors with copal incense and feather bearers shading Jaguar Paw from the sun. The cool had already given way. The air was now pleasantly warm, and the sun smarted on his skin. One of those who joined was a youth in ball-playing garb, hip and chest protectors with shin guards.

The sajal from the Lost World hamlet was warming up between the low walls of the court, kicking the ball against the wall and fielding it as it shot back at him. On seeing Jaguar Paw, he greeted him with an informal, "I see you have brought a substitute to play against me, oh mighty lord, Jaguar Paw."

"As is my right," Jaguar Paw returned.

"Indeed, it is, lord," his subordinate said. "Are we ready to begin?"

"Go, boy," Jaguar Paw told the young man. "Do not be concerned. You cannot lose." Under his breath he said, "The same cannot be said of the pipsqueak lord of the Lost World. Are we ready to do what is required after the match?"

"Yes, my lord," a courtier replied also under the breath. "The men are ready to secure him. A bucket of indigo paint is handy to drench his body with. A ceremonial flint knife is at hand to severe his head, which I shall do myself."

Jaguar Paw gave the sign for the match to begin. Much of the normal ceremony had not been conducted, but that was just fine. The grounds around the ball court, though crowded, were not yet packed to overflowing. There were even some spots still not filled on the temple mound beyond the sajal. But no matter. This was by no means an ordinary match. Jaguar Paw, divine king or not, did not want to give the sajal's followers time to consider what to do when he was grabbed and quickly dispatched. Everyone would agree that on certain occasions the state had the right — the need even — to sacrifice the loser. But was this one of those occasions? Jaguar Paw's father had assured him in his conjuring event that it was, but the sajal's followers — stirred up by the snake people's raids — may have tried to intervene if things were not handled expeditiously. The promise of a feast for the commoners and a feast and prizes for the nobles would calm them down, Jaguar Paw assured himself.

Jaguar Paw's ball-playing proxy put the ball in play. He threw it down the alley, the ball dribbling to the sajal. The sajal, to everyone's amazement, ran toward the ball. He clashed into it, smacking it against the wooden yoke around his hips. The ball shot up the inclined wall toward the vertical hoop. It glanced off the hoop and right to the young man. He kicked it toward the sajal, and the ball sailed past Jaguar Paw' rival.

One point for Jaguar Paw's side.

The young ballplayer served the ball to the sajal. Again the sajal attempted to knock the ball through the hoop and win the game. The ballplayer easily fielded the ball and scored a point.

"Is the sajal mad?" the lord of the chamber asked. "It is almost impossible to knock the ball through the goal hoop. The ball chosen for this match is only a fraction of a particle smaller. The angle must be just right. It is an impossible shot."

The next time the ball came to the sajal, he shot the ball at the hoop. It went through.

For one second, Jaguar Paw was stunned. As were the fans of both sides. Then someone let out a yowl. Then others were hollering. And they were running. "What is this?" Jaguar Paw wondered. Even some of his retinue broke and ran. Then Jaguar Paw saw why. A short fat spear zinged out of the sky and plowed into the earth near the young ballplayer. Momentarily, a second arced down and impaled the young man, whose chest spurted blood as he fell.

Flying spears? What was that? Maya spears were long and thin. They were used to jab an enemy. Occasionally, someone might throw one, but then the man would be unarmed, except for a war club or flint-inlaid sword, not much of a weapon against another's long spear. But these spears were short and they came raining out of the sky. No one was in throwing distance from them.

Wait. There, in the distance, approaching across the market square on the East Plaza, a phalanx of warriors approached. Those squatting over their goods ran leaving baskets and bundles, which the warriors kicked out of the way. They marched in lockstep. They paused, their arms cocked, and into the air went a shower of short spears. The spears rained down around Jaguar Paw. He heard the chamber lord grunt and drop. He looked and saw red, highly oxygenated blood spill onto the ground. The lord looked at Jaguar Paw, his eyes asking what was going on? Then his eye went glassy, and he gurgled the death rattle. Jaguar Paw, standing alone now, looked at the advancing line of men. They were dressed in the garb of the Mexican highlands. Teotihuacanos! He had been betrayed by his old trading partners. They wore the warrior's goggles and heavy cotton armor. A thought gathered in his mind. Before he could completely articulate it, the men cocked their spearthrowers and let loose with another fusillade. Two spears entered Jaguar Paw's torso in quick succession.

"What will happen to my wife?" Jaguar Paw wondered. "What will happen to my kingdom?"

Jaguar Paw's queen was killed as were his other wives and all his children. The Mexican wife was spared but her children were slaughtered. The sajal of the Lost World didn't make out much better. He too was assassinated, but his six-year-old son, First Crocodile, was installed as a simple ahaw the following year. He had a regent or overlord. That was Fire Is Born, the commander of the Teotihuacan forces, who gave himself the title of kaloomte or emperor.

Interpreting Jaguar Paw's Tale

The above scenario mixes what is known about the most peculiar and mystifying chapter of early Classic Tikal history with a likely, but at points hypothetical, explanation for it. All of the ethnological and most of the archaeological details are accurate, but some of the characters, notably Great Jaguar Paw's Mexican wife, were pure fabrication. (Another assist to history came in the way of the ball court which wasn't constructed until later and the stone hoops that never were characteristic of central Peten but were a normal feature elsewhere.) Archaeologists have long been puzzled by the evidence indicating considerable contact between Tikal (and the Maya) with Teotihuacan. For instance, many "cylinder-tripod" ceramic bowls have been found at Tikal of a type associated with the great Mexican capital. Not only the style but the painting of the vessels have central Mexican imagery. On a macro level, pyramids of a sort called talud-tablero (one or a series of slant walls layered between boxy platforms), long identified with central Mexico and Teotihuacan, were constructed in the Peten in this period. On stelae, images of men in full Mexican ceremonial dress were found. All of this engendered speculation that the flowering of Maya civilization starting in the Early Classic may have come about by pollination from Teotihucan, perhaps by the setting up of a colonial outpost by armed invasion at Tikal. Nowadays, it is known that lowland Maya civilization was flourishing in the Mirador Basin and elsewhere long before the Teotihuacan intrusion, in fact even before there was a Teotihuacan. If anything, this only makes the puzzle of the relationship of these two great capitals more confounding.

Tikal was hardly the only place that Teotihuacan influence turned up. In the Mexican Yucatan (at Becan), in Belize at Altun Ha, Teotihuacan also left its marks—and as much as a hundred years prior to the intrusion during Great Jaguar Paw's time. However, it was in the highlands at Kaminaljuyu (near Guatemala City) that the most evidence of Teotihucan was found, starting at a time well before the 4th century A.D. For instance, many of the temple pyramids were in pure talud-tablero style. This led early archaeologists to theorize that Kaminaljuyu had been an outpost of some kind. More recent analytical studies, however, showed this theory probably unfounded. Though the pyramids might look to be the spitting image of Teotihuacan talud-tablero architecture, the construction techniques were considerably different, indicating that Kaminaljuyu building engineers only modeled their edifices on those of the central Mexican highlands. The builders may have seen Teotihuacan buildings, either in person or in images, but clearly they were not instrumental in planning or erecting the real thing in the Central Valley of Mexico.

When the hieroglyphs began to give up the history of the Maya, more information came available, but it did little to settle the question of Teotihuacan's role in Early Classic Maya history. For instance, the hieroglyphs tell us that Great Jaguar Paw died on the day the strangers somehow connected to Teotihuacan arrived, eight days after they conquered El Peru. About a year later, the young boy, First Crocodile, was installed as "king" under the watchful gaze of Fire Is Born, presumably the commander of a Teothucan force. Fire Is Born also installed another vassal as ruler of nearby Uaxactun, which he appears to have conquered almost immediately after the fall of Tikal. In coming years, he seems to have savaged other cities in the region, some as far away as Rio Azul in the northeast corner of the Peten and Oxkintok in the Northern Lowlands. These new kings called themselves vassals (or yajaw). The overlord they acknowledged was not Fire Is Born. Rather he was a person called Spearthrower Owl. He was also designated kaloomte, super king or emperor. And art work at Uaxactun shows lords and ladies of the city painted black (the color of death) greeting warriors or lords in Mexican style dress. The arms of these black-painted people are slanted across their chests in the Maya gesture of submission, the gesture of captives about to be sacrificed.

Many have assumed, with no hard evidence, that Spearthrower Owl was the ruler of Teotihuacan. The spearthrower or atlatl was a device which used leverage to sling short spears with compelling force. It was the arm of choice of Teotihuacan. Owls, perhaps the night version of eagles, were birds much admired by the Teotihuacanos. The name Spearthrower Owl would be a fitting moniker for a Teotihuacan ruler. It was impossible to cross-check for a king by that name at the city in the highlands because Teotihuacanos left no written records, and not a single ruler's identity has ever been determined. The Tikal king, First Crocodile, called himself the son of Spearthrower Owl. He was always depicted wearing Mexican garb. Therefore, it was assumed the skeleton in Tomb 10 in the North Acropolis identified by hieroglyphs to be First Crocodile (along side lay the headless skeleton of a real crocodile) would be of foreign origin. Recently, forensic archaeology was able to put that claim to the test. The tester was Lori Wright of Texas A&M. She applied isotopic analysis to the teeth in the grave of First Crocodile. She found that the person in the grave had spent his entire life, from the time he was an infant onward, in the lowlands of central Peten (Wright 2005). One set of bones found at Kaminaljuyu in the highlands of Guatemala, however, did appear to have spent its youth in central Mexico, perhaps at Teotihuacan. Even if archaeologists do not as yet know what role Teotihuacan played in the Maya area, it is certain its effects were felt there as well as throughout all of Mesoamerica.

Teotihuacan and Its Legacy, Circa 100 B.C.–A.D. 600

Teotihuacan was a city of hundreds of thousands of people nestled in the basin of Mexico, 7,000 feet above sea level. It was about thirty miles from modern Mexico City, today again — as in Teotihuacan times — the most densely populated area of North America. By A.D. 100 it was a thriving metropolis, and it appears to have gotten its start less than two hundred years earlier. It is an article of faith that Teotihuacan was the most important city in Mesoamerica during the next several centuries (material in this section from Cowgill 1997).

Strangely, little is known about the culture or governance of the city. No accepted authority hazards a guess as to the origin of its inhabitants or the language they spoke. It is not even known what happened to the hundreds of thousands that called Teotihuacan home when the city fell, although it is pretty certain the city perished by the sword and the inhabitants were scattered to the winds in the 6th or 7th century A.D. Compared to Teotihuacan's veiled history, the Maya seem almost transparent.

The layout of Teotihuacan, on the other hand, suggests military precision and describes

The Pyramid of the Sun, Teotihuacan.

perfect grids. The principal thoroughfare, the Avenue of the Dead, runs for a mile and a half. It is oriented 15 degrees east of true north, as are almost all structures in the city. A cross street seems to intersect the avenue at midpoint. At the north end of the Avenue of the Dead stands the Pyramid of the Moon, excavations into which have turned up interesting graves including the skeletons of many caged animals — at least one puma and several coyotes — which appeared to have been interred live with bodies of notables, probably in the belief they were the animal familiars of the dead. Along the eastern perimeter rises the Pyramid of the Sun, an artificial mountain going up over two hundred feet, and arguably the largest construction in the pre–19th century western hemisphere. Its base rivals that of the great pyramid of Cheops. As we have seen, all the peoples of Mesoamerica shared core religious concepts, and it is believed this pyramid, as its name indicates, was used for rites to ensure the continual rising of the sun similar to those the Maya practiced. A cave found not long ago over which the pyramid built was probably ritually significant.

    The Feathered Serpent Pyramid is much smaller than either of these two and is contained inside the walls of the citadel-like Ciudadela, at the intersection of the Avenue of the Dead and the east-west cross street. It is adorned with many copies of a feathered rattlesnake. Also adorning this pyramid are cookie-cutter sculptures of an extremely toothy cat monster and of a deity in squarish headdress and goggle eyes representing Tlaloc, the god of storms and war (and rain). Inside this pyramid was found a mass grave of over two hundred men dressed in military garb. It is assumed these gents were the palace guard of a toppled regime whose ambivalent loyalty demanded they be dispatched. Or they could have been captives or slaves garbed in military uniforms and then sacrificed. Until the discovery of this massive grave, it was thought the Teotihuacanos had been relatively unmilitaristic until late in their history. The dating of the burial in an early phase of the city convinced archaeologists the polity lived by sword from near the start.

The residential housing is among the more interesting hallmarks of the city. Everyone — with the exception of a few in residential palaces in the city center — seemed to live in one story apartment complexes. Each "apartment" building was about 65 yards square. Probably for security reasons, it had a limited number of entrances. Up to two hundred people may have resided in each compound. The buildings were stone cemented together by concrete and coated with lime plaster. The more modest had dirt or stone floors; and the wall decorations varied from elaborate murals to whitewash with a modest painted trim. The warren-like rooms of the complex were connected by labyrinthine companionways. As interesting as these complexes may have been archaeologically, they made for deadly places to live. Ventilation was limited, as was sewage and garbage disposal. The evidence indicates a high incidence of infant mortality. Some archaeologist postulate that this infant death rate may have hampered the expansion of the state in later years, as the population seems to have remained fairly stable. Evidence of small enclaves of foreigners including Maya have been found in the city. It is believed that some of these were artisans adept in specialty trades. Because Teotihuacan was probably an empire, some of these foreigners were probably honored relatives (read hostages) of the rulers of foreign lands. The Maya artists and artisans may have been sent as tribute payments.

The economy of Teotihuacan, like most everything else about the city, is puzzling. The area just west of the city was suitable for irrigated agriculture, but that area could not have grown enough food to take care of the 150,000 or so residents of the city. The Aztecs, who occupied the Basin of Mexico many years later, practiced a unique kind of horticulture. They developed floating fields that were self-watering from the lake on which they floated. The Teotihuacanos did not employ this method. So how were all those people provided for? The most valuable nearby commodity was the green Pachuca obsidian. Teotihuacan traded in this commodity, but it does not appear to have maintained an exclusive trade. Strangely, Teotihucanos appear not to have been fond of luxury imports to any great extent. Presumably, they consumed food imported from elsewhere, but no evidence remains of what those comestibles might have been or where they came from — or what, if anything, was traded for them. It is possible the city lived from tribute. Tribute payments did much to enrich the Aztec empire at the time of the Spanish contact (and tribute also supported the rise of the larger Maya cities).

Teotihuacan art is vivid and some of the figures display considerable tension and interest. But many are stiff and primitivistic. Its best features are stylized and abstract. Human faces rarely show any individual traits and most of the time they are covered with regalia which seems the focus of the artwork. In short, there is no hint of a cult of personality of the kind shown by modern dictators — or the more modest sort displayed on the stela of the Maya kings. All this has led archaeologists such as George L. Cowgill to hypothesize that Teotihuacan may have been a non-egalitarian republic representing some coalition of aristocrats who passed around among themselves the supreme rulership of the city.

The extent of the Teotihuacan territorial control is not well understood. It seems apparent that the ruling authority of the city swept the Valley of Mexico clear of inhabitants and resettled the chosen in the city's residential complexes. Cities beyond 60 miles or so from

Teotihucan appear to have maintained their autonomy. Teotihuacan's influence was seen throughout Mesoamerica in durable artworks. As noted earlier, almost no imported products of any kind — craft, art, food — have been found at Teotihuacan making it difficult for archaeologists to chart exactly where Teotihuacan economic or military interest may have focused.

Writing in the culture never got much behind a set of notational symbols whose utilitarian value is not yet understood. But Teotihuacan established outposts of influence and probably at least occasional control through much of Mesoamerica, including among people whose intellectual merits were clearly much superior. In this regard, as warriors and perhaps engineers, the Teotihuacans have been likened by Simon Martin as the Romans of Mesoamericans (Martin 2008a). Cowgill doubts that a sizeable Teotihuacan colony was established at Tikal. Martin and Grube, on the other hand, cite a ceramic vessel showing numerous men in Mexican garb leaving the land of the talud-tablero edifice and entering the land of the Maya pyramid (Martin and Grube 2000). They see that as evidence for a formal Teotihuacan intrusion at Tikal. David Freidel holds that the Teotihuacan salient at Tikal was the work of Teotihuacan warlords (Freidel 2008).

Archaeologists do not know what happened to the inhabitants of the city of Teotihuacan — aside from the fact they disappeared. What happened to the quasi-colony of Teotihuacans in the Peten is pretty surely known. The Teotihuacanos — whether regular forces directed from the Basin of Mexico or simple thugs who saw an exploitable situation — regarded the political instability in the central Peten as opportunity. There may have been endemic warfare between the burgeoning city-states, such as the hypothetical skirmishes between the Kan Snakehead people and the Tikalese in our sketch above. Fire Is Born with his relatively small force of Teotihuacano legionnaires arrived. His men trained in military discipline with long-range arms cut through the Maya noble warriors and their irregular militia helpers like a knife through butter. Fire Is Born conquered El Peru. Eight days later he entered Tikal, subdued the city and deposed and killed Great Jaguar Paw. All this was probably done as colonizers have done in time memoriam in the name of restoring order. Fire Is Born went on to conquer other polities such as Uaxactun and Rio Azul (50 miles away) and the nearby hamlet of Bejucal. He put the six-year-old First Crocodile on the throne at Tikal, but kept the real power for himself as regent. In payment to his overlord in central Mexico, dozens of Maya artisans/slaves were probably transported to central Mexico to work. The granaries of the Tikalese and other subject folk were plundered in the guise of taxing them for the government that brought stability to the land. The Maya king, First Crocodile, was shown in artwork only in Teotihuacan dress.

A generation went by. The son of First Crocodile ascended the throne. On his monuments he was shown in full Maya regalia. True, he paid appropriate fealty to his supposed grandfather, Spearthrower Owl, by alluding to owls and spearthrowers; but more importantly, he claims to be in direct line of succession from Great Jaguar Paw. By now Fire Is Born is dead. His legions are creaky old men. The enormity of the distance between Teotihuacan and central Peten has thwarted Teotihuacan's attempt to take permanent control of the Peten (or the warlords have grown old and passed on). Almost all allusions to things Mexican have disappeared; even the picture of his own father on the stela the son commissioned gives two images. In one he is shown in Mexican dress and in another Maya attire. Teotihuacan ambitions have been swallowed by the immensity of the tropical lowlands. Their hand-picked puppet has returned to his Maya roots.

This, however, does not mean the Teotihuacan (inspired) intrusion has not had permanent effects. Formerly, Tikal skirmished with neighbors as close as Uaxactun, a mere twelve miles away. Fire Is Born had neutralized that polity and, though still a city unto its own, brought it into the Tikal fold. Other minor states within twenty or so miles were also semi-incorporated into a sort of over-state or empire, which, though not large, did establish Tikal as the major player in the central Peten. In response, other "divine kings" strengthened their military capabilities. Eventually, warfare between the cities became fairly systematic. As noted earlier, the purpose of these wars is not well understood. Cities fought in part for prestige and glory. But the economic and territorial ambitions, so often the practical motives for war, were by no means unimportant. Although no city-state is known to have been completely absorbed by another, some appear — for a time — to have become abject vassals of their conquerors. In these cases, a puppet king was installed in place of the deposed one. Hand-picked quislings, as we will see, in time forgot their devotion to those who put them on the throne and began to indulge independent ambitions for their city-states. In any case, war seems to have been an important means of developing the Maya political and economic structure.

The Late Early Classic Period, A.D. 495–562

For more than a hundred years, the kings of Tikal reigned in central Peten with little evidence of palace intrigue. The next blip on Tikal's historical record came at the end of the century in A.D. 495 when Great Jaguar Paw II was king. Given Jaguar Paw I's fate, it may seem strange that he was revered by later kings — but clearly he was. His palace, for instance, was the only building in the central acropolis not decommissioned and built over. (The common practice of ritually killing a building and erecting another structure on top of it played into the Maya belief of death followed by resurrection.) Jaguar Paw I was even designated as "Great," when so far as we know, his most notable feat was being deposed by that shadowy outside force.

In any case, Great Jaguar Paw II fared no better than his namesake. The city of Tonina, far over on the other side of the Usumacinta, records his death in July 508, and one of his vassals was put to the sword by miniscule Yaxchilan located on the banks of the great river (Martin and Grube 2000). This no doubt indicates a trans–Usumacinata adventure gone wrong. Shortly, a six-year-old girl dubbed the Lady of Tikal was established on the throne. And a wily fellow calling himself Kaloomte Balam (Emperor Jaguar) became first her regent then later her "husband."

The Maya historical record, which is usually opaque, gives interesting clues about this fascinating blip in dynastic history (Guenther 2000). Years earlier, in A.D. 486, Kaloomte Balam had conquered the site of Masaal ("axed it" in the Maya idiom). Therefore, it was clear he was a fierce war captain for many years prior to his taking over as "emperor" of Tikal. He even went so far as to call himself the 19th in line of succession from Yax Ehb Shock. However, he appears to have come of humble origins and didn't presume to prepare a tomb for himself on the North Acropolis, the burial place of royal blood. He passed on in due course, and was buried in a peripheral site now designated Group 7. His grave goods are lavish and include a jade mask of the kind that only the best-heeled Maya kings could afford, along with many polychrome bowls (no doubt once filled with the finest foods). A quetzal bird and two human sacrifices complete the inventory of grave goods. Nearby in a chultun (or storage pit) was found the skeleton of a much younger woman. She was deposited face down, and her sacrificial companion was a spider monkey. (A child's body was deposited in the tomb later.) She was fortified on her journey to the other world by the goods in one small ceramic bowl, pretty slim pickings. The face-down burial was also peculiar, typical of sacrificial victims, not royalty, which she appears to have been. Stanley Guenter has determined this was the grave of Kaloomte Balam's Lady of Tikal. Guenter speculates that after her great protector, Kaloomte Balam, died, an heir, probably the son of Jaguar Paw II and her brother, reclaimed the throne. Lady of Tikal, now without a protector, was assassinated, or perhaps she was allowed to kill herself.

In any case, her sibling, Double Bird, became the 21st ruler of Tikal (Martin and Grube 2000). He erected a stela in A.D. 557 to celebrate the passing of the katun or twenty year cycle. He was the son of Jaguar Paw II, born in 508, three years before the "Lady of Tikal." Like the reigns of Jaguar Paw I and II, his was not to be smooth. Also like them, he was not aware of his limitations. In what probably appeared to him as a masterstroke, Double Bird presided over the swearing in of the king of Caracol in A.D. 553.

Caracol was to become a huge city-state located high up in the hills called the Maya Mountains, forty miles from Tikal in present-day Belize. It was among the most potent almost first-rate state in the Maya realm. Having the king of Caracol acknowledge his supremacy was quite a plum — Double Bird thought. This meant that Caracol was not in collusion with its archenemy the Kan Snakehead people of the north.

From a local perspective, Caracol's swearing fealty to Tikal was a relief to Double Bird. Naranjo, almost on the present Belize border, 24 miles from Tikal and also 24 miles north-north west of Caracol, had come completely under the dominance of Caracol. This had come about through a star-war attack when Venus reappeared as the morning star (Chase and Chase 2004). Caracol was growing fat from tribute payments. Its population was mushrooming. Causeways were being built connecting the various quarters of the extremely large municipality, and the standard of living was increasing for all classes. At present, Caracol was by no means as large or powerful as Tikal, but clearly the rulers of Caracol were becoming a potent threat. Double Bird was pleased to keep it under his control.

By A.D. 556, Double Bird realized he had to knock Caracol down a peg. He captured and sacrificed a lord of the city. The presumed lesson obviously was lost on Caracol. Timing the blow with the appearance of Venus, Caracol unleashed a full-fledged star war on the queen city of the Peten. The date was A.D. 562. It is also the death date of Double Bird. What is known of Double Bird (aside from Caracol bragging) comes mainly from Stela 17 in Tikal, which he erected at the katun ending in 553. That stela was found defaced and lying by the side of a causeway by archaeologists 1,500 years later. Not only had Double Bird been dispatched in the flesh, but the spirit force in the stela had been ritually killed.

When 20th-century archaeologists found that fallen stela, it puzzled them mightily. The date on the monument was the last posted at Tikal for more than a century and a third. They then jumped to the conclusion that all of the Peten went into eclipse along with Tikal. The period was given a name, the Mid-Classic Hiatus. Learned papers were published as to its cause. The fall of Teotihuacan, more or less at about the same time, was bruited as the possible reason for Tikal's dark period. It was later determined a drought hit the area about the middle of the 6th century, and therefore the decline was attributed by some to meteorology (Hodell et al. 1995).

Starting in the 1980s, Arlen and Diane Chase of the University of Central Florida began documenting Caracol's role in Tikal's Mid-Classic eclipse phase. They were surprised to learn that while Tikal slumped, Caracol prospered. In time, the city grew to a population that nearly rivaled that of Tikal itself. So finally the cause of the Mid-Classic Hiatus had been found. Caracol's defeat of Tikal was the reason mighty Tikal went into its downhill slide. It was a nice theory. But unhappily, the evidence did not add up.

Caracol had not been able to pull off this stunning upset on its own. The power behind it, archaeologists came to understand in the 1990s, was the dreaded Snake or Kan people of the north. The rivalry between Tikal and the Snakehead dynasty went back hundreds of years. As noted earlier, Tikal may have had a hand in the collapse of El Mirador, where the Snake-clan people appear to have originated (Freidel 2008). We ended the last section atop the second highest pyramid at El Mirador. Obsidian spearpoints littered the site indicating a battle of warriors armed with Teotihuacan atlatls in Classic times. It is presumed the Teotihuacan-inspired soldiers were tussling with Kan forces on an abandoned but highly symbolic field of battle. Given the advances Tikal made on all fronts at the time, they obviously carried the day.

But now two hundred or so years later, Tikal had finally been brought to heel. The decline Tikal suffered would, as noted, last for a century and a third. During the period the Snake or Kan dynasty would rule supreme. The next section details the glory of the Kan empire.

4

Calakmul and the Snakehead Dynasty, a Maya Superpower

Discovery and Exploration, A.D. 1931–1994

No Classic Maya site has a history of discovery and recognition more intriguing than Calakmul. It was among the last of the important Maya cities of the Classic era to be found, having been discovered in 1931. Today, it is universally considered one of the two most important cities in the Classic period (A.D. 250–800). Yet Calakmul's rightful place in the Maya order came to be widely recognized only after the turn of the 21st century.

Even today, Calakmul has the reputation of being one of the most remote Maya ruins. Like many reputations, it is not entirely deserved. If you catch an early flight into Cancun and hire a rental car, you can arrive by midafternoon. You would only have to drive the two hundred odd miles paralleling the Caribbean to Chetumal on what increasingly comes to resemble a freeway. Then you'd have to go another hundred or so miles due west toward the Gulf Coast on the Chetumal-Escarcega road. This road is called the International Highway because a side road near Chetumal leads to Belize. In spots this highway is an improved two-laner. It drives like a superhighway, thanks to the courteous Mexican habit of slower vehicles pulling far over onto the paved shoulder. Not long ago it was very narrow and potholed from eighteen-wheeler traffic. The fly in the ointment comes when you turn off the asphalt at what is known as Access Calakmul. Once you pay the toll and the guard manually raises the tollgate, you have another forty miles to go.

After a while the pavement narrows and the forest closes in; but all things considered, the road is not that bad. The recommended driving speed is thirty-five kph, a lousy 22 mph. At that velocity you don't have to worry about hitting the game that wanders across the tarmac. You'll see ocellated turkeys (lots of them) and the occasional coatimundi or whitetail deer. After a few miles, you come to another gate barring the road. This one indicates that you are about to officially enter the Calakmul Biosphere, billed as the largest chunk of protected tropical forest in Mexico and the second largest left in the Western Hemisphere. The guard will let you through after asking your nationality and taking your license plate number. You continue on, passing perhaps one or two vehicles on your way. You could probably arrive by three in the afternoon. You would have time for a very brief tour of the two large plazas open to tourists before the INAH guards close up shop at five P.M. and shoo you out. On average, about forty visitors a day make their way to the ruins. Few stay much longer than the two hours you'd have. That's time enough to walk the half mile into the site and get a quick eyeful of and even climb the towering Structures 1, 2, and 7. You can also briefly view the residential and ceremonial complexes. During high season, the small parking lot may be almost full of passenger vehicles and a bus or two. On many days in the off-season, the site is almost deserted. When Calakmul was discovered in 1931 by an American biologist working for the Mexican Exploitation Company, the situation was quite a bit different.

The reason Calakmul was discovered was chewing gum. In the 1930s chewing gum was a derivative of the sapodilla tree. At the time, few North Americans had heard of that tropical tree. Fewer knew of its fruit, about the size and shape of an apple with a brown sandpapery rind and meat that resembles a pear drenched in molasses. The fruit is too perishable to ship and too cloying to appeal to Euroamerican tastebuds. All the same, the average American consumed an astonishing amount of the product of that tree, 109 units per person in 1929. The sap of the tree is known as chicle. The raw product was boiled by collectors to a rubbery latex for storage and shipping. Then it was sent to North America. Northern factories made it into chewing gum. Only mature trees could be tapped, so the vast hinterland of the Yucatan where the sapodilla grew had become for the first time in almost a millennium an economic zone worthy of note. Twenty-three million dollars worth of chicle was imported into the United States in 1929 (Landon 1935). Adjusted for inflation, the raw chicle market was a $250 million a year business.

A defining characteristic of the tropical forest is its high number of species. Whereas in the far north entire forests may be composed of just one species of tree, in the tropics a species may be represented by a single specimen in an acre. Under certain conditions more specimens of the target species may be encountered. To determine the growth conditions favorable to concentrations of mature sapodilla trees, twenty-four-year-old Cyrus Lundell was sent in 1931 into what was effectively an unexplored wilderness (Lipscomb 1995). The area was penetrated only by the small trails and tramways used by chicle tappers (or chicleros).

At first blush, Cyrus Lundell appears dull, almost colorless. About the best one could say of him is that he was a quiet member of that legion Tom Brokaw called the Greatest Generation. That was the energetic and talented group that without fanfare pushed the U.S. into a position of global leadership in the first part of the 20th century. Later in life, when he had obtained a PhD, he was described as "a slender, rather quiet, self-contained scientist; a trained, exceptionally able botanist; a scholar; for all his enthusiasms, a circumspect and cautious speaker" (Haynes 1946). Lundell's supposed mission may have been as a botanical surveyor. But that wasn't the only thing the twenty-four-year-old college dropout from Texas was looking for. He was hoping to find Maya ruins because he had a passion for archaeology. Lundell had schemed for three years to become a Maya explorer. In 1928, when he was only twenty-one, he had temporarily quit college to go to British Honduras as a research assistant (Lipscomb 1995). There he formed the idea of searching for ruins in the great forests of the Peten and Yucatan. After he secured the appointment with the Mexican Exploitation Company to do a botanical survey, he was ready to get down to business.

He knew the Peten district of Guatemala to the south of the company's vast concession had been designated the Maya's Old Empire. The conventional archaeological wisdom held that the many ruins dated no later than the 8th century. The northern Yucatan, including the sites of Tulum and Chichen Itza—not far from Cancun, was called the New Empire. The ruined cities in this region were then believed to have flourished after the first millennium

A.D. Ruins of both the New and Old Empires had been known for more than a hundred years. In the intermediate region, away from the coasts, not a single Maya site was known to exist. And little wonder, given the conditions there as Lundell described them.

"The jungle of southern Campeche," he wrote, "begins at the coast and stretches, an unbroken forest, across the Yucatan Peninsula from the Gulf of Mexico to the Caribbean Sea" (Lundell 1933). The town of Champoton abuts the sea, forty miles south of the capital of the state of Campeche on the opposite side of the Yucatan Peninsula from Cancun. Lundell boated up the Champoton River to the village of Kanasayab, a distance of perhaps twenty miles. There he found a narrow-gauge tram. The "platform cars" were pulled by two mules in tandem without reins, controlled like old-time freight wagons by whips and curses. They were used to lug huge blocks of raw chicle to the sea. Lundell rode on top of cargo "through a low narrow tunnel in the dense and ever encroaching vegetation." By the end of his first day, he'd crawled forty or so miles into the interior and found his first Maya artifacts at the village of Pustunich. The objects were three stelae inscribed with Maya hieroglyphs. When he resumed his journey on the flatcars the next morning, he was confident his quest to find Maya cities would not be in vain.

Late in the afternoon of the following day, Lundell arrived at the village of La Gloria. Now the easy going was over. From here, he mounted a mule for two days of hard riding. The rainy season made "the trail almost impassable, and many times the mules wallowed belly deep, and constantly lurched against the tree trunks in their effort to find firmer footing." Given his travails so far, it may seem strange to learn that Lundell was thrilled with conditions as he found them, in terms of his scientific explorations. "The exploitation of the sapodilla forest for chicle," he wrote, "has made the remote interior accessible. Roads and trails have been opened to bring out the chicle, and as the demand for [chewing] gum has increased, the chicleros penetrate deeper and deeper into the great forest. These chicleros, many of whom are Maya Indians, have opened the way for scientific explorers who have long delayed entering these regions which appear formidable, yet in reality are not too difficult to traverse."

Tuxpena, a village not far from modern-day Escarcega and seventy miles north of the Guatemala border, became his base camp. It was the company's headquarters in the interior. This was the collection point for raw chicle delivered by contractors and chicleros. Lundell returned to the site as an oasis in his wanderings. By Christmas he had heard whisperings of the existence of a huge site near the Guatemalan border. This was the same site that Madeira and the University Museum aerial expedition had been told to look for by executives of a chicle company in coastal Cuidad del Carmen. But Madeira's pilot spotted Danta pyramid and made for El Mirador, a mere twenty miles away, instead. Lundell used the New Year's break to do his ruins hunting. He followed an old Indian trail through "akalches (wooded swamps) and bad terrain" to the village of Central Buenfil. Quite near this old village is where the modern tourist turns off the International Highway to the site. In Lundell's time the village was the center of the largest chicle contractor in the Yucatan. There he acquired a guide and advice from the brother of Don Manuel Oscorno, the facility's manager. The brother, Enrique, had visited the large Maya site and left graffiti with his name to commemorate the occasion.

The last leg of the trek into Calakmul takes a bit over an hour of leisurely driving today. It took Lundell about the same amount of time it would take you to get there, starting from any major city in North America, if you caught an early flight. Lundell began at dawn and spent the day in the saddle of a mule "following a narrow muddy chiclero trail." But the payoff was the same to Lundell as to the modern tourist. "At half past three I saw, standing in the trail before me, a huge sculptured monolith. We passed it, and a pyramid to our right, and entered what I found to be the main plaza and ceremonial center."

Lundell and his guide, Garcia, spent three days at the site, meticulously surveying and mapping the main group of buildings. He was greatly impressed by the two tallest pyramids. He judged them both to be about 160 feet high. He discovered more than sixty stealae covered with hieroglyphic writing, a larger number than had been found at any other site. Chicleros called the location the Spanish equivalent of "Woman Cooking." But Lundell, not thinking that name dignified enough for a major city, renamed it Calakmul. He devised the name himself. In Yucatec Maya the term means "the place of two adjacent pyramids." He departed from Calakmul on New Year's Day, going to the Buenfil chicle camp for more supplies. He then returned to the area and continued his exploration for neighboring sites. He reported passing by ruined buildings for miles. Because of the large number of inscribed stelae, the height and size of the pyramids, and the extent of urban development, he accurately judged Calakmul to be "one of the most important cities of the Southern Maya culture."

When Lundell finished his botanical survey of the forest in late February and returned to the civilized areas of the Yucatan, he wasted no time presenting a copy of his report to Sylvanus Morley—in person. Morley headed the Carnegie project at Chichen Itza. He was, as noted earlier, arguably the world's leading Mayanist. If Lundell was a quiet member of the Greatest Generation of Americans, Sylvanus G. Morley was a noisy and sometimes controversial one. Morley has been described as a small, near-sighted bundle of energy (Coe 1992). He stood five feet two inches tall, and he weighed 105 pounds sopping wet. He was practically blind without spectacles. But he was endowed with something that more than made up for these supposed limitations: abundant charm. It was said Morley could talk a snake out of its skin. Once, early on, Morley's social sense betrayed him when he ran afoul of Charles Bowditch. At that time, in 1909, Morley was twenty-five. He had just gotten an MA in archaeology from Harvard and was shooting for the PhD when he published one of his first papers on Maya hieroglyphs. Bowditch, a major donor to the Peabody Museum and the Harvard archaeology department, was an amateur epigrapher (or interpreter of ancient languages). His specialty was the Maya. He sponsored expeditions to Central America, and he took umbrage at Morley's gall for crossing him. It is claimed that in a brazen exercise of clout, Bowditch prevented Morley from finishing his degree (Harris and Sadler 2003). As though that punishment was not enough, Bowditch also made sure that Morley's research was never underwritten by Harvard's Peabody Museum, a major funding organization.

Not abashed, Morley applied to the Carnegie Institution of Washington to sponsor an expedition to Central America. The president of the Carnegie, Robert Woodward, summoned Morley in order to tell him in person that no funds would be forthcoming. But Morley's enthusiasm for the Maya turned Woodward's head. Morley won a slice of the Carnegie's $22 million endowment. Some things Morley's charm could not avoid. One of these was the ambush of his mule-back expedition deep in the forests of the Peten. Morley was riding behind the guide when a squadron of drunken Guatemalan soldiers, thinking Morley's group were insurgents, prepared to open fire. Just before the Guatemalan fusillade, Morley's eyeglasses dropped to the ground. He dismounted, retrieved them, and the others in the mule train pressed ahead. Taking Morley's place behind the guide was a medical doctor from Louisiana. The doctor and the guide were shot dead.

Although he looked down on Europeans who "went native" in the tropics, Morley himself was a womanizer. He once brazenly propositioned a female bareback rider in a Honduran circus; another of this complex man's passions was the circus and similar entertainments. Unhappily, the woman was married to the troupe's strongman, who threatened to shoot the archaeologist and throw him in the Caribbean. Morley's luck again spared him the bullet, and his charm led to him getting falling-down drunk, arm in arm with his new comrade, the strongman.

Much of the controversy surrounding Morley didn't surface until many years after his death in 1948. By the turn of the 21st century, it became widely known that "Vay," as he was known to friends, had used his archaeological cover to spy for the U.S. Navy during World War I. His primary mission was to ferret out any possible German submarine bases in the Caribbean area. The secondary mission was to determine the extent to which German nationals or sympathizers influenced the local governments and popular opinion. In the salad days of the early part of the 20th century, the United States did not have an international presence to speak of. Most American scholars, without much international experience, would probably have praised such activity. But the intervening years have shown that mixing research and espionage, poisons the well for academic work. Foreign governments — and local folks — tend to look suspiciously at projects with even the remotest political or military value. Morley had no qualms, though, and he was able to have his way equally with Central American strongmen who admired the rising European fascists and socialist Mexican governors and generals who followed the red star.

Morley's most controversial ideas, however, were scholarly. He was the leading proponent of the empty-ceremonial-center theory of the Maya. This hypothesis held that the Maya were a peaceful, agrarian people who built great temples that were used by a few priest-scholars. These individuals supposedly spent their time contemplating the cosmos from atop their pyramids and devising complicated calendars. The peasants, according to the theory, had courteously built these great structures and then melted back into the jungle to tend their slash-and-burn gardens, showing up only occasionally to provide levees of food and labor and to worship at the shrines. Such things as monarchs, real cities, wars of aggression — known to practically every other civilization in history — had, according to Morley, somehow bypassed the Maya Old Empire. The so-called New Empire centered on the northern Yucatan more closely resembled the doings of most historical states. The reason for this, according to Morley, was foreign conquest and domination. Today almost none of Morley's Old Empire–New Empire theory is held as accurate by professional Mayanists. When Lundell reported to Morley, these ideas were the reigning wisdom regarding the Maya. Morley's great enthusiasm led him to such unconventional ideas. Evidently his charm persuaded the close-knit group of Maya scholars to endorse them, at least provisionally.

Lundell was surprised and pleased to learn that Morley had already set in motion preparations for a major expedition to Calakmul. The formal report about the ruins which Lundell had submitted to his employers had been forwarded to the archaeologist. Even better, the company put at Morley's disposal their considerable infrastructure in the jungle. Had they stonewalled him, it would have been impossible to mount an expedition. With incredible dispatch, Morley and his archaeological assistants arrived at Calakmul on April 9, slightly more than three months after the discovery of the site. The expedition was prepared to stay fifteen days. Traveling with Morley were a number of local helpers, two archaeologists, and an engineer. Morley's wife, Frances, was the photographer. She was also "in charge of the camp commissary" (Morley 2001).

Carnegie archaeologists and helpers at work at Calakmul in the 1930s. From interpretive sign at Calakmul (courtesy INAH).

Morley was suitably impressed by the site. He wrote, "The next day was one of the most remarkable in the writer's twenty-five years of tropical exploration." Morley's team found forty-one stelae in addition to the sixty-two stelae Lundell had discovered. Tikal, the supposed first city of the Old Empire, could boast only seventy-five stelae; but of that number, just eighteen were sculpted. At least eighty of the Calakmul stelae were inscribed. Of these stelae, fifty-one carried Long Count dates.

Morley was delighted with all these dated monuments for two reasons. Numbers and dates were among the few items Maya epigraphers, such as himself, could read. More to the point, Morley believed the Maya elite spent most of their creative energies contemplating numbers and time. Dates and numbers, therefore, to his way of thinking, provided the raw material for cracking the Maya puzzle. Morley believed (more or less correctly) the Maya commemorated time periods by erecting monuments in multiples of approximately twenty years, known, as mentioned before, as a katun. At Calakmul, as many as three or even four stelae were put up on one of these dates. No other site was nearly as well populated with stelae. All this led Morley to conclude that Calakmul was an important religious or ceremonial center. Nevertheless, he deemed it a second-tier city. "Provincial as the city seems to have been, judging from the art of its sculptured monuments, when it came to mass production, Calakmul may be fairly to be said to have surpassed every other site of the Maya civilization now known."

Despite this judgment that it was a fairly unimportant, if large, city, Morley felt Calakmul and precincts deserved further study. Altogether a total of four Carnegie expeditions were sent there during the 1930s. Karl Ruppert and John Denison published the findings of these expeditions in 1943. Nothing in them altered the perception Morley first gave of the site. So matters stood, as far as Calakmul's archaeology was concerned, when Proyecto Calakmul, sponsored by the state university of Campeche, began studies in the 1980s. By now a vehicle road of sorts wended its way to the site; but in bad weather, sometimes four days were required to make the passage. William Folan, the director of the proyecto, was an interesting complement to Lundell, the diffident, focused amateur without archaeological training, and Morley, the errant archaeologist whose strong point was his showmanship. A native of Chicago, Folan was the consummate professional. He eschewed the easy career of a professor at a northern university with only occasional forays into the field. He devoted his life to field archaeology, working at points as divergent as British Columbia and Peru. But mostly his research had been conducted in Mesoamerica, and most of that in the Maya area. As early as 1960 he'd conducted investigations at Dzibilchaltun near Merida, Yucatan, and later at Coba. He had explored the famed cenote (or well) at Chichen Itza. Anyone who has ever met him is impressed with his single-minded interest in the truth. And to William Folan, the only truths worth having are archaeological truths (Folan 2007). In 1982 he was fifty-two years old, at the height of his powers. He eagerly looked forward to the daunting task of making sense of what was one of largest, most perplexing of all Maya sites. Among his staff during his various investigations were his wife, Lynda Florey Folan, and Maria del Rosario Dominguez Carrasco.

Since the last investigation of the site — nearly a half-century earlier — there had been a sea change in the understanding of the Maya. The first chink in the dam began spouting water shortly after World War II. A draft dodger or a photographer, accounts vary, was the first to bring to the world's attention an obscure temple at a small Maya site in the hills of Chiapas, Mexico. The place was called Bonampak. The walls of the three small rooms of a fairly small stone building were adorned with an astonishing full-color mural of a Maya court. The Maya were decked out as never seen before. The first scene in Room 1 showed fourteen lords in long white garments. Being presented to them was a young man and his mother. Thanks to the breaking of the hieroglyphic code in the 1970s, archaeologists now know this man's name and that he was the heir apparent of the nearby kingdom of Yaxchilan. The date of all this was A.D. 790. Right after World War II the name couldn't be read, but it was apparent that the subject matter was political, not religious or vaguely scientific. Scene two shows a period almost a year later. Preparations for the coronation of the heir-apparent are taking place. Scene three shows the coronation procession. The pageantry was the sort of thing that Hollywood could have dreamed up in the days of Cecil B. DeMille. There is a figure in a Las Vegas style headdress. Musicians are banging on drums, blowing into conch shells, and shaking rattles. Lords are dancing. This scene was disturbing to the conventional wisdom because only the most convoluted interpretation could yield anything but a secular scene. These folks were not priests studying the stars, religion, or philosophy.

As difficult as the scenes on the walls of Room 1 were to the believers of the conventional archaeological wisdom, Room 2 was even more challenging. Three of the four walls were decorated by what can only be described as a good old-fashioned rumble. A spear point bursts through the head of one warrior, and prisoners are being taken. Teams of warriors snatch unfortunates who have been separated from their comrades. These sorry folks are grabbed by the hair and led away to what literally is a fate worse than sudden death. Their demise is shown on the north wall. It is presided over by the new reigning monarch of the kingdom. The captives are painted black and arrayed on the steps of a palace. The POWs look dejected, and their fingernails leak blood from tortures already inflicted. More is to come. A severed head lies on the steps, and a body appears lifeless and dead. Room 3 presumably shows a great celebration taking place with elaborately costumed figures gloating over the great victory.

Early Mayanists had been aware of the practice of human sacrifice, but that didn't concern them particularly. Almost all societies, including our own, observed that custom. But these scenes showing widespread battle with the taking of captives for sacrifice didn't square with the idea of humble priest-scholars. Nor did the elaborate pageantry on what appeared to be the accession of a king.

But the murals at Bonampak did not provide the only new evidence. The second piece of disquieting information was harder to overlook. Maya pyramids, the conventional wisdom stated, were used for religious purposes or astronomical laboratories. In other countries, such as Egypt, they may have been built as elaborate sepulchers for political authorities, and indeed, no one else would be able to command the sort of labor required to erect them. But such was not the case with the Maya. Well, as a matter of fact, it was so with the Maya. The evidence was provided by Mexican-Cuban archaeologist Alberto Ruiz. In the late 1940s he noticed something that had escaped the eye of observers for over one hundred years.

By rights, the Maya ruin of Palenque in the foothills of Chiapas should have been one of the most obscure of all sites. It wasn't. It had been visited by archaeological expeditions for almost two hundred years. One of its best known buildings was called the Temple of the Inscriptions, and even today this small, mansard-roofed temple is a poster child for Maya art. It is extremely attractive, set as it is on a modest pyramid against the verdant green of the Chiapas rain forest. Any number of 19th century would-be Mayanists had visited the site. These included the great American-British duo Stephens and Catherwood, and the merely colorful, the so-called Count Waldeck, the Mayanist Munchhausen. None of them noticed what Ruiz did. He became suspicious of a flagstone on the floor of the main chamber of the temple. It was a bit out of alignment. He lifted it and found rubble beneath it. Removing the rock revealed a staircase. Three field seasons later workmen had cleared a passageway more than a hundred feet down. Then finally came the pay-off, a burial chamber to the side. The fill was carefully removed and a wonderfully inscribed sarcophagus lid weighing tons was revealed. This lid later became famous when the Swiss charlatan Erich von Däniken claimed it showed a Maya interpretation of a spaceman blasting into the heavens. In fact, it portrays an image of the body found in the tomb, King Pacal, falling into the underworld down the axis mundi, depicted here as the trunk of the cosmic ceiba tree. When Ruiz made his discovery Pacal's name was not yet readable. The jade death mask and the elaborate funerary ornaments told the story. These items belonged to a wealthy monarch, not a humble priest-king.

Professional Mayanists were able to discount Ruiz's discoveries — for political motives of their own. Ruiz was a first cousin of Fidel Castro. Politically he was sympathetic to his cousin. He was not shy about letting his political beliefs be known (Coe 1992). By now, Morley had been gone for a few years, but the new leading proponent of the priest-king school was the British J. Eric Thompson, later Sir J. Eric Thompson. He was High Church with archly conservative political views, like Morley's, that made it difficult for him to countenance anything coming from a socialist's mouth. Scholars are not supposed to let such considerations get in their way, but, being humans, on occasion they do. All this made it easy for Thompson and those who agreed with him to dismiss Ruiz's discoveries. The next major element was also not paid a great deal of immediate attention to by the Anglo-American contingent. This discovery came from an expatriate German living in Mexico City by the name of Heinrich Berlin.

From the very beginning of Maya decipherment, many of the landmark turns in the road came from those without a real first-hand knowledge of the Maya. The initial symbols for the Maya numerals one and five were puzzled out by an eccentric French naturalist living in the United States in the 1830s, Constantine Rafinesque. He studied crude drawings of Maya hieroglyphs produced by early travelers. Another frontiersman, the Virginia City, Nevada, newspaperman Joseph Goodman was responsible for correlating, more or less, the so-called Long Count to the modern calendar. (As an aside, Goodman also gave a young Civil War draft dodger his first job as a writer for his newspaper. This young man signed his stories Mark Twain.) A 19th century Tennessean, Cyrus Wright, did pioneering work, identifying a few Maya words here and there. His small vocabulary, plus his belief in the phonetic elements in Maya writing, proved extremely helpful to epigraphers in the 20th century.

Berlin noticed that many Maya sites had a particular hieroglyph — along with grammatical identifiers — associated with them. In other words, each city, or perhaps its ruling family, had a name. He identified eight places, including several well-known sites such as Tikal and Copan. This concept is not difficult for the modern reader to understand, but the prevailing wisdom was that ceremonial centers did not need names. The next discovery was harder to overlook. It was made by Tatiana Proskouriakoff. She was a White Russian émigré right out of central casting, a chain-smoking woman of mystery given to the occasional emotional outburst. The artistic temperament was due to the fact that she was an artist. She had been hired in the 1930s by the University of Pennsylvania Museum to make drawings of Maya monuments. For almost thirty years, she had traveled from site to site throughout the whole of the Maya world recording the art of her subjects. One day while drawing a series of stelae at the remote site of Piedras Negras on the Usumacinta River, she made a startling discovery. It became apparent to her that the figures in the stelae she was reproducing were of rulers of the site. She showed her evidence to her coworkers, and they had to agree that the monuments were dedicated to the rulers. By now the empty ceremonial center theory was leaking badly. As German scholar Nikolai Grube puts it, these celebrated discoveries "led to the collapse of the old view of Maya civilization as a theocracy guided by a priestly elite without interest in politics" (Grube 2000).

All this made for new puzzles, which in the upshot bore directly on the identity of Calakmul. Stela A at Copan in faraway Honduras listed four emblem glyphs clustered in a manner to suggest the important capitals of Maya polities. The names of the three of those cities had been determined by Berlin. Copan was located in the southeast corner of the Maya area (the name it went by in Classic times, *Xukpi,* means "corner"). Palenque occupied a similar position on the northwest perimeter. Tikal was more centrally located, but given its presumed preeminence in the Maya world, its inclusion was not a surprise. The fourth emblem glyph was a complete cipher. It included a snake's head. One of Berlin's partially identified emblem glyphs was just such a figure, but he couldn't associate it with a locale. In the 1970s Joyce Marcus of the University of Michigan proposed Calakmul as this site. Marcus is one of the better published Mesoamerican epigraphers, but her judgment was not based on analysis of the hieroglyphs. Calakmul's

Calakmul emblem glyph. Note the three-fanged snakehead. From interpretive sign at Calakmul (courtesy INAH).

apparent immensity prompted this suggestion. But her evidence was slim, and Morley's view that Calakmul was too provincial to merit inclusion with the first cities of the Maya lingered.

Presently another puzzle began to occupy archaeologists, the solution of which would have a huge impact on understanding Calakmul's place in the Maya world. This mystery was brought to light thanks to the work in the 1970s of a brilliant graduate student, Australian Peter Mathews (who as it happens was the major advisor of Armando, one of the authors of this book). Also responsible was a "paradigm shift" in the chicle industry. The chicle industry began to fall apart in the early 1950s when American chewing gum manufacturers switched to a petroleum-derived product. Many former chicleros now either out of work or woefully underemployed turned to a new line of employment. They became art collectors. The art they collected was supplied by the unprotected Maya sites in the hinterland. Their manner of removing their precious objects was none too subtle. With saws, or even axes, they reduced large limestone monuments to small parcels that could be packed out. Many a delicate frieze or glyph crumbled in the process. But there were many more pieces in the thousands of unexplored mounds in the Mesoamerican jungles. Willing participants in this trade were northern museums and collectors who grabbed up what was offered. Although aware that it was illegal to export such items, they rationalized their acquisitions, claiming if they didn't buy the items, they would be lost. In many instances, as far as archaeologists were concerned, the pieces were already lost. Without a context, including not only the site but the position within the site, the information saved by the museum was next to worthless. But taking what was at hand, Mathews conducted a study of looted Maya objects in museum collections in the United States. The result of his study came to be known as the Site Q controversy. The name was given on account of the word *que* in Spanish, which means "what" for what is it. This intellectual brouhaha raged until just recently, when it was conclusively resolved. Among the questions answered was the identity of the city-state the Snakehead dynasty ruled.

Mathews, who had already helped break the Maya hieroglyphic code, identified more than thirty art objects that had elements in common. Among those common denominators were impressively fine workmanship and the high quality of the limestone. Most important, though, were the identifying markers on these objects. The text accompanying the friezes identified a site known as Three Stone Place. Also found in many passages was that mysterious snakehead figure that Berlin had been unable to associate with a specific location. The dean of Maya archaeologists, Michael Coe, chair of the anthropology department at Yale, immediately identified the limestone as the sort of high-grade material common to the Usumacinta River basin. This, plus other factors, gradually pointed to two sites in the western Peten, near a major tributary of the Usumacinta, as the most likely candidates as Site Q. Those sites were known as El Peru and La Corona.

The problem with one or the other being Site Q was that since the late 1970s when Mathews begun the Site Q investigation, references to the Snakehead glyph had been found at almost fifty other sites. Geographically, these Snakehead sites spanned the whole of the Maya area. They were etched on stone monuments at Quirigua, Guatemala, in the southeast, not far from Copan in Honduras. They were also found at Moral almost on the Gulf of Mexico in today's state of Tabasco, Mexico, and at Dzibanche in the northeast Yucatan state of Quintana Roo, Mexico. It was clear that when a scribe etched a foreign emblem glyph into a stone monument, the mention was not just casual, like a snapshot with a brownie at a picnic. Archaeologists had gradually pieced together the reasons for this strange practice.

Not surprisingly, cities that were directly under the control of distant rulers were not allowed to display emblem glyphs of their own — but they did display the distant city's glyph. Another class of city, which was merely an ally, or probably more properly a vassal, could show its glyph. The city acknowledged its indebtedness to the foreign ruler by having a member of the superior city's family present at important occasions, such as accessions to the throne, all being duly noted on the monuments.

The year in which Site Q's identity was finally settled was 2001. The instrument that resolved the dispute was dull, plodding scientific analysis. Stone from the site of La Corona was correlated with the mystery monuments in American museums. The discovery at La Corona by Marcello Canuto of Yale University of a magnificently inscribed tablet in 2005 put the icing on the cake. It was a match piece to one of the key friezes in the Art Institute of Chicago, which served to excite Peter Mathews's interest in the first place. But by the time the mystery was resolved, the major question about where the Snakehead dynasty was seated had also been settled (Guenter 2005). Many of those taking an active part in the inquiry felt neither La Corona nor El Peru could successfully challenge Tikal.

To David Stuart and Stephen Houston went the honor of proving Joyce Marcus's surmise about Calakmul was on the mark. Stuart's father was a Mayanist who did field work in many areas throughout Mesoamerica, and young David grew up speaking Mayan languages like a native. Not surprisingly, he became a leading epigrapher (reader) of written Mayan. Stuart and Houston made a tentative identification of Calakmul with the place name called Ox-te-tun, Three Stone Place, associated with the Snakehead dynasty. To do so, they studied texts from other sites, notably Dos Pilas far to the south. Finally, in 1994 the first written evidence at Calakmul itself was found linking it to the Snakehead dynasty. This was discovered by Ramon Carrasco on a fragment from a hieroglyphic staircase. Subsequently, seven additional Snakehead glyphs have been found at Calakmul, proof positive that the mysterious Snakehead dynasty called Calakmul, or more properly Ox-te-tun, home. At least, as we will soon see, the Snakeheads called it home for a while (Folan, Gunn, and Dominguez 2001; Marcus 1987, 1992).

The Discovery of the Two Empires and Calakmul as the Superior Rival City, A.D. 431–537

In the very first years of the new millennium, scholars have finally assembled a tolerably complete history of the Classic Maya. Their methodology was incredibly painstaking. Most Maya books written on bark paper perished long ago. Fragments of only four books remain. The raw materials of history, then, are the text on monuments or ceramic pots. These sources are among the worst imaginable. How would you like to piece together the history of, say, the Cold War, using the captions on Soviet-era monuments and the slogans on American coffee cups? All this demanded the most finely honed critical sensibilities. Then there is the fact that the pots are frequently only sherds and the monuments are almost always eroded. After months or years of discussion and contemplation, a panel of hieroglyphs might suddenly yield a sentence. A paper might then be written on that one panel of glyphs — or even a single glyph. A great deal of information might be something on the order of the name of a prospective ruler, the name of his enemy city, and an event, say, "of flint and shield falling." At least two other experts will have to judge the paper worthy of publication. Once the paper sees the light of day, it might be accepted at face value. Or it might spark a vigorous discussion. Other scholars might claim, for instance, that the ruler was brought down, rather than bringing the enemy down. Ultimately, however, something like a consensus is arrived at and another piece of the mosaic goes into place.

Essentially the history of the Classic Maya is a tale of two cities, Tikal and Calakmul. We have Simon Martin and Nikolai Grube to thank for pulling this information together in their superlative *Chronicle of the Maya Kings and Queens,* published in 2000 and republished in 2009.

Before delving into the clash of these ancient cities, let's look at the site of Ox-te-tun, as Calakmul was referred to by those who lived here. Let's climb to the top of a short mound on the western perimeter of the Central Plaza. It is about twenty feet high. If you look across the middle tower of the building across the way at sunrise on the equinoxes, the sun

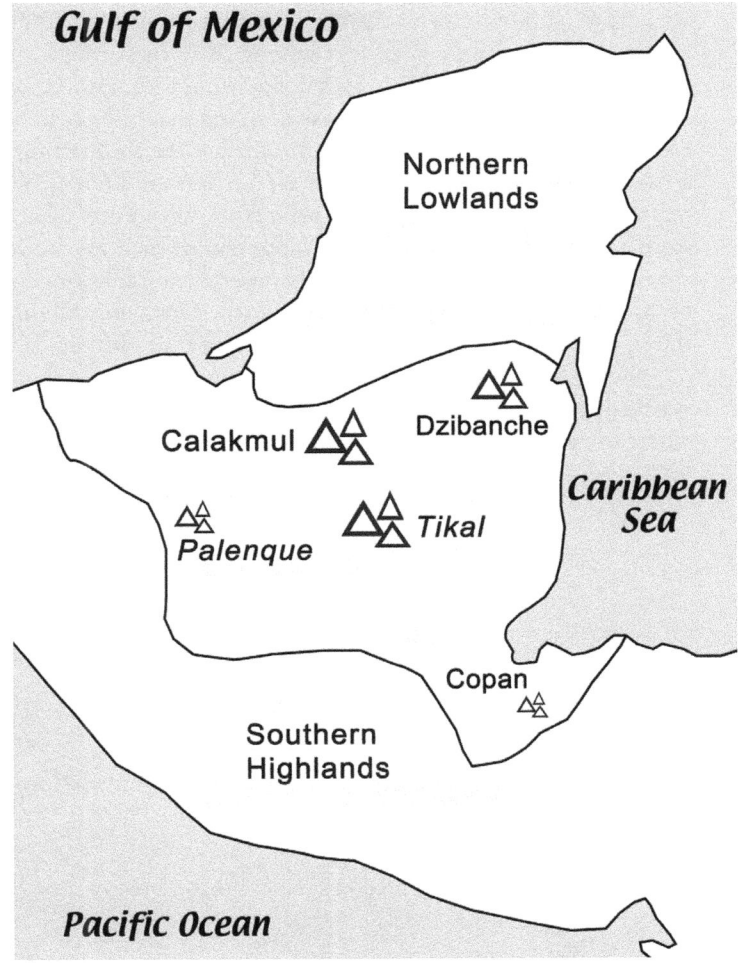

Calakmul and its allied site of Dzibanche. Tikal and its allies Palenque and Copan.

would be square in your face. At the winter solstice, you'd have to pivot a bit to the right and line up with the tower on the right flank of south tower. You'd be in perfect alignment. A left pivot would square you with the sunrise on the summer solstice. We have just surveyed Calakmul's E Group. As you remember from the last chapter, the E Groups at Tikal disappeared by the Early Classic. At Calakmul, whose legacy goes back — possibly — to cities in the Mirador basin, the E group remains in the Central Plaza. Anytime from about A.D. 908 until the present, the plaza and the surrounding campus have been thoroughly overgrown with vegetation. You are lucky now to have light enough at ground level to take a photograph at mid-day without a flash. The trees are also the reason you cannot get a good photograph of Structure 2.

But even if the National Institute of Anthropology and History (INAH) had completely denuded the Central Plaza, you'd still have a hard time getting a frontal shot of Structure 2 from anyplace other than Structure 7, far across the plaza and eighty-five feet up. Your only other choices would be a side view from Structure 1 or chartering an airplane. And actually all good photos of the building have been taken from the air. Its base is about four hundred fifty feet on a side. It is among the largest Maya buildings, judging by mass. An endless succession of dump truck loads would be needed to fill it. But the Maya had no dump trucks, and the laborious task of filling that huge structure was done by hand. Neither animal nor wheel was employed; for all the Maya's learning in certain spheres, they were amazingly deficient in others. Wheeled toys were known; wheelbarrows were not. In the matter of erecting buildings with solid cores, they knew what they wanted. Their structures were meant to replicate the sacred mountain of their mythology. The doorways were caves, the nexus in the Maya belief system between the middle kingdom of man and the underworld or Xibalba where people went after death. Even their divine kings went to Xibalba, but they — unlike we mere mortals — were capable of escape.

Let's climb Structure 2 and see what we see up there. Not many years ago, the building was a pile of rubble. The only easy way to get to the top was to stay to the far right where the rocks more closely resembled steps. Nowadays INAH has reconstructed the tem-

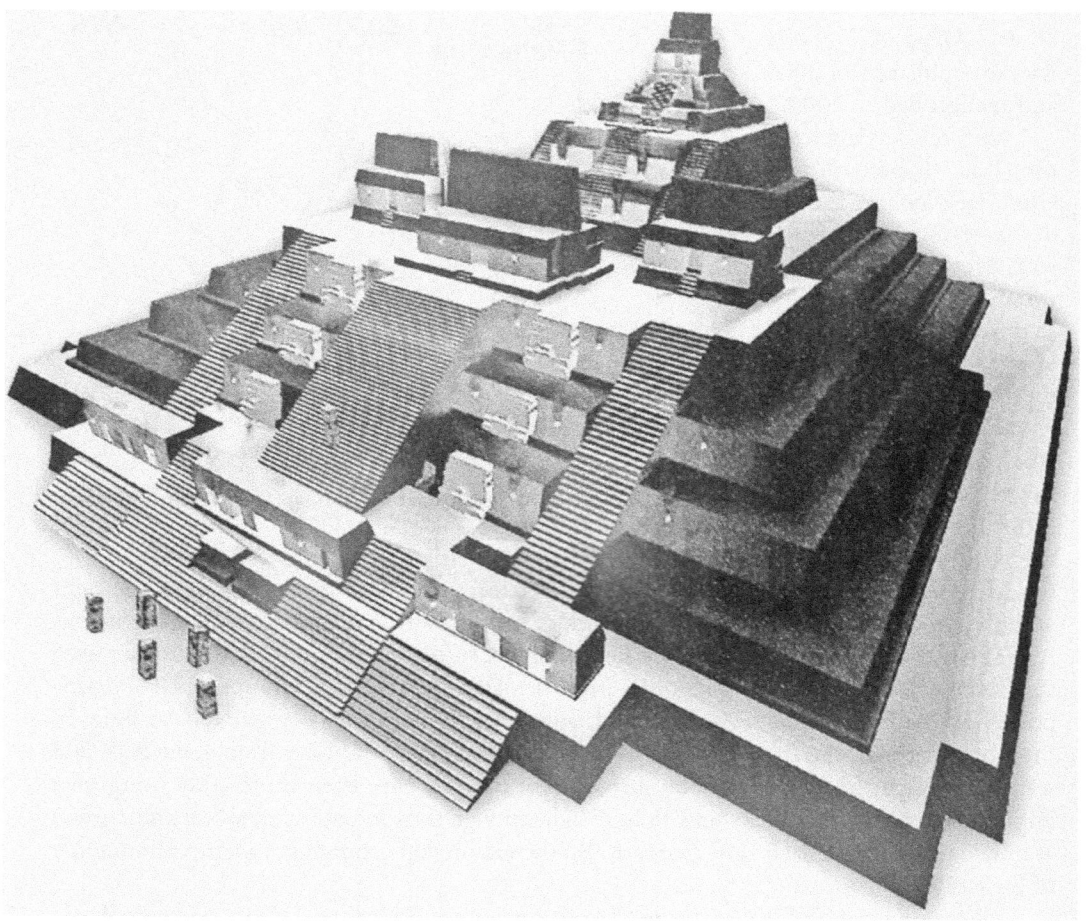

Reconstruction of Structure 2, Calakmul. Note triadic structures on false summit which hearken back to the triadic arrangement of the Mirador Basin in Preclassic days. From interpretive sign at Calakmul (courtesy INAH).

Aerial view of Structure 2, Calakmul. From tourist office poster (courtesy INAH).

ple, and you can go up any of three staircases, east, west, or central. Going up the center staircase would be a mistake. It ends in a small temple that box canyon-like blocks progress to the top. That small temple obscures the view of the true top and is another reason a good photo can't be taken from down there. So it's best still to go up on the right or west side. It's 180 feet to the top. There is no shade, and the north façade can get very hot in the summer when the sun has passed to the north of this latitude and is shining directly onto it.

But 180 feet up a breeze is always wafting. No matter how warm the day, the zephyr will refresh you. Looking at the forest canopy, almost twenty stories up stretching as far as the eye can see, may make you a little giddy if you let yourself think about it. Except for that slender blacktop thread coming in from the north connecting you to the modern conveniences, you could hike briskly in a straight line for days in any direction without encountering a human being, with the exception of the occasional poacher, looter, or squatter. In Calakmul's heyday, the scene would have been quite different. The forest canopy would have been much diminished. In the Terminal Classic, A.D. 800–900, period, it may even have been almost denuded. The massive population of the town required lots of firewood for processing corn and for making plaster to build and stucco temples. Folan estimated the population of the city's core at fifty thousand. That number of folks may seem only a moderately sized town today. But those fifty thousand were supported almost entirely by local resources. Those local resources had been taxed for a very long time. The building that you are taking this survey from, Structure 2, has been standing here for at least 1,750 years, as it was basically completed before the end of the late Preclassic era, A.D. 250. Enough people lived at the site then to pile up dirt and rubble in a pyramid measuring 450 feet by 450 feet by 180 feet. That high mass of population thrived in the area until about A.D. 800, and a diminished population stuck around until at least A.D. 908 (Folan 1992).

The most important ingredient to supporting a human population is water. All major cities are located on a source of water. In Calakmul's case the great seasonal swamp known as El Laberinto provided the supply during the wet months. El Laberinto rises directly west of the city's downtown area and runs about twenty miles off to the southeast. It was as much as five miles wide. Like other such bodies, it may have been a shallow lake before sediment washed from fields, city streets, and lime kilns clogged it up. The early construction of a series of reservoirs (aguadas) and canals connecting them shows El Laberinto was always temperamental source of water.

The months of February to April can be almost bone dry, and many of the trees will lose their leaves. The karst limestone underlying the thin soils absorbs rainfall like a sponge and prevented Stone Age peoples from digging deep wells. Had you spent the previous night camping in a Maya homestead nearby, as the authors have done on occasion, you'd be struck by the paucity of water. No showering or washing facilities are provided, as the sole source of water is catchment tanks. As one moves west or south, the rainfall is more plentiful and more consistent. So why, one may ask, would one of the Maya's great cities be situated in a marginal area? That question, as we shall see presently, is strategic.

During the Classic period, you'd probably be able to see glinting from atop Structure 2 the surface waters of El Laberinto. The swamp (or shallow lake at the time) served various functions. Its position to the south helped erect a defensive barrier. Bajos (swamps) almost always were associated with chert deposits. Chert provided the raw material for spear and knife blades. To a Stone Age people it was an extremely important resource. Something else that no longer can be seen gleaming from up here are seven long straight white causeways. These *sacbeob* were built much like modern highways with stone bases, the roadbed raised above the surrounding lands. One leads just a bit west of south toward El Mirador, a shade less than twenty miles away. You could sight down that sacbe and note the slight uptick on the horizon. That was — is — the giant pyramid known as El Mirador's Danta, discussed in chapter 2. Structure 2 is almost an identical, but slightly smaller, duplicate of it. Early on, it was believed the sacbeob were used only for ceremonial purposes. That such great labor — the sacbe from Coba to Yaxuna, for instance, stretched for sixty-two miles — would be used only for ritualistic endeavors beggars the imagination. These causeways must have been employed to communicate with the hinterland area of the empire for political and perhaps economic reasons. No doubt in times of war they were also used to move troops, for good or for ill, from the point of view of the state they led to. Two of Calakmul's sacbeob, though, were short, eighty and five hundred yards, and these obviously would have been used for intra-urban purposes.

As noted above, the view from Structure 2 extends on for at least twenty miles. Probably not all the area you can see from up there was under the control of Calakmul. But most of it was. And even more territory than was visible to the naked eye was administered by the city's ruling dynasty. Based on a study of the cities that displayed Calakmul's emblem glyph and other factors, William Fallon estimated that Calakmul controlled about 5,000 square miles. That would be an area about 70 miles by 70 miles, vastly larger than Rhode Island and about twice the size of Delaware. The highly urban core of the state took in an area slightly larger than a square three miles. In this area, Folan's team from the University of Campeche discovered 6,250 structures. On the basis of this, he estimated the city was a third larger and 37 percent more densely populated than Tikal. Tikal, as we have seen, is usually accorded a somewhat higher population (owing perhaps to different means of computation). Hundreds of thousands probably populated the larger area Calakmul controlled. The inner zone of about a mile square contained almost a thousand buildings, nearly a third of which contained a sophisticated vaulted ceiling, the so-called corbelled or Maya arch. Almost a hundred buildings were set on pyramids, and all these were arranged in plazas and courts. One particular feature must be noted; "an impressive wall," six-tenths of a mile long, 20 feet tall and two yards wide. It functioned as the northern boundary of the ceremonial center. It runs just behind Structure 7, three hundred or so yards north of the massive Structure 2 where we stand. Archaeologists hypothesize that this wall may have had a defensive function, but how a simple wall, not enclosed in a box, fortification style, could be useful is not easy to see. Certainly, though, it stopped foot traffic from the Central Plaza into the residential area behind, but at a great cost in labor. A wooden fence could have done the same thing.

Descending, we find the small building at the top of the center staircase, which makes a sort of box canyon. It blocks the view of the summit from the ground. This little building was added in the Late Classic. Its nine rooms functioned as a palace or living area high above the city. But we are not interested in that late-time period — yet. Looking down into the central plaza, we will pretend we can see a pile of rubble off to the right. We have to pretend to see it because the forest canopy blocks our view.

In Early Classic times, though, you could have seen this building, which has been dubbed Lundell Palace. In those days it would have been a small but elegant palace with three roof combs. A roof comb is a stone superstructure projecting above a temple. It is characteristic, as we have seen, of Maya architecture in the Peten region. The term evidently was suggested by the comb on top of a rooster's head.

Those three roof combs symbolized the name of the city, Ox-te-tun or Three Stone Place. This name had been associated with the city since the Preclassic period. It referred to one of the most powerful images among the Maya, the three stones of the hearth. The Maya hearth, like the fireplace in the cabin of our forefathers, suggested familial warmth and the basic family unit central to any society. We have seen the triadic arrangement was common at El Mirador and Nakbe. When Ian Graham explored the Mirador basin, he was struck by that architectural peculiarity. Calakmul's architecture, though dating hundreds of years later, was shot through with triadic images, as was appropriate for a location known as Three Stone Place. Structural collapse has robbed the modern visitor of a view of Ox-te-tun's artistic unity, and today you have to look at archaeologist's reconstructions to appreciate this feature.

The Lundell Palace in ruins may seem a unprepossessing building. It has only twelve small rooms which housed between twenty to thirty people, probably high-status individuals and their retainers. Room 6 is located in a maze, far away from the entrance. Folan and his colleagues were tipped off that something unusual was to be found beneath the floor of this

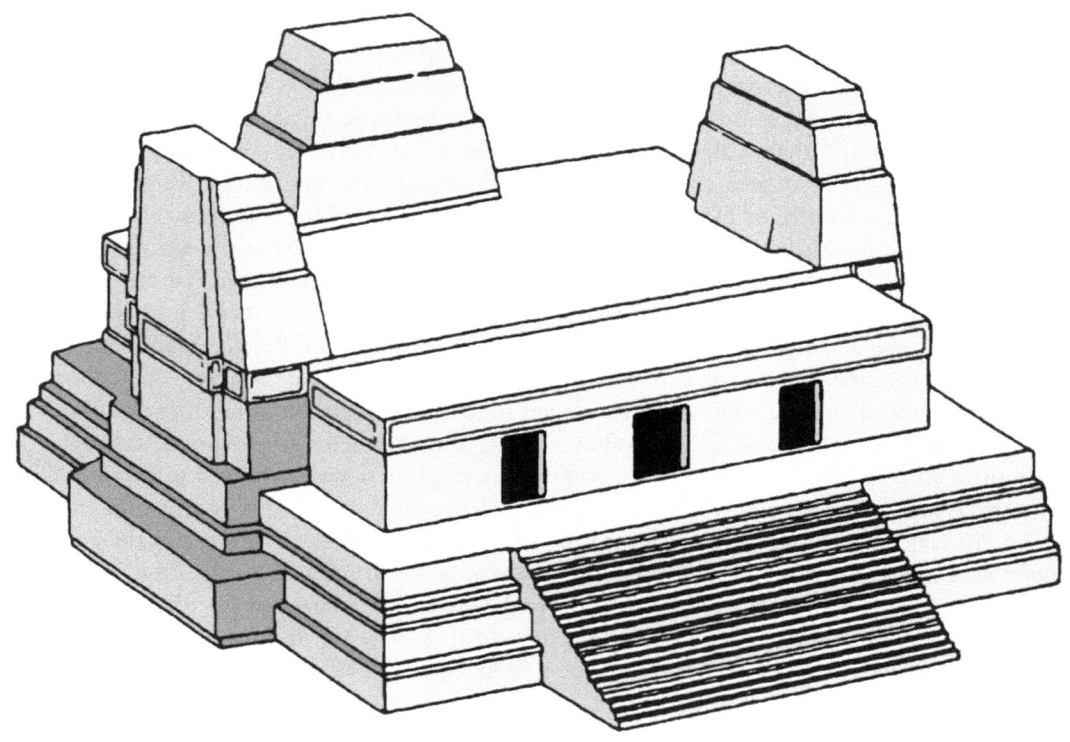

Top: Structure 3 or Lundell Palace, Calakmul. William Folan notes Three Stone Place, the translation of the ancient name for Calakmul, is an apt moniker owing to the triad roof combs and triadic structures characteristic of the site. Illustration by John Wilton after a drawing by Luis Fernando Alvarez Aguilar. *Bottom:* Interpretive drawing of Lundell Palace (courtesy INAH).

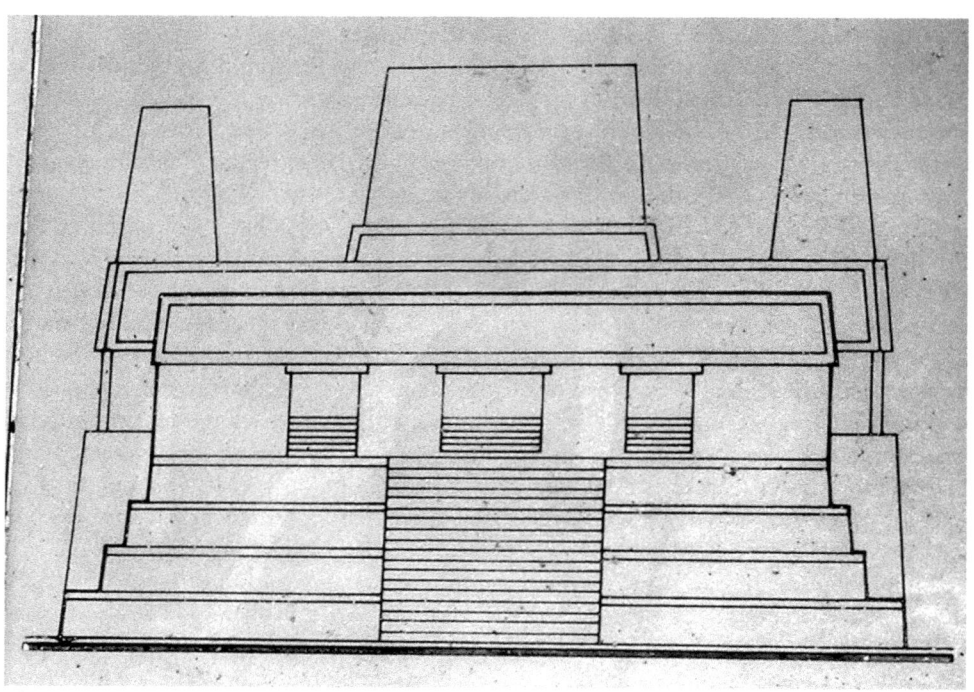

room because three of the entrance ways were blocked by a surface uplifting. Two of Folan's team, Alvarez Aguilar and Armijo Torres, excavated the room in 1989 (Folan et al. 1995). They found a male "at least thirty years of age, lying fully extended on his back on a woven mat." It is supposed the man was an early ruler on account of the richness of funerary goods interred with him. The body and the materials surrounding it were impregnated with expensive red cinnabar. The mat was placed on top of several intricate ceramic pots. The most spectacular find was a cache of jade. A death mask composed of one hundred seventy pieces of jade rested on the skull.

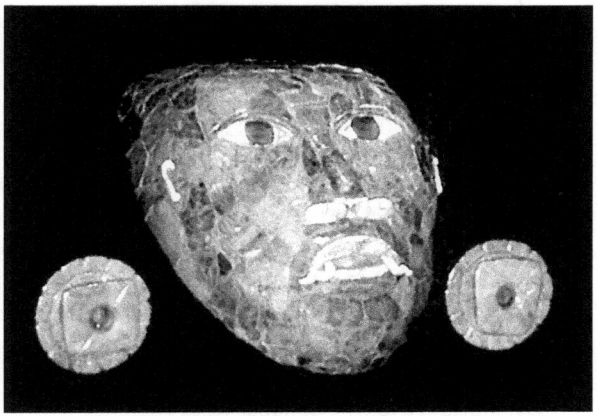

Jade mask found in Tomb 1, Lundell Palace. Illustration by John Wilton of photograph of mask in a museum in Campeche, Mexico.

The mask may actually have been worn while the decedent was alive because there are holes to secure it by a cord to the face. The mask has a stucco backing and shell eyes, lips and teeth. A second mask made up of one hundred twenty-five jade pieces rested on his breast. It probably depicts a long-fanged jaguar with a hieroglyphic disk in its mouth. Depending from it are three inscribed disks. A third mask, of ninety-two pieces, was a sort of belt buckle. This too appeared to have three jade pieces dangling from it which clanked when this important personage made his imperious way in processions and in court. Jade ear plugs complemented the death mask. These were adorned with pyrite and mother of pearl. A jade ring, thirty-two jade beads — many of which were inscribed, 8,253 shells, several large oliva and spiny-oyster shells, a stingray spine, and a block of red pigment completed the burial treasure. A number of extremely fine ceramics, several with handles that appeared to be likenesses of the deceased, were also recovered.

Who did the skeleton in Room 6 belong to? The ceramics could be dated to the Early Classic. It seemed Folan may never be able to answer that question because INAH, the bureau in charge of archaeological ruins, revoked his permit to excavate. The reason: he had been too successful. INAH's own team, under Ramon Carrasco, was designated to take charge. With only three days left, Folan's team discovered a mysterious stela. This stela had escaped notice because it was inset into Structure 2 in its own vault. The niche was dead center in the north face of the large pyramid opening onto the Central Plaza, a position of the utmost honor. Although covered with hieroglyphs on the sides and back, it was placed flush against the walls, keeping the text from probing eyes. To intensify the mystery, this stela had obviously been moved from its original location. Two boa constrictors and charred human bones were found as offerings in the rededication.

Astonishingly, similarities pointed to a link with the body in Tomb 1 of Lundell Palace. The characters and art on the belt masks of the two individuals appeared identical. Even more convincing, however, is the fact that a name occurs on the mask in the tomb. The eroded name on the Stela 114 belt mask appears to be the same. The Long Count date correlated to A.D. 431, making it the earliest known date at Calakmul by more than a hundred years.

So what was going on here? Of the various possibilities the most likely, Folan decided, was that a new ruler, or dynastic line, reset the stela to claim the old king as a direct forebear. As we have seen in the case of the Teotihucan-backed First Crocodile at Tikal, this was an old Maya dodge. It was also one of the reasons for the supposedly long dynastic heritage at many sites. A pretender would slip in and claim false kinship with the old dynasty. Now comes a bit of speculation based on hints by the archaeologists. The reason we have to guess, among other things, is because there is a hundred year gap in the evidence. That's right. A whole century elapsed before mention was made of the next Calakmul ruler. And this king was definitely of the Snake or Kan line. Early rulers of Calakmul, probably including the man in Tomb 1 in Lundell Palace, belonged to the Bat dynasty. We can therefore assume those boa constrictors left as offerings at the rededication of Stela 114 were placed there by the Snake clan that was claiming the Bat king as an ancestral figure. The Snake dynasty, it is worth repeating, appears to have become first known in the El Mirador basin south of Calakmul. After the collapse of El Mirador a quarter of a millennium earlier, the Snakeheads moved north and east, apparently to the area around Dzibanche, one hundred miles from Calakmul. Perhaps that dynasty had only recently routed the Bat dynasty at Calakmul. Calakmul, slightly north of the old homeland, would have been attractive for sentimental, economic, and strategic reasons. On the other hand, it could be that the Snake dynasty had been established at Calakmul for all of the hundred-plus year period for which no monuments have been found. It could be many tributes to Snake kings have yet to be found in far flung corners of this very large city. Or it could be the Spartan-like Snake people were simply modest and went through a period in which they didn't believe in erecting monuments.

This announcement to the Maya world of the appearance of the Snake dynasty at Calakmul was not found on a monument at Calakmul. Rather it was found at Naranjo. This city, to say again, is in eastern Peten, not far from the border of modern-day Belize. A Calakmul ruler, Stone Hand Jaguar, is cited on a monument as presiding over the accession of the local king. In short, the Naranjo monarch is admitting he is a vassal of Calakmul's Snakehead ruler. The year was A.D. 537.

The War of the Worlds, A.D. 537–690, More or Less

Consider the Maya world as the American states at the time of the Civil War. Think of Calakmul as Washington, D.C., the northern capital. Pretend Tikal is Richmond, the southern capital. What was Lincoln's strategy to subdue Richmond? Lincoln attempted to cut the southern lines of communications. To do this, his navy in the Atlantic blockaded southern ports preventing aid from Europe. Lincoln also attempted to gain control of the Mississippi River. After these strategic elements had been accomplished, Union troops sliced the South in half, driving to Atlanta, Georgia, and then to the sea. The point was to isolate the various parts of the Confederacy from one another and hem Richmond in. During all this period Washington was unassailable, thanks to the superior number of Union forces guarding the city.

The Snake rulers at Calakmul pursued a strategy similar to Lincoln's during the Civil War. When we first hear of them, they are making Naranjo an ally by supervising the accession of their king. Naranjo, not surprisingly, lies on the headwaters of the Belize River, the major waterway flowing from the Peten into the Caribbean. Later, the Snakeheads befriended Caracol, an even more powerful city on the headwaters of a different branch of the Belize

River (Martin and Grube 2000). Calakmul allied itself with Caracol by the most egregious Machiavellian turn—letting Caracol turn Naranjo into its own milk cow. Think of the Belize River, in terms of its ability to carry vessels, as the equivalent of the Atlantic Ocean. The headwaters of that great river were now under the control of a powerful ally, Caracol, the equivalent of talking South Carolina into switching to the Union side.

The next we hear of the Snakeheads, they have gained control of El Peru on the tributary of the Usumacinta River that penetrates closest to Tikal. The Usumacinta, like the Mississippi, is a huge river, and, like the Mississippi, it flows into the Gulf of Mexico. One of Lincoln's purposes for securing the Mississippi was to stop the flow of foodstuff from the states to the west. The Snakeheads had control of the Usumacinta for long periods of time. Their hegemony prevented or hindered Tikal's association with the powerful western states such as Palenque with which Tikal

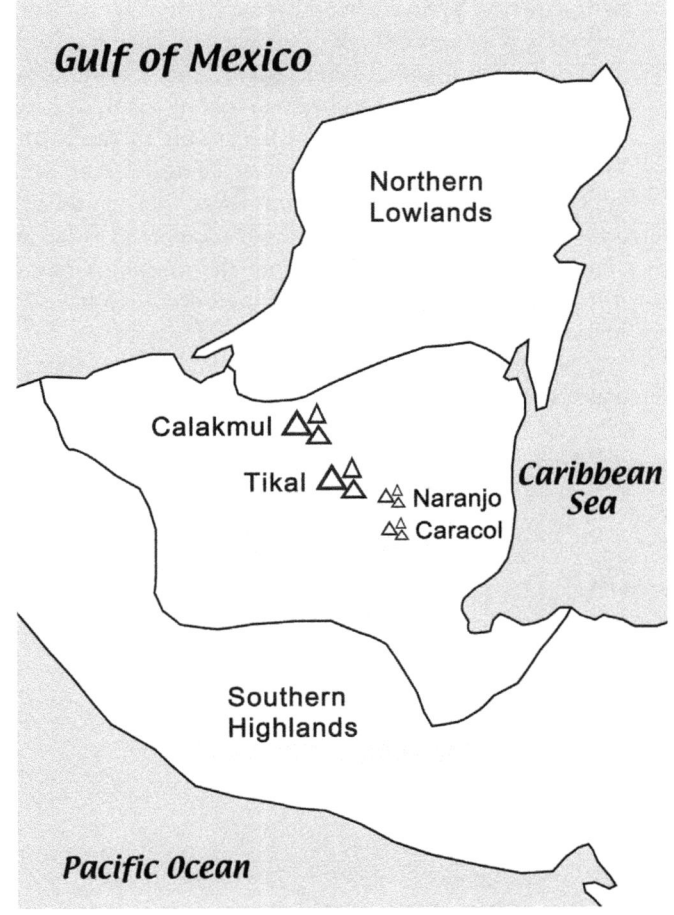

Relative position of Calakmul and the two Tikal allies it lured away.

was at least sometimes allied. Lincoln's prize at the mouth of the Mississippi was New Orleans. Sure enough, the record shows, the Snakeheads attempted to place an ally in control of the area almost directly south of Tikal on a major branch of the Usumacinta. Although the Maya area was considerably smaller than the United States at the time of the Civil War, the strategic thinking employed by the Snakeheads to subdue or control their rival capital of Tikal was similar to that employed by the Union forces under Abraham Lincoln.

Sky Witness succeeded Stone Hand Jaguar (he who had presided over the accession at Naranjo in 537 and who started the wars that brought Tikal to heel). He picked up where Stone Hand Jaguar had left off. One of his vassals was captured and presumably sacrificed by Yaxchilan in the far southwestern corner of the Maya area (in what would be Texas, to continue the Civil War metaphor). This indicates Sky Witness had directed a salient almost two hundred miles from home base, showing an astonishing strategic capability.

By now Sky Witness's strategy, and the long-term strategy of the Snakehead dynasty, is apparent. The Snake people were attempting to turn what had been one of Tikal's natural advantages — interior lines — against her. Tikal was located in the heart of the better-watered and densely populated Peten. All around it were formerly autonomous cities which it had subjugated. Naranjo had been an ally of Tikal, as had Caracol.

Even though Sky Witness's first sally to Yaxchilan and the southwest appeared to have been thwarted, he felt ready to strike again. And strike he did. His forces, including his allies, made a frontal assault on Tikal. This could be likened to the Battles of Bull Run, only Sky Witness's armies did what Lincoln's failed miserably at. Tikal was overrun, and Tikal's monarch was driven from the throne. A new Tikul king, Animal Skull, ascended the throne. Tikal, already in eclipse, seems to have little hope for ever emerging from its period of darkness.

Maya warfare was rarely aimed at totally destroying an enemy state. Rather, a new ruler was installed, one who swore fealty to the one responsible for his rise in the world. Shortly, however, the logic of his position and his city's needs (and his need for maintaining internal control) would overrule his sense of allegiance. And the two city-states would again tussle. This inability to completely destroy an enemy and sow salt in its agricultural fields, as Rome did to Carthage, speaks volumes about the political organization of the Maya state.

Calakmul understood it had always to maintain its strategy of containment of Tikal, no matter how close to heel it believed it had brought its enemy. As the nobility played with geo-politics, the dreary life of the peasantry droned on pretty much the same in both defeated Tikal and victorious Calakmul. The farmers were told the kings, who underwent the appropriate ritual no matter how they came to office, were divinely ordained to rule them, much as modern religious folk believe their leaders' religious pronouncements, despite their peccadilloes. The monarch's divinity — and the rituals they enacted — ensured the timely and plentiful fall of rain. As in Europe, there was horizontal mobility among monarchs. In other words, a family wasn't necessarily tied to a particular locale. As long as the monarch's ritu-

Calakmul completely surrounded Tikal with hostile city-states.

als — including auto sacrifice — caused the crops to grow, the burdens of peasant life were acceptable. The levees of food crops demanded by their lords would be steep. Warfare probably mobilized all phases of society to some extent, but the burden fell on the aristocratic class. Little did the peasants know how lucky they were to be taxed mainly for their corn and labor. A city could be overrun, its monuments razed, even its temples ritually destroyed, and the effect on the peasants was slight, at least in the Early and Middle Classic periods.

Sky Witness's next long-term successor, Scroll Serpent, moved to consolidate Calkamul's control of the Maya lowlands. Twice he attacked Palenque. Today, Palenque is the best part of a day's drive from Calakmul — or in other words, a long way. In Scroll Serpent's time, moving a force of men into position would have been formidable and included crossing the Usumacinta. The first foray in A.D. 599 did not succeed. The second one, twelve years later, resulted in the death of the Palenque ruler. Presumably, Palenque, for a time at least, became an ally of Calakmul.

Naranjo, no doubt chafing as the fiefdom of Caracol, broke with its former allies about A.D. 626. For five years, it skirmished with Caracol and probably Calakmul. Then in 631, its ruler was subdued by Scroll Serpent's son, Yuknoom Head. The fate reserved for that ruler was the special one of the fallen-away ally. He was transported, not to nearby Caracol, but to distant Calakmul. Imagine him suspended from a pole as his captors lugged him along the jungle trail, alternately taunting and scourging him. After a suitable amount of public humiliation and torture at Calakmul, he appears to have been killed, barbecued, and eaten. And evidently not satisfied that that ruling dynasty was appropriately put in its place, these events were etched into a hieroglyphic staircase at Naranjo. The Maya were not prone to boast of their defeats on public monuments, so all this was an additional punishment inflicted by Calakmul.

The brother of the man who devoured the ruler of Naranjo was also named Yuknoom, and he is believed to share the same father, Sky Witness. He has been dubbed Yuknoom the Great by Simon Martin and Nicholi Grube. Yuknoom the Great began the program of public improvement that saw as many as eighteen stelae erected. It is also believed he was responsible for building many of the smaller plazas and ceremonial complexes in Calakmul. But of course, his intervention, usually armed, in the affairs of other states is the principal reason he gained "the Great" title. During his fifty-one year reign, he again had to deal with Naranjo, which in A.D. 680 overran its neighbor and Yuknoom ally, Carocol. Within two years, the Naranjo dynasty was totally eradicated, and a Yuknoom-supervised monarch ascended the throne. All this points toward a revitalized Tikal, one fanning the flames in peripheral city-states, and Yuknoom was not behindhand in meeting the challenge. At El Peru, he installed a vassal, Great Sun Jaguar. Yuknoom traveled the Usumacinta, installing rulers at Moral in the delta near the Gulf of Mexico in A.D. 662. Twice he oversaw the accession of vassals at Cancuen hundreds of miles to the south on the Rio Pasion, one of the Usumacinta's headwater rivers.

Calakmul scored a major victory in internal Tikal politics by encouraging a pretender to the Tikal throne. Yuknoom forced the recognized Tikal monarch out of the city. The year was A.D. 657. Unfortunately, he was unable to consolidate these gains by placing his ally on the throne and keeping him there. Shield Skull, the "rightful" monarch, managed to reclaim his seat. In the meantime, Yuknoom's ally established himself at Dos Pilas far to the south on the Rio Pasion. Now Yuknoom had Tikal completely boxed in. To add insult to injury, the pretender at Dos Pilas used the Tikal emblem glyph, claiming Dos Pilas was the real Tikal. Understanding the precariousness of his position, Shield Skull marshaled his forces, attacked Dos Pilas, and drove the rival claimant from his seat of power. Yuknoom arrived with a force in time to send Shield Skull's armies fleeing. In short, Yuknoom ended his reign, vis-à-vis Tikal, with a sort of split decision in his favor. Both sides had managed to draw blood, but Yuknoom, the Snakehead Dynasty, and Calakmul were clearly preeminent. Still, there was a cloud no bigger than the hand of a man on the southern horizon. It was called Mutal (as Tikal was known to the Maya). Yuknoom had not totally subdued it. It would be the undoing of his successors. And the fall came much faster than one might expect, given the victories to date.

The Worm Turns, A.D. 695

When we started this historical digression, we were in the ruins of a small palace called II-B, on Structure 2 high atop the quiet city of Calakmul. Literally beneath our feet, in what is called II-Bsub, another richly adorned tomb had been discovered by Ramon Carassco in 1997. It has been dubbed Tomb 4. These bones were wrapped in the remains of a jaguar pelt, and all the riches of Tomb 1 in Lundell Palace were replicated in this burial place, including fine ceramics, a wealth of shells, and jade — lots of jade. The man's name apparently was Fiery Claw. His coronation was duly recorded by allies at El Peru and Dos Pilos. In A.D. 693, he presided over the accession of a five-year-old monarch at Naranjo. So Fiery Claw had Tikal boxed in again, right? Well, apparently not. By A.D. 691, Fiery Claw sent an emissary to Tikal. Given their clashes in the past, such an ambassador could only be said to be tugging the forelock of submission. Four years later, in August of 695, Fiery Claw was attacked by Tikal. It is recorded that "Fiery Claw's flint and shield were brought down," meaning he was captured and/or killed. One of the Snakehead's principal deities, carried into the battle on a palanquin, was captured. Fiery Claw's corpse seems to have been spared untold indignities. It was interred in Structure 2. For more than a millennium, it reposed there before being discovered by Carrasco.

Although Calakmul would carry on for two hundred more years, its glory days were over. Tikal had risen from the ashes and would once again reclaim its role as first city of the Maya.

5

The Tale of Two Cities, Concluded, A.D. 695–869

Copan, A.D. 427–822

By any accounting, the most important early Mayanists were John Lloyd Stephens, often called the father of Mesoamerican archaeology, and Frederick Catherwood, his artist companion. Born in 1805, Stephens came from a wealthy New York merchant family. He graduated from Columbia and read for the law at Tapping Reeve's law school in Connecticut, the nation's first law school, through the portals of which passed the likes of John Calhoun and many of the political and judicial leaders of the young republic. Though Stephens passed the bar, he never really practiced (von Hagen 1990). Or rather he practiced too much by squandering his time in New York coffee houses with those who became America's first literary school, the Knickerbockers, Washington Irving being the best known today of that movement. Stephens himself later became one of their luminaries. Politics and literature have always gone hand in glove; and Stephens, an ardent supporter of Old Hickory, spent much of his time not occupied chinning in the Astor House bookstore making stump speeches for Tammany Hall candidates. All this led to a case of strep throat and the doctor's recommendation for a change of venue.

The young lawyer was packed off to Europe with ample funds to take jaunts to far eastern Europe including Russia and the Ukraine and the Mediterranean with side visits to Egypt and the Sinai. In fact, disguised as a Muslim, he was one of the very few foreigners ever to penetrate to the lost city of Petra in the Sinai. The ruins of the city had only been discovered in the early 19th century. Its discoverer had been killed because he was found to be an infidel.

All this excited an interest in lost cities in the youthful Stephens; he was still in his twenties at the time. In London on the way home, he met Frederick Catherwood, an artist who had spent years in Egypt drawing ancient statuary and ruins. The biographer of the two men, Walter Wolfgang von Hagen, dubbed Catherwood the preeminent architectural artist in the world at the time, having spent years in Egypt. Catherwood appears to have been Stephens's complete opposite. Whereas Stephens — judging by his prose and life history — was lively and charismatic, Catherwood, born in 1799, was older, more stodgy, and self-effacing. But both shared an abiding interest in lost cities, and despite or because of their differences in character, the men became fast and lifelong friends. Pure happenstance also took a hand. Just at the time Stephens and Catherwood met, an article was published in northern newspapers by one Juan Galindo.

In actuality, the "modern" discoverers of the Maya probably should be thought of as a triumvirate, with Galindo being the third member (Brunhouse 1975). He was one of those wondrous 19th-century characters that could be described either as a polymath or flimflam man, and perhaps both. His origins are murky. It has been claimed that by birth he was Irish by the name of Paul Gallagher. Another claim is that he was a black Irishman named Galindo who's earliest male Irish descendent arrived in the Emerald Isle thanks to British guns and the huge storm that destroyed the Spanish Armada. It appears most likely that he was a native-born Central American, the son of a colonial official. In any case, young Juan Galindo rose to prominence in the army and government of the infant Central American republic, which split into the modern states in the 1840s and never has reunited, despite supposed interest by the peoples in all the countries of the former republic to do so.

Stephens and Catherwood were lucky. Galindo, though not without a certain amount of good fortune, was born with a bad-luck rabbit foot. For instance, he was appointed governor of the district of Peten. Up until recent times, the Peten has been a hot, sweaty frontier province—especially as compared to the cities in highland Guatemala with their eternal spring climate and many years of colonial urbanism. To most an appointment in the Peten would have been anything but a plum. Having an interest in antiquities, Galindo made his way to Palenque in neighboring Chiapas, Mexico, over difficult jungle trails. He missed discovering magnificent Tikal less than forty miles north of his Peten base! So that sow's ear of a job never quite got redeemed.

In time, however, Galindo worked his way up to become a diplomat to the U.S. and Great Britain. He offered his services to both countries in ways that today may not be considered exactly of the most honorable sort. While in the Peten he acquired a grant for a huge piece of territory. His grant unfortunately was in the area also claimed by Great Britain, known in later times as Belize (British Honduras). He had earlier been the agent to the U.S. in talks about rights to developing a canal across the isthmus. He spilled the beans to Lord Palmerston about the United States' efforts to acquire rights for a canal. The British government was supposed to recognize his land grant in return. The wily Palmerston, after ferreting out supposed U.S. intentions, reneged on the deal. Galindo returned to Central America, visited Copan in Honduras, excavated a tomb, and penned the article that drew the interest of Stephens and Catherwood.

Despite his economic machinations, Galindo's analysis of the Maya displayed a level-headed, common-sense approach to the ruins that became a model for Stephens. For instance, when describing the Temple of the Cross at Palenque, Galindo merely noted the resemblance to the Christian symbol without making an inference about direct Christian influence. In this he showed a discipline sorely lacking in many 19th-century writers. He also intuited that the hieroglyphics were a form of writing. Galindo made a connection, despite the large number of differences, between Copan and Palenque, arguing that they were of the same cultural origin, if perhaps not of the same culture. He noted that the tools of daily life found in the ruins (metates and manos used for processing corn) were similar to those used by local natives in his day. Finally, Galindo claimed that the builders of the ruined cities he visited were the ancestors of the present Indians of Central America and that the vernacular of contemporary natives was likely related to the language of the builders of the cities. As free of controversy as these ideas may seem today, it was many years before Mayanists agreed to all of them. Stephens much wanted to meet Galindo—probably as much for matters of state as for archaeology.

Stephens had used his political connections to get himself appointed as American minister to Central America, That was a good thing, too, because without the official charter he could never have made his way through that tumultuous and civil war-torn land. His official mission had two charges. The first was to determine the state of governance, if any, in the Central America republic. The second was to ratify a treaty giving the U.S. sole right of passage for a trans-isthmus canal. He reported there was no government and gave up all attempts to gain legal claims for a canal. His failure to secure a treaty annoyed Daniel Webster, to whom he reported, the secretary of state for the successor Whig president Fillmore.

Webster had good reason to be unhappy with Stephens. On arriving in Central America, never minding his official duties, Stephens (along with Catherwood) made not for the capital of the supposed country, Guatemala City, but the ruins at Copan. They endured several of the minor tribulations of Job. They had to best the mud trail over the Mico Mountains, spend a night in jail, and suffer the inhospitality of a surly don whose "house had two sides, an inside and an out; the don [his far from obliging host] and his family occupied the former, and [Stephens and Catherwood] the latter."

The don also tried to thwart Stephens's access to the ruins. He had his reasons. The rebel conservative forces had gained the upper hand. All things that might smack of liberalism were looked on askance. Something as simple as showing a little hospitality to foreigners might end very badly for a Samaritan. For instance, the unfortunate Galindo had recently been put against a wall and shot at Tegucigalpa.

But at long last, Stephens procured a guide. Fording the Río Copan, he rode along the bank on a path that Jose opened with his machete "until we came to the foot of the wall. The wall was of cut stone, well laid, and in a good state of preservation. We ascended by large stone steps, in some places perfect, and in others thrown down by trees which had grown up between the crevices, and reached a terrace, the form of which it was impossible to make out, from the density of the forest in which it was enveloped. Our guide cleared a way, and we came upon a square stone column about fourteen feet high and three feet on each side, sculptured in very bold relief, and on all four of the sides, from the base to the top," and so Stephens began his description of Copan.

The first book went by the ungainly title of *Incidents of Travel in Central America, Chiapas and Yucatan,* but it took the U.S. by storm becoming a runaway bestseller, selling 20,000 copies in the first three months after publication. Against all odds, Stephens also pocketed a goodly sum for the publication in England. The prevailing custom among the British was to stiff Americans whose publishers ignored British copyright laws. But Catherwood's involvement in producing the illustrations garnered him favor in that country. In part, the secret of the book's success was Stephens's personality—or perhaps better put, the personality of the persona of the narrator. He was enterprising, industrious, cocky, good-humored, friendly, adventurous, a bit brash, inventive, and irreverent. Nineteenth-century readers responded to such a character just as the modern reader might. And of course, it didn't hurt that he had the ear of the Knickerbocker establishment, which put out the word to booksellers across the land. But at bottom Stephens's two-volume work was about archaeology and ethnology—and quite technically written with elaborate descriptions of sites and monuments—and antebellum American (and British) readers couldn't get enough of it.

For instance, here's his description of the statuary garden north of the acropolis now known as Copan's Great Plaza.

> The front was the figure of a man curiously and richly dressed, and the face, evidently a portrait, solemn, stern, and well fitted to excite terror. The sides were covered with hieroglyphics. This our guide called an "idol." Before it, at a distance of three feet, was a large block of

stone, also sculptured with figures and emblematical devices, which he called an altar. We followed our guide to fourteen monuments of the same character and appearance, some with more elegant designs, and some in workmanship equal to the finest monuments of the Egyptians, one displaced from its pedestal by enormous roots, another locked in the close embrace of branches of trees and almost lifted out of the earth, another hurled to the ground and bound down by huge vines and creepers and one standing, with its altar before it, in a grove of trees which grew around it, seemingly to shade and shroud it as a sacred thing.

And here's a much more detailed description of what has come to be called Atlar Q, which perhaps presents as curious a subject of speculation as any monument in Copán.

The altars, like the idols, are all a single block of stone. This stands on four globules cut out of the same stone. The sculpture is bas-relief, and it is the only specimen of that kind of sculpture found at Copán, all the rest being in bold alto-relievo. It is six feet square and four feet high, and the top is divided into thirty-six tablets of hieroglyphics, which beyond doubt record some event in the history of the mysterious people who once inhabited the city. The lines are still distinctly visible. The next two engravings exhibit the four sides of this altar. Each side represents four individuals. On the west side are the two principal personages, chiefs or warriors, with their faces opposite each other, and apparently engaged in argument or negotiation. The other fourteen are divided into two equal parties, and seem to be following their leaders. Each of the two principal figures is seated cross-legged, in the Oriental fashion, on a hieroglyphic which probably designates his name and office, or character, and on three sides of which the serpent forms part. Between the two principal personages is a remarkable cartouche, containing two hieroglyphics well preserved, which reminded us strongly of the Egyptian method of giving the names of the kings or heroes in whose honor the monuments were erected. The headdresses are remarkable for their curious and complicated form. The figures have all breastplates, and one of the two principal characters holds in his hand an instrument which may perhaps be a scepter.

As it happens, Altar Q turned out to be one of the most important of all Maya monuments, and Stephens pretty much had it right.

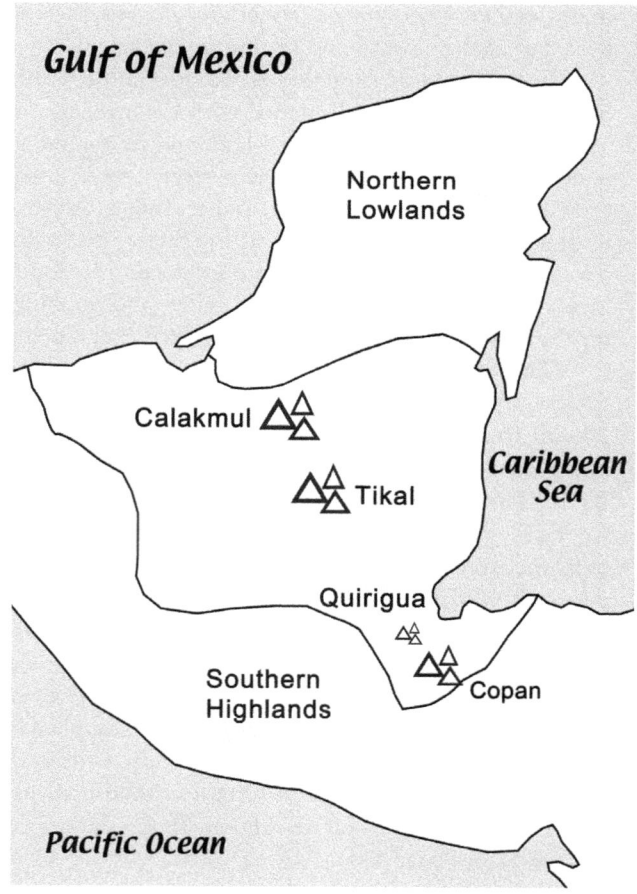

Copan and its dependent site Quirigua in relation to the megacities of Tikal and Calakmul.

The sixteen figures are all chiefs (or kings; even today archaeologists are split as to what would be the better designation, most tilting toward kings), and fourteen of them are sitting on hieroglyphs giving their names. The principal two are indeed identified by the cartouche between them in what Stephens called the Egyptian manner. The bar in the hand of the man to the left is a scepter, as Stephens speculated. All of this Stephens, following Galindo, deduced using those arcane analytic principles of common sense and an understanding of world history.

The New Order in the Deep South(east), A.D. 427–822

But Stephens did not get it all right. Had Stephens and Catherwood been a touch more astute — and as we have seen they were very astute compared to Mayanists for a 130 years after them — they could perhaps have guessed the 16 figures on Altar Q were the fifteen in line of succession after the founder. But lacking a crystal ball, it would have been nigh unto impossible for them to know that the intergalactic warfare of the Tikal-Calakmul tiff played into the dynastic politics even in this far corner of the Maya world. Even more astonishing, it was long after the balance of power had shifted back in Tikal's favor that Calakmul would score a stunning victory in the southeast corner of Mayadom (Sharer 2003).

Regarding Atlar Q, hardly anyone would have been happier than Stephens to learn that the gentleman handing the scepter off may have been from Tikal, the putatative city that the old Spanish priest in the highlands thought was still going strong in the lowlands. Even better, that man's name was Yax Kuk Mo (First Quetzal Motmot). He arrived at Copan perhaps at the head of an invading force about A.D. 427, or a half century after Fire Is Born and his Teotihuacan (inspired?) warriors barged into Tikal. After what probably was a brief skirmish, he imposed a new dynasty. The person Yax Kuk Mo is facing is the 16th in line of succession, Yax Pisaj. This remarkable carving was dedicated in A.D. 776, one thousand years before the birth of the republic of the north Stephens represented, and after three and a half centuries of the dynasty. How do we know this? Because that's what the hieroglyphic text on the top of the monument says.

Copan is pleasantly located in a mountain valley on the southeastern perimeter of the Maya world, the major Maya site in Honduras, a country with few other Maya sites. The name most associated with Copan in Maya times — it is worth repeating — was Xukpi, meaning corner, as in corner of the Maya lands. Its elevation is 3,000 feet, high enough to mediate the surly climate of the lowlands, but low enough to produce the many products of the tropical flatlands. Nowadays, for instance, tobacco for fine cigars is produced in the area. Nevertheless, at the end of the Classical period a population of 25,000 or so sorely taxed the valley, and many of the inhabitants suffered from malnutrition. So why would the rulers of a state far away bother with Copan?

The answers are jade and trade. Jade, of course, was the most precious commodity of Mesoamerica during Classical times. The only known quarries of this important stone were found on the upper Motagua River, sixty or more miles from Copan (Wagner 2008). Understanding this, a new ruler was named also for Quirigua situated directly on the Motagua. But thinking strategically, Copan was designated the superior of the two sites, and Quirigua's ruler was sworn in by Yax Kuk Mo. Presumably the fact that it was several mountain ranges from the quarries and Quirigua gave Copan a strategic advantage. Copan was too far away

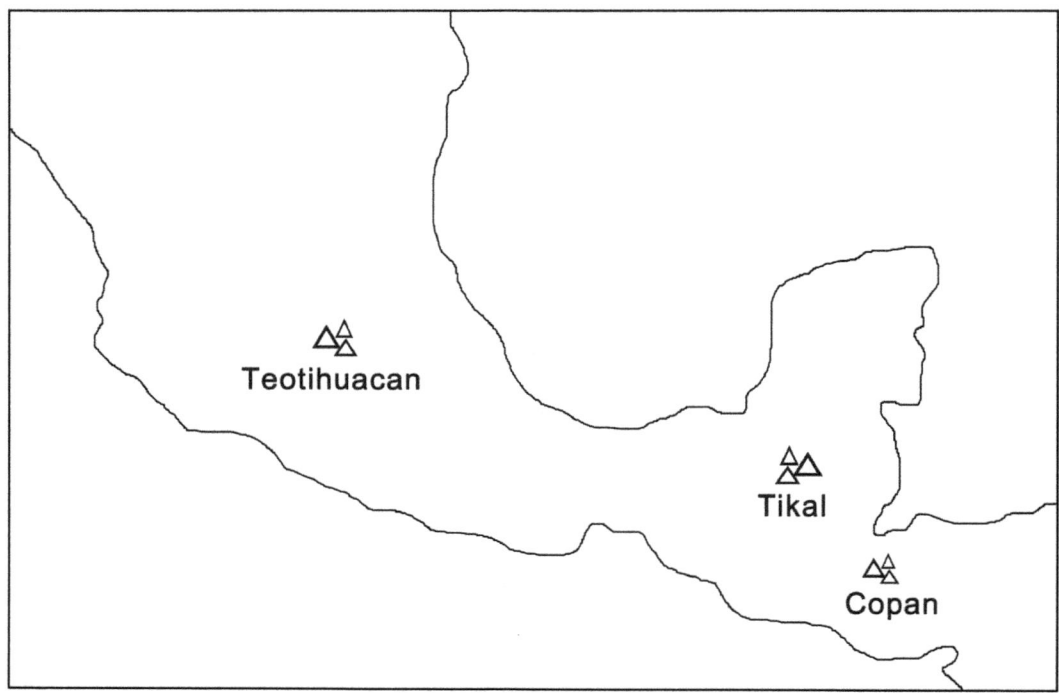

The place of cattail reeds where Yax Kuk Mo was affirmed as king of Copan could have been Teotihuacan, 700 miles away in the Valley of Mexico, or Tikal, 168 miles away in lowland Peten.

for an invader to seize the quarries and attack Copan simultaneously. If Quirigua was smashed and the quarries seized, Copan's armies could swoop down from its secure location to quell internal or external threats.

Early on, archaeologists were not certain if Yax Kuk Mo hailed from the Peten or Teotihuacan. Either seemed possible. The hieroglyphs on Altar Q told them that on September 5, 426, he took the "snake-footed jaguar-sun god scepter and rose to kingly status." Three days later a "coming" event occurred at the Foundation House. It was apparent this event occurred not at Copan, but at some distant and unspecified location and that distant place was known as a place of cattail reeds. It took Yax Kuk Mo and his retinue 152 days, almost half a year, to reach Copan. Martin and Grube speculate that the column moved under the banner of a jaguar-sun-god image, much as a Roman Catholic procession under the auspices of the appropriate saint or a military column with its standard. These banners were on prominent display during Maya battles and their capture during skirmishes was considered a major disgrace just as the capture of standards during 18th- and 19th-century Euroamerican warfare also produced enormous loss of face. The place-of-reeds imagery, oddly enough, had long been associated with Teotihuacan, even though it was situated in a semidesert. The allusion did not refer to a physical location. Rather, it hearkened to the cleft in the back of the mythological reptile which to the Maya was the primordial marsh from which sprang the fourth creation, the present world. It was here that potential rulers had to go to receive confirmation of their right to rule. There appear to have been more than one possible cattail reed place. Tikal, positioned between two sawgrass marshes, also was known by a cattail image, which archaeologists believe was acquired by its association with Teotihuacan and not its marshy location (Schele and Mathews 1998). Later ages would regard Tula in the Mexican highlands as the mythical cattail place, Tollan.

The Copan valley, because of its good soils and water, had been inhabited for almost 1,500 years when Yax Kuk Mo and his retainers arrived. Long Count dates for events hearkening back as far as the 4th century B.C. have been found, and a king by the name of Foliated Ahaw appears to have dedicated a stela in A.D. 376. Did Foliated Ahaw not leave any claimants to the throne? Or were there perhaps too many? Did the people of the valley ask a foreign ruling family to give the Copan valley a new royal house? That is possible, and although given the fact that a king of Quirigua was installed at the same time, it does not seem particularly likely. Conquest on the order of that seen in the Peten after the conquest of Tikal seems more probable. Then, as we remember from chapter 3, after Fire Is Born proclaimed himself kaloomte (emperor) of the area around Tikal, new rulers were installed at Uaxactun, Rio Azul and other locations (such as Oxkintok in northern Yucatan) under his leadership. It very well may have been that Yax Kuk Mo was a contender for the throne at Tikal. What better way of ridding oneself of a possible usurper than giving him leave to set up a satellite state in the far corner of the Maya area 170 miles away? In any case, Yax Kuk Mo's dynasty lasted going on four hundred years.

To return to the question of where Yax Kuk Mo received his charter to colonize Copan. A stucco portrait of him on Temple 16 of the Late Classic period shows him wearing a pair of goggles. Teotihuacan warriors wore goggles perhaps to deflect atlatl darts, perhaps in homage to the owl motif so common to that megacity in the basin of Mexico. But earlier depictions of him, on the other hand, show him in Maya costume. Some of the buildings he constructed were in the talud-tablero style common at Teotihuacan. This early building, nicknamed by archaeologists the Hunal, after the jester-god ornament of Maya kings, also appears to have been decorated with Teotihuacan-style murals (Sharer 2003). The body of a mature woman was buried nearby bearing images of the long-tailed motmot bird, which forms the "Mo" part of Yax Kuk Mo's name. This woman was not the bearer of Yax Kuk Mo's successor, but she evidently was an early wife. Isotopic analysis of her bones show she was a foreigner. Three male trophy skulls were buried with her. Sharer notes that it is possible these skulls were of the ruling family of Copan when Yax Kuk Mo appeared on the scene.

In 1995, the body of Yax Kuk Mo himself was discovered in the apparently Teotihuacan-inspired Hunal Temple deep below Temple 16 on Copan's Acropolis. The skeleton was in the appropriate place for the founder, the Hunal temple which Yax Kuk Mo was believed to have started; it lay under at least seven other temples like a series of nesting billy pots, and each of the seven temples were dedicated to him. Also, the many battle wounds of the figure in the sepulcher included a broken and poorly mended right arm. The portrait on Altar Q shows Yax Kuk Mo favoring that arm, and such a battle-scarred skeleton would be just the sort that could be expected to belong to an adventurous, possibly regime-threatening fellow sent off to found a dynasty far away.

The isotopic signature of the teeth showed that the corpse in that tomb had spent his youth in the Peten — not Copan, not the Guatemalan or Mexican highlands. So going on this evidence, it is clear that Copan was, early on, a dependency of one sort or another of Tikal, again reinforcing the supposition that he may have been a worthy candidate to found a new colony — and be gotten away from the central palace.

Yax Kuk Mo did not last long as king of Copan, about ten years (Martin and Grube 2000). His successor was nicknamed Popol Hol by archaeologists. As we have seen, before

Yax Kuk Mo, left, the founder of the Copan dynasty, passing scepter to Yax Pasaj, the 16th in the line of succession. Note Yax Kuk Mo's right arm, which some archaeologist's believe indicates battle injuries similar to the skeleton found below Temple 16. Detail Altar Q, Copan.

the breaking of the hieroglyphic code, many Maya personages were designated by fabulous monikers suggested by their portrait or their as-yet-unread name glyph, some of which seem a bit irreverent today. The cartoon character Casper turned up in more than one regal name, such as the founder of Quirigua who Yax Kuk Mo swore in, Tok Casper. Popol Hol, the second king of Copan, is a more sedate nickname being the Maya for Mat Head, which is entirely appropriate for a king. To the Maya, "mat" was sort of code for throne, a regal place for a king to sit. Popol Hol was a vigorous fellow, commissioning Copan's first ball court which he named for Seven Macaw. Seven Macaw was, as we recall from chapter 2, another name for the Principal Bird Deity. The first born of the Hero Twins dispatched with his blowgun, issuing in the present Fourth Creation, and later the father of the twins assumed the identity of the bird.

Popol Hol also was responsible for many more monuments and buildings. After burying his father in the Teotihuacan-inspired Hunal, he ritually killed the building and put up an east-west oriented Maya building similar to what would have been found in the Peten. A burial chamber was included in the building. Before his body was laid to rest, this building

Modern Maya in Yucatan with bones of his grandfather. Some Maya today believe, as those who visited the bones of Yax Kuk Mo and the Lady of Copan also did, that the remains of the ancestors are sentient.

too was ritually terminated and another built over it, decorated with effigies of two species of long-tailed birds, quetzals and motmots, representing the founder, Yax Kuk Mo, First Quetzal Motmot. In this building the body of an aged female was interred. She is called the Lady of Copan. She is the presumed widow of the first king of the line and the mother of Popol Hol. Archaeologists have designated her as Yax Kuk Mo's wife because she was buried near the founder and also because of the wealth of jade and art found in the grave. Isotopic analysis shows she was from the Copan area (McNeil, Hurst, and Sharer 2006). It can be assumed then that, as with many an imposed ruler, a local wife, perhaps even from a local ruling house, was taken to cement local alliances. This mausoleum is called the Margarita. Even after successive temples were built over the burial vaults, passages allowed access to the queen's bones. The Hunal with Yax Kuk Mo's bones was also visited. Smoky ceilings and organic residue of the sort left by dried up flowers indicate that the remains of both Yax Kak Mo and his local queen were worshipped, prayed to, and consulted for many generations after their deaths (Sharer 2003) Today, modern Maya in some villages continue to hold the belief that the bones of the departed are sentient and they disinter them and communicate with them in practices probably similar to what went on in these burial chambers.

After about twenty years, more or less, as ruler of Copan, Popol Hol passed on the torch (Martin and Grube 2000). And so it went for almost two hundred years when Smoke Imix was installed as king in A.D. 628. Smoke Imix distinguished himself by three things.

Number one was his tenure on the throne, almost seventy years, which would probably get him at least honorable mention in the *Guinness World Records* book for long-serving monarchs. Secondly, he dotted the Copan valley with monuments. Each of his stelae was huge and intricately carved. The reason he placed the monuments throughout the area is debated today. Some claim mundane reasons of state such as territorial markers. Others see them as paying religious homage to the mountain gods or quasi-scientific solar observation points or even as signal posts. Though covered with extensive texts, his monuments — owing to erosion and the poetic nature of the texts — have not been interpreted to the satisfaction of epigraphers. One of these monuments talks about one of the favorite topics of the Maya, the beginning of the present creation in August of 3114 B.C., much as Popol Hol was preoccupied with the same event when he named the ball court for Seven Macaw.

The third of Smoke Imix's three memorable events became known with the decipherment of a text sixty miles across the mountains at Quirigua. He was named in an A.D. 652 event. Generally, kings of one city-state mentioned those of another as a means of showing fealty. However, this kind of event, a "conjured arrival here," sometimes occurred between cities that had recently been at war. The monument could indicate that for more than 200 years Copan had maintained Quirigua as a sort of satellite entity. Or it could mean that the cities had become neighboring rivals and were now kissing and making up — with Copan the winner. Either seems possible. That the two polities would be enemy states seems natural given the distance — sixty miles, same as the distance between Calakmul and Tikal — and several ranges of mountains intervened. Then, too, there was Quirigua's independent economic base of river trade and precious stone quarries.

On the other hand, Quirigua had not made much of its possible sources of wealth, and in size and monumental constructions it was far inferior to Copan. The influence of Copan, by contrast, during Smoke Imix's reign extended across the bay of Honduras to southern Belize. Protected from the Peten by the Maya mountains, the cities of Pusilha and Nim Li Punit seem to have fallen under his sway. For instance, the ruler of the former took Smoke Imix's name presumably in a show of obeisance, and the king of Nim Li Punit is shown wearing a Copan-style turban. Because of the influence Copan had in the area, it seems likely that Quirigua had also long been a satellite state of Copan.

In July 695, Smoke Imix's son became the 13th in line of succession to the throne of Yax Kuk Mo. Even for the Maya he has an incredibly difficult name, Waxaklajuun Ub'aah K'awiil. This name is variously translated as 18 Images of the Sun God or War Serpent Sun God. However, in English he is best known as 18 Rabbit because his visage on Altar Q sits on an easily deciphered number 18 (three dots and three bars), and early commentators fancied the rest of the glyph resembled a bunny. Archaeologists have tried to change this nickname to 18 Jog with little success. Owing to many factors, not the least of which is his memorable fate as well as his easy-to-remember name, 18 Rabbit is probably the best known of all classic-era Maya rulers.

Eighteen Rabbit inherited a storybook kingdom. It was situated in a mountain valley by a purling brook far from the feuding principalities of the Peten. Presumably a goodly amount of tribute came in annually from Pusilha, Nim Li Punit, and above all Quirigua. Eighteen Rabbit knew what to do with those surplus funds. He set about developing a statuary garden that was second to none in the Maya world. It would be the envy of any art museum in the modern world. His monuments in the Great Plaza have been ogled by commentators going all the way back to Palacio, the first Spanish chronicler of Copan. Eighteen Rabbit was also responsible for erecting a number of temples and starting the largest hieroglyphic text in Mayadom, the hieroglyphic stairway on the acropolis. In short, he would probably have become a well-known Maya king even without his easy-to-remember name — and his fate.

Every one of his six stelae in the Great Plaza contains portraits of 18 Rabbit himself. There may well be an element of narcissism in his motives for commissioning this vast undertaking. But the portraits of him are the least interesting things on the statues, and sometimes there is a face on both sides. The portraits appear very wooden, like a man posing for a daguerreotype. His fists are usually clubbed and held knuckle to knuckle. But even if 18 Rabbit's primary motive was self-adulation, it is the sophistication of the abstract elements that cause the modern viewer to swoon when viewing them. This sophistication is in the service of depicting the king as the divinely designated ruler of his people. No doubt monarchs the world over commissioned similar works of art to remind their subjects that they needed to pay taxes to the state and march their husbands and sons off to war. Why? Because the stars in the heavens and god himself ordained it to be, the monuments tell them.

Portrait of 18 Rabbit. Detail from east side of Stela C, Copan.

The intricacy and execution of 18 Rabbit's sculptors wowed Stephens and Catherwood. They proclaimed, as we saw above, his works to be on a par with those created by the Egyptians. Being men of the world, they probably intuited that the elaborate scrollwork and the hieroglyphic texts gave the ruler depicted on the monuments rationalization for his right to rule. Today, thanks to the pioneering work of Linda Schele and Peter Mathews and many others, we know how exactly 18 Rabbit claimed he was so ordained by the celestial sphere.

Quite literally, ropes tied him to heaven. These drop down over him — from the scepter — and symbolize cords binding him to the celestial plain, the sacred realm. We know this only because Schele and Mathews tell us. It would be impossible to comprehend this notion by simply viewing the stela. It is much too busy in the way oriental art is too busy to allow a naïve viewer to ferret out such secrets. How many of the Maya in 18 Rabbit's time would get this? No doubt, the educated nobility would, and because 18 Rabbit was making claims based on a mythology known by the entire populace, the majority of the populace would at least dimly understand the claims made on this stela.

For instance, at the foot of the west side of the monument is a turtle-shaped altar. Aside from having two heads, the turtle form is almost a perfect image of the large leatherback sea turtle. This sculpted reptile is obviously a representation of the cosmic turtle swimming in the cosmic sea in August of 3114 B.C., at the time of the creation of the present world. If one views head-on the turtle altar and the visage of 18 Rabbit on the stela, it is apparent he is shown in the guise of the Maize God rising from the back of the turtle. On the date of the dedication of the stela, December 5, 711, Orion would have been straight overhead, and the three stars in Orion's belt represented the three sacred hearthstones around the cleft in the turtle's back (from which the Maize God levitated). Eighteen Rabbit is therefore claiming kinship to (and impersonating) the Maize God. This imagery reminds the populace that it is through the king's good offices that their corn patches keep producing. He jabs his penis with stingray spines and offers his blood to the gods for them. In the vision caused by this pain, he journeys to the otherworld and communes with the ancestors. He learns the secrets needed to keep the state prosperous and peaceful. Although all Maya let blood, no one aside from the rightful king could perform the ritual required to keep the city-state in harmony with the universe.

This stela was commissioned to be set for a ten-year period (hotun) ending. Maya astronomers timed this event with the first appearance of Venus as the evening star. As we have seen, Venus was revered as the embodiment of the elder of the Hero Twins. It was considered among the most important forces in the universe; and in fact, the patron deity of Copan was a jaguar god that was sometimes depicted as the sun and other times as Venus. (Not surprisingly, Tikal, Copan's patron city-state, also claimed this deity as its own.) Venus could not be taken for granted. It governed war and the taking of prisoners for sacrifice (Sheets 2003). One of the most important tasks of the ruler was to keep it appeased. The numerous glinting flint blades accompanied by emerging heads of gods or ancestors on Stela C assured the folks of Copan that 18 Rabbit was fully up to the job (Schele and Mathews 1998). And even if he were not, the fact that Copan was an ally of Tikal could never be forgotten. Along about the time that 18 Rabbit ascended the throne, the king of Tikal, Heavenly Standard Bearer, had begun to push back against Calakmul. In a very nice turnaround, he even took war right to the center of Calakmul, as we will see in the next section when Calakmul's king Fiery Claw was killed in A.D. 695. And even without its ally, Copan was insulated from the turmoil of the Peten by distance. The people of Copan, under the leadership of 18 Rabbit, had nothing to worry about.

Or did they?

For 43 years 18 Rabbit went about the business of a kaloomte, the supreme ruler of his city-state and several others. Among other things, in the 29th year of his reign, he crossed the mountains to Quirigua. The site was hot and wet with fertile river bottom soil. Today, a vast banana plantation occupies the area not reserved as an archaeological park. In those days perhaps cacao, a tree on which money literally grew, was produced in the area. For certain, as noted several times, jade was procured from quarries nearby. Despite all these riches, 18 Rabbit no doubt looked down his nose at Quirigua with its oppressive climate and its minor monuments of a few stunted stela. He did this because he was able to, owing to his city's domination of the site for more than two centuries. Eighteen Rabbit oversaw the installation of Kak Tiliw as ruler and returned to his pleasant life in his mountain valley.

For a dozen more years things went on as they had for the past centuries. But in the 13th year of his reign, Kak Tiliw received at Quirigua a visitor. He was a divine lord from

Stela D, Quirigua. The figure shown on this 19.5 foot tall monument is Kak Tiliw, the man who captured and sacrificed his former liege, Copan's 18 Rabbit.

a site designated as Chiik Naab. It took epigraphers some sleuthing, but they finally learned this was an alternate name for Calakmul. Two years later, in 738, Kak Tiliw set a trap, and the victim of his treachery was his former liege. Eighteen Rabbit was captured by Kak Tiliw — and, after a suitable amount of torture, he was beheaded.

Now, Kak Tiliw called himself a kaloomte and the ruler of Copan as well as his own formerly minor principality, Quirigua. Population began flowing into his city, presumably as tribute thanks to his stunning victory. Among those new residents were craftsmen from Copan. Kak Tiliw began erecting stelae, much taller and, to his eye, more interesting than those at Copan.

Such perfidy against the ally of a powerful and resurgent Tikal could be dealt with severely. But Kak Tiliw chose his moment wisely. Tikal's ruler, Heavenly Standard Bearer, died at about the same time the king of Quirigua moved against 18 Rabbit. The new king of Tikal had such things to do as erect Temples I and IV, two of the finest achievements of the ancient world. He could not be bothered with a mosquito in the corner of the realm. Kak Tiliw was left to do as he pleased. He raised the tallest stelae in the entire Maya world, two of which went up almost twenty-five feet. He also produced — or rather the sculptors working at his direction produced — huge altars with finely etched mythological yarns on their sides.

One of these altars depicted a huge sea turtle, and it told of Kak Tiliw's own hallucinogenic journey millions of years into the past. His dream ordained Quirigua as a mystical portal into the underworld, and thereby one of the great cities of the Maya realm. In terms of realpolitik, its population never reached more than a few thousand, a fourth or a fifth of Copan — itself quite small as Maya cities went. Quirigua's population was just a sliver of the megacities of the Peten. In terms of art, though not quite the equal of Copan in an aesthetic way, there can be no gainsaying of the achievement of Kak Tiliw's statuary garden. The ruler himself died peacefully in bed in A.D. 785, after 60 years in power and 47 years after he duped 18 Rabbit and sacrificed him at the behest of Calakmul.

Kak Tiliw might have gone on to be resurrected as the Maize God, as he believed. According to the belief, he first descended to Xibalba and then up into the heavens. He was attended by beautiful young women bedecked with jade. One might assume, never minding his pleasant fate, the kingdom he left stood in jeopardy. Strangely, his successor, Sky Xul did not seem to understand that within a quarter century of his "father's" death, his own successor would be deposed and the population of the town scattered. Although it is by no means certain where the threat came from, it is clear the villain was not the one we'd first suspect, a vengeance-reeking Tikal ruler.

Sky X's monuments continued in the rococo tradition of his predecessor. His best is called Zoomorph P. It was dedicated in A.D. 795, fifteen years before the fall. It was made from a huge boulder intricately inscribed with a hieroglyphic text. The front shows a king emerging from the gaping maw of a fabulous monster in sort of a throwback to Altar 4 of La Venta. The figure is double life-sized. He carries a shield — evidently denoting his prowess in war — and a scepter, letting the viewer know he is a king. As Martin and Grube say, "Every inch of the great beast is crowded with an exotic tangle of leafy scrolls and serpents, animated deities and glyphic panels." And this is just one of four such intricately inscribed boulders Sky X has left as his great life work. Altogether 900 hieroglyphs adorn his altar-like boulders, but they are eroded and not easily read. However, epigraphers have puzzled out some of what is said. Kak Tiliw, the conqueror of Copan, is paid homage to, and "dancing" is alluded to in conjunction with the grave of 18 Rabbit, no doubt boastfully. The place of Quirigua as the center of the cosmos is, of course, discussed as is Copan's status.

When Sky X passed on after only ten to 15 years as king, the Maya cities in the Peten were in steep decline. Part of the reason appears to be another terrible drought had descended on the landscape. The first iteration of the dry period fell about A.D. 770, and the worst years were to come in the 9th century. This drought was similar to that beginning early in the millennium when El Mirador fell. But this drought dovetailed with other problems in the political landscape. Perhaps owing to Quirigua's favored location on a major river, Sky X carried on in the imperious way a Maya divine lord would have during any of the favorable decades during the Late Classic period. The same cannot be said of his successor Jade Sky, who came on the scene about A.D. 800. His first monument was a stunted stela, hardly taller than a man. Though quite ornate and nicely done, it was a far cry from the stunners five times its height of the decades before.

The text on this stela again brags about the capture and sacrifice of 18 Rabbit and tells of Calakmul's role in this duplicity. It was dedicated in A.D. 800. Ten years later, a text on a building constructed by Jade Sky talks about Copan in an entirely different light. Now it appears Jade Sky and Yax Pasaj, the Copan lord who commissioned Altar Q, are friends and allies. They may even have co-celebrated the last katun ending together. Clearly, the forces of darkness were gathering, and both "divine kings" seem to have understood the need for common cause to keep matters from getting completely out of control.

But realignment with Copan did Jade Sky little good. His last dedication occurred in A.D. 810. In just a few years, not only was he gone, but — river with its life-giving properties of irrigation and drinking water or no — Quirigua was abandoned. Some of the satellite communities in the Motagua River Valley hung on with vastly reduced populations, but most of those villages were abandoned too (Martin and Grube 2000). The Motagua River with its enormous natural resources was once again a wilderness, broken only by the cries of the howler monkeys in the trees.

Could the twin maladies of drought and political instability have been enough to do Quirigua in? The winds of political change, by itself, may have been enough. The process by which the divine kings lost their supposed god-given rights can be seen a bit more clearly in the Copan record.

Sixty miles across the mountains, Copan came slowly back on the scene as a major power. Seventeen years passed after 18 Rabbit's beheading before the city erected a stela, indicating it was no longer under the political thumb of Quirigua. The sixteenth ruler, Yax Pasaj the man who commissioned Altar Q, ascended to power in 763. Was Altar Q an early distress signal? It reminded his people that his reign was part of a 350-year dynasty, and that the institution of kingship was not something to slough off lightly. By the end of his reign in 810, clearly the belief in the divine right of the likes of Yax Pasaj was waning. In the hamlet called Los Sepulturas a mile from city center, his supposed vassal had taken unto himself some of the trappings of royalty. Other supposed vassals such as the ruler of the hamlet known as Los Higos erected his own stela, generally only the prerogative of the holy king. He also possessed a hieroglyphic bench as sumptuous as Yax Pasaj's own. Even more telling, iconography on a palace-style building in the residential area behind the grand acropolis seems to indicate it was a "council house," indicating Yax Pasaj, divine lord or not, appeared to be sharing power with nobles (Fash and Agurcias 2001). In the last texts Yax Pasaj commissioned, sometime after 800, he speaks of the fall of the Foundation House.

This seems to indicate a gang of nobles grew tired of the dynasty that had lost one of their number, 18 Rabbit, in a manner that embarrassed the city of Copan and which was not supplying the rainfall needed for crops. Folk from all classes were suffering from malnutrition. The infant mortality rate was skyrocketing. The highest mountains within sight of the city had been stripped bare of every stick of wood. As a result it appears a "council" or some other entity had taken political control of the realm. Yax Pasaj, though apparently deposed, appears not to have been harmed and died a peaceful death about A.D. 810.

For that, Yax Pasaj was not the last personage who designated himself divine lord of Copan. Probably there was a royalist or monarchist faction — shades of the Scarlet Pimpernel — and it managed to elevate to the throne one final king. His name was Ukit Took. His only monument says he was "seated" in February of A.D. 822. The monument was to be an altar something like Altar Q with Yax Pasaj playing the role of the new dynasty founder. The monument was crudely done. And it was never finished. And no more was heard of Ukit Took. Unlike the Motagua River Valley, the Copan Valley did not completely depopulate immediately; but the density of people dropped off sharply, and nothing more is known of the system of rulership — if any.

As Stephens wrote just about one thousand years later, "In the solemn stillness of the woods, [the monument] seemed a divinity mourning over a fallen people. We asked the Indians who made them, and their dull answer was 'Quien sabe?' Who knows? Architecture, sculpture and painting, all the arts which embellish life, had flourished in this overgrown forest. Orators, warriors and statesmen, beauty, ambition and glory had lived and passed away, and none knew that such things had been or could tell of their past existence. Books are silent on this theme. The place where we sat, was it a citadel from which an unknown people had sounded the trumpet of war? Or a temple for the worship of the God of peace? Or did the inhabitants worship the idols made with their own hands and offer sacrifices on the stones before them. All was mystery, dark, impenetrable mystery, and every circumstance increased it. The city was desolate. The only sounds that disturbed the quiet of this buried city were the noise of monkeys moving among the tops of the trees, with a noise like a current of wind, passed on into the depths of the forest. With the strange monuments around us, they seemed like wandering spirits of the departed race guarding the ruins of their former habitations."

Star Wars II, The Empire Strikes Back: Tikal, A.D. 695–869

When Shield Skull acceded to the mat (Maya talk for coronation) at Tikal in A.D. 657, he was concerned about a great darkness over the land of the Maya. But to him that darkness was not the coming oblivion of the A.D. 800s, which swept into extinction all the cities of the central core of Maya civilization. Rather, the darkness was that which had settled over what he believed was the first city of the Maya, his own Tikal, about one hundred years earlier. As we remember, beginning in A.D. 562, Tikal had come under attack by Caracol, the huge city in the Maya mountains of Belize, some fifty miles away. The king of Caracol, Wak Chan, had been a vassal of Tikal's Double Bird, having been sworn in by him. But treachery similar to that of Quirigua against 18 Rabbit was afoot. The lords of Calakmul had talked Caracol's Wak Chan — probably by giving him his way with Naranjo — into switching sides and striking at Tikal. And Tikal was subdued (Martin 2005a).

For 95 years Tikal had not exercised the prerogatives of an independent city. No dated stela were erected to commemorate important dates. The peasants of the city had not been called on to build monuments. Their spare corn and labor were going to construct monuments elsewhere. It is entirely possible that from time to time the political-religious authorities of Tikal summoned the resources to put up monuments; but these erections, if they occurred, were destroyed by Calakmul or its allies during raids or temporary occupation of the center city. In any case, the upshot was the same. For the best part of a century, Tikal was lost to the annals of history.

Shield Skull determined to change all that. At first his prospects appeared dim (Martin and Grube 2000). Not long after his accession, Yuknoom the Great of Calakmul sent a coronation gift in the way of a star-wars attack. Shield Skull fled from his city. He had two great allies. Copan lay 168 miles to the southeast. The Maya and Mico mountains made it more or less

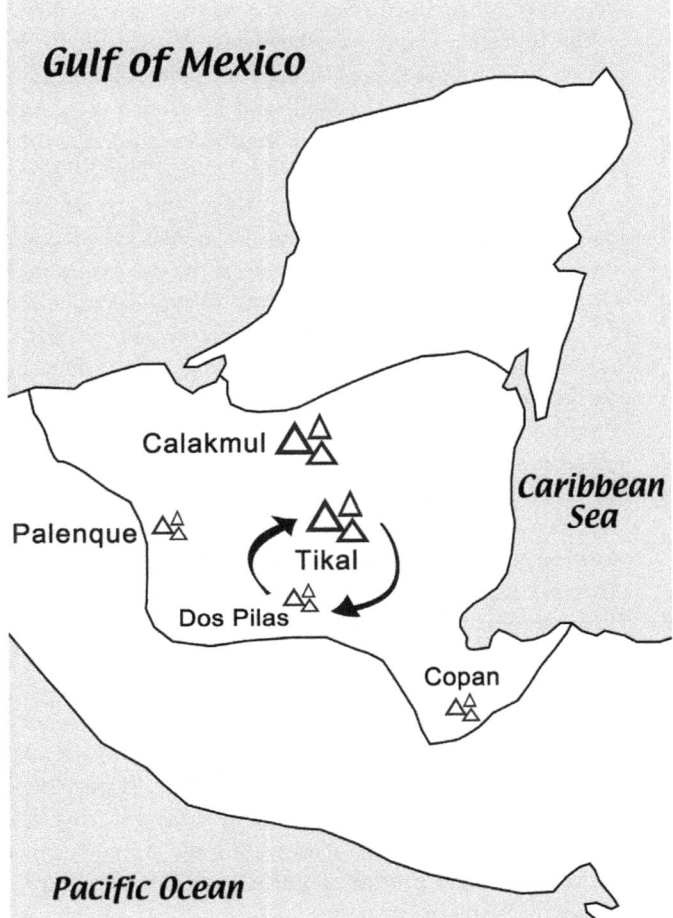

Tikal attacks Dos Pilas and occupies the site for a time, but Dos Pilas with the help of Calakmul turns the tables and strikes at Tikal.

invulnerable to attack from the Peten. By the same token, it was pretty much worthless as a refuge from which to mount a military campaign on the central Peten. The other ally was Palenque, under the very able ruler, Pacal. We have seen the relationship between Tikal and Copan. The reasons for the ties with Pacal's Palenque are not as well understood at present. It is known that they included marriage alliances. The affinity of the cities could have been principally strategic as both were targets of Calakmul's raids. A dynastic element similar to the commissioning of a founder of a line of kings as at Copan may have played into the equation. In any case, Palenque lay almost as far distant as Copan from Tikal, 155 miles to the west-northwest. Shield Skull fled to either Palenque or a location close enough that Pacal's warriors could protect Shield Skull's flanks. He remained in that area at least two years.

Maya warfare, as we have seen, was puzzling. A city whose ruler had debouched with his militia would by standards of modern warfare been ripe for disaster. But the practice of Maya victors appears to have been much less draconian. Economic and political institutions were only lightly burnished by the temporary occupiers of cities, although agricultural land in the hinterland may have been lost control of. Be that as it may, a formidable array of armed cities on the great Usumacinta River, almost all of whom had thrown in with Calakmul, lay between Shield Skull and his queen city. And Tikal does in fact appear to have been under domination while he was in exile. Yet the next we hear of him, he is back at Tikal and threatening the pretender Tikal, Dos Pilas. As you may recall, Calakmul induced a younger brother of the Tikal ruling family to set himself up as the rightful Tikal king in exile. It seems the ahaw of Dos Pilas had taken over as ruler at Tikal in Shield Skull's absence — all of this reminding one of the two popes in the medieval period when the French king sponsored a temporary schism in the Catholic church.

Now in an amazing turn of the screw, Shield Skull not only threatened the false Tikal, Dos Pilas, he actually succeeded in conquering her and the other polities in her domain. For five years he reigned as monarch of both Tikals. But the screw continued to burrow. Shield Skull had not destroyed the ruler of the false Tikal; and in 677, his old rival in concert with Yuknoom the Great of Calakmul, forced him from Dos Pilas. In so many ways, Maya warfare seems more akin to modern professional sport than modern warfare. The participants of both seemed to know each other and be on, if not friendly, at least communicating terms. It was a very serious game to be sure — as modern professional sport is. At times it could be deadly, and it always involved a great deal of economic wherewithal. But there were times when no one doubted it was real warfare. One of those times came in A.D. 679. That was when Shield Skull evidently was killed in yet another attack on Dos Pilas.

His bones were recovered and brought home to Tikal. But his remains are the only thing of Shield Skull's at Tikal. Everything known about him comes from textual sources produced outside of Tikal (Harrison 1999). If he erected any monuments in his home city, they were destroyed by occupiers or raiders during his tumultuous reign. In terms of his burial, he lies among the many royal and noble crypts on the North Acropolis, in Temple 33, the first great production of his son, Hasaw Chan, whose name in English is rendered Heavenly Standard Bearer.

Today, Temple 33 does not look like much. To the casual tourist it seems another of the many moldering piles of stones on the North Acropolis. True, it is centered on the first rank fronting the Great Plaza, and also it is taller than any other building of the North Acropolis. But compared to the restored Temples I to its east and Temple II to its west on the plaza, both world-class icons of ancient civilizations, it has little presence. That is today. When it was built, it pushed the envelope. It was centered on the sacred north-south axis of the acropolis that ran perpendicular to the highest point in the city. It was the most sacred spot in the most holy necropolis. (In chapter 2, we showed how modern lime kilns can still be models of a Maya comosgram — Maya cities, also developed on a cosmogram model — big cities like Tikal may have had several cosmogram-like arrangements.) Shield Skull's funerary temple covered that of an earlier Tikal king and hero. As we have seen, no disrespect was intended to that king. A ritual would have been performed showing his mausoleum had been ritually "killed," symbolizing the Maya belief in death followed by rebirth, in this case the birth of Shield Skull's funerary temple. The scandalous element regarding the temple was its height. Its roof comb pushed above Temple 22 which had occupied the highest point on the summit of the necropolis for generations. Temple 22 may contain the bones of the founder of the Tikal dynastic line, Yax Ehb Shock. Architecturally, though retaining the roof comb that had long been the mark of the Tikal (and also the Peten style), the building was taller and steeper than any yet erected. Temples were meant as sacred artificial mountains; and this one, indeed, gave the impression of such a mountain better than anything built on the Great Plaza at Tikal to date. It would become the template for Temples I and II — the east and west points of the Great Plaza cosmogram — and the other temples built by Shield Skull's son and grandson.

The erection of Temple 33 was Heavenly Standard Bearer's way of telling the world he was taking after his father (Martin and Grube 2000). He was announcing to Calakmul and its allies — in particular — that keeping him down would not be easy. Aside from Temple 33, the record is silent on what Heavenly Standard Bearer did for the first thirteen years of his reign. Clearly, he marshaled forces. Perhaps he stored grain in secret chultuns (caches) in case of a prolonged struggle. He could have recruited the peasantry to fight more effectively than in earlier battles. None of his strategy or tactics is known.

But it is certain that Heavenly Standard Bearer realized Tikal's war strategies had failed during the past century and a third — by now a full 33 years had passed since his father had set out to avenge Tikal's position without any conspicuous success. But it was apparent to Heavenly Standard Bearer that Tikal's problem was that it played the enemy's game. Calakmul had ringed Tikal with an alliance of friendly states. It had taken advantage of what in most military circumstances would have been Tikal's great advantage, internal lines of communication.

Theoretically, Tikal should have been able to employ its forces more effectively than the enemy because it could deploy them across the shorter distances between fronts (Harrison 1999). But Calakmul had kept Tikal on the defensive by urging its client states to attack at will, turning its supposed advantage into a hundred miles-long front that needed to be constantly defended. In terms of offense, Heavenly Standard Bearer's father concentrated on Dos Pilas, the false Tikal. The direction was south, as far away from Calakamul as could be got. To say again, Tikal had been doing exactly as Calakmul wanted it to do — directing its military force away from Calakmul.

Heavenly Standard Bearer broke with the past century and a third. He went on the offense. It is entirely possible that his hand was in the attack of Naranjo against Caracol. Both of these city-states were clients of Calakmul. But their enmity reached into the far distant past, in the time before a Pax Calakmul descended over the central area when both vied to control the resources of the area along the western border of what is now central Belize (Chase and Chase 2003). If so, the result didn't turn out well for Naranjo, as Calakmul's stone-shod sandal came down on its neck and the rebel ahaw was not only subdued, but possibly tortured and eaten. All this occurred just before Heavenly Standard Bearer was sworn in as king; but presumably he was functioning in some capacity for his luckless father. In the thirteenth — the number of the celestial realms — year of his reign, Heavenly Standard Bearer struck.

He may have concluded a deal with the ahaw of Masaal. Masaal is located on the northern rim of the Mirador Basin, and only about ten miles from Calakmul. We know the two rulers collaborated on a matter of repatriating the bones of a mutual relative. Whether this sort of dynastic rapport carried over to the military sphere is not known. If so, Masaal would have been playing a very dangerous game (Martin and Grube 2000). Yuknoom the Great had been dead less than ten years. And Calakmul seemed an empire very much at the pinnacle of its power — until Heavenly Standard Bearer's warriors tore screaming through the center of the city. Women and children fled (or ran into hiding) as Tikal warriors stabbed at fleeing males and chopped the stone faces of past rulers on their stela — and started fires around the bases of some of those they particularly hated. They incinerated all the thatch houses into whose fronds they could heave a torch. With the entry of Heavenly Standard Bearer's men into Calakmul, the balance of power in the Maya world tipped like a seesaw with a three-hundred pound man on one end. With that one strike, in Heavenly Standard Bearer's 13th year, the teeter-totter never again leveraged in favor of Calakmul, although that was not yet completely apparent. Tacitly, though, even the most partisan of Calakmul rooters would admit the city had fallen on hard times.

Among the luckless snared in Heavenly Standard Bearer's blitzkrieg, was Fiery Claw, Yuknoom the Great's son and successor. Apparently, he was tortured and sacrificed, but his body, as noted in the previous section, was interred in the giant pyramid that is known as Calakmul's Structure 2 today. Also captured was the great war standard of Calakmul. It bore the likeness of the patron god of Calakmul, a jaguar-god, similar to Tikal's own. (Some speculate that at some time in the distant past Tikal and Calakmul were closely related, perhaps like Tikal and Dos Pilas.)

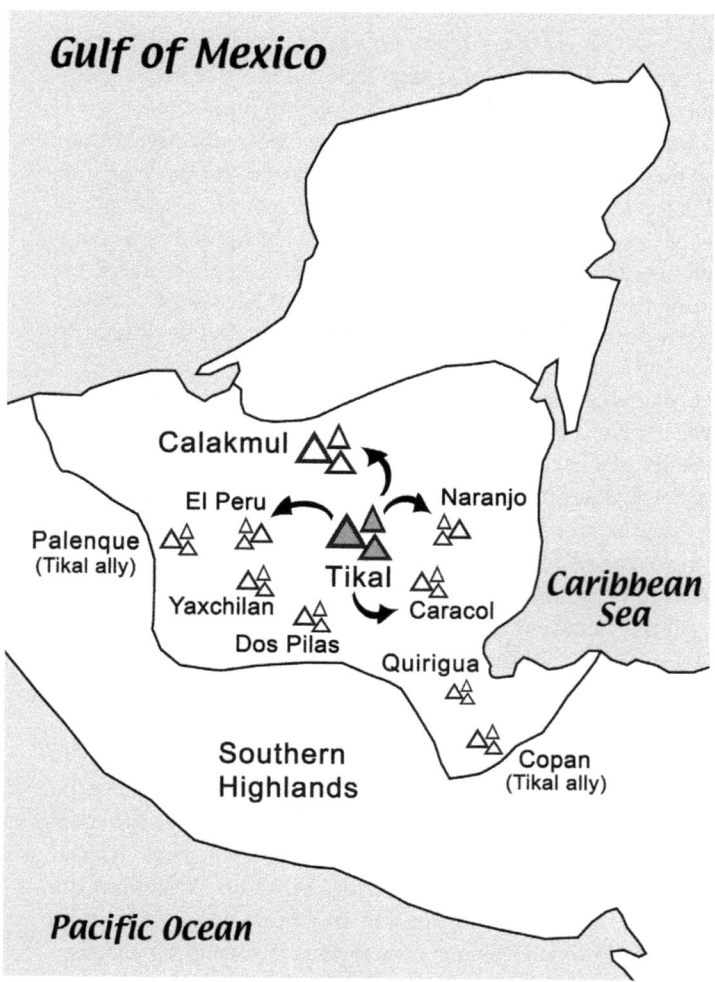

Tikal's king, Heavenly Standard Bearer, strikes a blow at Calakmul. Later, its principal allies are also successfully attacked.

Back at Tikal just before the turn of the 8th century, Heavenly Standard Bearer returned triumphant to his city. He entered the city riding the palanquin of the Calakmul emperor-king, he who had for so many years brought under his domination every city on the periphery of Tikal. The palanquin, like so many items used or touched by Maya royalty, was sacred in and of itself. It possessed the power of the great city. Over his head flew the great banner of Calakmul's jaguar-god. It was under that banner that Calakmul's forces had made so many successful raids on Tikal and her allies. Losing such a standard would be extremely shameful to military men the world over. To the Maya, the loss resulted in more than a simple loss of face. The banner itself, like so many of the appurtenances of Maya power, was considered a living source of magical power, power that now was controlled by Heavenly Standard Bearer.

Emboldened by this campaign, did Heavenly Standard Bearer set about on similar campaigns to punish former allies of his great city? Perhaps. Caracol, the city high in the Maya mountains of Belize, as may be remembered, was Calakmul's catspaw. Its turning coat and the subsequent successful foray against Tikal was responsible for Heavenly Standard Bearer's city's 133-year hiatus. As we recall back in the 6th century, Caracol's holy lord had been sworn in under the aegis of Tikal—but scant years later she attacked and evidently sacked Tikal, all urged on and helped by Calakmul. Now Caracol suffered a similar hiatus, lasting about a hundred years, during which period no monuments were erected or any textual references of any kind produced. It was as though it was a city under heavy tribute burdens to some other entity. No evidence remains of Tikal's involvement in this hiatus. During this period, Tikal's probable client state of Ucanal, about halfway between Tikal and Caracol, frequently brags on its monuments of victories over Caracol. All this could perhaps have been Tikal's way of paying Caracol back for her perfidy, by allowing her to be dominated by a fairly insignificant minor polity. Tikal herself does not deign to mention the perfidious enemy, at least on any text yet discovered.

What Heavenly Standard Bearer's role in all these events can only be speculated on. He helps us by leaving portraits of himself in full military panoply—with a rather archaic touch of heraldry hearkening back to Teotihuacan (Harrison 1999). That city in the Valley of Mexico by now had been sacked and abandoned. Heavenly Standard Bearer's outfit displays perfect geometrical grids—like Teotihuacan's streets—a neatly trimmed brush-like headdress and shell body armor. Clearly, he is proclaiming that the ruling line that Fire Is Born bestowed on central Peten is marching on once again. By the same token, he did not forget the original dynasty begun by Yax Ehb Shock. Most of the kings of Tikal lived in palaces in the Central Acropolis on the south side of the Great Plaza. Heavenly Standard Bearer chose to revitalize the palace of Great Jaguar Paw, the king who perished during the entrada of Teotihuacan-inspired troops in the 4th century A.D. It was the only building in the whole of the Great Plaza area that had been preserved intact, that is it had not been decommissioned and built over as was common for Maya structures. Clearly, the dynastic connection with Yax Ehb Shock which ran through Great Jaguar Paw remained of enormous importance to all claimants to the throne of Tikal, all of whom claimed allegiance through Jaguar Paw to Yax Ehb Shock, even if that claim was patently false (by the way we see things). A frieze high on the wall of Heavenly Standard Bearer's palace in the central Acropolis shows a Calakmul lord tied by the neck being brought back to Tikal. Owing to more than a thousand years exposure to the elements, his name glyph is obscure, but we assume the victim is Fiery Claw himself. Clearly, he was later sacrificed—probably after a great deal of torture to insure the sun would come up and the rain would continue to fall on the corn crops.

Heavenly Standard Bearer's further military victories, if any, evade the modern scholar (Martin and Grube 2000). It appears that he was unable completely to wrench the neighboring city-states of Naranjo to the east and El Peru to the west out of the grasp of Calakmul. And the false Tikal to the southwest, Dos Pilas, continued to taunt its mother city. Heavenly Standard Bearer's architectural accomplishments, on the other hand, loom above the canopy of the forest now covering Tikal for all to see.

At each *katun* (twenty-year) commemoration during the mature phase of his reign, A.D. 692, 711 and 731, Heavenly Standard Bearer erected a complex of twin pyramids. Most kings simply commissioned a stela, sometimes just a plain stone not even inscribed with hieroglyphs or art work. Heavenly Standard Bearer built temples. Was this a result of the

Temple I, Tikal. This building, as tall as a 15-story high-rise, must be included on any list of the world's most graceful and elegant structures.

tribute pouring in due to his victories over Calakmul and perhaps other cities? Or perhaps was he attempting to erect monuments that future raiders could not easily deface, break up, or carry away? In any case, these three twin-pyramid groups set the stage for his great work that would become one of the planet's icons of preindustrial architecture, Temples I and II facing each other across the Great Plaza. It is known for sure that Temple II was put up by Heavenly Standard Bearer. In truth, it is a bit squat, sort of the foil for the tall, elegant, graceful Temple I on the east side of the football field-sized plaza. Temple II is dedicated to Lady 12 Macaw, believed to be his wife. Archaeologists have sought in vain for her crypt inside the large structure. Because it is located on the west — the direction of death — side of the plaza, some speculate that Temple II may simply be a cenotaph or non-burial monument to Lady 12 Macaw. In any case, there is no doubt that Temple I is dedicated to Heavenly Standard Bearer because his bones have been found in a crypt inside the building.

5. The Tale of Two Cities, Concluded, A.D. 695–869

How do we know this skeleton is that of Tikal's greatest king? Firstly, his effigy — quadruple life size — was stuccoed to the roof comb in the year of his death, A.D. 734. (You can make out the seated figure only vaguely today.) Secondly, the eight-and-a-half-pound, 114-bead jade necklace atop the skeleton's rib cage resembles that shown on several of his visages on stelae and elsewhere. Also, a jade mosaic vessel with a male head projecting from the lid as a handle resembles one dedicated to Lady 12 Macaw, his wife. Among the items are some 37 bones inscribed with miniature scenes and hieroglyphs. One of these is among the most often replicated pieces of Maya art. It shows an image of the Maize God sitting amidships in a canoe, borne away to who knows where, possibly the Maya version of the Elysium fields. The god holds his wrist to his forehead, fingers extended forward. A paddler sitting on the bow appears to be a Maya king with a jester headband on in sort of a comic gesture. The stern paddler is fully costumed with a bone in his nose. He appears to be a god of some kind. Four anthropomorphic critters, a peccary, a monkey, a macaw and a furry rodent-like creature, ride along as passengers. They all appear to be whooping it up at the absurdity of the boat bearing them off presumably to Xibalba. (This is a literal rendering of a piece of art much explicated in many different ways by archaeologists and art historians.)

Another bone commemorates the presumably peaceful death of his uncle, Ruler 2 of Dos Pilas (Harrison 1999). As we recall, Heavenly Standard Bearer's father's half brother had long ago been set up as king of Dos Pilas and turned against Tikal, becoming an ally of Calakmul, claiming among other things to be the true king of Tikal. Was Heavenly Standard Bearer showing his pleasure for his distant relative's passing on to Xibalba ahead of him? Or was he honoring a fallen relative of great status? At this point, archaeologists can only guess as to which of those alternative interpretations — or possibly another — is correct.

In any case, these grave goods show a refined, ironic side of Heavenly Standard Bearer's personality quite at odds with the visages of him on some of the stelae that showcase a figure with shrunken heads dangling from his costume. Other images are of a man very full of himself as a regal prince holding an outsized centipede-bar scepter. This more delicate side is by no means difficult to reconcile with what is known of his deeds. Though Tikal's greatest late classic warrior — by dint of his defeat of Calakmul and capture of the rival king — he is known to us today as the man responsible for the Tikal skyline as 21st century tourists know it. He probably had little to do with the peculiarly Tikal style of ornamentation, which had grown up over the years. This included fairly elegant step pyramids with a tall roof comb and what archaeologists call apron molding — a series of overlapping, slant upper walls above a recessed vertical one — characteristic of Tikal. Roof combs are features of Maya temples in the Peten and in places as far to the west as Palenque and north as Uxmal in the Yucatan. Tikal's unique roof combs partake of a high-arching elegant simplicity that, among all else, were structurally stable, as most have survived to this very day. Only the front portion of the topmost register of Tikal temples were ornamented with stucco figures, providing — again — an elegant simplicity in marked contrast to the pleasant busyness of much of Maya art.

The man who may have actually been responsible for Temple I was his son, Yikin Cahn, translated into English as Night Sky (Martin and Grube 2000). He had lintels installed which bragged on Heavenly Standard Bearer's victory over Calakmul. Night Sky ruled from 734 to 746, for certain, and he may have been in power even longer; the record is unclear. Much as 18 Rabbit at Copan took advantage of the stability and wealth his father amassed

Top of Temple I, Tikal. This scale model of Temple I at the museum of natural history in Chetumal, Quintana Roo, Mexico, depicts the four-time life-size effigy of Heavenly Standard Bearer.

to restructure Copan artistically, Night Sky's artistic output challenged Heavenly Standard Bearer in terms of artistic and architectural production. He built Temple IV, the tallest structure at Tikal. It follows the norm developed by his father (and earlier Tikal builders). It consists of a series of telescoping platforms, ending in a temple with one doorway and a roof comb the peak of which soars at least 212 feet above the floor of the city. It is dedicated to Heavenly Standard Bearer, and originally his seated effigy lolled on the roof comb. (Today, those who know what to look for can still see the outlines of this figure.) In days of yore, the visage of Heavenly Standard Bearer looked from the western edge of the city a half mile across the structures of what — thanks chiefly to him — was the first city of the Maya. There he saw the other likeness of himself on the comb of Temple I overlooking the Great Plaza.

Although Night Sky's architectural development of Tikal was important, his skills as a general were probably of much more importance. Two cities were the lynchpins in Calakmul's containment of Tikal. They were Naranjo, twenty-four miles east, almost on the present border of Belize. Militarily, Naranjo dominated the eastern frontier. Just as importantly, economically, it controlled the headwaters of the clear-flowing Mopan River which a few miles below becomes the Belize River. To the west of Tikal lay El Peru. It was one of the formidable array of enemy cities on the Usumacinta drainage. In fact, it straddled the San Pedro Martyr River, which had canoe access to the great river. As we recall from the development of Tikal during the Early Classic period, control of the east-west trade across the Yucatan Peninsula was responsible for the development of Tikal as a superpower in the first instance. Wresting back control of these key elements of the economic infrastructure would benefit Tikal immensely.

Whether Night Sky actually came to dominate these venues is not spoken to in the extant documentation. What is known is that his forces gave El Peru a sound thumping. Its king was captured and sacrificed, and Night Sky rode into Tikal on that king's sacred palanquin. A similar fate occurred to Naranjo, and both cities — like nemesis Caracol in the Maya Mountains already in this state — fell into hiatus for a generation. We can only guess that the energy that may have gone into local monuments for those municipalities was paid to Tikal as tribute, and as such, funded Night Sky's ambitious building program. Almost as importantly, Tikal's share of the trans-peninsular trade increased substantially. The longest feather in his quetzal headdress also is known only by indirect sleuthing.

This has to do with the final iteration of Calakmul's power. It was during his reign that the dynasty changed at Calakmul, The Snake (or Kan) dynasty under which Calakmul rose to the height of its empire was deposed, and the Bat Dynasty under which Calakmul rose was restored. This signaled — we must assume — the end of most of the organized warfare between the empires of Maya's two megacities.

Although firmly under the domination of Tikal as far back as Heavenly Standard Bearer's first victory over Fiery Claw, Calakmul itself didn't know it was a goner (Martin and Grube 2000). By A.D. 702 — just seven years after the death of Fiery Claw — a new Snakehead lord calling himself King Scrollhead had sent forays into Tikal territory. He also set the monument workshops going. He dedicated seven stelae in that year. He also maintained relationships with the city-states that shared a frontier with Tikal. Naranjo's king openly proclaimed on his monuments that he was a vassal of Scrollhead. Perhaps to show that Calakmul was back on the scene, Scrollhead visited the far-distant Dos Pilas in 702, and at some later time he installed a new vassal at El Peru. Scrollhead exceeded even Yuknoom the Great in the number of stelae that he commissioned. The number seems to be twenty-one, including seven in A.D. 731. Understanding that the local limestone was inferior, he imported more durable materials. Probably in 731 he dedicated Stela 54 and 51 at the foot of Structure 1. It is an impressive pyramid almost as tall as Structure 2, and one of the two adjacent pyramids that gave Calakmul its made-up name in modern times that means Two Pyramid Place. Luckily for Maya enthusiasts, Stela 51 fell face forward onto the ground, preserving images and glyphs in a near-perfect state. It is nice that we have this view of Scrollhead. Otherwise, we might have only the perspective found on a Tikal altar dating 736 or so. It shows a bound Calakmul noble, who presumably was tortured and sacrificed. The name glyph is damaged and unreadable, but epigraphers think it reads Scrollhead.

With one exception, Calakmul was finished as a mover and shaker of Maya cities. That exception is a dandy: Quirigua's capture and slaying of Tikal's ally, 18 Rabbit at Copan, which we discussed immediately above. This event, as we have seen, occurred in A.D. 738. Quirigua lay far away. Lakes, rivers, and the dread Mico Mountains stood between it and

Tikal. The new first city of the Peten — or as Tikal thought of itself, the properly restored capital of Mayadom — had turned its attention to problems closer to home. In 743 and 744, Tikal's Night Sky, as noted above, smashed the nettlesome states of El Peru and Naranjo. At about the same time, Calakmul erected five massive stelae, as though to proclaim to its clients that nothing was amiss. In truth, the world was falling apart around its ears. Nearby cities began developing a new architectural style called the Chenes and Rio Bec, and former subject cities carved their own emblem glyphs on stone monuments. All these cities apparently slipped the collar, and the ruling dynasty at Calakmul was unable to do anything about its loss of power.

The so-called Rio Bec style must have been particularly galling to Calakmul — and pleasing to Night Sky and the royalty at Tikal (Braswell et al. 2004). It features roof combs similar to those found on the temples of Tikal. By the time these buildings were erected, the Snakehead dynasty had long been consigned to the dustbin of history, the place the Romanovs were heading and all dynasties eventually end up. The Bat dynasty had been restored. With the exception of a late monument dated 908 chiseled by illiterate sculptors who decorated it with make-believe hieroglyphs, no more was heard of Calakmul until Lundell discovered it in 1931, and William Folan, Joyce Marcus, Ramon Carrasco, and Martin and Grube pieced together its history more than a thousand years after its demise. By this time, Calakmul had fallen so far from grace that even the inhabitants of Calakmul were decorating their city in the Rio Bec style! Just as strangely, the last inhabitants of massive Structure 2 were not conquered in battle, they appear simply to have stowed their belongings in caches for future use and left Calakmul, never to be heard from again. In short, Calakmul ended not with a bang, but a whimper.

The restoration of the Bat dynasty in the fourth decade of the 8th century was celebrated at Tikal by allowing the palisades around the city to lapse into abandonment. The Tikalese no longer had to fear outside attack, even though under the restored Bat-dynasty kings a little sniping went on here and there. Only two temples — in a twin temple complex common to the city — pay homage to Night Sky. These commemorate a victory over a city in the eastern border region. They may have been built by Night Sky or by his son and successor called Ruler 28. Ruler 28 is known to have occupied the throne for a very short duration, from 766 to 768. He may have had to deal with the first iteration of great drought, which it is believed had much to do with toppling the cities of the central region. The first band of this drought began about the time of his reign, and could have been severe enough to cause complete crop failures in areas, but it probably was a cause for little alarm in Tikal. Owing to the city's varied economy based on trade and tribute, the drought seems not to have affected her production of great monuments. Under Ruler 28, Temple VI, used as a sanctuary for a god effigy, was dedicated. But the turning point had come — just a few short decades after his father had secured victory in the long running war against Calakmul.

The next king was another son of Night Sky. He took the name of First Crocodile, hearkening back to the king who blended the warrior traditions of central Mexico with the Maya ones of the central lowlands. Perhaps the need to call himself after one of the city's great icons indicated he smelled trouble brewing. If so, the record shows he erected two large but undistinguished twin-pyramid complexes. The difficulty comes mainly in the renewed activity at sites under the heel of Tikal. El Peru, Naranjo, and Caracol all began building programs, and presumably they felt free once again to attack, if not Tikal, her allies. The last great pyramid, Temple III, to go up at Tikal was dedicated sometime after A.D. 800. It rises to 180 feet and appears to be the work of a king by the name of Dark Sun.

His image — richly caparisoned in a jaguar skin — can be seen (albeit dimly) on the lintel of the still unexcavated temple. His bones were found inside the building. His father's name is known, but the father's reign and how he fits into the dynastic scheme is lost to history. What this appears to say about Tikal's dynastic history is that, like the sites in the southeast, the institution of kingship was being called into question. Was the stress induced by drought-hungry bellies responsible for the diminution of divine kingship? Or was it the diversion of too much of the city's resources to monument building? Did the normal grumbling of those made to fork over labor or grain develop into more ominous rebelliousness? Or could it have been the infernal warfare as assertive nobles clashed with a king with diminished powers owing to drought or infirmity? Though no longer directed by the two great cities, wars between cities continued unabated, as we will see in the next section. Or did a combination of two or more elements cause the political collapse that was growing ominously closer. For instance, did peasants under the leadership of minor war captains defy the king and attack neighboring principalities, willy nilly, to gain something to eat? Did these same folks, in desperate times, attack different quarters in their own cities? In any case, it is clear the land of the Maya suffered onslaughts of lawlessness during the years of the worst drought.

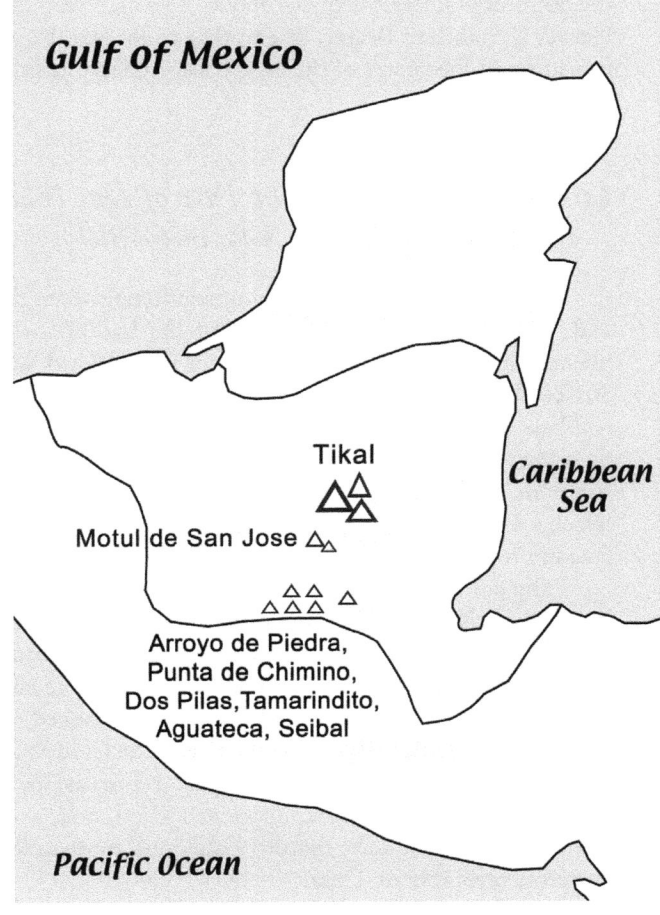

This map shows the tiny city-states of the Petexbatun region.

After Dark Sky and his memorable achievement in the dedication of Temple III, Tikal falls into another hiatus (Martin and Grube 2000). For three decades there is no building of note. The population begins to diminish. By now the droughts, which began sixty or so years earlier and which saw periods of several years, here and there, of relatively normal precipitation, appear to have settled in in earnest. Desertification was the rule, and it was taking a toll.

The next and last time a monument went up in Tikal was 869, marking another twenty-year katun, the previous two of which had not been observed. It was a modest stela — by this time an ambitious twin pyramid complex would have been completely out of the question; the manpower diverted to work on a pyramid had more pressing concerns, such as finding something to eat. It was set in the Great Plaza between Temples I and II and along the boundary of the North Acropolis. The man who commissioned the stone called himself Heavenly Standard Bearer, attempting to invoke the power and influence of the ruler who transformed the center of the city. It was the last heard of him. Mighty Tikal had crumpled to her knees.

Living by the Sword: The Fate of Dos Pilas, the Pretender Tikal, A.D. 646–810

As we have seen, the on-going conflict between the two Maya superpowers, Calakmul and Tikal, dominated the history of the Late Classic epoch. Many commentators have likened this period to the Cold War of post–World War II when the United States and the Soviet Union squared off against one another — at long distance. During the Cold War, conflicts were numerous, but usually these were conducted by one of the superpowers taking on a client state of its rival. For instance, the U.S. fought the Soviet surrogate regime in Vietnam, and the Russians tussled with U.S.-backed "freedom fighters" in Afghanistan. Israel, a U.S. ally, took on a Soviet one when the Jewish state confronted Nassar-era Egypt, friendly to the Soviet Union, and so on.

The pattern was similar during the prolonged Calakmul-Tikal struggle. The very first indication scholars had of this conflict was the so-called mid–5th-century hiatus when Tikal suffered a decline. It was many years before the reason for that decline was discovered, a major defeat at arms dealt to Tikal by Caracol, the city in the Maya Mountains in Belize. Ultimately, scholars determined Caracol was backed in this attack by Calakmul.

One of the main differences between the Cold War and the Late Classic Maya struggles was the fact that each of the principals did occasionally attack each other in Maya times. On several occasions, Calakmul sacked Tikal, and, as we saw in the last section, Heavenly Standard Bearer took the fight to Calakmul, more or less ending the centuries-long conflict on terms favorable to Tikal.

After the Cold War, many knowledgeable commentators spoke of a "peace dividend." It was assumed military spending would trail off to an insignificant level, both in the principal countries and the world at large, and wars of so-called brushfire sort would be a thing of the past. Although the threat of nuclear annihilation by major powers that had hung over the world disappeared, it wasn't long before tensions that had been kept in check in client states by the superpowers boiled over. A nasty civil war with genocidal overtones broke out in the disintegrating Eastern Bloc country of Yugoslavia, and former client powers such as the Islamic fighters against the Soviet Union in Afghanistan turned on their backer, the United States.

No doubt, the inhabitants of Tikal in A.D. 695, the year Tikal sacked Calakmul (and in about 735 when the Bat dynasty was restored), also expected a new era had dawned, a sort of Age of Aquarius, when vicious warfare and rivalry between the states was a thing of the past. We have seen in the last section how without the calming influence of Calakmul, serious warfare broke out again between Naranjo and Caracol, to the detriment of Caracol. Now we look at the equally unpleasant fate of the cities in the area of Dos Pilas, which we have termed the false Tikal because a breakaway member of its royal family established the city during Shield Skull's time.

The area around Dos Pilas is known to archaeologists as the Petexbatun region, because of the dominant topographical feature, Lake Petexbatun, which feeds into the Pasion River, one of the headwaters of the mighty Usumacinta. The region is located about fifty miles south-southwest of Tikal. Area-wise, it was quite small as Maya city states went, being only about twenty miles square, about half the size of the average. Aside from the city of Dos Pilos, four other major centers occurred in that area, Aguateca, Tamarindito, Arroyo de Piedra, and Punta de Chimino. Seibal lies just outside the twenty-miles-square region and figured largely in the politics of the area.

Dos Pilas, the supposed capital of the Petexbatun, was founded on swampy land far from a permanent source of water in about A.D. 646. This leads some researchers to suspect that a royal house from Tikal was invited to become the ruler of the area (Inomata 1995). A conquering king would probably have chosen the best city and simply taken it over, dispossessing or sacrificing the current ruling family. The first king of Dos Pilas, Balaj Chan Kawiil, who we will call Ruler 1 as he was long known, was born in 625 at Tikal. In 646, he fought and possibly killed a holy lord, probably the king of Tikal, who may have been of a dynasty installed by Calakmul and Caracol in the previous century. This led to civil war, and when the dust settled Ruler 1 was at Dos Pilas and Shield Skull was king of Tikal. The two were brothers or half brothers. Tikal was a large if cowed city of tens of thousands. Dos Pilas's population was no more than a thousand or two.

Yuknoom the Great of Calakmul, of course, did not like this turn of events. The compliant king of Tikal had been replaced by two other royals, both of which were sure to be trouble in the long run. Yuknoom attacked and subdued Dos Pilas in 650, when Ruler 1 was still a tender 25 years old. Tikal's Shield Skull was a tougher nut to crack. It wasn't until 657 that Yuknoom brought Shield Skull and Tikal to heel. He proved his mastery of both when he made both brothers attend a successor-naming ceremony. This occurred at the supposed Tikal ally, Lake Yaxha. Perhaps both Shield Skull and Ruler 1 swore fealty to Yuknoom the Great and his successor, Fiery Claw. Ruler 1 really meant it, and he operated under Calakmul's patronage throughout his career. If so, Shield Skull had crossed his fingers. As soon as he was able, he attacked Calakmul's new client, Dos Pilas. As we saw in the last section, the attack succeeded; and for five years, he reigned at both Tikal and Dos Pilas while Ruler 1 went into exile at Jaguar Hill, an as-yet undetermined site somewhere near or in Calakmul. Five years later, when Yuknoom was good and ready, he sent a force against Dos Pilas, restoring Ruler 1. In the fracas, Shield Skull was killed, and Ruler 1 returned to Calakmul to dance with Yuknoom at this great victory. In time, Heavenly Standard Bearer replaced his father and began gaining control of forces that would successfully challenge Calakmul. In the meanwhile, Ruler 1 lived the good life of a quisling, compliantly showing up at Calakmul for the coronation of Fiery Claw and allowing Calakmul sculptors to chisel a hieroglyphic staircase lauding his exploits. He apparently died peacefully and is probably buried in a as-yet undiscovered tomb in the largest temple at Dos Pilas called El Duende.

Ruler 2's position was anomalous. He came to power shortly after Heavenly Standard Bearer captured and sacrificed Calakmul's Fiery Claw (Martin and Grube 2000). There would be no easy life of a turncoat for him. He concentrated on consolidating political control of the Petexbatun. He appears to have succeeded in this, and all the cities in the area erected monuments with his name indicating their fealty. Even Seibal almost twenty miles away mentioned him, although some years later his successor dramatically conquered the city to make sure there was no doubt of Seibal's loyalty. He appears to have left the glory to his successor, a war captain who began his career as he ended it at Seibal by capturing and killing a Tikal lord in 705. Ruler 2 concentrated on making sure Tikal did not establish a diplomatic beachhead in the Petexbatun.

And so it went until Ruler 4 came to power. He began his reign in A.D. 741 by capturing and immolating nobles from El Chorro, Yaxchilan, and Motul de San Jose. Diplomatically, he made sure he had a hand in all the goings on in the neighborhood, as was his perfect right as the kaloomte. Then suddenly in 761 things went terribly wrong for Ruler 4. A hieroglyph found at Tamarindito says Ruler 4 "went out." And a week later Tamarindito came under an "axe" attack. No more was heard of Ruler 4 — and the city of Dos Pilas came to be a ghost town.

Why had Dos Pilas gone from a swaggering bully to a bankrupt in the course of little more than a twenty-year katun? Scholars cite the demise of Calakmul's overlordship as one of the reasons. True, but Calakmul had not been able to render much assistance for many decades. The root of the problems can be traced to the inherent weaknesses of the institution of divine kingship itself (Demarest 2004a). For starters, polygamy was practiced. This meant entire crops of possible pretenders to the throne were being generated, making for increased violence and strife. But on a quiet, everyday level, the royal class was also drag on society. Its members absorbed an enormous amount of the wherewithal of their communities to pay for exotic trade goods, and they demanded the peasant population erect ever more monuments. Fernando Tzib of San Antonio Cayo in Belize notes the word for "lord" or "ruler" was the same as vulture, and the divine lords do not appear — even after hundreds of years — to be remembered fondly. Even in Classic times, one of the six ways to write the word "king" or "lord" showed a vulture image.

The Petexbatun area provided a test-tube microcosm of the coming collapse of divine kingship, and with it, the central Peten. The population of Dos Pilas never amounted to more than five thousand, and it was dominating five local municipalities some much larger than itself, the rulers of which owed their position as community leaders to the sanction of the divine lord of Dos Pilas. It is theorized that the kings of Dos Pilas believed too much in their divine status and became too dependent on the loyalty of their vassals (Martin and Grube 2000). Seeing the opportunity to stake a claim as kaloomte of the region, the king of Tamarindito overran Dos Pilas. But this victory did the king of Tamarindito little good. That monarch crowed about his defeat of the king of Dos Pilas on a monument dated a year afterwards in A.D. 762. He also presumably claimed to be the new divine lord of Tikal, but that is the last heard of him or the nearby town of Arroya de Piedra. He was probably defeated by the headman at Aguateca. Agauteca lay just a few miles from Dos Pilas. It is supposed that the elite at Dos Pilas fled there after the rout in 761. Little is known about the king at the time. He is simply called Ruler of Aguateca. He too claimed to be the true king of new Tikal, and the flag he flew over his city had the exact emblem glyph of the old Dos Pilas and the real Tikal.

Among his achievements was ringing his city with a wall, the circumference of which ran to more than three miles. The wall protected cornfields and gardens and a source of water. The nearby town of Punta de Chimino lay on a peninsula projecting into Lake Petexbatun (Inomata 1995). The settlers there, whose fealty presumably extended to the Ruler of Aguateca, excavated three canals across the peninsula, removing 50,000 cubic yards of spoil. The ditch closest to the community was protected by a wall thirty feet high. In short, both communities were loaded for bear — or least expecting an enemy that was loaded for bear.

Who could that have been?

Seibal had been a vassal of Dos Pilas for two generations. But the fall of Dos Pilas allowed Seibal's king, Master of Fire, to not only claim independence for his city, but to be able to boast his was the true seat of the new Tikal. He too used the emblem glyph of

Tikal. Two other rulers in the area claimed the right of independent communities. And about this time, a group of peasant farmers recolonized Dos Pilas. But they feared attack. So they pulled down the stone off the façades of buildings the divine kings of earlier years had erected as monuments to their divinity. With these stones, they encircled the old center city and the nearby El Duende pyramid — with a double wall.

And then all of these communities attacked each other like male stickleback minnows in a jar. It is possible that outside groups also tried to horn in on the area. This area was extremely desirable because of its deltaesque fields and proximity to permanent water. Attacks came as fast and as furious as any outpost in the Old West. Among the first to go was Aguateca. It was stormed in a lightning-like blitz. Its elite class took to shank's mare, heading probably for nearby Punta de Chinimo, which they probably believed would welcome the additional hands and eyes to man the ramparts.

Coming upon one of those villages suddenly abandoned, Roanoke-like, for no discernable reason was downright spooky for 20th-century archaeologists (Inomata 1995). Expensive and portable goods, such as shell and jade beads, were left in place. Domestic pottery sat where it had been put for ordinary household reasons more than a thousand years before. Not only had the owners not had time to finish their meals before absconding, the attackers had not bothered cleaning out all the loot.

When the smoke cleared, by the second decade of the 800s, no one — despite temporary reoccupation such as at Dos Pilas — had been able to reestablish control. And indeed, in the opinion of most archaeologists, all the sites of the Petexbatun and surrounding territory had been abandoned, by everyone including the peasant population. The exception was the remnant population under permanent siege at Punta de Chimino. It grew its food in kitchen gardens using night soil as fertilizer, its population fearing to venture beyond its walls.

We saw in chapter 2 that a severe drought developed some decades before El Mirador collapsed. It seems likely that drought had much to do with the fall of that large early Maya high culture. But drought had little to do with the collapse of the Petexbatun, owing to plentiful orographic rainfall provided by Caribbean sea breezes and the Maya Mountains (Demarest 2004a). But imagine the stress on the political fabric of Maya societies in general if drought were added to their burden.

As we remember, El Mirador was especially vulnerable to drought because its water supply was dependent on shallow lakes or swamps that had over the centuries slowly filled with a substance known as Maya clay, indicating that the precipitate was a byproduct of Maya agriculturalists and, in particular, builders. As noted earlier, beginning sometime within a half century of A.D. 770, another dry period commenced. This dry period lasted about three centuries. The corn and other crops would have been severely reduced, although some production would have been possible. Climatologists have deduced this drought by several means. For instance, the composition of small shellfish known as ostrocods changed in area waterways and the isotopic signature of key elements in snail and other shells also indicated an increased salinity in some lakes, meaning less rain was falling. Lesser sedimentation at the mouths of major rivers was yet another indication of drought (Hodel, Curtis, and Brenner 1995; Folan et al. 2000).

Several periods of a few years duration within this cycle saw almost no rainfall whatsoever, meaning there was no crop production. Because of the various indirect methods climatologists use to determine drought, synchronizing their studies to specific dates has proven difficult. One of the dire periods most climatologists agree on was about A.D. 810, the exact year many struggling polities appear to have been pushed over the brink. The

Mirador Basin contained a population of several hundreds of thousands, but the rest of the Maya lowlands was relatively sparsely populated during the Late Preclassic. By the Late Classic, the Peten region was thickly populated with a population estimated from 3 to 13 million people. Any diminution in the food supply would have caused major disruption.

The period beginning about A.D. 770 was not the only droughty time since the fall of El Mirador. Climatological studies have shown, as noted previously, that the mid 6th century also hosted a drought lasting until about A.D. 600. As we recall, from the section on the Early Classic, during this period no monuments were erected at Tikal; and because of that archaeologists designated the time the Mid-Classic Hiatus in the belief that all of Mayadom fell into a state of malaise. We know now the first recognized "star war" attack occurred then when Caracol — at Calakmul's bidding and with its assistance — attacked Tikal. Was this new level of naked aggression the result of drought? Arlen and Diane Chase have shown that Caracol attempted a war of conquest on Naranjo for economic — not ritual — reasons (Chase and Chase 2003). Drought may or may not have been one of the factors that drove the highland city to such dire tactics.

In any case, by A.D. 770 when a much more pronounced and long-lasting dry period ensued, the 60–80 city-states of the Maya lowlands, mostly aligned with one or the other of the two principals — had been star-warring with each other for centuries. Their military skills had been sharpened. Should the need arise to use those skills for survival, the upshot could be something terrible.

On the other hand, the institution of divine kingship was particularly vulnerable to the misfortunes of drought. As we have seen, the divine king — as all political rulers must — made certain implicit promises to his constituents. Among the most important was that he was able to manipulate the universe by magical powers to insure rains fell for agricultural production. On a more practical level, one of the mainstays of the divine kings political leverage was control of water resources. Access to drinking and irrigation water in city reservoirs during the dry season was, it is believed, controlled by the state. Control of water was both a major source of power and revenue. If there was no water to mete out, the king's power of the polity was sorely challenged. Then too there were the inherent weaknesses of the hereditary political model (Demarest 2004a).

How many generations can be made to believe — even with the sanctions of the state religion — that a son (or less often daughter) of the ruler has the best vision for the city-state in an increasingly complicated world? Inbreeding among the various royal houses probably produced the usual number of imbeciles and misfits, which, as we have seen, the system accommodated by considering as demi-gods themselves. More importantly, the Classic Mayas acceptance of interlopers claiming fealty to a former ancestor probably refreshed the institution of divine kingship and kept it working longer than most such systems. And it did function going on a thousand years.

Early on, the institution of divine kingship organized the peasantry and secured the borders from all but ceremonial raids. The demands the kings made for grain and corvee labor were paid back by religious edifices that infused the ordinary citizen with civic pride and religious grace. But over the course of a thousand years, the occasional raid that cost a life or two became destabilizing wars of royal conquest. Even without the additional burden of a debilitating series of droughts, it is unlikely the institution of divine kingship would have long survived (Demarest 2004a). By the end of the Classic period, a sophisticated culture had developed world-class artworks and literature, and in some cities such as Caracol, evidence of a burgeoning middle class has been found (Chase and Chase 2004). It is unlikely the men and women responsible for such a system would long slough off all political decisions to a divine king. Unfortunately for them, the normal yearnings for political liberty came at just the wrong time.

First, the large city-states fragmented. Then in each city-state, the ruler lost control of outlying townships. Finally even hamlets and parts the city center began opting for autonomy of sorts. The rulers or ruling councils or mobs who took over were no better able to deal with drought and anarchy than the divine kings they deposed. The dire condition of the time allowed no learning curve. The centuries of sharpening their fighting skills in service to the Tikal-Calakmul rivalry were now used by former allies and fellow citizens against each other. The purpose of this warfare was mere survival. One wonders how many luckless peasants caught by their neighbors were sold as sacrificial slaves to better watered areas for a few pecks of corn. And how long it was before the sellers of the first batch met a similar fate themselves. Such were probably the fates of many of those who perished during that long dry period.

Individual city-states ceased to exist as viable political entities at different times over a duration of almost two hundred years. For instance, when we broke off the narrative, not a single city in the Petexbatun was a going concern, even though a few folks were hanging

Stela 2, Seibal. The effigy of Aj Bolon on Stela 2 at Seibal at 10.2.5.0.0 in the Maya Long Count calendar or about A.D. 874. Seibal was one of the few cities in the southern lowlands thriving at this late date.

on in a well-fortified peninsula jutting into Lake Petexbatun. Then about A.D. 830, a man named Aj Bolon recolonized Seibal (Martin and Grube 2000). Ironically, he hailed from Ucanal, the former vassal of Tikal. His reign lasted until at least A.D. 900. Taking advantage of the local rainfall as well as the fact that Seibal fronted the Pasion River, his city prospered. He erected stela as profusely as any king during the Classic heyday. Early on, in 849, he invited kings from Calakmul, Tikal, and Motul de San Jose to participate in a katun-ending celebration.

In days gone by, such a gathering would have been a tale to be sung from the rafters. It appears not even Aj Bolon was impressed. Many of his seventeen or so stela were adorned with men, probably images of Aj Bolon himself, wearing contemporary Mexican attire and sculpted in Mexican style. In days gone by, these monuments gave archaeologist pause. Did this mean an entrada of Mexican warriors penetrated the southern lowlands? It seemed that way. Now it is clear that the classic Maya model of divine kingship did not inspire even the local man who claimed to be a divine king. He sought his model of kingship elsewhere.

By the same token, the collapse of the political leadership which had erected monuments and other telltale signs of a vibrant population did not mean a population no longer inhabited an area. For instance, at Tikal, the population peaked shortly after A.D. 700 at something between 50,000 and over 100,000. By A.D. 850 it had fallen to about 20 percent of its highest number (Haviland 2003). In A.D. 950 five percent of the peak population could still be found in the area. During these bad years, scrapes over water and the more fertile lands were incessant. Finally, the forces of disorder and drought overcame even the few favored enclaves like Seibal where some sort of civil order had been sustained. The population of the Peten collapsed to an insignificant level.

True as this may have been for the Peten and sites ruled by divine kings, it seems much less true in outlying areas such as Belize to the east and the northern Yucatan Peninsula. Laminai, for instance, the great Preclassic site in northern Belize, appears to have continued through the Classic period into the Postclassic without suffering any "collapse" at all. Other smaller sites in Belize may have survived because the institution of kingship had never taken hold in the same way as in the core area of the Peten. Always, in Maya political organization there was tension between kinship and kingship.

In the Peten, kingship won out as the more important of the two and the needs of family — as expressed by the family patriarch — took a backseat. Patricia McAnany argues that in some outlying areas the family patriarch continued to function as an effective counterbalance to the overweening political dominance of the king. These areas tended to fare much better during the period of the central core collapse (McAnany 2000). Interestingly, McAnany argues that the rule of the family patriarch, so far as women and other low-status retainers went, probably was no less harsh than that of the king. But familial cohesion and traditional organization of the community presumably allowed these sites to endure through the hard times of the Terminal Classic in fringe areas of the southern lowlands.

By the beginning of the 12th century, the population in all areas of the Peten had collapsed on itself to a very small number, although always a remnant population remained. By that time, some elements — years before — had migrated to the north and at times returned to the Peten, in back and forth movements. We will discuss their fate in the next section. In any case, the rains returned in the 1100s. And when the rains came back, they were much heavier than in the period in which the Maya flourished in the lowlands (Leyden 1984). The great forest sprouted and grew to climax, making the environment more difficult for those in the Peten. And the vast forest remained pretty much unchanged, just as the Lindbergh and University Museum aerial expeditions witnessed early in the last century. The quasi-rain forest of the Peten and surrounding area had been seemingly undisturbed for a millennium.

6

Terminal Classic in the Yucatan, A.D. 800–1100

Discovery and Exploration, Circa A.D. 1830–1970

Thanks to the outlandish resume Jean-Frederic Waldeck concocted for himself, he is now remembered as the Maya Munchausen. According to himself, he was an intimate and confidant of King George III, Lord Byron, Baron von Humboldt, and — most impressively — the fictional character, Beau Brummell. If all that wasn't enough, he also claimed to have visited Marie Antoinette shortly before she trekked to the gallows. Among his acquaintances were those that sent her there, specifically Robespierre. He sometimes claimed to be a count, other times a baron, and sometimes a duke, as the circumstances demanded. For all this, Waldeck's CV is interesting enough to stand on its merits (Brunhouse 1975).

Born in Paris in 1768, Waldeck boasted of having studied art with the great Jacques-Louis David, and probably really studied with the almost great, Joseph Vien. In any case, his training was substantial. It was through his artist craft that Waldeck was introduced to the Maya. He was hired to engrave the plates of the Del Rio expedition to Palenque in Chiapas commissioned by the Spanish crown. Smitten by the Maya bug, which has bitten hundreds of thousands since, Waldeck applied for a job as hydraulic mining engineer for an English firm in the Sierra Madre of Michoacan, Mexico. At the time, according to the best guesses of modern scholars, he was in his mid fifties. Left behind in London were a younger wife and infant son, Fritz. After three years of indifferent success as an engineer, Waldeck and the mining company parted ways. Rather than use his separation monies to return to his family, he made his way to Mexico City and earned a living catch-as-catch-can while plotting strategies to visit the fabulous ruins in lower Mexico.

It took him six years to find the wherewithal to wend his way to Palenque where he endured more than a year at the jungle-shrouded site in pouring rains and grinding poverty. To the modern traveler, Palenque is one of the most glorious of all Maya sites, owing in no small measure to its tropical verdure. In the days before electricity and sheltered transport, it could be a hellhole. Even the indefatigable Stephens and Catherwood, men half Waldeck's age, who on muleback had traveled the best part of a thousand miles around Central America, showed the white feather at Palenque. The heat and downpours tried their souls, but the site's insect population, notably the ticks and bot flies, were what did them in. After a sojourn of a couple of weeks, they moved on to the drier Yucatan. They made vague plans to return to the beautiful ruins in the great forest — but they never did. Waldeck, on the other hand, stayed for more than a year. When a completely empty wallet made it impossible for him to afford the scant luxury of the nearby village, he fashioned a hut at the ruins (or renovated a standing Maya building) and stayed there, living on goodness knows what.

Despite the purity of his lifeways, Waldeck's Munchausen–like properties found their way into his drawings and writings. He is perhaps best known for his depiction of certain Maya hieroglyphs as stacked masks that can be mistaken for nothing but pachyderms, owing to the enlarged ears and so on. If Waldeck was still with us to defend himself, he would probably note the state of erosion of many of the glyphs and point to the mammoth bones he'd seen in Mexican collections. He was merely, he'd claim, connecting what he supposed were the dots. Understandable as that may be, it does not explain the four identical statues with European faces clothed in nothing more than straw mantles and helmets which he placed atop the Pyramid of the Magician at Uxmal — in the Yucatan where he moved on to from Palenque.

According to Waldeck's drawings, there were four such guardians of the topmost tier of this building, all of which, he claimed, to have carefully buried to keep safe from looters (and later archaeologists). Waldeck returned to Paris from Mexico at the age of seventy. He spent his remaining years telling whoppers and cadging drinks in the city of his birth. He lasted another thirty-nine years dying at the supposed age of 109. Not a whiff of evidence has ever been found of his buried guardians from the Pyramid of the Magician. Nor have the models been located for many other fanciful drawings he made.

So was Waldeck an outright fraud? An extremely hard heart would be required to claim that a man who had put up with what he did for his archaeology, peculiar as it might be, as an outright mountebank, even if the evidence points in that direction. Augustus and Alice (née Dixon) Le Plongeon can be regarded in a similar vein. Augustus was born on the isle of Jersey in 1825 and compiled an even more impressive resume than Waldeck (Desmond and Messinger 1988). He graduated from the Ecole Polytechnique in Paris at the age of nineteen and almost immediately thereafter managed to get himself shipwrecked on the coast of South America.

Augustus made a living as a teacher in Chile until news of the gold rush drew him to California. There he apprenticed himself to a medical doctor. He then returned to Europe, England this time, and learned photography. Back in San Francisco he opened a photo studio. In the early 1860s, he relocated to Lima, Peru, where he photographed ruins for Ephraim Squier's archaeological investigation of Inca sites. Then came another sojourn in England. He studied ancient texts in the British Library and upgraded his photo technique, the latter of which earned him a wife and photo apprentice. Then it was off to the Yucatan. For the best part of a dozen years he and Alice Dixon poked about the peninsula. Though drier and less insect-ridden than Palenque, the Yucatan for much of the year can be incredibly hot. A much worse trial by far, though, was the War of the Castes, then in its twenty-fifth year.

As we will see in the final section of this book, the War of the Castes was the last Maya attempt at setting up an independent state. During the prolonged struggle, native peoples warred against Mexican authority in all quarters of the Yucatan. Owing to indifferent interest in the task, the government secured the settled northern and western portions of the peninsula and allowed the rebel Santa Cruz Maya to have their way elsewhere, including the location of many ruins. Equal to the task, the Le Plongeons learned to speak Yucatec Maya and shared their views that the Maya was the protocivilization of the entire world.

All this was not always enough to insure the cooperation of the locals so Le Plongeon resorted to hocus pocus. For instance, one December day in 1875, a group of foreign visitors came to visit the Le Plongeons working at the great site of Chichen Itza. The male member of the investigating team could hardly be bothered to welcome them. He was in a trance-like state (Brunhouse 1975). All of a sudden, he stalked to a mound not far from the great ball court and pointed at the ground. His workers excavated the spot, unearthing a sculpture of a human-headed jaguar. Le Plongeon directed the men to keep digging. When more than twenty feet down, they came upon a larger-than-life-size monument of a man on his back, head and knees raised, wearing a peculiar square headdress with a hollow vessel in the chest cavity. He called this statue "Chacmool." The term means red jaguar. The name was suggested by his workers.

Le Plongeon's performance was so impressive that grandchildren of the workers related similar incidents to the sometime American consul of Merida, sometime amateur archaeologist Edward Thompson. (Thompson dredged the sacred well at Chichen Itza recovering at least sixteen pounds of gold artifacts, most of which ended up in collections at a famous university in Boston. The socialist Cardenas regime of the 1930s demanded the return of these treasures. At last check, the Mexican government was still asking for their repatriation.) No doubt Le Plongeon's foreign visitors may have suspected artifice in his remarkable method. But could it have been entirely fake? The first increment of this performance could be easily a matter of sleight of hand, but how could Le Plongeon possibly plant a motor scooter-sized artwork twenty feet down? Clearly, Le Plongeon had the intuition shown by many archaeologists. Stephens, at Uxmal, dug a hole and found the two-headed jaguar throne on the east side of the Place of the Governors. As we have seen earlier in these pages, Blom and Stirling made intuitive guesses on meager evidence that later yielded pay dirt. At the very least, Le Plongeon was an unusually lucky excavator.

In the choice of his theoretical superstructure, he was not nearly so fortunate. Nor was luck with him in being exposed to the ideas of Brasseur de Braumbourg. A French cleric, Brasseur was the most learned man working in Mesoamerican studies in the middle 19th century (Coe 1992). He was conversant with a number of Maya languages, and his reputation allowed him access to the Spanish archives of the Indies in Seville, a place few foreigners (or even Spaniards) were admitted. Among Brasseur's great works was the discovery and translation of Bishop Landa's *Relacion*. Landa's book provides the best eye witness account of the Yucatan Maya at time of contact. It also contained the so-called Maya alphabet which allowed 20th-century scholars to crack Maya hieroglyphs.

For all this, Brasseur was given to wild speculations. His worst was a belief in the continent of Atlantis acting as a land bridge between the civilized parts of the Mediterranean and Mesoamerica. Brasseur was hardly alone in the belief of a lost continent. The great classic Greek philosopher, Plato, who we may remember placed the sun at the center of the solar system, posited such a large island beyond Gibraltar. That a civilization which erected pyramids and wrote in hieroglyphs would somehow be in contact with others which did the same is reasonable, almost everyone would admit—at least as a starting point of an investigation. The theory's name was diffusionism, and variants of it have been in good odor up until almost the present day. Claiming the diffusion occurred via a landmass in the Atlantic that all trace of has since been lost, as Brasseur did, did not stretch 19th-century sensibilities to the breaking point. Brasseur even went so far as to say it was the Maya who influenced the ancient Egyptians, and from there his ideas got weirder and weirder.

Le Plongeon's theories went beyond Brasseur. For a time, his ideas were taken up by the Theosophists, a group founded by the Russian spiritualist Madame Blavatsky and a couple of like-minded Americans. Today, the Theosophists are credited as the fountain source of New Age thinking; and in their day, they proclaimed all religions held but a sliver of the truth. Among the points on which the founders of this society and Le Plongeon agreed was the proper way to have one's photo taken. One's eyes must bore into the viewer with a penetrating gaze hinting at great but as yet unexpressed truths. For that, support for the Le Plongeon's excavations and theories dried up perhaps because of Le Plongeon's insistence on ideas such as the Maya first discovered and used telegraph-like devices. First, Pierre Lorrilard, the French-American tobacco magnate who underwrote in part archaeological investigations in Mesoamerica, cut them loose, and finally even the Theosophists could not see merit in their ideas. Though close to dead broke, the Le Plongeons retired to an apartment in Brooklyn and self-published their last work. Both died in the first decade of the 20th century, he in his 83rd year, she in her 59th.

History has judged the Le Plongeons harshly. However, it might be fairer to evaluate them on their lasting contributions rather than their eccentricities, a few of which even the most workaday scientist exhibits. (It's reputed, for instance, that Isaac Newton, the father of physics and calculus, believed in astrology and other outlandish pseudo sciences.) The discovery of the chacmool figure at Chichen Itza was a major find, even if modern archaeologists would be appalled at Le Plongeon's excavation technique. The chacmool figure can even be considered a major diagnostic feature of Chichen Itza and its boon times. Subsequently, ten similar figures were found at the site, all of which are called by the generic term, chacmool. Then, even more startling, chacmools turned up in excavations at the site of Tula, eight hundred miles away in central Mexico. Closer examination showed many similar artistic motifs at both sites, such as atlatl-bearing warrior sculptures, buildings with rounded column galleries, and so on.

In the intervening years, archaeologists have tussled with explanations for the similarity between these ancient cities — Tula in the highlands of central Mexico and Chichen Itza, in north central Yucatan, an entire country distant. Truth to tell, the conventional archaeological beliefs even during the 20th century in the hands of men from the best universities — looked at through the prism of the conventional wisdom of the early 21st century — seem almost as fantastic as Le Plongeon's theories.

Desire Charnay, 1828–1915, was another French archaeological explorer who stopped off in the United States on his way to Mexico (Brunhouse 1975). Although an "amateur," his ideas profoundly influenced the 20th-century professionals. As a young man in New Orleans, he was exposed to Stephens' narratives of Maya discoveries. He admired the success of Stephens' books, and evidently in order to emulate it, he tried to copy the objective, empirical approach of Stephens and Catherwood. His photographs of the ruins are, even today, stunning, and he labored under the tropical sun using the latest papier-mâché technologies to produce casts of Mexican monuments. But his early immersion in continental rationalism got the better of him.

Charnay was impressed by some of the material he found in the "ethnohistories" left by the Aztecs. The Aztecs were Johnny-come-lateiles to Mesoamerican civilizations, having arrived from the frontier provinces of the desert Southwest scant centuries before Spanish contact. They in fact seem to be related to the Shoshones and Comanches of North America. In the valley of Central Mexico, the Aztec quickly brushed off their bucolic ways and pushed to the political forefront. As with many folks lacking a proper pedigree, they concocted their own. After the conquest, Spanish monks encouraged Aztec intellectuals to chronicle their past. (Maya in the Yucatan also set chronicles to paper.) The resulting "ethnohistories" have given Western scholars much food for thought. Although for the most part written in Spanish, the philosophical concepts and the way of rendering historical events reflected a native American viewpoint. The Aztecs looked back to a people they called the Toltecs as their spiritual and political forebears. The identity of the Toltecs had been an open question before Charnay came on the scene. Teotihuacan, the great ruined city, less than three dozen miles northeast of the Aztec capital was an early favorite as their seat.

Charnay proposed as the Aztec ancestral capital Tula, Hidalgo. Tula lies just forty miles north of Mexico City (and the old Aztec capital) and not far from Teotihuacan, which had been abandoned before the rise of Tula. In the intervening century and a third, Tula has generally been the seat of choice for the homeland of the "Toltecs." Conferred on it was the ancient title of Tollan, the place of the reeds or cattails. The image of the mat as the figurative throne of Mesoamerican kings has come up before in this narrative, and it is believed that the cattail rushes were the material the mat was constructed of. As we may remember from our discussion of Copan, the place of reeds where the king of Copan was affirmed in office could not have been Tula, as that city came on the scene much later.

It is entirely possible that the image of a place of cattails was metaphorical and may have changed with the times. It probably harkened back to the cleft in the reptile's back at the beginning of the fourth creation, which presumably was a primordial marsh. But in regard to the mysterious "Toltec" forebears of the Aztec ethnohistories, Charney designated as their homebase, Tula, the place that is still most favored by a preponderance of archaeologists as the Aztec place of cattails reeds or Tollan.

Charnay visited Uxmal and Chichen Itza. He found architectural and artistic similarities at both places. These similarities include atlantean (sculpted column) figures, images of eagles and jaguars eating human hearts, galleries of columns supporting large open-air rooms, jaguar-snake-bird images, reclining chacmool monuments, rattlesnake banisters or columns, and warriors in pillbox hats with butterfly breast adornments carrying atlatls (Kowalski and Kristan-Graham 2007). For Charnay that was proof positive, not only of "Toltec" culture but of its preeminence in Mesoamerica. Try as he might to emulate Stephens's empiricism with its deafening lack of speculation, Charnay was unable to resist the temptation. He posited an invasion of the Yucatan by Toltecs which brought a flowering of Maya culture. As though that claim was not wild enough, he went completely haywire with the assertion that the Toltecs were the mother culture of every civilization in Mesoamerica. He believed this claim was backed up by the ethnohistories of the Aztecs. The chronicles told of the expulsion of a great lord, Quetzalcoatl, from the place of reeds. This great lord and his army made an exodus to the east — the direction of Chichen Itza.

The 19th century gave way to the 20th. Professional Mayanists came on the scene. The new generation of archaeologists were educated in top-tier universities and supported in their field work by grants from major institutions. The new "scientific" archaeologists decried their forebears excavating techniques as ruinous, and the individuals themselves frequently as little better than treasure hunters. But they sometimes admired the evidence these individuals produced — as they rued their theories.

Early on — in the first years of the 20th century — scholars such as Leopoldo Batres and Herbert Spinden unearthed evidence that supported Charnay's belief in a Toltec intrusion in the Yucatan. Charnay said, regarding a column that he excavated at Tula and a similar one at Chichen, "If, as we firmly believe, the Tula column is Toltec, the other must be so too for it could not be the result of mere accident" (quoted in Kowalski and Kristan-

Chacmool framed between Atlantean columns, Temple of the Warriors, Chichen Itza. Note the sculpted Atlantean figures on the columns.

Graham 2007). As the 20th century progressed, the fly in the ointment was the conditional "if." Indeed, "if" one believed the Tula folk were Toltec, then some of the architecture at Chichen was Toltec, and therefore, those buildings would also be somehow tied to Toltec builders. The similarity between the sites, it was believed, was undeniable. But what was the evidence that Tula actually was the Toltec homeland of the Aztec ethnohistories? And as far as that went, why believe the Toltecs were anything more than a figment of Aztec imagination? Two camps evolved. The first held that Charnay, though grossly overstating the case, had hit on a core of truths about Tula as the Toltec homeland with Chichen Itza as an outpost of it. The second doubted the very existence of a "Toltec" people.

Confirmation (of sorts) of the first theory came when two Mexican archaeologists, Wigberto Jimenez Moreno and Jose Acosta, using accepted modern methodology, identified Tula as the homeland of the Toltecs. Among the many traits that pointed to Tula as the mythical Tollan or Place of Reeds was a sunken courtyard in a main plaza that seemed to hearken back to a reed-filled swamp. This courtyard, it was claimed, was the foundation house where divine kings of far-flung municipalities received their sanction. Even before these discoveries, Sylvanus Morley had begun a large-scale examination of Chichen Itza with the support of the Carnegie Institution of Washington. Morley, it may be remembered was working at Chichen, when word of the discovery of Calakmul reached him. Showing the incredible energy that characterized the man, he assembled an expedition and headed off into the hinterlands of southern Campeche in a matter of months. In the decade before his jaunt to Calakmul, Morley formulated an Old Empire–New Empire theory of Maya history. The Old Empire consisted of the sites in the southern lowlands during the Classic period. All Maya sites in the Yucatan were New Empire built by the Maya fleeing the catastrophic collapse of the southern lowlands. The New Empire had two phases, one wholly Maya and a second later phase that was influenced by foreigners, when Maya sensibilities were altered considerably.

According to Morley, the purely Maya architecture at Chichen comprised a style known as Puuc. The word "puuc" means hills in Yucatec Maya, of which there is one range that runs up the coast of the Yucatan from the southwest and then juts inland. Sites such as Uxmal, Sayil, Kabah, and Labna, just to the south of the Puuc hills, hold the buildings best known for the style, and it is perhaps the most esthetically pleasing of all Maya architecture. According to Morley the Puuc buildings at Chichen, such as the Red House and Monjas in the southern plaza, were pure Maya. The Castillo, which one sees on entering the site from the main gate, the great ball court, the Temple of the Warriors, and the Skull Rack, among other buildings in that location, were constructed after the foreign entrada (conquest) from central Mexico. Morley had deduced the date of the entrada in the twenty-year katun designated at 4 Ajaw, some time in the 10th century, he believed. He was also aware of the stylistic similarity of the architecture at Tula to that of the later-phase buildings at Chichen.

About the time of World War II, Morley retired to Santa Fe, New Mexico, and penned a classic called *The Ancient Maya*. Even though Morley died shortly after publication, the book has remained in print, in seven editions to the present. In his first edition, Morley beat around the bush regarding the identity of the Itza, as he called the people who changed the architecture of the city. He did not specify the place of their provenance nor did he claim they conquered a prior Maya settlement at Chichen. In short, he was not prepared to say the refugees that settled Chichen in the second wave came from Tula, although he did concede there was such an emigration. The third, revised edition came out in the mid fifties. It was authored by George Brainerd who had no such qualms. He identified the incoming force as Toltecs, made no bones about their forceful conquest of Chichen Itza, and stated that they were led by the exiled king Quetzalcoatl (called Kukulkan in Maya), as specified in the Aztec and Maya ethnohistories.

In the years before and after World War II, scholars had poured over the various ethnohistorical accounts, from both the Yucatan and central Mexico; and the textual — as well as the architectural — proof appeared to be conclusive (Kowalski and Kristan-Graham 2007). The Toltec homeland was Tula. Lord Quetzalcoatl and his troops were forced from that city. After a brief stay on the Gulf Coast in present-day Campeche, they canoed around the peninsula and marched inland. At the site of Chichen Itza, Quetzalcoatl led his men on an attack which laid the inhabitants waste and took over.

All this proved the theory of a central Mexican Toltec invasion of Chichen Itza had been confirmed by the ethnohistories so far as these archaeologists were concerned. First, there were the archaeological parallels between the two sites of Tula and Chichen Itza. Then there were Aztec accounts that detailed the expulsion of a Lord Quetzalcoatl, and the Maya accounts that named a figure called Kukulkan arriving in the Yucatan. Both names mean "feather serpent," and the accounts were almost identical, given the divergences expected in histories of two peoples widely separated in space and time. Archaeologists were even able to synchronize these accounts with Long Count dates found at Chichen Itza. Analysis of paintings and bas reliefs at Chichen by Alfred Tozzer provided the final evidence. These images showed warriors in Mexican attire clashing with Maya-clad peoples. According to Tozzer, this was clear evidence of the successful invasion of Chichen Itza by the Toltecs.

The pieces of the puzzle fit together so well it almost seemed too good to be true. And as the 20th century progressed, that is exactly what most leading archaeologists thought, that the theory was too good to be true. Stratigraphic dating using pottery fragments showed that many of the supposed imported elements from Tula, central Mexico, such as the chacmool, were first developed in the Yucatan, and that they grew out of Maya traditions (Miller 1999). Also, it was pointed out that the art work and architecture at Tula were more coarse than that found at Chichen, almost as though the latter were the model and the former a poor imitation. By the 1980s, Susan Gillespie of the University of Florida showed that the historical accounts that had supposedly exhibited such amazing concordance of historical stories had actually been massaged by various sources to line up as needed (Gillespie 2007). The iconographic evidence yielded by Tozzer's reconstructions showed — all agreed — pillbox-helmeted, atlatl-carrying warriors going hammer and tongs with Maya caparisoned warriors. But there was no clear indication that this fight occurred at Chichen. The images could just as well depict new-mode Maya warriors clashing with provincial Maya at some other city.

Today, few scholars hold that there was a single central–Mexican ruler known as Quetzalcoatl that headed a "Toltec" invasion of Chichen Itza. Indeed few hold there was any Toltec invasion at all, much less that Chichen was an outpost of Tula. In short, it is clear that in archaeology, as elsewhere, things that look to good to be true, almost always are too good to be true. Also, in archaeology, as in other life followings, the very best people from the best universities can be just as wrong as anyone else. Fortunately, in academic disciplines there is sometimes as much to be learned from the process of investigating discredited ideas as from imbibing sound ones.

Chichen Itza, Circa A.D. 800–1100

Today, millions of daytripping tourists from nearby Cancun flock to Chichen Itza every year. What they see is a superlative Maya city — but also a unique one. Chichen Itza may well have been the largest Maya polity in terms of population. Many estimates range to over 100,000 (with some as small as 50,000). It was also, in significant ways, the least characteristicly Maya, and, by the same token, the most Maya, of all known ruins (Sharer 1994; Sharer and Traxler 2006).

Located in the dry scrubland of north central Yucatan, Chichen was colonized by a Maya-speaking people known as the Itza. Though not in use during the city's heyday, the term Chichen Itza is ancient. It was bestowed on the city after its abandonment but before the arrival of the Spanish. Unlike most Maya cities which grew up in the far distant Preclassic period and had a history stretching back hundreds of years, Chichen was settled late, A.D. 750 to 850. And it flourished for a surprisingly short duration. Mary Miller of Yale University gives a figure of ten generations, two or three hundred years (Miller 1999).

Who were these people, the Itza? The locals in the Yucatan called them "They Who Speak Our Language Badly," probably indicating their home language, at least early on, was not Yucatec Maya. Traditionally, it was held the Itza were a Chontal Maya-speaking group from the Gulf Coast area of the southwestern corner of the Yucatan. This folk were canoe traders and warriors. The great 20th-century archaeologist Eric Thompson suggested the Itza originally hailed from coastal southern Campeche and eastern Tabasco. He called them Putun Maya. Today, the matter is still under debate. Some of the hieroglyphs at Chichen seem to have Chontal components. Their residence in this borderland with people more exposed to the cultural influences of central Mexico, Thompson theorized, accounted for their "Toltec" habits. Schele and Mathews disagree. They have designated the Itza homeland as the central Peten, not far from Tikal. It is known with absolute certainty, as we will see in the next chapter, that some Itza migrated to central Peten after the fall of Chichen. It may well be that several different non–Yucatec-speaking Maya groups came together to settle the site of Chichen Itza (Miller 1999). If this is true, Chichen would be among the most Maya of cities. At the same time, it would be the least characteristic Maya in the sense that its architectural and artistic traits are much different from those developed in the Classic southern lowlands.

What is certain about the Itza is that they were sea-going canoe traders. Their main canoe port was fifty miles due north on the coast at Isla Cerritos, where a sea wall enclosed a portion of the lagoon allowing docking in any weather conditions (Andrews 1999). Stone jetties and numerous sherds indicate a great deal of commercial activity at the spot. The Itza's central industrial facility was also located nearby and a bit to the east at Emal, another of their ports. The industry was salt making. Salt pans filled with seawater during the monthly full-moon high tide then dried by sun evaporation. This single facility was capable of producing about 4,000 tons of salt a year. Archaeological evidence shows Itza activity at Isla Cerritos began about A.D. 900, a little bit more than a century after the city appears to have been founded.

Chichen, though situated in a barren and hot locale, was blessed with natural resources. The first was water. Thanks to the permanent water supply, it was able to grow into a megacity. The fact that the water sources had a larger supernatural significance added to the luster of the spot. The other significant resource was Chichen's location. It was situated at a strategic trading juncture. West of Chichen lay the heavily populated Puuc region with its rich agricultural soils. Also to the west were the cities of the Northern Plains such as Itzamal and Dzibilchaltun. To the east were the equally well-peopled Ek Balam and Coba, the latter in particular favored by rainfall almost as plentiful as in the southern lowland regions.

El Mirador, Tikal, and Calakmul all rose to prominence owing to their ability to control cross-peninsula trade routes. Chichen straddled a similar route in the far north of the Yucatan. Twelve miles to the south lay another city, Yaxuna, which profited from the cross-peninsula trade. We will see below how Chichen dealt with this city later in this chapter. But the case of Chunchucmil will give a hint.

By the 10th century Chichen controlled the salt pans and ports on the north coast of the Yucatan. Chunchucmil shared many similar business practices. It was a large market town twenty miles inland from the Gulf of Mexico on the northwest coast. Its inhabitants numbered as many as 30,000 (Hutson et al. 2001). It was a very unusual Maya city. Rather than erect monumental architecture to its lords, its population built ten identical pyramid-courtyard complexes for public worship, each site large enough to accommodate about a tenth of the city's population. The polity was completely devoted to commercial activity. Chunchucmil's main business, like that of the Itza, was servicing the salt pans along the northwest coast and trading product to the cities of the Puuc region (Foster 2002). In any case that was its business until it was sacked and razed to the ground, its population killed or scattered. Because activities such as killing and scattering leave little archaeological evidence, there is no definitive proof regarding Chichen's role in the city's demise or even the manner in which it so abruptly ended existence. But archaeologists connected the dots. The dots formed an arrow pointing at Chichen Itza. In short, it seems the Itza wrote the book when it came to cutthroat competition.

Chichen traders offered new products to their many customers. Turquoise from New Mexico became first widely available during this period, and it quickly became a valuable commodity finding its way into cache vessels that imbued the life-force in buildings at Chichen Itza and elsewhere (Andrews 1995). Also coming on the scene were easy to work metals, first gold and then later copper. The source for gold lay far to the south in Central or South America and also central Mexico. In Chichen itself, gold was worked mainly by flattening out product from elsewhere and then hammering images on the reverse side. The final outcome was a raised image, usually a battle scene in which the pillbox-hatted warriors (from Chichen) bested traditionally Maya-garbed ones (Sharer and Traxler 2006). Obsidian, jade, and volcanic ash (as temper for fine pottery) continued to be imported in quantities. In addition to salt, textiles woven of native cotton were produced in the Yucatan for trade elsewhere in Mesoamerica. Also, a limited amount of that most valuable tree product, cacao, was raised in favored sinkhole gardens.

The Itza's great innovation stemmed from vertical integration of production, distribution, and trade. During the Classic period, the power of kings came in a large measure from their control of trade. There is little evidence that the kings actually oversaw the manufacture of their products. The exception to the rule may be some prestige art goods and water. The divine kings claimed responsibility for making water fall from the sky and they probably claimed control of the substance once in reservoirs in the ground.

While the institution of divine kingship was collapsing throughout the southern lowlands, the Itza began establishing trading stations along the coasts, generally about one day's voyage apart. The Caribbean was dotted with wholly owned subsidiaries of the Itza state. On Cozumel Island, for instance, evidence still remains of such a way station and trading port. Similar stations can be found down the coast along the offshore island keys of Belize to present day Guatemala. In Guatemala, Itza traders paddled up the Motagua River.

As we remember from the first part of the last section, the Motagua River city of Quirigua controlled the only jade quarries in all of Mesoamerica. This source of wealth presumably goes a long way to explaining the splendor of both Quirigua and its patron city, Copan. Quirigua fell early in the Classic-era collapse. Then it was later settled by a people foreign to the region. Archaeologists have unearthed a chacmool figure at Quirigua, proof positive that the outsiders were Itzas (Sharer and Traxler 2006). The monopoly they had first come to exercise in salt commodities they now exercised in jade. In short, the Itza controlled the two most valuable substances; one essential to everyday life, salt, the other, jade, most precious in the way of prestige goods and essential for those claiming kingship.

Was the Itza hand in the fall of Quirigua? Given their trading habits, they may well have been exchanging Yucatan salt and textiles for Quirigua jade for years, even if their documented presence at their main ports occurred after the fall of Quirigua. Given their aggressive ways, it would not have been out of character for them to take advantage of the weakness of the Quirigua state. At present, archaeologists do not appear to have produced evidence for this scenario — even if the Itza were the clear beneficiary of Quirigua's demise.

Likewise, the role the Itza played in other areas of the southern lowlands is murky. Nevertheless, it has been speculated on for many years. Early on it was believed the Itza (or some other Mexican-influenced Maya group) had founded an inland state at Seibal, far up the Usumacinta River. As we saw in the last section, it is now known this state was a satellite of the central Peten city of Ucanal. But Jeff Kowalski of Northern Illinois University has shown that the hand of the Itza can be discerned in art work at the site, indicating pretty cozy relations with one of the few successful states in the lowlands at the time (Kowalski

1989). Farther downstream at the site of Piedras Negras, the story was considerably different. Mary Miller has noted that one of the murals which early archaeologists took as depictions of a Mexican takeover of a Yucatan city, include water and lush, well-grown tropical trees. She has deduced this battle occurred at the site of Piedras Negras (Miller 1999).

The buildings at Chichen lack an architectural unity, which might perhaps be expected from a multi-ethnic seafaring nation. The Itza also traded along the Gulf of Mexico where they picked up their "foreign" Mexican manners. Because there was no indigenous style of architecture or time enough to develop one, ideas (and possibly personnel) were borrowed from many different sources. The Red House, for instance, has two parallel corbelled arches and a roof comb reminiscent of the Piedras Negras-Palenque region. Could it have been the product of the successful war against Piedras Negras which brought workers and architects north by way of tribute? The Temple of the Three Lintels, on the other hand, partakes of the style known as Puuc. Because of Puuc importance, we will discuss this style at more length below. Suffice it to say regarding the Three Lintels, that unlike the Red House, the technology displayed in its construction clearly was not produced by native Puuc artisans. The proportions and design look Puuc, but the masonry walls and individual stone fretwork of the upper register was crudely produced (Miller 1999). The Monjas, or Convent, situated nearby, partakes of the Chenes style, another characteristic architecture of the region and quite similar to Puuc, though much busier. Though Chenes buildings may be found throughout the Yucatan, they are characteristic of the area about midway between the western Puuc area and Calakmul.

The edifice known as the Caracol situated not far from these buildings represents a break with Maya tradition. The view of the exterior appears similar to a modern observatory. Like modern buildings fitted out with star-gazing telescopes, it is round with a dome like roof. The loop-holelike slits in the dome give credence to the view that the edifice was used as an observatory. These slits align with Venus (Miller 1999).

But more important than these small apertures is the reason for this peculiar and wholly unMaya–like structure. It is set on a telescoping platform and its doorway does not align with the platform stairs. This gives the impression of circular motion reminiscent of the central Mexican god of wind, Ehecatl. As we have seen before, the Maya (and peoples of Mesoamerica) believed in shape shifting in both people and gods. In other guises this god was known as Quetzalcoatl. (The proper term in Mayan is Kulkukan but this god is most commonly called Quetzalcoatl.) This deity was enormously important in both its standing in the pantheon of gods and to the people of Chichen. Ehecatl was considered the broom sweeping the way for the rain god. When the wind comes, rain is not far behind (Miller and Taube 1993).

Wind, therefore, was important for the growing of corn. In near semiarid areas like Chichen or droughty times, such as the Terminal Classic, his importance could well have been much magnified. The circular building with the domelike roof was reminiscent of a cave. The Maya held that wind issued from caves because of the draft present in such places. Ehecatl was something of the Mesoamerican Prometheus. He is credited with rescuing the bones of humans from the underworld. He also created the sky and the earth and gave humans corn, alcoholic beverages, and music. In short, he was quite a guy. Many of the circular buildings devoted to Quetzalcoatl have snake-mouthed doorways. The Caracol at Chichen lacks this feature, but it can be regarded as Quetzalcoatl (feather serpent)'s temple at Chichen all the same.

The nearby High Priest's Grave is noteworthy for three things. It provides the feather-serpent imagery the Caracol lacks by its enormous fanged rattlesnake balustrades. The latest

Caracol, Chichen Itza.

date at Chichen and the Maya world was found here, A.D. 998. (This date is much disputed.) Finally, it is a radial pyramid, meaning it has staircases on all four sides. This sort of stepped pyramid was a Maya specialty all the way back to the Preclassic era. So with the exception of the round observatorylike building, all the edifices in the southern quarter have obvious Maya affinities, and in days gone by, archaeologists noted even the round building had Puuc decorative touches.

From here we head a few hundred yards north to the Great Terrace. First, we see the Castillo, which is not particularly unusual from a Maya stylistic point of view. It is a radial pyramid much like the High Priest's Grave, and it too has feather serpent balustrades. Though only about 75 feet high, it dominates the Great Terrace as the Twin Towers dominated the

The Castillo at Chichen Itza is one of the signature Maya structures.

New York skyline. It is Chichen Itza's signature icon. It rivals Temple I at Tikal as the most pleasing — and well known — of Maya architecture. Consistent with Maya practice, an earlier version was found encased in the present one. The northern balustrades of both the Castillo and the High Priest's Grave have far-flung tourist fame. On the equinoxes a shadow slithers down the balustrade, like an undulating snake. Thousands queue up to see the spectacle. Schele and Mathews point out that more importantly the balustrades connect the Maya to the universe (1998). Like the cords on the Copan stelae (and similar lines which Le Plongeon claimed were telegraph lines), they assured the Maya they were properly tied to the cosmos.

Among the finds made in the exploration inside the Castillo were a chacmool and a throne in the shape of a jaguar, painted red with inlaid eyes. These statues were aligned, the chacmool before the red jaguar. It is believed the ruler sat the throne and accepted offerings placed in the vessel on the chacmool's belly. Mary Miller has shown that the chacmool figure evolved from native Maya traditions of a bound captive (Foster 2002). The chacmool, unlike the bowed and humbled captive with arm across chest in gesture of submission, lies on its back, knees and head raised at almost 90 degree angles. He wears a cap reminiscent of the pillbox helmet of the warrior (Miller 1999).

A quarter mile due north of the Castillo is the sacred cenote of Chichen Itza. A cenote is a waterhole wholly or partially underground. It source of water is the water table. The one at Chichen amounts to a small lake whose surface is 65 feet below ground level. It is also about 65 feet deep. It is a practically inexhaustible supply of the fluid of life. The fact that the area around it remained unsettled until the Itza arrived must be a testament to the technological sophistication of the Itza and the lack of the same by local groups. Sometimes the cenote is called the Sacrificial Well of the Itza, and it is true that many a sacrifice from gold ornaments to full-grown human beings went into the well. Long after Chichen was abandoned, pilgrimages were made to the site.

To the west across the Great Terrace lies the Ball Court, the largest in all of Mesoamerica. The playing alley is the size of a football field, the walls rise more than thirty feet high, with the goals 26 feet up — not many game-ending scores were hip-butted into them. The Ball Court, like all ceremonial ball courts in Mesoamerica, represents the cleft on the primordial reptiles back from which the first corn stalk issued. The ball court is sacred because from it (and the blood of losing players) the corn regenerates and future crops are assured. Murals on the walls and inside the building on the east wall tell the story of the Hero Twins and the Maize God. Twelve other, smaller ball courts have been found at Chichen, three more in the Great Terrace area alone.

Between the Castillo and the Ball Court are two small, very interesting buildings, and it is here that the Chichen begins to differ radically from Maya sites elsewhere. The Platform of the Eagles is a squat pyramid adorned with images of jaguars and eagles. These creatures are eating human hearts. Adjacent to it is the Skull Rack or Tzompantli. Register after register of skulls are clearly individuated in this singular piece of architecture. Each etched-in-stone skull presumably symbolizes an identifiable human being, captured or killed in battle. Early archaeologists up until the 1970s believed both of these artistic innovations were imported from central Mexico. However, during the 1980s and 1990s, a counterposition became fashionable among archeologists and art historians. The research during those times showed the heart-eating eagles and jaguars were a stylistic importation characteristic of Tula, Chichen's twin city high in central Mexico, but the grisly skull rack could have been a local invention. True as that may be, only one other skull rack has been found in the Maya realm, whereas they are quite common in central Mexico (Kowalski 2007.).

Eagle eating human heart. Detail from Platform of the Eagles, Chichen Itza.

A stroll to the east of the Castillo will take you to the Temple of the Warriors with its many columns sculpted to resemble atlatl-bearing soldiers, tribute-bearing (some women) priests, sorcerers and individuals in other offices of Itza life including prisoners. There are dozens of columns set quite close together. In days gone by, they supported a roof. While facing this temple, extend your right arm. You will be pointing across an open plaza to the Mercado, another building with a colonnaded gallery. This one was thatched during the 9th and 10th centuries. Despite the large gallery patio, access to the building was had through a single door. It led into a large auditorium-style room. The walls were adorned with images of self-sacrifice.

The Temple of the Warriors and the Mercado are the two buildings most similar to the structures found at Tula. Indeed, the Temple of the Warriors has a virtual double in the central Mexican highlands in Temple B at Tula. This innovation was such a radical departure from anything erected in the land of the Maya, it seemed clear the prototype came from central Mexico. Even more compelling was the fact that early versions of this sort of building had been known from sites in the northwest of Mexico at the cities of La Quemada and Alta Vista, areas that Tula traded with for turquoise. Was it possible that the Maya independently invented this style?

The answer is it is possible. Nikolai Grube and Ruth J. Krochock show that the first of the fifteen columned range-style buildings at Chichen is the House of the Hieroglyphic Jambs. It bears a date of A.D. 832 by their interpretation, three-quarters of a century before Temple B at Tula was erected. As for the eerie resemblance between Temple B at Tula and the Temple of the Warrior at Chichen, it turns out that Jose Acosta, the archaeologist who restored the site, used the Temple of the Warriors as his model for the restoration (Cobos 2006)! So the modern similarities of the two buildings have little real significance.

Does this mean that Chichen was actually the model for Tula? The probability is very small. Thoughtful commentators such as the art historian Jeff Kowalski admit the situation is confused and confusing. However, Kowalski feels a great deal of central Mexican cultural influence came to Chichen, rather in disagreement with many Mayanists in the 1990s who seemed to hold most of the influence went from the Yucatan to central Mexico (Kowalski 2007). Exactly how to account for the relationship between these centers is the subject of intensive debate and research at present — and few convincing answers (Cobos 2004). Kowalski assumes that because of the vast number of colonnaded halls in central and northwestern Mexico, the style had to have its origin there. However, his attempts to find a clear prototype that antedates the Temple of the Hieroglyphic Jambs at Chichen has been blunted by the lack of investigation at Tula Chico, Tula's ancient predecessor (Kowlaski 2007).

Even a cursory survey of the art at Chichen makes one thing clear. The institution of the divine kingship was not practiced, at least in the same way as the Classic period in the south. That is obvious because of the complete dearth of propaganda-style images of the king with his foot on the neck of some hapless arm-slanted-across-his-chest character. Those southern lowland images, usually on stela monuments, were accompanied by text connecting the king and his lineage to the cosmos. But the Itza learned from mistakes made in the southern lowlands. The death of a king there meant the lords of the city took time out from fighting their external enemy to scuffle among themselves to determine the next king. In an ongoing state of war, as we imagine the Terminal Classic period, this could be devastating to a community. The concept of divine kingship had other inherent weaknesses, such as the inability to allow structured input from constituents.

For this reason and also because Chichen appeared to be a multiethnic state, scholars have long held Chichen had a ruling council of some sort. Back in the 1960s, George Kubler theorized it was seated in the Mercado, with its one door and large auditorium-style room. Schele and Mathews cite the second story of the Temple of the Warriors as the seat of the council (1998). Kowalski believes an earlier version of the Temple contained a throne room depicting a single monarch in council (or court) with representatives of persons in the various stations of Itza life. Indeed, he indicates the sculpted columns of the temple hark back to the stelae of the Classic Maya. Stelae in the southern lowlands showed only kings; at rare instances important nobles who appeared to have wrested the privilege from the local king might also erect stela. The Itza column-stelae, however, show almost a cross section of

Itza life. Menial laborers are not depicted, but almost all other social positions are represented. As with the stelae of kings elsewhere, there is usually a supernatural element on the column — generally referring to a Venus cult. A name glyph is also usually present, and some of those names correspond to patrynyms known during Colonial times, such as Cokom and Chuc.

Most commentators no longer believe the figures in the Temple of the Warrior represent a ruling council. But there may have been some kind of council which formally contributed advice to the royalty. A political innovation of this sort would have been a huge improvement on the despotic kingship of the south. Hieroglyphs that have been recently deciphered show Chichen did have its own version of the divine king, at least early on.

His name was Kaku Pacal. He is known to have been active from A.D. 869 to 890. Archaeologists have deduced that he was quite proud of his mother, Lady Kayim, and less proud of his father, Jawbone. This leads them to believe that the form of descent was maternal; that is titles, privileges, and goods were handed down through the mother's side of the family. Such a practice would be consistent with an itinerant band of male Itza appearing in the area and taking highborn local women as their wives. Early in his career, Kaku Pacal is shown conducting rituals with two other figures. At one point he is depicted with the king of Ek Balam and his brother. At another time he is shown with a Cokom lord and his brother. His brother is mentioned almost as often as Kaku Pacal during a period of three years (Grube and Krochock 2007). There is no doubt that Kaku Pacal is the most important ruler in the city. His city, however, never developed an emblem glyph, which marked a city as a free and independent state during classic Maya times. Other cities in the area, some quite small, had emblem glyphs. By the time Chichen became the most important city in the Yucatan, posting emblem glyphs and many other customs of the southern lowlands had fallen out of style.

After Kaku Pacal leaves the scene, no other Itza ruler is known. Does this mean that some sort of shared governance was possible? Rafael Cobos of the Autonomous University of Yucatan does not think so. He believes the institution of a single ruler continued through the years Chichen came to dominate the Maya world. Today most knowledgeable commentators say that would be about a hundred years to A.D. 1100 or so (Kowalski and Kristan-Graham 2007). Others say it would be two or more centuries to A.D. 1250 (Andrews 1995). Those who hold the latter date are in the minority at present.

At least 50 percent of the surface in the area surrounding Chichen Itza is bedrock. It is not suitable for agriculture. It would seem a poor site for a city. How did the site's massive population make a living? It was not by growing corn. Nor is there any reason to suppose that the administrative and transportation needs of its fleet of trading canoes required a massive inland population. The Itza may have learned from the mistakes of their southern cousins by involving a wider segment of the populace in the affairs of state. But they misread the parable regarding war and conquest. They seemed to think what was needed was a more efficient system of belligerence, rather than avoiding the pestilence and dislocation of war altogether. Not all authorities agree that Chichen Itza made its living as a conquest state (Ringle et al. 2004). But at present most do.

Missionary zeal propelled the Chichen warriors. The cult they followed was that of Kukulkan (Quetzalcoatl) (Ringle et al. 2004). Lord Quetzalcoatl was praised for bringing a new cult of blood sacrifice and sacred war to the Yucatan as exemplified by the Temple of the Eagles with its birds and cats of prey feasting on human hearts. Of course, these concepts were not new to the Maya, but the vigor and energy with which they were practiced were.

The Hero Twins and their father the Maize God, though still worshipped, took a backseat to this Feather Serpent deity. The deity made its way over the years to Central Mexico where it grew into a major religion. The Gulf Coast Chontal Maya, who may or may not have been a major contingent at Chichen, brought the cult to the Yucatan with their cargoes of trade goods. It is believed the adoption of the cult of Quetzalcoatl by the Itza provided a common cultural denominator with the folks of Tula. This paved the way for the extraordinary — though as yet not well understood — relationship between the two cities. Both Chichen and Tula worshipped and admired Quetzalcoatl because of their slavish devotion to commerce and sacred war.

Ek Balam, Circa 500 B.C.–A.D. 910

Today Ek Balam is best known as a secondary tourist destination, a mere bump in a tourist's day to relieve the tedium of a long bus ride. Visitors frequently drop in on their way to the flamingo sanctuary at Rio Lagartos, which incidentally is located near the ancient Chichen Itza port of Isla Cerritos and the salt pans of Emal. The tourist whose favorite part of an attraction is the gift shop will be woefully disappointed by Ek Balam. There is not much infrastructure. At last check, not even the thatch huts that local folk often erect to hawk gewgaws had been set up near the parking area. Nor is the entrance from the backside of the main plaza very attractive. One sees simply shrub-clad mounds. But once you go into the main plaza, your opinion begins to change.

The plaza occupies an area the size of two football fields. The north side is bounded by a structure called the acropolis. It goes up almost one hundred feet into the air (Foster 2002). If you have come from the Maya sites to the west, you recognize immediately the difference here in vertical development. With few exceptions the architecture in the Yucatan is spread out in what archaeologists call range (or palace-style) buildings. Vertical relief was not paid much attention to, but here you have both, an acropolis — which by definition is a fairly spread out structure — that rises high above the flat plains of the Yucatan. On what would be the third or fourth story of a modern high rise, you see a long thatch roof protecting the west portion of the structure, the apex of the Acropolis rising behind. Drawing closer, you are startled by the brilliance of the material concealed under the thatch. It is pure white. Huffing up the central stairway for a closer examination shows the raw material is plaster stucco. The figures in the plaster you recognize as similar to Puuc or Chenes. There are the geometrical designs and the full-figured sculptures we expect in this Maya style. But the technology used to achieve the Chenes-Puuc effect is different. In many respects it is similar to the way the Red House at Chichen appears like a classical Puuc building. The ornamentation looks Puuc but it is constructed using quite different techniques.

The classic Puuc style used fitted stones to produce their effect. You are not sure that the innovation at Ek Balam, that is the use of stucco instead of individually sculpted pieces, is as aesthetically satisfying, but there is no doubt about the effect, taken as a whole, of the statuary under the palapa roof. It's spellbinding. Larger than life-sized figures cast in stucco stand out on horizontal plinths — also stucco — from the wall. These were shaped more than a thousand years ago. The feat of engineering strikes one as remarkable as the artistry of these stucco full-sized figures. They appear to hover almost in midair. On either side of the stairway are two large masks wearing the war serpent headdress. Hieroglyphs born on snake tongues attest that the staircase was dedicated by the founder of the line, probably as a war memorial.

Art historians have noted the similarity of many of the architectural features at Ek Balam to the sites in the southern lowlands area. Also, we have already noted the influence from the Puuc region in the western area of the state of Yucatan and the Chenes in the southern part of Campeche state where sculpted stucco was prominent at such sites as Balamku and El Tigre. And archaeologists are more or less in agreement that these influences also indicate movement of peoples from these regions to Ek Balam. Does that mean then that Ek Balam, like Chichen Itza, was founded late in the long arc of Classic Maya history?

Not Hardly. Unlike Chichen Itza, the area around Ek Balam has been settled since the Mid-Preclassic period, a half millennium before Christ (Ringle et al. 2004). The area was desirable for the most obvious reasons — its soils were heavy and rich (by Yucatan standards). In terms of rainfall, it is located on the outer rim of the only truly wet area in northern Yucatan, a thumbprint-like area inland from the island of Cozumel. Coba, thirty miles away as the crow flies, lay dead in the shadow of Cozumel and it gets pelted with as much rain as south Florida, enough to produce near rain-forest vegetation. That much rainfall leaches fragile tropical soils of valuable nutrients. On the other hand, not enough precipitation stunts the yield. By all indications, Ek Balam was the favored location that hit it just right. Chichen Itza, a mere 18 miles away, was located in a near desert, thanks to scanty soils. The corn yield per acre in the Ek Balam area today is among the highest in the Yucatan, and it is assumed the same was true in Preclassic times when rainfall appears to have been somewhat less. Abundant cenotes and sinkholes that would be quarried to the water table provided plentiful drinking water during the dry season.

Monumental architecture was erected at Ek Balam from the Early Classic. However, the site's artistic — and population — peak occurred during the Late Classic when the impressive Acropolis, GT-1, and two flanking structures called GT-2 and 3, were put up enclosing the double ball court on three sides. The southern end of the plaza is bounded by a fairly low pyramid and a palace-style building. Several smaller structures complete the picture of the central plaza, giving it the enclosed appearance typical in the Yucatan.

All these building were encircled by a double wall about six feet high. The primary function of this wall probably was to keep prying eyes out of the holy sanctuary of the ruling elite. The double wall, however, added what archaeologists call a "killing alley." An attacker who scaled the first wall — topped with a log palisade like an Old West fort — would find himself exhausted in the inner-mural zone. He would be vulnerable to relatively easy destruction. The second wall bespeaks the defensive nature of this architectural feature. However, the fact that in places the defensive perimeter runs just feet from a pyramid that towered above it, giving attackers a tactical opportunity, shows its slapdash quality as a military feature.

Legend credits a Lord Ek Balam with founding the municipality. That clearly is a wives' tale, but it may reflect the change in dynasty in the Late Classic. The first known king in this dynasty was called U Kit Kan Lek. He's associated with dates late in the 8th century, A.D. 770–801 (Grube and Krochock 2007). His visage appears on Stela 1, set at the foot of the Acropolis. Sharing the stela with him is a bound captive, reminiscent of monuments in the southern lowlands, and at nearby Coba, itself an outpost of the southern lowlands where stelae had been erected for two hundred years (Ringle et al. 2004). One unusual feature for the north was a Long Count date, one of two known for the entire upper Yucatan. (So-called Short Count dates found in the region, however, can be calibrated to the Long Count but not without controversy.) All this might make U Kit Kan Lek seem a gentleman of the old school, and one subservient to Coba and southern lowland traditions.

But the buildings he erected showed much Puuc, that is western Yucatan, influence both in their ornamentation and quadrangle positioning. Moreover, he was known as a ballplayer. The figure on a corner of the astonishing stucco section of the Acropolis wears a ballplaying yoke. That person may well be U Kit Kan Lek himself. His bones are believed interred in the Acropolis. Altogether, archaeologists have deduced the names of five kings of Ek Balam.

Hun Pik Tok may have cut the largest figure. A generation after U Kit Kan Lek, he is mentioned on a lintel at Halakal (a hamlet near Chichen) and is also named at Chichen where he appears with Kaku Pacal and Kaku's brother. It is assumed that his appearance at Chichen indicates the latter was a subsidiary state of Ek Balam. This means that at A.D. 870 or so, Ek Balam was the first city in the north central Yucatan. Another layer of construction was added to the GT-1 Acropolis after terminating and preserving the stucco figures that have come to be a treasure of Maya

Ek Balam king in ballplaying gear, including yoke around the hips. The monument probably is a likeness of the dynasty founder, U Kit Kan Lek (courtesy INAH).

art. At the community of Ichmul de Morley, halfway between Chichen Itza and Ek Balam, the influence of the latter city far outshone its sea-going rival, Chichen Itza. The rulers of the village of Ichmul showed their fealty to Ek Balam. Before assuming office, they dutifully trudged to Ek Balam, donned ceremonial ballplayer garb and let themselves be sworn in by the king of the larger city.

In almost all other ways, Ichmul followed Ek Balam (Smith, Ringle, and Bond-Freeman 2006). Its architecture reflected the rather eclectic influence of Ek Balam, and its domestic and imported pottery was nearly identical to Ek Balam. In only one important commodity did they fall under the sway of the newcomers near the large cenote 15 miles to the southwest. And that was obsidian. Ek Balam's supply of that most precious of goods used for cutting edges came exclusively from the mountains of Guatemala through southern trading partners. The good people of Ichmul tapped into the supply of their cosmopolitan neighbor, Chichen Itza, which got its supply from central Mexico and other sources.

So how did Ichmul remain more or less independent of Chichen if it was a conquest state? Ichmul developed an emblem glyph with apparent ties to Tikal and swore fealty to Ek Balam, the powerful neighbor to the north. At the same time, it stood between Chichen and its port villages. Could Chichen really be a militaristic conquest state and allow one of its neighbors to go peacefully about its business, acting as subsidiary of the large state of Ek Balam?

It is clear that relations between Ek Balam and Chichen changed dramatically sometime toward the end of the reign of Hun Pik Tok. That is obvious because Chichen slipped out from under the thumb of Ek Balam and became the dominant state in the area. The institution of kingship at Ek Balam, on the other hand, ceased to exist. But Ichmul continued to thrive. Why?

At present, there are no definitive answers to this question. Perhaps Chichen did not feel particularly threatened by a small city whose patron, Ek Balam, had been neutralized. It is known that sometime after A.D. 900 monumental architecture ceased to be erected at Ek Balam. Shortly thereafter a C-shaped building was put up. C-structures are rather mysterious buildings that share certain features with mysterious appearances in low-budget science fiction movies. These buildings went up in many sites around the Yucatan — shortly after the city where they were situated lapsed into paralysis. C-shaped buildings were remarkable for their shoddy construction. Material was often scavenged from existing buildings. And like the appearance of a mysterious icon in a science fiction movie, this new architecture always went hat in hand with a societal trauma. The social crisis at Ek Balam is shown by the cessation of construction of several buildings before completion. Also, the center city — the portion protected by that double-walled killing alley — fell into disuse. Then the population of the city as a whole disappeared.

Was the ruling elite wiped out by Chichen? Were the C-structures used by administrators from the winning side to collect tribute? William Ringle and George J. Bey, two leading researchers at this ancient community, are not willing to concede that point, at present. Though holding it is a possibility, they note the collapse in the north in general and Ek Balam in particular has too many contending possibilities to adopt any single answer. They credit climate change as a plausible agent, but note evidence suggests a drought severe enough to bring famine and devastation would still have been a hundred years into the future. Religious fervor brought about by the Quetzalcoatl cult seems a possible explanation for the collapse of the city center. As noted many times in this narrative, the myth of the Hero Twins supported the institution of divine kingship. Once the new cult of Quetzalcoatl was fervently adopted by the populace, the religious basis of the king was undermined. The worker bees had no reason to pay their mite in taxes to the state, and the institution of kingship and its associated structures may well have collapsed.

Whether the religious fervor of the commoners at Ek Balam had anything to do with the city's failure, it is certain it failed. And, just as in the south, along with that failure went not only the king and monumental architecture, but most of the population as well. Having said all that, a truer clue as to the fate of Ek Balam may be found on the murals in Room 22 of the Monjas palace at Chichen Itza. Depicted is a pitched battle at a site defended by double walls such as those at Ek Balam (Miller 1999). Given the subsequent rise of Chichen and collapse of Ek Balam, many (not including Ringle and Bey) believe the fate of Ek Balam is being graphically depicted on the walls of this building. In short, Chichen Itza conquered Ek Balam.

Uxmal, the Quintessential Puuc Site, A.D. 750–950

Hardly anyone would dispute the claim that Frank Lloyd Wright is America's best known architect. But many of the details of Wright's life, as true of many famous persons, are the subject of much controversy. The intellectual movements that influenced him are often debated hotly by scholars. Puuc architecture is one of the influences he acknowledged and one that is obvious in much of his work. How he became knowledgeable about Puuc styles is far from clear. Did he help assemble the papier-mâché casts made of Puuc sites for the Chicago World's Fair of 1893, as some claim? Did he pass by the Puuc pavilion which remained in place after the fair on his way to work in downtown Chicago as a young man, as others attest? Or was the Puuc architecture displayed at the World's Fair of no importance to him at all? Did he, as still others claim, simply adopt European architects' methodology. They looked to Egypt for new ideas for the new (20th) century. Similarly, these folks claim, Wright adapted artistic motifs from the New World and in particular from the Puuc.

In any case, it is clear that Puuc architecture has been known and admired in the United States and other northern countries all the way back into the middle of the 19th century. The explorers Stephens and Catherwood set up a Maya pavilion in New York before the Civil War featuring Maya art, not to mention the major display at the Chicago World's Fair. It is equally clear that the Puuc style has had far-reaching effects. This was particularly true in the middle part of the 20th century when Wright's so-called Maya Revival influenced the look of many large public buildings such as movie theaters, office and apartment buildings, and even churches. It is characterized by an entablature—a large rectangular table-like element—above the entranceway with geometrical designs. For instance, as an undergraduate one of the authors of this book passed daily under the Puuc style entablature of one of the classroom buildings on his campus. Though the Maya Revival style is no longer current, many of the decorative touches it spawned are still with us, such as cast concrete

The arch at Labna shows the hallmarks of Puuc architecture, a plain lower story with highly ornamented second story composed of mosaics of individually sculpted stones.

ornamentation in geometrical patterns. The U.S. Senate chamber is decorated with a chain of Puuc cloud designs.

Structurally, Puuc architecture is characterized by buildings with a thin veneer of limestone over a wall of concrete hearting. This makes for a more stable building than many early Maya constructions. Stylistically — and most obviously — Puuc architecture consists of a plain lower register with a geometrically ornamented upper register consisting of individuated sculptures (Sharer and Traxler 2006). The Chenes style in which ornamentation reached all the way to the ground is an obvious precursor to the Puuc. It is much "busier" than the Puuc and not nearly as pleasing to the modern eye. As we have seen, Puuc style architecture can be found throughout the northern Yucatan, but the sites called Puuc occur on the south side of the range of Puuc hills in the western part of the state of Yucatan. Like Chichen Itza, all these sites came into existence in the Late Classic, after other areas not far away had been inhabited for hundreds of years. The soils in the area are quite fertile, and modern farming techniques produce high yields. But the bane of this spot is lack of year-round water. Unlike much of the rest of the Yucatan, the water table was not accessible via cenotes. The Late Classic settlers had to rely on ponds or chultuns, cisterns carved out of the living rock. In an area with low rainfall, and a long dry season, this could be a perilous way to live. Nevertheless, in this supposedly unpromising spot, Maya architecture reached its apogee.

Uxmal is the largest and best known of the Puuc sites, such as Sayil, Labna and Kabah, all of which are within a dozen or so air miles of each other. According to Schele and Mathews, traditional ethnohistories credit the settling of Uxmal to a group known as the Tutul Xiu (Schele and Mathews 1998). These people supposedly came from the present state of Tabasco along the lower Usumacinta River, an area not far from where the Itza may have migrated to Chichen. A band under the leadership of Ah-Kuy-Tok-Tutul Xiu — it is claimed in the traditional accounts — settled at Uxmal in A.D. 751. Schele and Mathews note that archaeological data agree that the Puuc sites were settled about at this date, and other commentators more or less agree, though some put the settlement date at A.D. 770–800 (Kowalski 2007). The name of leader of the Tutul Xiu means owl flint, a loose translation of which probably means warrior and, in this case, conqueror. Forty years later a convocation of Maya elders was called by the Itza. It occurred at Dzibilchaltun, just north of present day Merida. Gravitas was conferred on the proceedings by representatives of Tikal as well as the major cities of the northern plains of Yucatan. The Xius of Uxmal may have been invited to this affair. The evidence is unclear and indicates the as yet undeveloped state of the city.

Over the next half century migrants continued to pour into the city. At least one documented wave came from Tabasco, but others may have migrated from the disintegrating polities of the lowlands further south. By the late 9th century, the Xiu rulers had established relations with Kaku Pacal of Chichen. This is known because his name appears several times in Uxmal inscriptions. His mother, Lady Kayim, is also named (although his father, Jawbone, is not). Just as early on in Kaku Pacal's reign Chichen was judged a subordinate because of the name of Ek Balam's ruler being mentioned at the site, Uxmal can also be considered a dependency of Chichen. The affiliation may be responsible for Uxmal becoming the leading state in the region. Despite its avowed relationship to Chichen Itza, the rulers of Uxmal — like those of Ek Balam — took care to construct a defensive wall around the sacred inner city.

The only ruler of the site known from archaeology — as opposed to ethnohistory — is Lord Chac. He appears to have come into his prime just as Kaku Pacal of Chichen Itza had passed his, about A.D. 890 or so. Lord Chac claims to have built almost all of the signature buildings at the site. The House of the Governors, which Frank Lloyd Wright apprized as the finest example of Maya architecture, is his. Also bearing his name is the ball court, and the Nunnery. The latter building is a quadrangle edifice, consisting of four wings. Astonishingly, all three — or actually all seven, as the Nunnery is really four buildings — of these great construction projects appear to have been built almost simultaneously. The labor and resources diverted to these great works boggles the mind. All Maya construction was labor intensive because of the lack of metal tools, beasts of burden or the use of the wheel. But Puuc style ornamentation consisted of mosaics of thousands of individually sculpted stones.

The Temple of the Magician at Uxmal.

The production of those individual sculptures with stone tools boggles the mind. Although copies of the mosaic sculptures could be produced by non-skilled workers, the façade still required an enormous amount of effort.

Today's tourist first encounters the Temple of the Magician, a massive "pyramid" that has been reconstructed with rounded corners similar to the apsidal corners of many Maya houses. This building is burdened with a lode of folklore about a dwarf who supposedly built it in a single night. In days gone by, the tourist could ascend this pyramid and look down into the Nunnery quadrangle. After viewing the very steep backside of the Temple of the Magician, you can slip between the east and south wings into the Nunnery. However, the way builders meant for dignitaries to enter was through the arch in the south building.

If you pause in the arch — more graceful and closer to a true arch than the earlier corbelled vaults of the south — and turn around, you will see the ball court below you. Its goal markers will stand out in the sun, and one of them bears a date of A.D. 901, similar to the dates of the dedication of the various wings of the Nunnery. Passing through the arch — as many a Maya procession did in Classic times — you enter what is now a grassy infield. The four wings of the Nunnery complex surround you. Each is about as long as a football field is wide. The platform the south wing is set on is noticeably lower than the east and west wings. The north building stands highest of all. True to what we have learned about Puuc architecture, the lower zones of all buildings are plain stone, the upper zones are filled with arabesque designs inset by larger patterns. Some of the designs are themselves geometrical and abstract. Others are representational sculptures.

From what we have learned of Maya site layout in the south, one might suspect the Nunnery quadrangle forms a sort of Maya cosmogram, which centered on the person of the Maya king. The cosmogram proved his being the pivot in the universe, the lynchpin that tied his people to the basic forces of the cosmos. Not incidentally, the cosmogram also showed how by obeying him or her the rain would keep falling and the corn growing. Jeff Kowalski and Linda Schele and Peter Mathews agree that the Nunnery does indeed conform to the cosmogram model, but at some divergence from the way this was accomplished in the southern lowlands (Kowalsky 2007, Schele and Mathews 1998).

Schele and Mathews point out that the south building is adorned with corn leaves. They also note that an abstract V of horizontal bars of varying length on the east wing probably denotes a corn crib. The whole point is that Lord Chac is promising to keep the people's larders full of corn, (providing of course they fulfill their part of the bargain by building his buildings and fighting his wars). Kowalski also notes that "the centralized column representing the world tree and [the] nearby jaguar throne can be associated with Maya creation mythology which served as a divine charter for kingship" (2007). And indeed, Uxmal was adorned with stela showing Lord Chac in full feather headdress. His feet were planted on the necks of unhappy captives who were about to be dispatched to keep the cosmos in good working order and the corn yielding.

All this, including his status as divine king, was in keeping with the traditions of the southern lowlands. The difference comes in a warrior bearing an atlatl standing behind Lord Chac on one of the stelae. The atlatl, as noted earlier, was always taken to be a symbol of warriors influenced by central Mexico. In this instance, most scholars believe the atlatl-wielding soldiers were from Chichen Itza. With their help, Lord Chac appropriated the territory (or labor and resources in the way of tribute) of other cities in the area. One of the construction projects of the peasants whose labor was co-opted was building a causeway to

Kabah, only five miles away. After its completion Kabah became, it is believed, a wholly-owned subsidiary of Lord Chac's ruling dynasty.

Such central Mexican imagery was not limited to stelae. An emblem centered in the corncrib motif on the east wing long puzzled scholars. Schele and Mathews deduced the tufts sticking out at the 11 and 1 o'clock positions were bundled atlatl darts. Kowalski determined the symbol itself stood for an owl, perhaps hearkening back to that mysterious figure Spearthrower Owl who was once believed to be the emperor of Teotihuacan and the father of the Tikal king, First Crocodile. The figure of Spearthrower Owl may have been four centuries in the past. Lord Chac was making no direct claims on kinship to him. He was simply claiming a right to rule based on central Mexican imagery as well as traditional Maya mythology. It was abundantly clear that, given the collapse in the south, Maya mythology had somehow failed — but the states in central Mexico were still going strong.

According to Kowalski, by staking his kingship to central Mexican authority symbols, Lord Chac believed he was rooting the Uxmal state on a firmer basis. The most obvious icon of central Mexico in the Nunnery can be found on the west wing entablature. As we recall, the west is the direction of death, and boldly adorning the west wall is a rather involved feathered serpent with several heads and prominent rattle tails. This sculpture clearly refers to the Quetzalcoatl cult of Chichen Itza and central Mexico. The most feared snake in the area is the fer-de-lance, the so-called "ultimate pit viper." Rattlesnakes are rarely mentioned by local folk. If the image on the west wall were locally inspired it would be of a fer-de-lance. Cradled in the crook of the Feathered Serpent's tail is a so-called "drum major headdress." This image that looks as much like a pineapple as a drum major's shako was suggested by neither. Now that many of the Maya glyphs can be read, it is known the pineapple is actually a human heart with associated vein work. As we recall, the cult of Quetzalcoatl was associated with "human sacrifice and sacred war." Venus was the astral body allied with it.

To the southwest of the Nunnery and almost directly west of the House of the Governors and the Great Pyramid is an unrestored building Kowalksi and Alfredo Barrera excavated in the '90s. Its floor plan describes a perfect circle. They suspected the structure might be a temple of Quetzalcoatl's alter ego, the wind god Ehecatl. Their suspicions were confirmed, giving credence to Uxmal's connection to central Mexico (Kowalski et al. 1996). Those ties were mostly ceremonial and useful in replacing or supplanting the discredited ideology of the southern lowlands. More importantly, this excavation plus the warrior atlatl on a stela and the feather-serpent imagery in the Nunnery proved a connection with Chichen Itza. This connection goes a long way to explaining how a site like Uxmal in a waterless plain could come to dominate its neighbors militarily, be recognized by the older, large cities of the northern plain as its equal or better, and bring to fruition an art style that a thousand years later would be admired around the world. So did Lord Chac and his city go on to a long and fruitful career?

Not at all. Shortly after Lord Chac passed from the scene, Uxmal fell into decline and was abandoned. Why? Archaeologists are not sure. Some even doubt the A.D. 950 date for the collapse of the central government, holding that Uxmal continued on much longer. But most agree its demise occurred in the A.D. 950 timeframe, and they finger Chichen Itza as the culprit. As that city expanded it may well have become a very uncertain ally. As we saw in the section on Ek Balam, many archaeologists believe Chichen was responsible for the fall of Ek Balam, Chichen's former superior. As at Ek Balam, after the fall of Uxmal, shoddy C-shaped buildings were erected. Were they some kind of Chichen-Ehecatl house used by an administrative staff to collect tribute and keep the peasants in line? If this narrative was a science fiction novel, the mystery of the C-shaped buildings would be resolved in the final section. Archaeology rarely ties things up as neatly as fiction writers, but the case of Yaxuna comes pretty close to doing just that. It also provides great insight into the dynamics of intercity relations in the Yucatan during the Classic through Terminal Classic periods.

Yaxuna at the Crossroads of the Yucatan, Circa 400 B.C.–A.D. 850–900

Yaxuna is a fitting community to conclude this chapter on the Terminal Classic in the north for two very good reasons. First, the city compares and contrasts nicely with Chichen Itza. In many ways the two communities, which were separated by only twelve miles, are alike. But even more importantly, Yaxuna's history from the Early Classic through the Terminal Classic provides a recap of much we have learned about the political history of the Maya during the Classic period. It is sort of a microcosm of the times.

Just as Chichen Itza developed because it lay at the crossroads of the Yucatan, more or less equidistant from the population centers of the north, Yaxuna traced a similar trajectory but much earlier. Chichen developed into a major center at A.D. 800 or later. Yaxuna, by contrast, had begun its development more than a millennium earlier in the Middle Preclassic period or about 400 B.C. Well before the time of Christ, Yaxuna had become integrated in a peninsular trade and ritual network headed by El Mirador (Freidel 2008). After the fall of El Mirador, it appears Yaxuna continued as a trading partner of the Kan people who ultimately developed an empire from their site just north of the Mirador Basin at Calakmul. This affinity with the peoples near the Mirador Basin is indicated by the triadic arrangement of the major early buildings at the site.

The first important event that archaeology has made known to us occurred about A.D. 400, shortly after Teotihuacan-backed forces under Fire Is Born installed a new king at Tikal. Fire Is Born then became the kaloomte or emperor of Tikal, Uaxactun, Rio Azul, and at least one other location in the Peten. Trade brought relative prosperity to Yaxuna. It also brought something else. Personnel of many kinds traipsed through the city. Most were there to trade, but some came as spies. In this case, agents of the prime city of the western Yucatan at the time, Oxkintok, appear to have gotten in touch with an opponent of the pretender to the throne of Yaxuna after the death of the king. The person set to succeed the king was a male about fifty-five years of age (Ambrosino, Ardren, and Stanton 2003).

His age is known because his skeleton was found in a crypt in the eastern pyramid of the triadic arrangement on the North Acropolis. The pretender's jade hunal was lying at his feet and an obsidian blade occupied the spot where the head should have been. He was lying on top of an ancestor bundle that had been desecrated by burning. Eleven skeletons occupied the crypt with him. Their ages and genders run the gamut from an infant to adult males and females. Some had been killed in the time-honored method befitting royalty, decapitation. The grave goods included with these bodies were fairly elaborate. Archaeologists recovered jade jewels, fancy foreign and domestic pottery, and elaborate mosaics. Some of the pots in the grave came from the large western Yucatan city of Oxkintok. They betrayed the Teotihuacan influence of the city. One of these, for instance, was a bowl with three incised faces. An almost identical pot was unearthed in a royal grave at Oxkintok.

Another plate had the iconic signature of Fire Is Born, the kaloomte of Tikal himself. He may have commanded the Oxkintok forces supporting the new king of Yaxuna.

Another bowl with the portrait of the imposed ruler of Yaxuna was also put in the grave. He is wearing Teotihuacan-style garments. To make sure the point was not lost on the spirits of the dead, the same individual commissioned a stela which was erected in the main plaza bearing an identical portrait. The building in which the deposed royal family was interred was ritually terminated. An axe head was stuffed between several royal jade pieces in a black pot. It was buried atop the structure. In short, the old royal family had been symbolically and literally "axed."

David Freidel directed the team of archaeologists who made this discovery (Freidel, MacLeod, and Suhler 2003). He notes that the skeleton of the deposed pretender was bracketed by those of two young women. One was pregnant or held a child in her lap. The other carried a doll. Both women had shell crowns including jade hunals. The positioning and gender of these three skeletons was reminiscent of the Maize God, frequently shown bracketed with beautiful and fruitful women. It also hearkened to the creation myth, which Maya royalty took as their license to rulership. Underscoring the creation mythology was the apparently defleshed skeleton of an older male in a sitting posture against the wall. Freidel judged him to have been made into an effigy of the Maya death god. The death god is a central player in the Maya creation myth that features death before regeneration. The young women with infants suggested regeneration.

The pot cached above the crypt with the "axed" jades was black in color. It was on the west side of the structure. A red pot was found on the east side. It contained what apparently was a stone portrait of the new king. Owl imagery was found in the black pot hinting once again at Fire Is Born and his apparent Teotihuacan patron, Spearthrower Owl. A crypt in the northern pyramid was found to contain the skeleton of he who Freidel believes to have been the king prior to the usurpation. Stones were piled neatly on both sides of his skeleton. These resembled "a clefted mountain, a symbol of resurrection" (Freidel, MacLeod, and Suhler 2003). The identity of the disturber of this grave is indicated by the owl imagery on the incised bone deposited in the crypt. In short, the usurper king was showing his allegiance to Oxkintok, Fire Is Born, and Teotihucan. Three hunal jewels of the dead king were redistributed throughout the crypt. All this was magic rites conducted by the new ruler. The rites allowed him to call himself a direct descendant of the old king. No doubt, the kings of Tikal such as First Crocodile who claimed kinship to the founder — even as they clearly broke the dynastic line by killing a legitimate king — performed a similar ritual.

Freidel believes the new king constructed the coronation platform directly above the crypt in which the twelve bodies were found. As noted earlier, human sacrifice was expected of a new king, and the dead pretender's family fulfilled that expectation.

In any case, the new ruler began constructing Teotihucan-style buildings such as a patio-quad-style palace on the outskirts of the city. Whether or not Fire Is Born actually led the military wing supporting the pretender, it is clear that Oxkintok became the local overlord of Yaxuna. This is apparent on the basis of the continued accumulation of Oxkintok ceramic sherds indicating Yaxuna became a depot for Oxkintok goods.

For the first 800 years of its existence, Yaxuna had been an ally of the peoples of the Mirador Basin. For the next 150 years its major trading partner, as judged by the ceramic sherds found on the site, was Oxkintok which had ties to Tikal. Then abruptly that all changed.

But first a word about Coba. Coba is a sui generis city in the Yucatan. Other polities, such as Ek Balam and Yaxuna, may have been founded in the Middle Preclassic at the same time as the cities of the Maya heartland. They may even have maintained contact with the city-states of the south, but Coba is the only one that really resembles a southern lowland megacity. Its population was huge, at least 50,000 (Folan et al. 1982). Because of a climatological anomaly caused by a thumbprint of higher rainfall on the northeastern Yucatan coast, its climate is practically identical to the northern Peten. Just as the meteorology was similar to the Peten, so was the cultural climate. The stela cult of the southern lowlands was fully developed at Coba. During the 1970s and early '80s William Folan and his team had discovered almost three dozen stelae, and they believed many more were concealed by the heavy brush. Given its large size, it is not surprising that the city contains three ceremonial centers. The largest is called Nochoch Mul. Its largest pyramid rises 150 feet or so above the site. No large city can carry on for hundreds of years without developing its own character. In Coba's case, these peculiarities centered on infrastructure problems that modern city planners would fully understand. The problems had to do with water and transportation.

Cyrus Lundell noted long ago that rainfall in the Yucatan varied from year to year by as much as a third or even half of average (Lundell 1937). This meant that the authorities in even well-watered spots like Coba obsessed about retaining as much rainfall as possible. Contained within the city were four lakes, a rarity in the Yucatan, and one bajo swamp that may have been a lake in Classic times. The people of Coba were not content to rely on these water sources. They dug wells and built check dams and catch basins. A canal connected Lakes Coba and Macanxoc between which the beautiful ceremonial center called Coba was located. Another canal was cut from Lake Coba to a small pond nearby. Dikes were also constructed around many of the lakes. Interestingly, there is evidence that some of these lakes may have been, in part, artificially excavated.

The activity that produced or enlarged some of the lakes was strip mining. The material the good people of Coba were quarrying is called *sascab* (calcareous sand). This material was used for fill for buildings. Coba with its three ceremonial complexes required a great deal of it. In chunk form, it could be burned in a kiln to produce lime. Granular sascab was mixed with lime for cement. The two lakes on either side of the Coba ceremonial center were modified by activities to procure sascab (Folan et al. 1982). Quarries usually were no deeper than six feet, but Coba miners followed veins of sascab underground, sometimes going a hundred feet into the overburden. Pillars of sascab would be left to support the limestone cap. In one instance, a shaft a kilometer long was sunk using 31 hourglass-like supports. By studying the marks left in the sascab, archaeologists have determined the tools used were made of hard stone or wooden wedges. Other substances mined in similar ways were salt, chert for tools, potter's clay for ceramics, and attapulgite clay, a kaolin-like substance used to control diarrhea. This sort of clay, by the way, was mixed with indigo to produce a brilliant blue ink-like paint. The paint, called Maya blue, was used in Maya codices (books) and to daub sacrificial victims. Altogether, Folan and other archaeologists determined Coba miners removed almost a quarter million cubic yards of calcareous sands. Some of this may have been reduced to lime and exported. Most of it was used to build Coba's other characteristic architectural trait — roads, of all sorts.

During the rainy season, clay paths turned into slippery quagmires, especially treacherous for people packing loads. Coba solved this problem by paving its walkways. House lots were bounded by stone walls that functioned as sidewalks, and larger intracity centers and out-area hamlets were connected by a system of *sacbeob* (roadways) that would have pleased any modern city planner.

Coba's sacbeob builders first established a line, usually between two architectural features visible above the forest and vegetation. When developing a road to a far-away village, it is possible they used celestial navigation. Folan points out that the sacbe to Chen Mul may have been aligned on Sirius, the brightest star in the sky. Stakes were then driven in the ground along the center of the proposed right of way. Corvee laborers or slaves were set to clearing the vegetation on either side of the stakes, and then the business of actually building the road was gotten down to.

Retaining walls from three to 18 yards apart were laid up on both sides of the road. The walls ranged from 30 to 40 inches high, although in one instance they went up over twenty feet. The workers then filled the area between with large chunks of stone. This stone was settled with the use of log rollers, then the retaining walls were removed and a finished wall was erected in its place using large, shaped stones, apparently without the use of concrete. Then a cap of smaller stones was laid up in a convex pattern to produce a face that would shed water. After thoroughly packing, a final layer of calcerous sand was applied to the surface and wetted. New layers of this sort of paving were added as needed. The sacbe was built in short sections probably as projects by local groups at the direction of central authorities. Sometimes a line of stones were centered along the road. It is theorized these stones were utilized as steps to keep from eroding the pavement.

Sacbes radiated out from the ceremonial core of Coba like tram lines running from the downtown area of any modern city. Cenotes along the way refreshed the traveler and provided the wet stuff to sprinkle the road surface to keep it compact. Sacbeob multitasked.

Some principle city-states of the Terminal Classic period in the Northern Lowlands. Shaded cities are those Kaloomte Fire Is Born appears to have conquered during the Teotihuacan-inspired salient into the lowlands in the Early Classic. Yaxuna, for a time, also came under the influence of this tide. The 62-mile *sacbe* (causeway), longest yet discovered, between Coba and Yaxuna is indicated.

Shrines along the way allowed the religious to do their devotions as they traveled. (In Landa's day, after the Conquest, travelers would draw blood by notching their ears when passing certain shrines.) No doubt they also were used for ritual processions. Their economic benefit of such a network of roads is readily apparent. The easier it is to bring goods to the consumer, the better for all individuals involved in the transaction and the economy as a whole.

The military applications are also apparent. In our section on the Olmec, Philip Drucker estimated a soldier could travel about eighteen miles a day on foot. He was assuming the infantryman was crossing the country on unimproved paths. Coba constructed the longest sacbe in the entire Maya area. It ran 62 miles. That it was used for military purposes is obvious by the defensive ramparts that occasionally cross the road.

This sacbe started at the foot of the greatest ceremonial center at Coba and ended in the main plaza of Yaxuna, indicating that Coba warriors sent the Oxkintok-backed regime packing (Ambrosino, Ardren, and Stanton 2003). Among the acts of the Coba conquerors was building a residential palace on the Acropolis and ritually terminating the Teotihucan-style buildings erected by the folks from Oxkintok. Pottery was smashed on the floor and white marl was poured over the floors, as was common in termination events. Also, a stela that commemorated the usurper Oxkintok king was moved from a place of prominence to a spot of minimal access. Researchers surmise this stela was not destroyed because the Coba force worked with a local quisling, the new king. It is assumed he was inserted into the founding dynasty — now including the Oxkintok usurper — by the working of ritual magic similar to that that allowed the Oxkintok-backed claimant to take the throne.

Coba was an ally of Calakmul. After Coba's successful takeover of Yaxuna, Tikal-ally Oxkintok's ceramics were no longer found at Yaxuna. In short, just as Tikal was falling to the spears of Caracol warriors (with Calakmul's assistance), Coba attacked the Oxkintok outpost of Yaxuna, supported at long distance by Tikal. Coba carried the day in the north, just as Caracol and Calakmul did in the south. Tikal went into a decline known as its Mid-Classic hiatus, as did its client state in the north, Oxkintok. And Yaxuna swung back into the orbit of the allies of the Kan dynasty where it had started out many centuries before.

All this occurred somewhere between A.D. 565 and 600. For a century or more, Coba dominated Yaxuna and the center of the peninsula. These years do not appear to have been prosperous ones for the good folk of Yaxuna. And they seemed to have worked up a fine resentment. Suddenly in the 8th century, they rose up and threw off the yoke of Coba. The temple at the end of the Coba road was stove in by what appears to have been a hostile termination rite. Likewise, residential structures atop the Acropolis and near the E-Group were ritually desanctified in a violent manner. Their central vaults were collapsed, the staircases destroyed, and pottery ritually smashed.

On a more positive note, the local Yaxuna folk erected a council house. Imagery in this house extols the warrior deeds of local nobles. For the first time, locals appear to have taken control of their city. Could the local nobles — with the help of the Yaxuna peasantry — have overthrown mighty Coba? The answer appears to be no. They received copious help from the Puuc sites to the west. Indeed, shortly the Puuc seem to have been running the show at Yaxuna. Puuc style buildings were being erected. Burials of important personages occurred in Puuc style crypts, and Puuc pottery appears in the garbage middens. Not only that but the population at Yaxuna exploded indicating Puuc immigrants moved to Yaxuna.

All this takes us to A.D. 850–900. Now the Itza have established themselves at Chichen

Itza, just twelve miles away. After a late start, their city is developing a warrior class with aspirations of empire. Kaku Pacal, his brother, and a Cokom lord have erected images boasting of their wealth and power. Probably all three were plotting means of becoming the ultimate king of their city. The best way of doing that was showing their prowess in battle. None of this boded well for the community a mere dozen miles to the south. And Yaxuna knew it.

The city's ruler threw up a wall around the city. The high points on the Acropolis were converted to watchtowers. But none of this did Yaxuna any more good than similar defensive preparations were to do Ek Balam and Uxmal. The city was conquered. But no C-shaped structures to accept tribute were built around Yaxuna. It became a ghost town. Its population completely disappeared. Presumably the laboring class was resettled in Chichen where it was set to work at the many building projects in the city. Only one small building was put up on the Acropolis. Guards there kept an eye on troop movements along the Coba sacbe and made sure no one attempted to recolonize the area.

Chichen Itza went on to become one of the largest and most powerful Maya city-states ever. We know what happened to its enemies, many of which like Uxmal were first its allies. They appear to have perished by the sword. But what happened to Chichen? After crushing all possible challengers did it go on to survive for many centuries? It did not. The best guess is that Chichen reigned supreme for only a century and a half or so after it rose to prominence (Miller 1999). The cause of its demise is less well understood than the reason for the collapse of the Maya cities in the Classic lowlands. As we saw, drought, endemic warfare, and, most of all, the implosion of the institution of divine kingship seem to be the root cause of the collapse in the south. In Chichen's case, only drought at present appears to have been a possible—but by no means certain—factor.

Chichen shared many traits with the other "international cities" of Mesoamerica such as Tula, El Tajin (north of Vera Cruz), and other cities of the time. One of these traits was the Quetzalcoatl cult. And all of these cities collapsed almost simultaneously at A.D. 1100 or so. At present, archaeologists do not have a clue as to the reason for the connection, if any, between these collapse events. But one thing is certain, these cities, spread out across the country now called Mexico—some in the highlands, others near sea level—all passed into oblivion at more or less the same time.

7

Mayapan, Tayasal, and Chan Santa Cruz

Cortes as the First "Modern" Maya Explorer, A.D. 1524–1525

Whether one loathes or admires Hernan Cortes (1485–1547), all agree that he was one of history's great men of action. With several hundred Europeans and a few thousand Indian allies, he conquered the Aztec empire, whose population numbered at least 5 million. Much less told is his countrymen's early confrontations with the Maya. In these encounters, they were infinitely less successful.

The east coast of the Yucatan Peninsula lies directly west of Cuba, a long-time Spanish stronghold in the Caribbean. Spanish ships first made contact with the Maya on Columbus's last voyage. When Cortes, on his historic expedition to Mexico in 1519, made landfall on Cozumel Island, he learned of two Spaniards that had been taken prisoner by the Maya (Dias 1963). He demanded these men be brought to him. One was a priest in his early life, Geronimo de Aguilar, who spent his time in captivity toiling in corn milpas and fearing he would end most ignominiously for a Catholic clergyman, as a sacrifice to a Maya god. He was ransomed and, owing to his understanding of Yucatec Maya, proved to be an invaluable asset to Cortes. The other was broadly tattooed with an ornament inserted in his face. This man had gone gloriously native and refused Cortes's offer to be returned to his countrymen. He not only melted back into the Maya population, he later became a noted war leader among the Maya in the battles with his former comrades.

Otherwise, learning from earlier expeditions, Cortes left the Caribbean Maya alone. He coasted around the northern portion of the Yucatan Peninsula, and when he landed on the peninsula's western shore, he was met by determined opposition. Again, he withdrew as gracefully as possible — although not without coming to blows — and shipped for his true destination, the mainland of Mexico. That was where he had high hopes massive treasure would be found. But after a scuffle as a sort of tribute with a Tabasco-area cacique (chief), he was presented with twenty slave women. Given the lowly stature of women in a macho society, it would be easy to imagine the leader of such rough men merely passing these slave girls out to his officers for domestic service without much regard for the intelligence they might convey. But one of these women was a remarkable person. Cortes called her Donna Marina.

Just how she came to be a slave is something of a mystery. The chief chronicler of the journey, Bernal Dias, claims she was the only child of a chieftain of a place about 24 miles from the town of Coatzacoalcos on the river of the same name. Her father died. The girl's mother remarried and bore a son. To avoid problems about inheritance, the stepfather and mother said Donna Marina died, substituting the infant corpse of one of their menials who expired about that time. The healthy girl child was passed off as a slave orphan to a distant tribe. In due time, he was presented to Cortes along with the nineteen other women. She appeared destined for patting corn masa into tortillas and warming a conquistador's bed, but she made her talents known to Cortes. She could speak one or more Maya languages, and she also was fluent in Nahuatal, the language of the Aztecs. She was able to converse with Fr. Geronimo, allowing Cortes to have actual conversation with the peoples he was attempting to conquer. Even better, she seemed to have an innate understanding of court politics and human nature which helped guide Cortes's actions. Several times her uncanny abilities were able to ferret out traps or ambushes. Cortes claimed that, after God, she deserved the most credit for his amazing conquest.

Her biography as a youngster, as sketched by Bernal Dias, does not impress modern historians for its accuracy, but there is little agreement on what her true history was. Suffice it to say, that Cortes first assigned her because of her good looks to a highborn nobleman as a sort of reward. But later he sent her protector away and took her for himself. She bore him a son, supposedly the first mestizo (Spanish-Indian) born in Mexico. Her nickname was Malinche. Donna Marina was not the only wily person in Cortes's company. When his ships anchored near present-day Veracruz, he nominated a group as the town fathers of a new Spanish city. These fathers then named him mayor of the new town of Veracruz. The point of this charade was to recharter the expedition. Until that point, the group operated under the authority of the governor of Cuba. But in point of fact, Gov. Velasquez had appointed Cortes as leader because he wanted the very junior Cortes to be a caretaker, one who would save the real job of conquering Mexico for himself. By founding a city and having himself named military governor, *adelantado* in Spanish, Cortes was able to give himself legal cover for that which he had all along intended to do, head inland — Gov. Velasquez's wishes or no — and seize the Aztec empire.

Cortes demanded all hands give up the considerable gold, silver, and jewelry they had confiscated on their way around the Yucatan. He wanted to send this treasure directly to the king. Most objected, saying the king only deserved the royal fifth, but Cortes carried the day. The largest of his ships was outfitted, and two of his officers were put in charge, one being Francisco de Montejo. The ship rode the Gulf Stream past Cuba without being detected and made good time to Spain. Cortes's mission was looked on favorably — helped no doubt by the quantity of treasure that accompanied it. The king recognized the self-appointed adelantado. He was tasked with pacifying the new territory but at Cortes's own expense.

Not bad for a man who started off life just seven years before Columbus discovered the New World as a hidalgo, the lowest order of nobility. His family, though not wealthy, sent him to study law; the smattering of knowledge he gained clearly coming in handy when he conceived of the legal dodge of making himself adelantado. But Cortes's high spirits got in the way of his legal training. He headed to Spain's New World colonies, which at that time amounted to little more than the islands of the Caribbean. Record there early on showed little of the character traits that later made him famous. He continued getting into adolescent scrapes to the annoyance of local authorities. Not content to eke out a living as a planter, he inveigled the governor of Cuba, to whom he was related by marriage, into allowing him to lead the next expedition to the recently discovered land

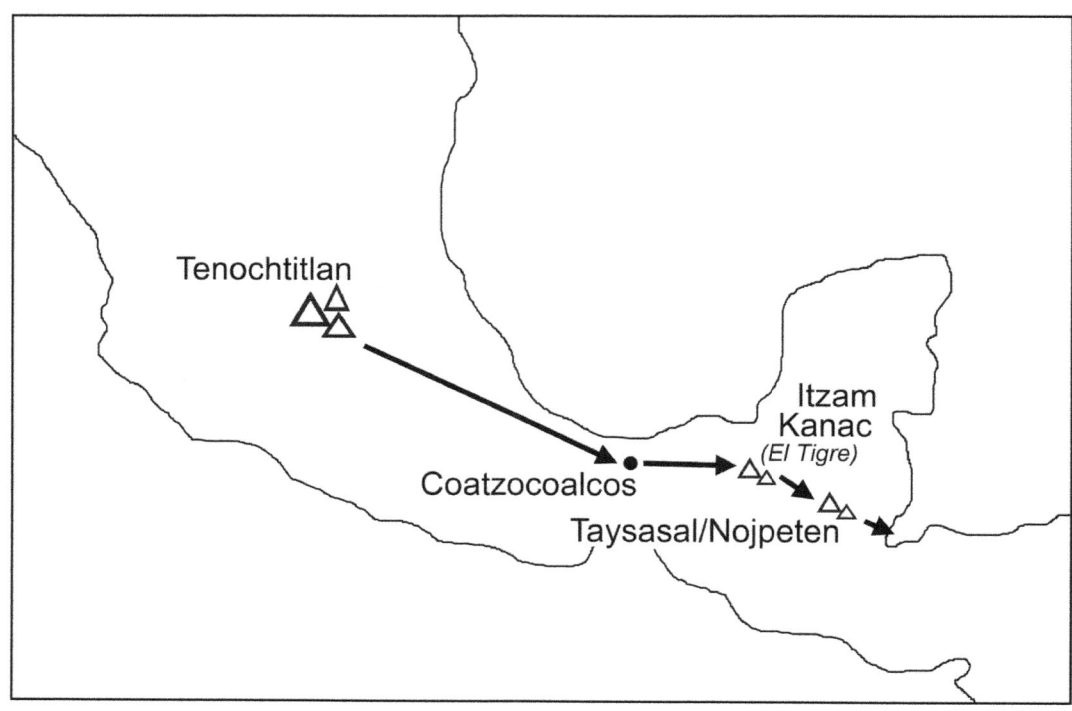

The solid line shows Cortes's march to the Bay of Honduras from the Valley of Mexico in 1524–25.

of Mexico. Governor Velasquez had a change of heart about Cortes just before the expedition was to disembark. He countermanded Cortes charter. But the ships of his command were laden, and the six hundred plus expeditionary force was ready to sail. Cortes slipped anchor and was on his way — and out of the grasp of what passed for legally constituted authority.

Now on the Gulf Coast, Cortes did not yet know that his legal stratagem — thanks in large part to the treasure sent the king — had worked. As a matter of fact, things were not going smoothly at all. Many of the men claimed loyalty to Velasquez. They demanded to return to Cuba. To stop such talk, Cortes scuttled the remaining ships in the Gulf of Mexico. He then rounded up his company of 600 or so men and marched inland. Also included in his arsenal were a dozen or so — the sources vary — horses, thirty or so crossbowmen, and fifteen musketeers. Each of these were made infinitely more effective by the discipline and strategy with which they were deployed. The musketeers carried harquebuses, actually small shoulder-fired artillery pieces.

When discharged in unison, their fusillade would terrify battle-hardened regular infantrymen. The effect of the flash and bang on those who had never witnessed such power — or sound — was predictably unsettling. Mastiff war dogs added an element of terror and surprise. Horsemen — invincible in full armor — joined the battle in formation. They routed the best Indian warriors, lancing them like targets at a medieval fair. Bodies piled up behind them in windrows. With these weapons — not the least of which was the formidable discipline of the otherwise individualistic Spaniards — Cortes took on friend and foe of the Aztec empire. He made directly for the highland lakes of central Mexico where the Aztec headquarters lay. His strategy seemed to be to show Aztec foes how strong he was in order to win them over. He attempted to avoid fighting Aztec allies so he could claim friendship, but many a skirmish ensued nonetheless.

The plan baffled Moctezuma, the king of the Aztecs. He was the ninth and very close to the last ruler of the Aztec empire. His ethnic group, known also as the Mexica, had begun immigrating toward what is now Mexico City from the deserts of northwestern Mexico two or three centuries earlier. Their language, Nahuatl, is related to Ute, Shoshone and Comanche. It was to become the most widely spoken language in Mexico. The Aztecs gravitated south — and up to the high valley of Mexico, some 7,200 feet above sea level. Much of the basin was flooded, thanks to summer rains and snowmelt from the snowcap of huge mountains to the east. On an island in that land of lakes, they founded a state and fought the other peoples on other island states. Gradually, they allied with two other city-states becoming the junior partner of the coalition. By about the turn of the 14th century, a hundred-some years before Cortes, the Aztecs became the leading member of the Triple Alliance and named the first Aztec emperor.

Moctezuma II, the ninth emperor of the Triple Alliance, had shown himself a fierce battle leader early in his career. But Cortes unmanned him. Moctezuma issued no end of contradictory orders regarding the Spanish. Sometimes they were to be accommodated. Other times, as at Cholula, modern Pueblo, he ordered an ambush attack to destroy them. Those captured were to be sacrificed to Aztec gods. In this last instance, Donna Marina learned of the plot, warned Cortes, and he turned the ambuscade in his favor. He then marched the hundred or so miles into the Aztec capital as an esteemed guest of the emperor. Cortes, playing the situation just right, insisted he be treated as the representative of an even greater emperor from across the sea.

Moctezuma did not know how to respond. In part, his problem was systemic. As a semi-divine emperor, his powers and perquisites were similar to those of the Maya kings during the Classic period. His subjects were forbidden from looking on his face, and his only true confidants were members of his own family. In short, he did not have a court of advisers competent to give advice about such threats. Falling back on his usual practice, he turned to the Aztec gods, to whom he sacrificed several victims a day. And he prayed for a strategy for dealing with the Spanish pestilence. But he received no clear answer from the gods.

The Spanish, on the other hand, were getting very clear messages. They watched the human hearts of the sacrificed burning before blood-smeared idols, and they were strengthened in the belief of the goodness of their mission to destroy such iniquity. By the same token, they discovered the secret treasury of Moctezuma and became impotent in the face of their desire to loot his holdings. But neither of these things were quite as strong as the fear generated by the precariousness of their position — a few hundred Spanish with a thousand or so Indian allies surrounded by one and a half million enemy, on islands in a lake more than a mile above the sea! Cortes's men beseeched him to take Moctezuma hostage.

Showing one of the many puzzling aspects of Cortes's multifaceted character, he seems to have struck up a genuine friendship with the emperor. He could see the utility of the course his officers urged, but he preferred not to violate the emperor's dignity. Nevertheless, Moctezuma was imprisoned. His coffers were looted, and ultimately the Aztecs staged something of a revolt. In the upshot Moctezuma was killed, evidently by the Aztecs themselves, and another was named emperor. The Aztec state set about ridding itself of the Spanish menace. But the most powerful force the Spanish had unwittingly brought along had been unleashed: smallpox. The new emperor died after less than three months on the throne.

Cortes had his men cut the aqueduct bringing the capital's only supply of water from the springs at Chalputepec. Smallpox continued to ravage the empire's warriors, and the Spanish mounted a naval attack on the island cities with the brigantines they had constructed. Somewhat more than two years after Cortes landed at Cozumel, by mid–August 1521, the Aztec empire, high in the Valley of Mexico, was secured by him and his troops.

After a bit more than three years of resting on his laurels, Cortes decided it was time to make another reconnaissance in force, this time through the Maya lands in lower Mexico and upper Central America. His supposed reason for this was to subdue a lieutenant that he sent to Honduras to secure that area. Cristobal de Oli, his former quartermaster, had—as ordered—established a beachhead not far from the present-day banana town of San Pedro Sula in Honduras. But Cores had asked too much of Oli. He tasked him to stop in Cuba on his way to Honduras to recruit more men. There, Governor Velasquez turned his head, and Oli claimed Honduras in the name of the governor of Cuba. All this put Cortes in a funk. For a time he appears to have dithered, something men of action are not supposed to do. But in due course, he outfitted an expedition of 100 men to go by sea to Honduras. In charge of the company was a newly arrived kinsman, Francisco de Las Casas.

Las Casas attempted to throw a little dust in Oli's eyes by entering the harbor under a white flag. But Oli sent an armed contingent to meet him. A fight ensued. Las Casas got the better of it. A cadre of Oli's men sent word they were in fact Cortes's loyalists and willing to do the needful in order to subdue the renegade Oli. But Las Casas failed to land his troops immediately. In the night a storm blew up, wrecking his ship. He and all his surviving men were captured. At first he was kept in chains. The men—after swearing loyalty to Oli—were mustered into the ranks. Oli then made war on another Cortes colony founded on the nearby Rio Dulce, in present-day Guatemala. However, the sun quickly set on Oli. Las Casas engineered a coup whereby he stabbed Oli, a man of immense strength. Though badly wounded, Oli ran into the night. The garrison declared for Cortes, and now Oli was a fugitive in his own land. Shortly, he expired from his wounds. Honduras was secure for Cortes.

But Cortes did not know that. And truth be told, he probably didn't even want to know that. He would merely have had to dispatch a ship to round the Yucatan Peninsula to get the measure of the situation. But Cortes was action oriented. He decided to mount a land expedition to Honduras. In October of 1524, he set out from Mexico City with 320 Spaniards, 93 of them mounted. In his train was a formidable arsenal of cannon and other weaponry (Jones 1998; Sharer and Traxler 2006). In addition, there were a number of irregulars. These included several pages including Cortes's private lance bearers, several grooms to tend to the horses, three muleteers, two falconers, and an entire company of entertainers including a band. The instruments in the band were a clarion, a dulcimer, and a sackbut, an early version of the trombone. The entertainers included a juggler and a buffoon who put on puppet shows (Dias 1963). Among the non–Spanish were 3,000 Mexican warriors including Diving Eagle, the last emperor of the Aztecs, nephew and son-in-law of Moctezuma. Abandoning his post in Mexico City was dicey enough, but leaving the last duly constituted emperor was unthinkable. So Diving Eagle, his courtiers, and the deposed rulers of the other states of the Triple Alliance were made to accompany Cortes.

The first phase of this great expedition was a march overland from the Valley of Mexico to the area where the country narrows at the Isthmus of Tehuantepec. The expedition passed in the shadow of snow-capped Mt. Orizaba, over 18,000 feet high. On the way, he paused to marry off his interpreter and presumably former mistress, Donna Marina, to one of the company. To insure that everyone understood this marriage was on the up and up, the consummation of the vows was publicly witnessed. When about 130 miles from Coatzacoalcos, almost all the colonists met Cortes. This very much pleased Cortes's vanity. Being a complex man, Cortes exhibited almost as many traits of the saint as the scoundrel, and his marrying off Donna Marina, his vanity, and his desire to take the land route through an impenetrable jungle to Honduras, are all examples of his difficult-to-comprehend character.

The staging area for the expedition was the town of Coatzacoalcos. As we recall from the first section, Coatzacoalcos is today a city on the banks of the river of the same name. Its main industry is oil and it supports what must be one of the largest oil refineries in the western hemisphere. Just upstream from Coatzacoalcos lies the ruined Olmec capital of San Lorenzo, which flourished at the time of the Battle of Troy and the oldest city discussed in this book. Also, near Coatzacoalcos, Donna Marina, Cortes's interpreter was born and grew up. And it was from the fairly well developed colonial town even in Cortes's day, that the chief historian, Bernal Dias, of his Mexican and Honduran expeditions, was quartered. As noted, a goodly number of seasoned conquistadors came along with Cortes from Mexico City. To this number was added a group of young adventurers newly arrived in the country, and all of the Spanish who had settled in Coatzacoalcos. The latter, including Bernal Dias the writer, was by no means pleased by Cortes's demand they join the expedition.

They had settled into estates which had almost come into production. But there was no point protesting. Cortes's order was law, Dias whispered to his narrative. As we recall from the first section of this book, the area around Coatzacoalcos is among the wettest lowland area in North America. Ten feet of rain falls annually. Many large rivers, including the largest in Mexico, approach the sea in this area. The rivers form deltas from which many finger-like waterways make their way to the Gulf. All of these had to be crossed, but Cortes, as usual, welcomed the challenge. Where available, canoes were pressed into service. Where none was to be had, rafts or even bridges were constructed, one bridge spanning more than a half mile. After crossing the marshy coastal plain of Tabasco, he crossed Mexico's largest river the Gijalva near present day Villahermosa, Tabasco (Jones 1998). He then made his way south and east ferrying the company across the Usumacinta River near present-day Tenosique where he appears to have pivoted south, paralleling the Candelaria River. If this reading of his course is correct — and scholars still debate his route — he traced a pathway, not dissimilar to the aerial reconnaissance of the University Museum of Pennsylvania, discussed in chapter 2. That expedition resulted, as we recall, in the discovery of the ruined site of El Mirador and the near miss of Calakmul. Cortes found neither of those long-since abandoned sites, but he did come on Itzam Kanac, at the time still a going city, with a population of about 4,000. Modern scholars have identified this site as El Tigre on the Candelaria in southwest Campeche (Sharer and Traxler 2006). Cortes was much impressed by Itzam Kanac (Villagutierre 1983). The city was the seat of Akalan. This was the homeland of the Cholan Maya whose name has appeared many times in these pages as mysterious canoe traders who navigated around the Yucatan and also along the Gulf of Mexico. But to Cortes this city was impressive for its population — or more specifically for the food supply that fed them.

Lord knew there was little to be had of the latter. Cortes's wily Indian hosts had evidently sent him off on a snipe hunt. They promised lots of people, treasure, and lands suitable for valuable crops such as cacao. Cortes and his men got only two things, hunger and rain. It poured down. Every rivulet turned into a raging torrent and had to be bridged in order to cross. As for food, the force of 3,000 plus lived off the land, which is to say the cornfields of the local peasantry. But the peasantry was frequently close to nonexistent, and those they came across were few and far between and hard to track down. When word of the strange bearded men arrived, the locals made off into the forest taking their stores of grain with them — or hiding it, or burning it. The forest provided almost nothing in the way of edibles. Sometimes they ate a root that made the mouth burn (Dias 1963). The situation was desperate. Men who would kill on the command of Cortes secreted away every morsel, refusing to share even a few grains of corn with their master. The juggler and buffoon no longer had the energy to amuse the men, and two of the musicians grew too weak to play. Only one tooted away, but rather than soothe the men, his infernal racket annoyed them. They threatened to kill him if he didn't shut up. Then more ominously two of the guides decamped in the night. Rats fleeing a sinking ship?

Actually, no. The guides had been slaughtered by the Mexican auxiliaries. After being gutted and properly dressed, they were roasted in an earth oven on hot stones, and then lovingly devoured. The Spanish were horrified and solemnly lectured their allies on the iniquities of cannibalism. But before they reached the coast, the Spanish, too, would turn to the dreadful expedient of cannibalism. In the meantime, it was clear the predicament was playing on the nerves of even Cortes. Word filtered to him that Diving Eagle and other of the Aztecs were plotting an insurrection. Cortes summarily hanged the former emperor and at least one other. Cortes's relationship with Diving Eagle, like many of his other relationships, was perplexing. On Diving Eagle's capture, the ruler asked to be put to death. Cortes refused, saying he would be treated respectfully because he admired his courage. In part, Cortes had an ulterior motive: the secret horde of gold it was widely believed the Aztecs held. Diving Eagle claimed there was no such stash. It wasn't long before Cortes ordered him tortured, his feet supposedly being literally held to a fire. Now in the jungles of Central America he was rashly put to death, without even the slightest effort of a trial that would allow Diving Eagle to attempt to refute the evidence against him. According to Dias, Cortes's hasty actions later haunted him. They may well have been because he suspected — and correctly — that he would have to answer for them to the king of Spain. (Monarchs don't take kindly to the killing of fellow monarchs, not wanting such behavior to become infectious.)

But in other ways, Cortes was still Cortes. When the men, including the officers, lost all hope, alternately beseeching Cortes to abandon the expedition and hinting at mutiny, Cortes set a henequen cloth on the ground. The cloth bore a rough map of the Yucatan with the geographical features they knew. He set a compass on the map, and oriented it to the north. The men may feel lost, Cortes said, but he wasn't. Science and common sense told them they were dead on track to arrive in Honduras. What he didn't mention was that they were not even a half of the way to their destination from Coatzacoalcos.

They continued on through the lightly populated area. The few population centers they found were sometimes at war. Once they arrived at a village full of thatch houses, all of which had been newly built. Surrounding the town was a tall palisade of posts in front of which was a deep ditch or moat. The town even had a watchtower reminiscent of those shown in Terminal and Postclassic Maya murals. Hanging from the rafters of the houses were dozens of roasted turkeys. The granaries were full of corn. Not a person was in sight. What was going on? After a time, a few of the leading men were found hiding in the forest. They explained that they were being besieged by their enemy. Their old town had been destroyed, and Cortes's men had been mistaken for their enemies, the Lacandon, coming back for a fight. Rather than let them have their livestock should they lose, the citizens determined to have a feast and eat every last morsel themselves. (If they won the fight, they sensibly supposed they'd help themselves to the Lacandon's fouls for brood stock.) But before they were able to tuck in, Cortes arrived — and the Spanish sat down to this Thanksgiving-like feast.

Cortes took possession of the village in the name of the king but apologized to his hosts that he was not able, at present, to bestow proper security on them. He would return and chastise their enemies at a later date. These people are known to modern scholars as Kejaches or the Itza, a branch that had left Chichen Itza long before and settled in what might have been the old homeland of the Peten (Jones 1996). By now, Cortes was in modern-day Guatemala, Peten district, the heart of the southern lowlands in the Classic period. As we recall from chapter 5, the institution of divine kingship collapsed here more than six hundred years before. With it went the trappings of the Maya state. But as we saw in chapter 5, a much reduced population continued in the area, and it was the remnant population with the occasional village that Cortes had to rely on for sustenance. Cortes's force of thousands had to pass very close to the ruins of Tikal. If they were stumbled upon — and it is hard to believe that at least a few of the thousands of hungry foragers did not come on the huge temples — not a word found its way into any of the chronicles of the journey, most of which were written long afterward. The Spanish were looking for food and people which meant food. Even gold held little allure, and ancient ruins probably had no appeal at all.

But Cortes did find the city on the hill that the old Spanish priest told John Lloyd Stephens about, mentioned in the beginning of chapter 3. And it did gleam from the brilliance of its whitewashed skyscraping temples. The city was also, as the priest confided to the American traveler, well peopled, and they spoke a Maya language very similar to Yucatec Maya. The city occupied an island in the largest lake in the Peten, Lake Peten Itza. It was called Tayasal or Nojpeten, and it was governed by a king called Kan Ek. The granaries were full, and the king shared generously with Cortes. Not a word was mentioned about chastising Kan Ek and his Itza for raiding his northern neighbors. In fact, just the opposite was the case. Cortes was so pleased by their generosity that he gave Kan Ek a horse. How the old adventurer gave away one of his most prized horses is a story in itself.

After leaving Tayasal, the Spanish came to savanna lands where deer were plentiful. The supply of meat and a for once sunny-to-the-point-of-boiling sky bolstered Spanish spirits. The horsemen went wild chasing and lancing deer. It was a silly sport, and Cortes knew it, but boys will be boys. One horse completely foundered and died. (The Spanish said its fat melted, killing it.) Cortes own favorite animal, a black horse, grew sick. The savage old conquistador could not see his way to putting it down. He sent it back to Kan Ek as a mark of special favor. We will see in the upshot that it was indeed regarded as a mark of favor.

In the meantime, Cortes continued by the needle on to Honduras. Local guides either willfully misguided him or Cortes refused their council. The rains returned, and the land tilted upward. They were in the Maya Mountains. Though low, the Maya mountains are rugged. Even today, it takes the best part of a week to ascend the highest peak and return to pavement. And Cortes's men had to contend with rain. Every valley and canyon had a roaring torrent in its bottom. Finally, Cortes sought the help of the locals. But they too were at a loss. So he sent patrols of men in all directions. They came back to say there was nothing but water, water everywhere. But the last patrol came in. It had captured three women — and some corn. The women supplied the intelligence that it was only five days march to the

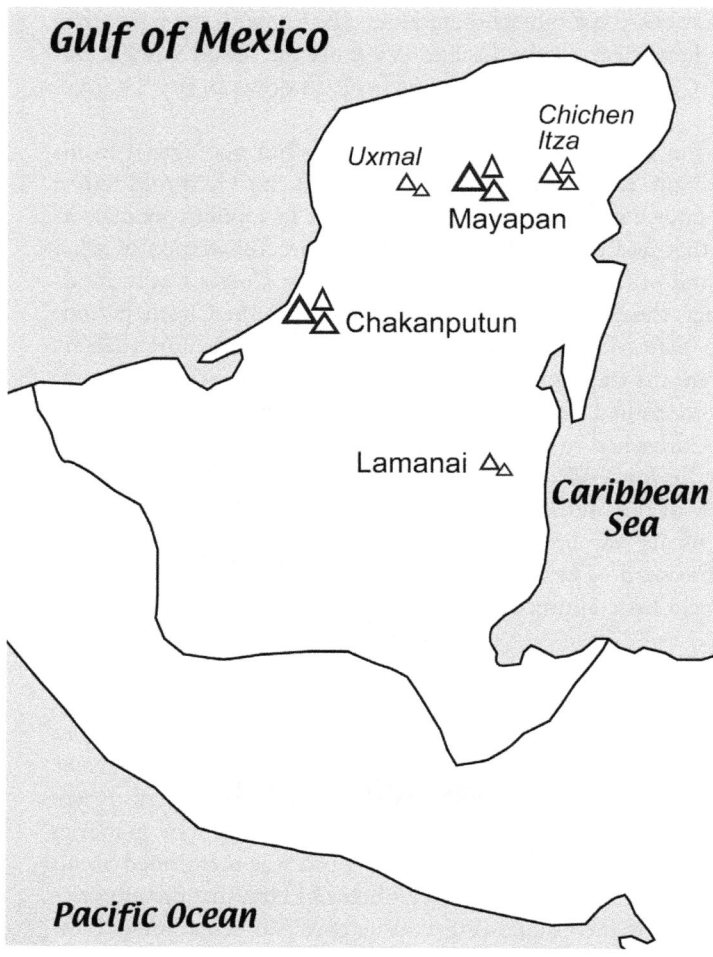

Mayapan and two principle late Postclassic sites are shown in relation to the abandoned Uxmal and Chichen Itza.

Spanish outpost on the Rio Dulce. By now it was April 1525. The travails of this misbegotten expedition were far from over, including Cortes's final call to justice for what came to be regarded as the lynching of Diving Eagle. The long decline in Cortes's fortunes had begun. But the expedition was invaluable for us. It gave a glimpse of the southern lowlands of the Classic Maya six hundred years later, and to it must be credited the western discovery of island kingdom of Tayasal, which gave rise to the enduring legend of the last Maya kingdom in the jungles, which, as we have seen, has raised hopes innumerable times of finding a populated and still functioning Tikal in the Peten wilderness. This Maya city, protected by the great wilderness which surrounded it, was to continue in existence for almost two centuries more. But before taking up the fate of the city of Tayasal (Nojpeten), we must return to the northern Yucatan and discuss the city of Mayapan that took over as the first city of the peninsula after the fall of Chichen Itza.

Mayapan, A.D. 1100 (1263)–1500

The Postclassic period, during which Mayapan was the undisputed leading city of the lowland Maya, is among the more confusing and least understood Maya epochs. This period concluded with the European conquest. Spanish chronicles, notably the *Relacion* of Bishop Landa, have left accounts of what the early Europeans witnessed. And — unlike any other period — the Maya themselves, the so-called jaguar priests, the chilam balam, wrote narratives that have been fodder for anthropological interpretation. The Postclassic period centered in the northern Yucatan and on the Caribbean coasts (and to a lesser extent the highlands of Guatemala), among the more accessible of Maya areas. Given all of this, it's rather a puzzle as to why the period should have been so misunderstood and for so long.

The Castillo at Mayapan was almost an exact, if much smaller, copy of the one at Chichen Itza.

The reasons, as usual are multiple, but the most obvious are the conclusions of the Carnegie Institution of Washington. That agency was the funding engine for much of the Maya research in the first half of the 20th century. Toward the end of its participation in Maya studies, during the 1950s, an expedition focused on Mayapan. It did not like what it saw. The centerpiece of the site was an exact replica of the Castillo at Chichen Itza, only much smaller. The population of the site was believed to have been no more than ten thousand. Many of the buildings were constructed of reused Puuc building stones, and those buildings seemed small, cramped, and shoddily constructed. Vaulted rooms were no longer built, the ceilings being flat and uninteresting. In the words of the final Carnegie report, "There seemed to be little striving for permanence. Just window dressing and false fronts." Indeed, some Mayapan buildings consisted of stone fronts with wood and thatch interiors, giving only the impression of a real Maya temple of yesteryear. "A coat of paint," the report went on, "will hide many faults and the ample use of plaster at Mayapan undoubtedly accomplished the same purpose" (quoted in Sabloff 2007).

The head of the Mayapan project called the culture of Mayapan degenerate. For instance, he wrote, "Mayapan was born when civilization was in eclipse and in spite of, or perhaps because of, the numerous foreign influences that moved across the peninsula and filtered into the city, culture never approached the excellence of earlier centuries." The chief reason for the decline, archaeologists at the time believed, was a loss of religious faith at the expense of materialism. "That personal comfort and glory came ahead of religious devotion is shown by the palaces and finer residences being built and apparently better furnished than the temples and other ceremonial buildings.... Over its life the city was subjected to numerous outside influences, but instead of finding a stimulus in them, the result was a sterile eclecticism, a culture without vitality." According to this archaeologist, Mayapan was "a degenerate civilization, devoid of great art," that had "reached a dead end." The great but often mistaken archaeologist J. Eric Thompson summed it up by saying, "I feel it is a manifestation of a great cultural dislocation resulting from a shift from a hierarchic to a secular and militaristic culture.... In compensation there was brisk trade and advances in material culture" (all quoted from Sabloff 2007). In short, the great pyramids and the satisfying vistas of the Classic and Terminal Classic were a thing of the past. Can a loss of aesthetic values in public architecture really be a marker of a society on the skids? If so, Lawrence Roys pointed out, modern American culture is clearly heading downhill. Not long ago, according to Roys, our buildings were constructed of stone (like the classic Maya). Nowadays, all great buildings have steel or reinforced concrete skeletons, with stone or faux stone facings. The reason for this is that we build our edifices for the here and now, not for distant societies to admire and pass judgment on — as did the Maya, and all other peoples. Maya civilization, therefore, should be judged accordingly. And in fact, though archaeologists might grouse about the degenerate Postclassic architecture, what they really were talking about was an assumption that we now know to be false. It was believed prior to the 1980s or so, that the Classic Maya were a peaceable people who devoted themselves to working in the fields and erecting temples for pious worship and intellectual study. The Postclassic period, it was believed, was a time when human sacrifice and warfare in large scale was introduced to the Maya area by outside cultures. As we have seen in these pages, the Maya practiced both warfare and human sacrifice from the beginning. As we have also seen, the religious expression of the Classic Maya that Thompson so admired was what caused the Classic and Terminal Classic downfall. The entire society was organized to support a quasi-divine king and his retainers. The peasant class was squeezed to the breaking point, and the society did break, with individual divine kingships collapsing one by one during a period of a couple of centuries at the end of the Classic period.

Without divine kings to organize state religious spectacles, religion became a matter for the home shrine. The new organizing principle for the society during the Postclassic, as Thompson noted disparagingly, was trade. The buildings and residences of Mayapan may appear cramped and small to modern archaeologists. But consumer goods and resulting comforts provided by Mayapan trade were passed more equitably among the population as a whole than at any other Maya center. As we saw in the last segment, sea-going traders coasted around the Yucatan Peninsula during the heyday of Chichen Itza. They were responsible for the rise of Chichen Itza as a great Maya power. This trade continued during the three hundred or so years that Mayapan was the first city of northern Yucatan. The ports used by Mayapan traders were the same or near those Chichen Itza traders used. Examples of these ports are Cozumel, Tulum, the keys off the Belize coast, and so on all the way to Honduras and perhaps beyond. On the Gulf of Mexico side of the Yucatan, Mayapan traders interacted with "Mexicanized" peoples in Tabasco and southern Campeche. These folk spoke Nahuatl, as a trading or home language, and practiced many of the customs of Central Mexico. In the last hundred years of Mayapan's existence, Aztec customs and personnel arrived in the city through the Tabasco connection. Locally produced trade items again were those Chichen offered. "White gold" (salt) came from coastal saltpans, and cotton and honey were major products of the peninsula. Various dyes could only be found in the lowlands. The most valuable dye product was a pigment called Maya blue that was much in demand in the highlands. The dye coloring was provided by the indigo plant, and clays found in Coba and other parts of the Yucatan incorporated mineral ingredients that made for a brilliant and long-lasting blue. The paint, as noted earlier, was used for mural painting—and daubing the bodies of sacrificial victims before undergoing the knife. Slaves were also a staple export product of the city.

Mayapan is located about 60 miles west of Chichen Itza and about 25 miles southeast of Merida. It is at almost the same latitude as Chichen (Milbrath 2005). The center of the city is encircled by a wall three miles long. There are 4,000 buildings inside this core zone. The area had been lightly populated for centuries before the development of Mayapan proper. In the time just prior to Mayapan's founding, a Puuc town may have occupied the locality. Traditionally, Mayapan was believed to be founded about A.D. 1263. As we will see in more detail shortly, a political cataclysm hit the town in the mid A.D. 1400s, and it was abandoned at about A.D. 1500 owing to an epidemic. Nowadays, scholars favor a founding date for the city earlier than A.D. 1263, such as about A.D. 1100 or even 1050. The Carnegie project estimated the population to be about ten thousand. Recent estimates range from slightly more than ten thousand to about twenty thousand.

The ceremonial heart of Mayapan centers on the Cenote Chen Mul complex. Among the most striking features of this group is a Castillo that looks remarkably similar to the one at Chichen Itza. It is a radial pyramid with stairs ascending all four sides, and like Chichen's Castillo it has nine terrace platforms, but the Castillo of Mayapan is a diminutive version, being only about fifty feet high. There is also a round caracol-style building. As you recall, temples with serpent balustrades were a feature at Chichen Itza. Both the High Priest's Temple and the Castillo are examples. Mayapan has five serpent temples. They are located in the ceremonial core of Mayapan.

The distinguishing feature of a serpent temple is dual serpent columns or balustrades. At ground level, the fanged mouth of the snake welcomes the visitor. High above are sculpted rattles—not now always present—indicating the venomous nature of the mythological beast (Pugh 2001). Often, the skin of the serpent is imprinted with stylized feathers. The first known example of a serpent temple, according to Timothy Pugh of Queens College, Flushing, New York, was the Feather Serpent Temple at Teotihuacan. It dates to about A.D. 250. The temple is usually called Quetzalcoatl's Temple, and all serpent temples seem to evoke Quetzalcoatl. A round temple near the Castillo gives a good clue that these temples at Mayapan were also ones devoted to Quetzalcoatl. As we recall from Chichen Itza, the round temple or Caracol was dedicated to the god of wind, one of Quetzalcoatl's alter egos. At Mayapan an underground passage or cave connects the round temple to a cenote providing an ongoing draft for the god of wind.

The Maya were artists with genius. They knew how to make their images do double duty. According to Pugh, the reptiles of the serpent temples also evoke the vision serpent. As we saw going all the way back to the Olmec era, royalty (and every one else) in Meso-america sought guidance by hallucinogenic visions. These visions could be induced by pain or use of drugs. Ancestors would often be the conduit for the guidance. In art, the ancestors are shown as being presented to the person seeking the vision by a snake, the vision serpent.

Also according to Pugh, the serpent balustrades (or columns) are sometimes depicted with tiny forefeet. In this case, that balustrade—though also equipped with a rattle tail—suggests the crocodile present at the creation of the present age. As we recall, the Maya creation myth begins with darkness and a primordial sea. A mythic reptile floats on that sea. Usually the reptile is depicted as a giant sea turtle, but at times it is crocodile-like. As a crocodile, the beast arches upright separating the sea from the heavens, creating light and earth into the bargain. The upright crocodile becomes the cosmic world tree that continues to separate the sky from the earth and hold back the great deluge that one day will inundate the earth again, starting yet another creation cycle. The crocodile can also be regarded as the earth monster or mountain monster, which has the same function of keeping earth and sky separate.

Four of the five serpent temples in the ceremonial core at Mayapan lie on each of the cardinal points of the compass about the fifth and largest serpent temple, the Castillo. Most of the serpent temples came equipped with stone rings to tie sacrificial victims, human and

Feather Serpent balustrades on the ultimate Feather Serpent temple, the Castillo at Chichen Itza. The balustrades were symbolic of cosmic ties.

animal. Blood sacrifice was common in the Maya area, of course, but the cult of Quetzacoatl with its special affinity to Venus, the fickle planet of war, demanded victims be offered on a routine and frequent basis. According to Pugh, the five temples can be regarded as a Maya cosmogram. The concept of the Maya cosmogram was introduced in the second chapter of this book when discussing the Preclassic period. Then we associated the east with the sunrise and the color red and west with the sunset and the color black. North and south were associated with up and down, rather than the directions of the compass. The fifth point of the cosmosgram was the most vital. It was the center, represented by a cornstalk — the staff of Maya life — or a tree such as the ceiba or the vertical crocodile mountain monster. Early Maya leaders understanding the power of this myth took it over. They claimed the center devolved on a divine king whose supernaturally endowed duty it was to care for his people (and for his people to care for him). The image of the cosmosgram survived among the Maya for two thousand years, and during most of that time it was used to back up the power of inherited royalty. But at Mayapan, while there may have been a monarch, there was no divine king in the same sense as in the Classic period.

So it may be wondered why did the cosmogram persist as a means of organizing the central ceremonial core of the city? A closer examination of the serpent temples gives an answer. The Castillo in the center stands alone. It was meticulously tended including the repaving of the plaza surrounding it thirteen times. Four temples at the cardinal points are part of a group of buildings which always includes a shrine and various small outbuildings, all probably used for religious purposes. A larger component of the assemblage is a colonnaded hall — with or without sculpted columns — similar to those we viewed at Chichen Itza. Pugh conjectures that social groups used the hall for public worship and ritual. No

An interesting feature of Mayapan architecture was stucco effigies with niches presumably for the skull of subject of the artwork.

doubt the other buildings of the assemblage were used by leading figures of the social group, who built (or rebuilt), maintained and owned them. But who were these mysterious social groups?

Actually, their names have been known all along. They are specified by Bishop Landa in his *Relacion* and in the books of Chilam Balam. A reader of this book will know two of them. The Xius were one group. They were, as you recall, the people credited with the founding and maintaining of Uxmal. Although only one Uxmal king, Lord Chac, has been named his family group, the Tutul Xius have long been known. Another group were the Cocoms. You will recall that one of hieroglyphic panels at Chichen Itza named Kukul Pakal, his brother, and a Cocom lord. It is believed by some that the first of the line of Cocoms at Mayapan were called Itza, but that the Cocom branch revolted against the larger group and took over that Itza linage at Mayapan. The other two groups were the Chels (also mentioned at Chichen Itza) and the Canuls, who as we will see, were a Johnny-come-lately group from southern Campeche or Tabasco. Pugh denominated the smallest and latest temple as belonging to the Canul linage. Other authors assign the western precincts of the city — the direction of Uxmal — to the Xius. The eastern parts — where Chichen Itza lay — in this ordering were the Cocoms (Sharer and Traxler 2006).

It is difficult to determine how such as strange amalgam of ruling lineages or houses should all end up in one city. The leading families specified here were not the only ruling families that lived in Mayapan. The rulers of all the provinces of Yucatan, and there were more than fifteen of them, lived in the city. They were sustained by food and other supplies sent to them by their vassals. These lesser families, it is believed, were virtual hostages of the rulers of Mayapan. No doubt they paid tribute and in other ways sustained the leadership by stiff taxes. In this way, Mayapan maintained itself as not only the cultural capital of the Yucatan, but the political one as well. But how did the imperial government of Mayapan function?

Until recently the archaeological consensus was that Mayapan was governed by a sort of council of the leading families called *multepal*, meaning joint rule. As we recall, this was also believed for some time to have been the means by which Chichen Itza governed itself. Recently, some leading northern lowland scholars such as William Ringle and George Bey have swung to the belief that Chichen Itza always was ruled by a monarch, and the same goes for Mayapan, with both the Cocom and Xiu families exerting a great deal of power and influence in the monarchy at Mayapan (Milbrath 2007). The actual king was probably of the house of Cocom, most or all of the time. Later on, the Cocoms may have felt they were slipping from power. They hired or invited the Nuahatl-speaking Canul as mercenaries to help keep them in power. The Canuls obviously made the best of the situation by erecting their own serpent temple and quickly becoming one of the leading groups of the city. Their rise and their arrogance was deeply resented. The Xius used this resentment to organize the other leading houses into a revolt. All Cocoms were killed with the exception, it was reported in the ethnohistories, of a younger son away on a trading mission in Honduras. The Canuls were exiled from Mayapan. The temples and houses of the Itza and Canuls were looted, burned, or otherwise ritually terminated — these destructive events were discovered by archaeologists. All this occurred about the middle of the 15th century. Mayapan was pretty much abandoned fifty or so years later when an epidemic struck, perhaps one of the first loosed by Europeans in the New World.

None of this explains how the ruling families of all the provinces of the Yucatan were huddled together in Mayapan. Archaeologists think something called the *may* cycle may explain it. In chapter 1 we were puzzled by the Olmec capital of San Lorenzo losing its status and power. As one of the possible answers we cited the may cycle, the doctrine that a particular city would be the capital or *may* for a cycle of 13 periods of katuns (usually about twenty years). In the case of Mayapan, it is believed the capital of the Yucatan was Chichen Itza until between A.D. 900 and 1000. At that time, the Itza transferred the *may* to Chakanputun (present day Champoton, Campeche) for one cycle (Schele and Mathews 1998). During this time, the Xius were the rulers of Mayapan. That is shown by early practices carried over from the Puuc regions, such as the erection of stela at the end of each katun and the incorporation into their buildings of Chak masks brought from Puuc sites. At the end of that *may* cycle, the Itza conquered Mayapan and transferred the *may*—or capital—there. The timeframe is about that of the traditional founding of Mayapan, A.D. 1263. It was at this time that the Castillo, which is a perfect albeit shrunken version of the one at Chichen was reconstructed. Thirteen new pavements were laid in the courtyard of the Castillo. It is assumed one pavement was put down as part of the renewal ceremony for each katun period. In other words, those 13 pavements account for one complete *may* cycle. At approximately the terminus of that *may* cycle the Xius rose up and overthrew the Cocom/Itza. By the Maya way of thinking, the cycle was about to expire. The idea of revolt to kill the old order and regenerate a new one would have been perfectly consistent with Maya ideology. The notion that the old order was ready to fall—by dint of calendrical prophesy—may even have assisted the Xius in rounding up support for their revolt. Scholars have debated the concept of the *may* cycle for about thirty years. There is not yet agreement on how the concept influenced the course of Maya history through the various ages from the Early Preclassic through the Postclassic. The clearest instance of its effect appears to be in this instance, which is the transfer of the *may* from Chichen Itza to Chakanputun to Mayapan. Many known dates can be correlated to the cycles starting from the fall of Chichen Itza, but two different katun lengths (the other uses a 24-year katun) must be used, and even then all dates cannot as yet be reconciled. In any case, archaeology and the ethnohistories both agree a destructive event took place at Mayapan within a hundred years or so of the arrival of Europeans in the Yucatan.

To return to the question of the vigor of the civilization at Mayapan, it was one of the few core urban areas in Mesoamerica where metallurgy was practiced (Paris 2008). Archaeologists have uncovered two locations that appear to have been metal-working shops, both in what were elite areas of the city close to ceremonial centers. Not even the Aztec capital of Tenochtilan, with its vastly larger population, had any metallurgical production within its limits. Metal production in highland areas occurred closer to the source of the metal. Altogether almost 400 metal objects of all kinds have been found in or near Mayapan. Fifteen percent of the items were utilitarian or miscellaneous in nature such as tweezers (three in number) or needles (just one) or pieces of metal sheet or ingot. By far the largest percentage, 85 percent, of the metal items were bells, some of which were imported. The more specialized items such as tweezers, needle and ring also appear to have been imported.

Bells were multifunctional. They, along with cocoa beans and shell beads among other things—could be used as currency, and they could be applied ornamentally to gowns as sort of fashion statement. Very small bells lacked clappers. They are called tinklers because they tinkled by clicking against one another. Somewhat larger bells were fitted with a clapper. They came in a variety of shapes—globular, pear, or rather vee-shaped—none being "bell-shaped" in the form most commonly known today. All had suspension loops to attach a thong. That the bells were incorporated into items of dress can be told by the green threads attached to some when discovered by archaeologists. Archaeologists believe the copper kept the cotton thread from rotting completely away. Rattles of various sorts had been long associated with Maya costumes. Metal bells probably replaced them, but the people of Mayapan had special reason to venerate bells.

Quetzalcoatl was associated with bells. The Chilam Balam of Mani, the colonial town to which the Xiu family moved after the fall of Mayapan, states that "Kukulkan beckoned with his hands, his bells tinkled, and he gathered his tribute of honey and quail. In the nineteenth year Kukulkan beckoned a second time, and again his war bells were heard, and he took his donation of the miserably poor ones." In short, Kukulkan rang the bell of war — with its attendant unpleasantness (Paris 2008).

The method used to produce these items was lost-wax casting. In this process, a wax mold is fashioned and filled with molten copper. A fair amount of practice is required to turn out product of consistent quality, but not a great deal of industrialization is needed. Excavations have turned up just four crucibles at Mayapan. These were simply clay pots of the tecomate variety. No specialized features like pour spouts or handles were added indicating the art of copper work had not developed greatly. The copper product was simply heated to the melting point, apparently without the use of a forge. Miscast bells and casting waste were found, half melted, in one of the crucibles. On Columbus's last voyage, he spied a Maya canoe in the Bay of Honduras. Copper-working tools were carried by its occupants. This has led to speculation that itinerant coppersmiths might have moved around the Maya area. Two of the four crucibles found at Mayapan were in burial goods in a grave. Five skeletons were interred with them, presumably one of which was the coppersmith. The other two crucibles plus 282 bells were cached in the foundation of a building. In short, about three quarters of the copper items discovered at Mayapan were cached in that one building.

Comparing the metal work found at Mayapan to that discovered at Chichen Itza does little to enhance Mayapan's reputation as a leading trade or industrial center. Although no casting of metal objects occurred at Chichen, gold work did occur there as noted in the last section. Many items of engraved and hammered sheet gold such as masks, both miniature and life-sized, effigy items such as spears, disks, ornaments and so on were discovered in the sacrificial cenote. Many more items cast of gold or tumbaga, an alloy of gold and copper, included figurines of many shapes. All of the sorts of bells found at Mayapan were also found at Chichen as well as a much wider assortment of bells both in terms of method of construction and shape, such as human and deity effigy bells. The Chichen bells were far more intricate and they necessitated more technical knowledge to cast (Paris 2008). It is clear that in terms of mettalurgy and metal products Mayapan — and perhaps the late Postclassic as a whole — took a backseat to earlier places and times.

Mayapan's leading artistic and cultural innovation came with what is called the Chen Mul modeled effigy censer (Milbrath et al. 2007). Censers are vessels used for burning incense, such as are currently used in Catholicism and other faiths. The Maya used them in a similar way in a number of different ceremonies. Archaeologists named this censer for the Chen Mul ceremonial area at Mayapan that includes the Castillo and the other serpent temples discussed above. In particular, Chen Mul is the name of the cenote roughly in the center of the ceremonial core. The term "effigy" is included in the name censer because the clay vessels, which are usually about twenty inches high, were shaped in the form a god. Ten gods were depicted on the Chen Mul censers.

A study of these censers provides an interesting view into the world of both Mayapan and the late Postclassic age. Images of many of the ten deities would have been found in Maya cities from the Preclassic period onward. According to Milbrath, the most common four gods are Chac (Maya god of rain), Itzamna (the creator god often depicted as the Principal Bird Deity), the Death God, the Maize God (which we have discussed at some length), and the Merchant God. Others effigies seem to be a blend of Maya gods and those from other areas of Mesoamerica, reflecting the cosmopolitan nature of late Postclassic times. An example of such a deity would be Tlaloc, the Mexican rain god. This personage had been known and depicted in the Maya area for centuries. Clearly, it is related to the long-nosed Chac, but Tlaloc was usually shown without a snout and wearing goggles, and it had war aspects that Chac may have lacked. But many of the effigy censers depict gods that are wholly foreign and can be identified with Central Mexico. These are Tlahuizcalpantecuhtli, Tlazolteotl, and Xipe. As we have seen, Maya deities could be demanding of the flesh and blood of their subjects. Central Mexican gods trumped them exponentially. Tlahuizcalpantecuhtli was the god of the morning star aspect of Venus. It was believed this god could inflict terrible damage not only to humans in war but to the corn crop and the water supply. Tlazolteotl was called earth lord or earth lady. Its aspect was usually feminine and shown in the guise of giving birth, in a squatting position with a horribly grimaced face. It was every bit as menacing to humans as Tlahuizcalpantecuhtli, seeing how her mouth was made of flint blades. Xipe was known as the lord of the flayed skin. Its devotees flayed a human victim and wore the rotting skin like a cape for twenty days. Xipe was associated with agricultural fertility.

How did these central Mexican deities come into the pantheon at Mayapan? Archaeologists say the answer is trade. (The merchant god — one of the more common depicted on Chen Mul censers — is shown with cacao beans, money, in his hair.) And clearly Mayapan was top of the heap in terms of trade in the Yucatan. This assertion is shown by the locations in which Chen Mul modeled censers have been found: everywhere in the Maya part of its trading sphere. Starting at Champoton (Chakanputun) on the southern coast in the Gulf of Mexico and going all the way around the coast of the peninsula to the Caribbean and south to Belize and inland to the Peten, these censers are the most common sort of ceremonial goods. Strangely (to us), few have been found in a whole state. Most had been smashed into bits in a ritual manner. Often times only some of the sherds were left indicating that other sherds were scattered in another location or locations. Materials from Chen Mul censers have been found in burials, caches, and around altars in association with a number of gods, especially Venus. Some also been found discarded in garbage middens. Censers received their power by dint of their ability to communicate with the gods through copious amounts of billowing copal smoke. Archaeologists believe the censers may have been used in calendrical celebrations, notably katun ceremonies. This may account for the high percentage of smashed crockery, representing the death of the old katun with another censer replacing it. At the end of the katun the replacement censer would be smashed and so on.

The vessels used outside of Mayapan were occasionally manufactured in Mayapan, but more often they were of local production and only modeled on the original Chen Mul censers. The locally manufactured ones were generally smaller. The best emulations of Mayapan censers came from two widely divergent sources, Chakanputun on the Gulf Coast and in inland Belize at Lamanai, which as you may recall was the second largest city during Preclassic times and which continued to thrive right into the Postclassic. The Chakanputun censers were for a time believed to be imports but modern analysis showed local clay was used in their production. Censers produced in outlying areas tended to be considerably more generic (and cruder) than those in more cosmopolitan areas. Eye holes in the better grade became dots in the outlying ones, and fully molded teeth become vertical lines, and so on. Chen Mul censers came into use about A.D. 1250, or about the date it is believed the Cocom Itza took control of the city. They survived until the Spanish conquest or about A.D. 1540.

The Next to Last Maya City State, Tayasal (Nojpeten), A.D. 1400–1697

Francisco de Montejo, as you may recall, was one of the two men Cortes sent to Spain with Mexican treasure for the king. He successfully pled Cortes's case to the royal court, and while he was at it, he secured for himself the title of adelantado of the Yucatan, which at the time was considered a separate entity. In 1527, he attempted to subdue the northern Maya peoples. He was destined for no end of trouble. After the fall of Mayapan, the provinces that had been loosely amalgamated by Mayapan became fiercely independent. There were at least sixteen provinces, and each fought the Spanish with determination. Even worse for Montejo, Francisco Pizarro hit the mother of all lodes of gold bullion in Peru. Montejo's soldiers abandoned his enterprise to try Peru where they expected to fill their pockets with Inca plunder. After almost thirteen years of trying, the Montejos — father, son, nephew — were about broke. The Yucatan was still in the hands of the Maya. In a desperate last attempt, Montejo's son moved north from the secure area of Tabasco to Campeche. He established the city of Campeche in 1540, the first Spanish city in the Yucatan. From there he called all Maya to come and submit to him as the true representative of the King of Spain. Not surprisingly, at first, this strategy did not succeed any better than force of arms.

But then Montejo got a lucky break. Representatives of the Xiu family, now based in Mani, heeded the call. The Xius, as we have seen, were one of the oldest and most powerful lineages in the Yucatan. They founded the Puuc state of Uxmal and maintained a leadership role at Mayapan. Why would they agree to submit to the Spanish? Even worse (or better for the Montejos), they agreed to take up arms against the other Maya of the peninsula. The reason was simple, and their old nemesis, the Cocoms (from Chichen Itza and the other major ruling house at Mayapan), had a hand in their turning against their own (Jones 1996).

The sacred cenote at Chichen Itza had remained after the fall of the city as a site of pilgrimage for peoples through out the peninsula. The Cocom maintained control of the cenote, charging a toll to anyone who wanted to do devotions there. They also controlled the town of Sotuta. A party of Xius wanting to make the pilgrimage applied for assurances of safe passage. They received even more. They were invited to Sotuta where they were treated like kings. The Xius had been apprehensive because of the uprising they had staged against the Cocom leadership at Mayapan almost a hundred years earlier. Then just about every male Cocom from Mayapan had been exterminated. Let bygones be bygones they were told. The partying went on for four days, long enough to convince even the most suspicious Xiu that the Cocoms understood the Maya had to stand together against the Spanish. Then when their guard was down, the Cocoms fell on the Xius and massacred the entire party.

So the Xius that had escaped the massacre by dint of staying in Mani went to Campeche. They promised to convert to Catholicism and assist the Spanish as needed. And they did.

Even with their help, it took the Spanish six years to pacify the peninsula, but by then the pagan gods (as the Spanish saw them) had been destroyed and the local Maya were rounded up into villages that often resembled concentration camps. The euphemism for this gathering of Maya was called being "reduced." The year was 1546.

But there was a fly in the ointment so far as the Spanish were concerned. It was that island city deep in the Peten that Cortes had visited in his march to the Rio Dulce, 21 years earlier. It exerted an ill effect on the northern Yucatan. Hardly had a year gone by after the pacification when the first rebellion against Spanish authority was launched by Maya. This occurred in the area below Chichen Itza and along the Caribbean coast making the Spanish stronghold of Bacalar in southeast Yucatan vulnerable. This seat, just north of the present Belize border, was located at the south end of the multicolored lake of that name inland from Chetumal Bay.

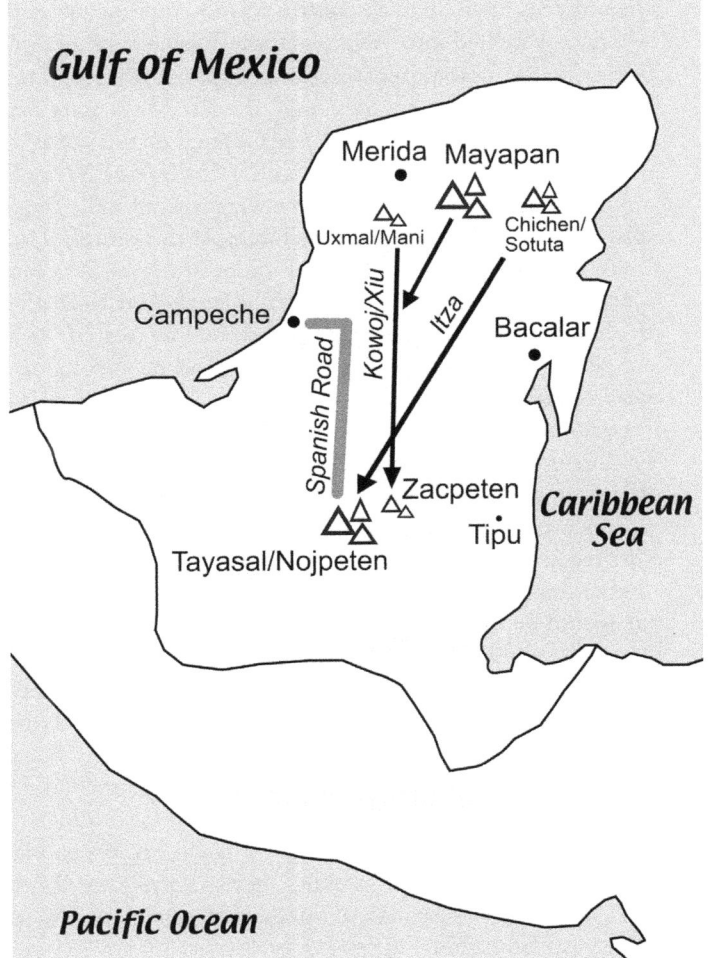

This map shows the movement of the Xius and the Itza from the northern Yucatan to central Peten at about the time of Conquest. The Spanish road was constructed to the last Postclassic Maya sites in the 1690s.

The first rebellion was put down but the area to the west of Bacalar remained wild and attractive to recalcitrant Maya. This was the territory just north of the Peten where the Itza remained in their island bastion. Also, from time to time the Itza staged raids on friendly Maya, sometimes far to the north and west. Courageous Franciscan monks led with their chins. They had built a mission station within fifty miles of the Itza city of Tayasal (Nojpeten). This mission was called Tipu. It was located on the Mopan branch of the Belize river near present day Benque Viejo, Belize, on the Guatemalan border. There were no permanent Spanish at Tipu, but itinerant monks visited—and the Itza raided. Another problem was refugee Maya from the Yucatan. As the demands of Spanish overlords intensified, more Maya voted with their feet. They headed for the lands loosely controlled by the Spanish, such as the province of Tz'ul Winikob,' which today we call Belize. Those who felt even the most nominal Spanish control was too onerous headed for the lake district of the Peten where they melted into the population. In short, a functioning Maya city-state in the neighboring wilderness posed a serious threat to the economic and political stability of the Yucatan. Much talk of "reducing" the last Maya state occurred in the Spanish capitals of the New World — and even in the Council of the Indies in Spain. But little was done.

Over the century and a half after Cortes's visit, the island capital had been visited by a number of Spanish priests. Some were treated well. Two that would fall into that category discovered a stone idol in a thatch temple that simply appalled them. This idol was shaped like a horse, and it was called Thunder Horse or War Horse. It was an effigy of the horse Cortes had gifted Lord Kan Ek. The horse had been gloriously cared for, being fed only the best meats and flowers, as a god should be treated. As a surprise only to the Itza, it died. An effigy of the horse was constructed, and Fr. Orbita on seeing it, sprung on its back and began beating its head with a stone. The head fell off, and the Itza fell upon the good padre. He was saved being sacrificed to the Thunder Horse by the quick thinking of his companion. Fr. Fuensalida broke into an inspired sermon, and both padres were allowed to leave the island on good terms with Kan Ek and other townsmen. Two or three years later the two padres returned. This time they had a formal proposal to make Kan Ek. If he accepted Christianity, he — and his heirs — would be allowed to rule his island kingdom without a "reduction." They would have to pay no tribute for ten years, and then afterward the tribute tax would be light. Kan Ek liked this arrangement. He agreed. He even erected a cross next to his dwelling. However, there were others, notably the priests and prophets who would be put out of business by this deal, who did not look so favorably on what they heard. They vetoed the idea. Kan Ek told the padres he had consulted the prophesies, and they had told him not yet, in so far as accepting the word of Christ. The good fathers returned to northern Yucatan disappointed. All this happened in the second decade of the 17th century, almost a full century after Cortes "discovered" Tayasal (Nojpeten).

A few years later — by now the Pilgrim Fathers had landed at Plymouth Rock and had consumed the first Thanksgiving feasts in the New World — another padre, Fr. Delgado, took up the work Orbita and Fuensalida started. As a matter of fact, Delgado's project was even more ambitious. He began trying — and succeeding — in bringing the faith to semi-rebellious Maya in that vast hinterland west of Bacalar and southeast of Campeche, an area that even today is still largely undeveloped. He was accompanied by a Spanish officer who saw the economic benefit in "reducing" the Indians to concentrated towns. Annoyed by the officer's violence and outright profiting from Maya labor, Delgado abandoned the soldiers and made his way to Tipu in Belize. He sent word to Kan Ek of his presence. Would he be welcomed? The answer he received was yes.

Fr. Delgado was escorted by 80 Christian Maya from Tipu. In the meantime, a party of twelve soldiers had caught up to him. They came along. As soon as they arrived at Tayasal, all of them were seized and sacrificed to the gods by the ripping out of their hearts. Their heads were cut off and impaled on stakes. The last to go was Fr. Delgado. He was informed that the reason for this massacre was Fr. Orbita's destruction of the Thunder Horse god — and the carrying off of other gods. Delgado, it is claimed, was still preaching as his beating heart was extracted from his chest.

Word of this massacre was taken to Bacalar. A messenger was dispatched to tell the soldiers working west of Bacalar. The messenger was denounced as a liar. The soldiers were in no danger, the officer interested mainly in Maya hands to do his work, said. In order to make the messenger recant of this massive lie, he was tortured. Then the officer, men and recently "reduced" Maya repaired to the thatch church for Sunday services. Naturally, they stacked their arms outside the church as it would have been an affront to God to appear in a holy temple armed. It was then they were fallen on — evidently by a party of Itza led by a prominent priest. All were killed. The Spanish were ritually sacrificed and beheaded. The Christian Maya were merely killed. Their bodies were not mutilated. Later, a detachment of soldiers tracked the Itza war party down. They found chalices and other ecclesial equipage from the church and the commander's dagger. They had the right group. They killed them all. It is clear that the Spanish were correct in their belief that the Itza kingdom functioned as cat's paw in their flank. Itza attacks on Spanish mission settlements encroaching from the Guatemalan highlands soon followed. Then they sparked a rebellion in the native province that covered most of what we call Belize. The town of Tipu, a mission center for over a hundred years, rebelled against the Spanish. Interactions of this sort made the Spanish chary about a direct confrontation with the Itza, while still very much wishing that sore on their southern flanks would disappear. And so the Itza remained unmolested until the last decade of the 17th century, or until about the time the witch trials got under way in Salem, Massachusetts.

The various Spanish missions to the Itza had acquired a great deal of information about the island kingdom. For instance, the island bastion was almost perfectly round and consisted of sixteen city blocks. In the center was a hill about fifty feet high and on that hill sat a temple of nine terraces, evidently a spitting image of the castillos at Chichen Itza and Mayapan, though smaller than either and probably only having one staircase. The island pyramid and many others were plastered with coats of lime cement producing a dazzling appearance from the distance. Thatch houses and temples stood shoulder to shoulder throughout the island. The padres reported that the Itza had fled the area of Chichen Itza, perhaps the very town of Sotuta where the Cocoms evened the score with the Xius, about a century before the coming of the Europeans. The reason for their departure was a woman (Jones 1998).

The Itza leader had taken a fancy for the bride of another chief. The two eloped and a sizeable number of his relatives and retainers had followed him to what might have been, as noted earlier, the original homeland of the Itza in the forests of what we now call the Peten district of northern Guatemala. Scholars are always on the lookout for European corruption, in particular religious imagery, pervading the ethnohistories of the Amerindians. This story certainly appears to have elements that could have come from classical European mythology, notably the Troy legend with Helen as the temptress. But human nature is a constant, and the scholar who has paid closest attention to this matter, Ralph Roys (the translator of the books of Chilam Balam), believes there is evidence to support this story. Roys reported that the Itza suspected some Xiu trickery helped precipitate the love crisis that caused their departure from northern Yucatan (Jones 1996).

In the Peten, the missionary Spanish padres determined that at least four ethnic groups occupied the lakes region, all of whom like the Itza spoke a variant of Yucatec Maya. The Kejaches stayed as far to the north as they could and still remain out of Spanish sight. They were the group whose roasted turkeys Cortes helped himself to. The Itza plundered them, and quite reasonably, they feared the Itza. The Mopan Maya were subject to the Itza. This group may have been long-time residents of the area, or they could have immigrated from the north. Scholars have not determined their homeland for certain at present. The second strongest Maya group in the Peten, after the Itza, were known as the Kowojs. They claimed the lands along the north shore of Lake Peten Itza and the territory to the east of it. Their capital was Sacpeten. They too had migrated in mass into the area fairly recently. They had left the area near Mayapan at the time of the Spanish entrada. Scholars have equated them with the Xius.

In short, the two most powerful occupants of the Peten were also two old rivals and enemies from the northern Yucatan. This fact played into the demise of the last kingdom of the Maya, just as it went a long way toward causing the downfall of the Maya in the Yucatan. Grant Jones, the scholar to whom we owe a debt of gratitude for most of the detailed information about the central Peten during this period, has determined about 60,000 persons inhabited the lake district of Peten during this time. Of those, probably about 25,000 were inhabitants of the Lake Peten Itza kingdom, with 5,000 in the island town of Nojpeten (Tayasal). Five thousand Itza occupied each of their four mainland provinces. These states were positioned around the island center in a sort of Maya cosmogram. This area was the heart of the Classic Maya lowlands. A thousand years earlier the population would have been closer to a million. Also, it is worth noting that the climate had changed considerably in the interim, going from a drier, warmer climate suitable for corn culture to a wetter one that favored the development of a forest. Presumably, it was much more difficult to support a large population with extant technology at this time, despite the lavish vegetation all about.

So as the 17th century ground slowly toward the 18th, the last stronghold of "wild" Maya lay deep in the jungles of Peten. The stories of the savagery of the Itza had lost their sting—but the romance of conquering the last province of Spanish North America still beckoned. And that romance also promised wealth, of sorts. Perhaps all of the mineral gold and silver in Mexico had been found. The riches of the land were to be had in the product of the country, honey, beeswax—and the labor of the Indians. The early conquistadors that missed the silver strikes had grown if not rich, then comfortable, by collecting annual tribute from Indians allotted to them in a system known as encomienda. It was a holdover from feudal times, and obligations supposedly went in both directions. The encomiendero was tasked with ensuring his charges were properly instructed in Christianity. The subjects paid tribute. It was a reciprocal—but vastly uneven—relationship.

The man whose lot it was to conquer the last ancient Maya stronghold was Martin de Ursua. The Council of the Indies granted him the official responsibility of building a road through the Peten that would connect to the capital of Guatemala. But paying for that road was up to him. He intended to repay himself for the expense with the labor of the Indians. The king was interested in the Indian souls. It pleased him that they would be saved for the true religion by virtue of the encomienda granted Ursua. In theory, this system made a perfect match of Old World aims and New World circumstances. The king and the royal court appear in most instances to have been absolutely genuine. But they were not fortunate in those who they selected to assist in this noble but misguided enterprise. So Ursua began his road south from Campeche. The trajectory of this trail was roughly similar to the one Cyrus Lundell traveled in the 1930s on his journey that resulted in the discovery of Calakmul.

At the same time another company of Spanish—directed by the Council of the Indies—began making road from the highlands of Guatemala into the Peten. Clearly, the days of the independent city-state in Lake Peten Itza were numbered. Among those who agreed was the present Lord Kan Ek. His predecessor had passed on not long before. Among the new king's first acts was to send an emissary to the government in Yucatan asking that missionaries come and baptize his people. He wanted to accept Spanish authority. This was music to the ears of Yucatan's interim governor and Peten road builder Martin de Ursua.

He dispatched four monks under the leadership of Fr. Andres de Avendano. Fr. Avendano's party made their way down the crude trail hacked out of the jungle by Ursua's men. Progress had been slow, and they found the trail head near the present-day Campeche-Guatemalan border. Fr. Avendano pushed on ahead to Lake Peten Itza. There he was met by the present Kan Ek, a man in his mid forties, who professed great friendship. He held his hands against his chest and said his heart beat gladly in his breast because his Spanish friends had come. He held his hand against Avendano's chest and asked if his heart did not also beat gladly.

Avendano was not unmindful of the fate of the last monks who visited the lake. Their chests had been ripped open and their heart, still beating, pulled out. Rather ruefully, he said he was very pleased to be among the Itza. He was bundled in a canoe and taken to the island headquarters of Kan Ek. There he was feted and became absolutely certain of Kan Ek's good intentions toward him, not that Avendano had not learned a thing or two from earlier missions. For instance, he was shown a thatch temple with a basket suspended from the ceiling. What looked like a leg bone of a horse was protruding from the basket. Showing that even indomitable monks understood silence was often the better part of valor, he smiled pleasantly and said nothing. The truth of the matter is that what disturbed him more than the god-horse bones was the fact that many of the thatch houses appeared to be new.

Avendano deduced the buildings they replaced had been burned. And that this burning had occurred as a hostile act. Just as disturbing was the familiarity shown Kan Ek by many of his people. Avendano wondered if he would be able to deliver on his promise of allowing the baptism of the Itza. The answer arrived one day in a canoe. This vessel came from the north shore of the lake. That was the area occupied by the Kowoj, the Xiu immigrants. The leading figure in the canoe was the king of the Kowojs, known later to the Spanish as Captain Kowoj. He treated both Kan Ek and Fr. Avendano contemptuously. Among his many reasons for looking down his nose at Kan Ek was the fact that Kowoj's forces had raided and burned the thatch buildings in the island citadel some time before.

This incident points to one of the many puzzling elements of Maya warfare. There are many records of kings of Maya states that were feuding, even capturing and sacrificing each other's warriors, shortly thereafter engaging in, if not friendly, at least non-hostile intercourse, often of a ceremonial nature. The arrival of the Captain Kowoj clearly is such an example. Some sort of safe passage agreement allowed him to confront his enemy king in that chief's capital. In any case, the nonverbals of the message he delivered unnerved Avendano. And it appears to have had a similar effect on Kan Ek too. Shortly afterward, he told the priest that he consulted the prophesies. They said it would be four months before his people would be ready to accept the new religion. And as for right now, it was time to Avendano to leave. In fact, he was spirited off the island in the dead of the night. Rather than return north through territory controlled by the Kowojs, a canoe—with the three friars and Kan Ek's personal assistants aboard—sped to the eastern shore of the lake. Then the padres made their way back to safety, but not before getting hopelessly lost and almost perishing from hunger. One of the byproducts of their ordeal was blundering on and describing what were most likely the ruins of Tikal, the first Europeans known to do so (Sharer and Traxler 2006).

Avendano came to understand the reason for this strange behavior. The Itza line of succession ran through the mother's side of the family. Not only several brothers but also uncles were possible successors. As we saw during the Classic period, a good deal of tension could develop when one faction did not like the outcome of the selection of the ruler. In this case, Kan Ek's cousin claimed to be the true heir to the kingship. The peoples of Nojpeten appear not to have countenanced his claim. So he fled among the Kowojs and they were pursuing his candidacy by armed conflict. Kan Ek, therefore, removed the Spanish arrow from his quiver and sent the emissary to Merida promising fealty to the European king. The tacit hope was that the Spanish would secure his reign for him.

In the meantime, the Kowojs and some of the Itza from Tayasal warred on whatever Spanish they could find. Hapless parties that blundered to the lake from the Yucatan or Guatemala were set upon and killed. It was rumored they were eaten. All this strengthened Ursua in the belief that the island kingdom in the lake would have to be dealt a harsh lesson. He sent a military company down his road into the jungles of Peten. Soldiers were paid top wages of eight pesos a month, nine if they had their own gun. A force of sailors were recruited and these were given the princely sum of 40 pesos a month to head for the inland sea in the Peten. A full company of boatwrights, muleteers, and so on also were recruited and sent down the road.

It took a good bit more than a year for the preparations to be complete. But in March of 1697, the galeota was finished and riding the waves of Lake Peten Itza about six miles from the island capital. Ursua himself had made the trek down the jungle road to command the action. He was among the first to board the galeota on the fateful thirteenth of the month. The motive power of the vessel was oars, like the galleys of yore. Unlike them, this ship was outfitted with cannon, and up to two hundred marines shipped aboard with muskets, pikes, and broad swords. They nervously awaited the command to strike. As the galeota approached a bottleneck where the lakeshores pressed together, hundreds of canoes came out to meet it. The Spanish ship stayed on course, paying no attention to the canoes. The marines on board had been instructed not to return fire. The volleys of arrows clattered against the decks. A touch of the match to the fuse of the cannon would have taken out numerous canoes. A command to fire was not given. The galeota proceeded on course for the island. The arrows were paid no more attention to than mosquitoes.

As they approached the shallows of the island, the Spanish saw a wall of stone or mud lining the shore. The Itza in canoes shouted imprecations. The Itza on shore shouted imprecations. Volley after volley of arrows arced down on the galley. The Itza shouted that the Spanish were cowards. Still, Ursua would not allow the men to open fire. But then one of the arrows sliced through exposed flesh of one of the men aboard. His weapon discharged. Taking that as the command to fire, all blasted away. The marines went over the side of the vessel. They stormed the defenses of the island. The Itza had spent months, perhaps years, dreading this inevitable moment. As the Spanish laborers inched the road inexorably closer, they had to sense the floodtide that none of the peoples of the Americas had been able to resist would sweep over them too. As the marines stormed ashore, they stood fast. But only briefly. Then they took to their heels. It is only a few hundred yards from the island to the closest shore. Men, women, even infants plunged into the lake, trying to make landfall. But the bloodlust was on the Spanish troops. They lanced, hacked, chopped. Bodies bobbed in the water like apples in a Halloween tub. The Spanish troops searched room to room, killing and looting.

Ursua himself—the official accounts say—headed for the Castillo on the summit of the island. He planted a cross and destroyed the blood-smeared idols he found there. The chaplains said a mass. One of the items discovered was the leg bone of a horse. This was chopped into pieces and thrown in the lake. So much for the Thunder Horse god.

Lord Kan Ek made his escape but shortly he came back to the island and surrendered. Ursua got it into his head that he had acted duplicitously against the Spanish. He was clapped in chains. Captain Kowoj was arrested and brought to Nojpeten, and he professed the greatest friendship for the Spanish. He explained that he was on the outs with Kan Ek because he, Captain Kowoj, insisted the Spanish be treated respectfully, but Kan Ek did not listen. Kan Ek killed and cannibalized Spanish bodies, he said. Captain Kowoj was thrown in chains. But after a while he was released. Ursua went back to the Yucatan where he was placed under house arrest. The governor — his political enemy — had heard (truthful) rumors of massacre. Meanwhile back in the Peten, things were getting grim for the soldiers holding out on the island bastion. Their food supply was about gone. Captain Kowoj was plotting rebellion. But as always it seemed things broke in the Spanish favor. The Council of the Indies found that Ursua had used appropriate force. The governor of the Yucatan was booted, and Ursua given the job. Later, he was awarded the high position of Viceroy of the Philippines. The insurrection of Captain Kowoj came to nothing because European diseases gradually worked their way down the Peten road. In a few short years, the 60,000 Maya surrounding the lake were reduced to no more than about five thousand. The last of the traditional Maya kingdoms was history.

The War of the Castes or the Very Last Maya City-State, Chan Santa Cruz, A.D. 1847–1903

But the last Maya state was yet to rise. That occurred in the middle of the 19th century, long after the Spanish yoke had been thrown off— at least theoretically — by the peoples of the American continent. This state owed its emergence to the republic of Mexico's appearance on the world stage. The influence of the United States and Britain, one indirectly and the latter more firmly, were also instrumental in the coming about of the last Maya city-state.

For more than a hundred years after the fall of the Peten lake states, Spain maintained iron control of her New World possessions, and especially the Yucatan. The population of the peninsula is estimated to have been between 800,000 and 1,128,000 when the Spanish arrived. But dislocation and European disease took a heavy toll on the Maya. At about the time of the conquest of Tayasal, the Maya population reached its lowest ebb at 130,000–160,000 (Dumond 1997). At this time there were about 20,000 persons called whites or *vecinos* in the Yucatan. The law spelled out the relationship of both classes in terms of paying taxes and tribute, and clearly the mantle of civilization fell more heavily on Indian shoulders. During most of this time, each Maya male above the age of 13 and below 61 had to pay a tribute of 14 reales per year. (It took 12 reales to make a peso, and the peso was the equivalent of the American dollar with which it was freely exchanged in the period after the American Revolution. A real was the equivalent of a bit, two of which made a U.S. 25 cent piece.) Women from 12 to 55 owed 11 reales. This payment went to the *encomiendero*, the Spanish lord. If the *ecomienda* had lapsed (and by the end of the 18th century the institution had been abolished), the tribute went to the crown. In addition, the Indians were charged a head tax for maintenance of the church, called euphemistically an "alm." It amounted to 12.5 reales for a male and 9 for a woman. Then there was the fee for Catholic instruction for each child. This amounted to an egg or jar of oil per week. The monetary fees were payable in commodities such as corn, cotton cloth, chickens, and so on. And this was not the end of what the Maya campesino (peasant farmer) was expected to pay to the state. One day's labor a week went to civic maintenance activities, such as sweeping the plaza, repairing the roads, and so on. That most Maya did not find too onerous because of its obvious community good, but two other chores were widely loathed. Each Indian pueblo had a weekly quota of workers that needed to be supplied to vecinos (whites). Supposedly the vecinos paid these workers, but the pay was minimal at best. Finally, the *repartimiento* was an institution whereby cotton or other raw material was given to a Maya worker by the state. This material needed to be returned as a finished product at a specified date. Altogether about one half of the income from the milpa and the farmyard was destined to end up in the coffers of the encomiendero, padre, or local civil government, and that didn't include the in-kind contributions made as labor. As the years passed, the difference between the whites and Indians in terms of material culture grew closer, at least in rural Yucatan. It was often practically impossible to tell members of the two classes apart. They looked similar and they dressed similarly. Their means of getting a livelihood — through milpa horticulture or as hands on haciendas — was similar. But their last names told the story. Those with Spanish surnames — a few with Indian surnames made the leap to vecino status — were acknowledged as the social superior in all ways. At the village fiestas, the vecinos ate first. Then they danced. When they finished, they went home, and then it was the Mayas turn to cut up the rug. Life was rigorously regulated. The Maya seemed to endure their lot with something approaching equanimity.

But this system's days — like the days of Tayasal as the Spanish road inched closer — were numbered. Trouble was brewing in Europe — and North America. The first shot, the American Revolution made no more impression initially than the second shot, the French Revolution. Then the French Revolution spawned the Napoleonic Wars. Spain was overrun. The monarch fled. But a loyalist parliament in Cadiz, the port from which ships bound for the New World departed and returned, claimed sovereignty of the Americas. Initially, its aim was to preserve the legitimacy of the Bourbon realm. As a sop to those under Spanish control, it abolished tribute payments to the state. As time wore on, the body fell under the influence of the ideas of the French Revolution. It proclaimed as Spaniards and full citizens all adult freeborn males in both hemispheres. In a stroke of the pen, the Indians ceased being second-class citizens from a legal point of view. They became voters. Local elections were also mandated. Furthermore, the Indians no longer had to submit to onerous labor duties, either to civil or religious authorities. They were merely subject to the same obligations as all other citizens.

Overnight, Indians disappeared from the labor ranks. The church in the Yucatan was particularly hard hit by these decrees. It persuaded the governor to promulgate tithing for Indians, and it also insisted Indians be charged for church services, such as marrying and burying. They had been exempt on account of the "alms" payment. The governor agreed. Such a proclamation was prepared. Local liberals objected. The governor, not wanting to get crosswise with the legislative body in Spain, desisted. But shortly these squabbles became irrelevant. The British reinstated the Spanish monarchy. The old rules regarding church support by the Indians were held to still be in effect. The liberals braced themselves for revolt. None came. The Indians went back to the old system as though they always expected they would have to. For the time being, all was well.

It would continue to be well for more than a generation. In the meantime, two things happened. The first had been going on a long time. That was the quiet appropriation of Indian lands. Until independence, not much of the outlying countryside had been incorporated into haciendas. Cattle ranching was the chief moneymaking activity of the haciendas. The cattle haciendas were situated on the north and west coasts of the state. They employed few people, and generally counted their cattle in the hundreds. Most of the peninsula was classified as "wasteland," which simply meant it was unclaimed. This land was open for

Indian milpas and collection of honey and the like. With independence — in 1821, which had little effect on the Maya — private holdings expanded, at the expense of land claimed or used by the Maya. The Indians were forced by debt peonage to become laborers on the estates or they were pushed to unclaimed lands south and west from the coasts. Because there was plenty of land, at first this produced a little grumbling, but the Indians moved on, happy to be out of the reach of the grasping hacienado.

Campeche was the first town founded in the Yucatan, but the second in terms of population (19,500 in mid 19th century) and political and economic importance. Its rivalry with Merida (population 33,000), the official capital, was intense, and from time to time even came to blows. This feuding, along with the national and international climate of the times, bears direct responsibility for the uprising of the Maya. It was an uprising that lasted more than half a century. Both of these cities were "liberal" in terms of politics. "Liberal" is a term with variable meanings, almost none of which ever proved helpful to the Indian population. Liberal partisans at this time favored a federal state with decentralized government. The conservatives or centralists basically wanted to maintain a monarchy. The leading proponent of a monarch was Prince Iturbide. He was supposed to go to Europe and return with a suitable crowned head. However, he never bothered to leave Mexico and assumed the duties of king himself. He lasted just a few years. For much of the intervening years, between the fall of Iturbide in the early 1820s and the outbreak of the War of the Castes, the de facto head of the centralist party was a man widely known north of the border because he personally led the forces against the Texans at the Alamo and at the Battle of San Jacinto, General Santa Anna.

The people of the Yucatan had a natural affinity for the liberal cause because the centralists placed heavy tariffs on important staples such as wheat flour. Central Mexico grew its own wheat. The Maya Yucatecans ate little wheat bread, but the white population preferred wheat bread to corn products. Obviously, the engineers on the train of Yucatan politics were white. And Santa Anna himself once came to the Yucatan to salve their wounds and try to entice them into the fold. In the case of Campeche it worked. The reason it worked was that the major garrison of Mexican troops was stationed in the city. Going rogue politically was not easy when armed men were at your backside.

But the liberals in Merida had no such compunction. When an emissary from the central government promised the Yucatecans the moon and Santa Anna — as complicated and interesting as Cortes — reneged, the Merida liberals called out the militia. It was sent to Campeche. It clashed with the regular army. There was absolutely no way the militia could best the army at Campeche. A port city in the days of the British buccaneers, the city had been sacked more than a dozen times. In the 17th century the crown had decreed it be walled. The walls stopped the pirate attacks, and they prevented the army from being defeated in the mid 19th century as well. But the Army did not wait for the militia. It went to it and trounced the Yucatecans at the village of Hecelchakan. The year was 1834.

But the centralists overplayed their hand. The troops lost in the Texas adventure needed to be replaced. Santa Anna decreed the Yucatan militias be armed — most had drilled with brooms and hoes — and transferred to bases in central Mexico. Yucatecan forces had never left the peninsula. The order to move them to Mexico resulted in insurrection. The leader was Santiago Iman from Tzimin. His initial efforts failed, and he headed for the heavy scrub between the city of Valladolid and the coast near present-day Cancun. There he recruited local Maya. He promised to relieve them of their various payments to church and state, which had risen to pre–19th-century levels. In the upshot his promises would be a fatal mistake as far as the *blanco* population of Yucatan was concerned.

But for the moment, it provided the firepower needed. Shortly, militia commanders throughout the peninsula were declaring for Iman. Then they were on the high points above the city of Campeche, firing cannon into the garrison. The army maintained control of the city, but the hearts and minds of the citizens were with the insurrection. The central government, still weak on account of the monetary and troop loss occasioned by the Texas war, withdrew by sea.

Yucatan became a de facto independent state. Now Campeche radicalized. It openly courted the secessionist Texans. It wanted to form a political alliance. The Texans insisted as a precondition that all of Yucatan declare its independence from Mexico. Campeche was for independence. Merida favored waiting and seeing. But Texas did agree to patrol the coasts with its infant navy, and Campeche put its maritime facilities at the Texans' disposal. The central government, like the U.S. federal government after South Carolina's declaration, mobilized. First, it sent an emissary to talk the Yucatan back into the fold. The negotiator, a native Yucatecan, gave the store away. The Yucatecans agreed. Santa Anna did not. He sent the army back. The force was huge, almost as large as that sent against Texas. They occupied Carmen, right across the border from Tabasco. The Yucatecans began recruiting troops. They enlisted Indians wholesale.

The next stop north of Carmen was Campeche. But this time the Yucatecans were inside those impregnable walls. Even though the heights around the city were occupied by Mexicans, the Campechanos did not budge. The only pitched battle occurred about ten miles from Campeche at the village of China. Yucatecans ventured outside the walls to slam a bivouced force of regulars. Losses on both sides were high, and the Mexican army decided to try its luck against Merida a hundred miles farther north. Merida was unfortified, but it was much farther inland. Mexican attempts to promote a fifth column were comically inept. After a few indecisive skirmishes and the disabling of a Mexican steamship by a Texas gunboat, both sides decided to call it quits. They agreed to commence talks. But talks got nowhere and in the meantime the Polk administration, sensing Mexico's weakness, invaded from the north. The Yucatecans saw no reason to rush to the defense of the country that just sent troops against it.

In the meantime, the Maya expected the promises made them when they joined the militia to be redeemed. And this time they meant business. Revolution and the rights of man would not be only for the whites.

In the vacuum of government caused by the withdrawal of Mexican forces, the people of Campeche again decided on revolution. They called for a reduction of the Indian head tax to a mere 18 reales per year. Laws allowing for the freedom of worship found their way onto the books. In short, they were attempting to follow in the path of Texas. European or American immigrants were courted. All this may have seemed to favor the rights of the Maya; but in fact, it was only sowing the seeds for an Indian rebellion. In the meantime, they got some Americans they didn't want but which could be used to advantage. The U.S. Navy occupied Carmen, cutting off any possibility of reinforcements from Mexico. The (nominally liberal) government in Merida was isolated, as the militias in the surrounding countryside declared for Campeche and insurrection.

Valladolid, in the north central part of the peninsula, nowadays about an hour from Cancun, was one of the three original colonial towns. The citizens were also known as the most conservative—and haughty—in the peninsula. So far as they were concerned, the Spanish were still in charge, and the Spanish caste system still ruled. The people of Valladolid would not let Indians participate in their festivals. In fact, they sometimes barred poor whites from the center of the city during feasts. Naturally, they opposed the Campeche "revolution." But the local militias declared for Campeche. The local peasants, both vecino and Indian, were smarting with resentment. Revolution was in the air, and the time was ripe — the way they saw it — to even the score.

When the order to attack was given, the militias thronged into the city center. Eighty-four citizens were killed. Women were raped and homes looted. The body of the commanding officer of the Valladolid garrison, Colonel Venegas, was dragged to the nearby hamlet of Sisal where it was mutilated. One week later in January of 1847, the governor in Merida capitulated. The Campechanos had won their greatest victory over their rival city, but it was to prove a pyrrhic victory of the worst sort. For the best part of a year, the Campeche government ruled without elections. In the meantime, a partisan of the former Merida governor staged a takeover of the Merida citadel. Troops were evacuated from the eastern part of the peninsula to deal with the emergency. This was exactly the opportunity that the Maya rebels were looking for. They swarmed into the small towns where the troops had been withdrawn. A few citizens were killed in the ensuing scuffles. This inflamed the whites. They worried about a full-blown race war. The Maya were likewise annoyed by the treatment of churches by the Campeche forces. Being liberals, many of the Campechanos were professed atheists. It was claimed they stabled their horses in churches. Also, they used the sacred buildings as latrines. This did not go over well with the pious local Maya, whether allies or not, further radicalizing a population being pushed in the direction of rebellion.

Maya forces gathered at the gates of Valladolid — now protected by forces loyal to the Campeche government. At this point, it was believed — hoped — that the Maya rebels were merely jockeying for political position in the time honored manner of the area. The whites vacillated between abject hysteria at the thought of Indian rebellion to near denial. Some suspected the supposed Maya uprising was a ploy of the Merida party. To those with their heads in the sand, the burning issue was the removal of the U.S. Navy from the Yucatan. An emissary was sent to Washington asking for the removal of American ships — and also for an American guarantee that Mexico would not wreak vengeance on Yucatan afterwards. In the meantime, informal negotiations began with the Maya. Of the demands put forward, at least half had to do with abolishing civil and religious taxes. Permanent access to land suitable for milpa horticulture also ranked high on the list. Thinking it was getting somewhere, the government gave the Indian leaders a month to put their demands in writing. When the month expired, no written demands were forthcoming. But a military contingent at Valladolid kept trying. They were told to appear outside the city. When the delegation arrived, it was surrounded and spirited away. Once deep in the rebel stronghold, the military and civilians were hacked to pieces by Maya machetes. The clergy were spared but not released.

The fat was in the fire. The blancos learned how bad things were shortly. Valladolid, far to the east, was deemed untenable. Evacuation was ordered. It began orderly enough. The road was a poor trail to the north because the main western road was in control of the Maya rebels. Cavalry protected the column. Wagons and carriages went first and behind came those on foot. The last person had hardly left the city when columns of smoke trailed into the sky. A unit of Campeche soldiers mutinied. They headed off for their homes far to the west on the Gulf of Mexico. Then the Maya fell on the helpless trailing behind. What started as an orderly retreat turned into a rout. The worst fears of the blancos threatened to turn into a nightmare as the small towns and haciendas north of the Puuc hills and south and west of Merida fell to the rebels.

Serious negotiations were called for. Miguel Barbachano, the former governor from Merida, was back in office, in part because it was believed the Indians were a military arm of his political party. By now, the genie was out of the bottle and neither Barbachano nor any other white could get it back inside. But, good politician that he was, Barbachano was willing to try to turn the situation to his advantage. He appointed himself chief negotiator. He devised a treaty that pleased only one person, Barbachano himself—because by the terms of the treaty he would be made governor for life. The other provisions seemed old hat to the Maya. They were on the books, but not observed. The Indians responded by rolling through the delta of land north of the Puuc hills. They seemed bent on plundering the largest city on the peninsula, Merida. It was the dry season. Nothing was stopping them from sweeping over the capital like a floodtide. Simultaneous letters were sent Great Britain, the United States, and Cuba by the Yucatan whites. These letters offered Yucatan as a dependency of any of these entities. All respectfully declined the offer. Then Spain was approached directly, as Cuba was still a colony. The island of Cozumel was offered, and then peninsula's customhouses. The answer was still no. Most humiliatingly, a delegation was sent to Mexico City, now clear of gringos. Understanding of the need to woo the Yucatan back into the fold as well as not wanting the race war to spread, the Mexican cabinet immediately granted aid, which took some months to arrive. Before too much of 1848 became history, Yucatan had been readmitted to the union of Mexican states.

That made little difference so far as the relentless Maya tide was concerned. It surged across the peninsula. In the south, Campeche, which early on might have thought of itself as impregnable, found the rebels almost at its gates. But the city that was really in the Maya sights was Merida. The area around it had been completely gobbled up by the insurrectionists. Itzamal, the largest town to the east, was occupied when government troops evacuated. The rebels did not quite know what to do with the town. They entered, looked around, burned the thatch buildings and headed for Merida. But as they approached the capital city, a locust-like cloud darkened the sky

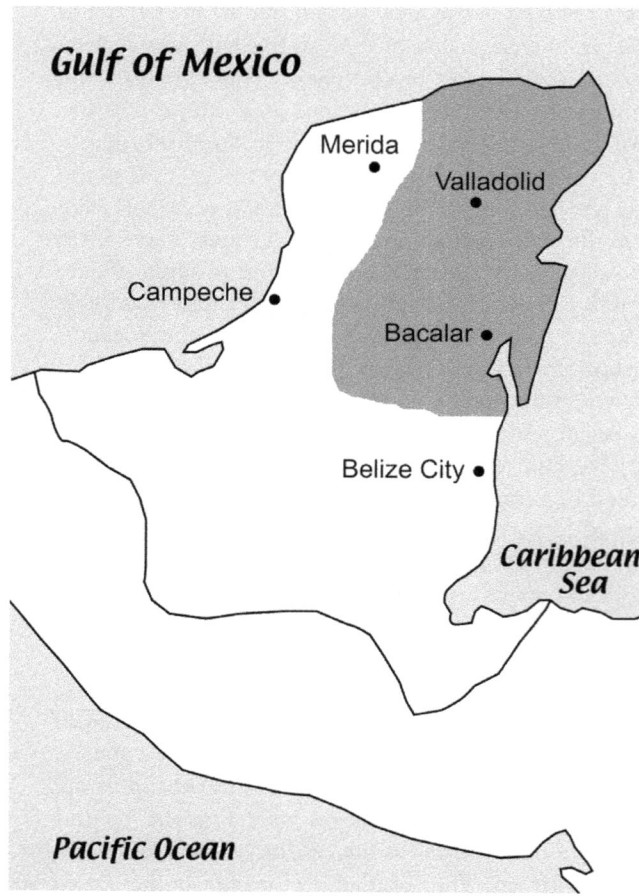

Shaded area roughly shows the farthest advance of the bravo forces in the War of the Castes. Valladolid was temporarily occupied. The villa (town) of Bacalar was ultimately wiped out.

on almost all sides. It was a throng of flying ants. Government guns might not have been able to thwart the Maya, but those flying insects stopped them in their tracks.

These ants were the precursors of the coming of the rains. The seed corn needed to be dibbled in the milpas. Otherwise, there'd be no corn in the granary for tortillas and tamales later in the season. The Maya turned, as one man, and headed for home. That is the story told by the immediate kin of veterans of the war. Don E. Dumond, the author of *The Machete and the Cross,* from which the material in this section is taken, has a fuller explanation. Dumond agrees the furthest expansion of the rebel frontier did occur in May of 1848. The rains begin, usually, in that month or June. Planting may have had an effect on hostilities. But according to Dumond, a far more serious cause of the collapse of the expansion was the local Indian population. It refused to rise up with the eastern rebels. The reason for this was the system of debt peonage.

In the western and northern Yucatan, landlords had been paying the taxes of the Indians (and some vecinos) on their estates for years. These debts fell much less heavily on the shoulders of those workers. True, they were forever in hock to the landlord. True, also, they had to get up every morning and do the hacienado's mayordomo's bidding. But it was a system they had long grown accustomed to. And it even offered security of sorts. Many of the rebel Indians, by contrast, had to hand over the meager proceeds they eked from their cornfields. Also, they were under pressure from grasping landlords. As the hacienda frontier moved east and south, fields that had formerly been theirs were claimed by whites. They were often asked to become indebted peons on those very same fields. Finally, the rebel Maya had been promised the rights and prerogative of full citizens of the republic. As reward for service — and thanks to the ideals of the French Revolution and the various constitutions that had been adopted and overthrown — Indians had been made equal before the law then reduced once again to second-class citizenry. In the west, a peasant mentality met the lack of political rights with a shrug. In the east, rebellion continued to be the result.

Early in the war, the Yucatecans had little experience in dealing with armed insurrection. Officers, chosen for political favor or by election, cut and ran when a little spine could have saved the day. The first months of war showed who the weak officers were. Because homes and lives were at stake, they were replaced with men more suited for the task. And loyal Indians in the west were recruited. Those who stayed for the duration were lured into service. Their reward was being granted the title of hidalgo. Not only would they become official gentlemen, but they were absolved of paying taxes for the rest of their lives. All told, nine thousand of these grants were passed out. Aside from bolstering the fighting force, it also provided a core of loyalists among the local Indians to help stabilize that population.

By the latter part of 1848, government forces had reoccupied all the hacienda lands of the western coastal and north-central Yucatan including Valladolid. In other words, approximately half the peninsula was controlled by government forces and half by insurrectionists. Lost and never regained by the government was the villa (or town) of Bacalar in the southeastern part of the peninsula. It had been stormed by rebels, and after a short siege, surrendered under an agreement of safe passage to British Honduras. The rebels very much wanted this strongpoint reduced. It had the capacity to block trade with Belize, and it was from Belize that powder and surplus flintlock muskets were obtained. Having lost the means of suppressing the trade by force of arms, the Yucatan government wrote the British superintendent of the colony asking that he prevent smuggling of arms and munitions. The superintendent offered soothing words but little in the way of active assistance. For this and other reasons, British motives were widely suspected during the course of the conflict. (In point of fact, the superintendant's office was a weak one, and the British, unable to control the populace of the colony of pirates turned traders, did what they could to suppress the worst abuses.)

Dumond estimates that about 100,000 Yucatecans could be counted among the rebels at its high-water point. Perhaps as many as 25,000 of these were combatants. But given the sort of warfare practiced by the Maya, the line between soldier and noncombatant was blurred. For instance, many of the combatants were armed only with machetes. However, in Maya warfare, irregular forces came in very handy. Those wielding machetes could chop brush, and those without arms piled the brush. Then when troops lured down the trail were confronted by the roadblock, those with firearms cut loose. In close-order fighting machetes took a toll too. Such tactics accounted for a frightening number of the unseasoned and untrained Yucatecan casualties. Likewise, many a walled pueblo was laid siege to. The weapons were such formidable things as wood drums, high pitched screams and so on. Noncombatants of all genders and ages could and did participate. The fear they instilled in combat-unseasoned civilians was often debilitating. The roadblock ambush was probably practiced by ancient Maya as shown by the periodic stone fortifications on the Coba sacbe (causeway), which could have been used for ambush as well as defense. One wonders if psychological operatives were also a feature of classic warfare. A third characteristic tactic could have been used against arrows or atlatls. That was the lying on the back and rolling a boulder forward with the feet, as a sort of mobile fortification. The Yucatan forces were schooled in the principles of European stand and fight warfare. The Maya practiced the guerrilla war common to the native peoples of the Americas to great effect.

The organization of the rebel army followed that of the Yucatan militia with a full colonel as commander, right down to the three drummer boys the government forces employed. Yucatecans got wind of a possible insurrection when Indians began appearing on the estate of Jacinto Pat, a Maya hacienado near Valladolid. For the first months of rebellion, Pat was the leader of the cause. But it was a revolutionary force, and it was not long before the revolution ate its first baby, Jacinto Pat. A death warrant was sworn out for him and signed by V. Pec and F. Chan. His crimes were the crimes of the white landowner. He wanted to claim forest for his estate. He taxed his soldiers in the way of asking for a share of the plunder. He flogged his men, and he asked the poor to contribute to the cause, presumably the cause of Jacinto Pat. This insurrection, unlike so many others, would maintain the purity of the cause. At least that faction would. And it did for over fifty years.

But it wasn't long before many campesinos had had enough. By 1851, the number of Maya still in a state of rebellion had shrunk to just a little more than half of those who so joyously struck a blow for liberty early on. Some of the pacified returned to the estates and gave up their weapons. But many moved to marginal areas and remained armed and became known as *pacificos*. The belligerents were called *bravos*. And they needed those arms because they were now warred on by their former comrades. In the meantime — four years into the rebellions — things were grim for the *masewalob* (poor people), as the insurrectionists called themselves. Constantly on the run, they could not always collect enough corn to feed themselves. There were actually instances of partisans starving to death. With their numbers shrinking, something was needed to bolster the spirits of those who remained. It was found near a cenote at the present-day town of Felipe Carrillo Puerto. One of the leaders, Jose Marie Barrera, carved three crosses in a tree near this cenote. As we have seen in the narrative, the classic Maya considered both water and caves — cenotes being sort of a mixture of each — as sacred. The crosses by the cenote began to be paid homage to by the rebels by burning of candles and so on. In time, three crosses were erected, and the devotions intensified. Shortly, it came to pass that the crosses began to exhibit amazing oracular properties including that of speech.

The talking crosses were exactly the sort of sign the partisans expected the rightness of their cause to engender—and it was the kind of thing needed to buck them up in the time of need. The crosses under the guidance of Jose Marie Barrera undertook to give advice regarding military and civil strategy. At one point it even dictated a letter to the English superintendant of British Honduras. It said, "The Holy Cross begs of you to give them powder, shot and all the implements of war. My beloved Sirs come and receive a holy benediction and enjoy the benefit of speaking with the True Christ who spilt his Blood for your sakes." The British superintendent was not impressed, but the *masewalob* were.

By mid 1851, the village of Santa Cruz was defended by 1,400 men, meaning the population would probably have been about 4,000. This is known because a Yucatec patrol fought to the center of the community. The houses were all brand new, and they had been set among the thick trees of the tropical forest. Water was drawn from the sacred cenote, and the brush around it was blackened from the soot of the candle fires always burning in devotion. When the Yucatan commander later again temporarily captured the village (at bayonet point by attacking in a driving rain storm), he found the crosses housed in a chapel. They were dressed in decorative campesino costume. The commander found out the secret of the "talking" crosses. He learned the sanctuary was off limits to the *hoi polloi*. A hollow drum stood at the foot of the center cross, which an accomplice of Barrera spoke into producing an ethereal god-like voice. The officer destroyed these artifacts of the rebel commanders hocus pocus. They were believed to be indestructible. When a captured cruxian rebel was shown the destruction, he is claimed to have said, "It cannot be. The cross does not lie." In short, faith trumped the evidence of his eyes.

The Yucatecans burned all the thatch houses of the village, leaving only the church which they stabled their horses in; clearly the Yucatecans knew a few tricks of psychological warfare themselves. Then they left. Barrera died. The rebels rebuilt their town and their crosses. A new leader took control of both the military and the religious side of things. The high priest or "Organ of the Divine Word" was, at this period, Tata Naz or Nazario Nah. Under him the Maya rebels renounced the old religion for that of the cross. All baptisms and marriages were conducted by Tata Naz, the former by anointing of water and the saying of the ritual words of the Catholic faith. Weddings occurred by each person merely saying, "I marry you," in the Tata Naz's presence. The two worst sins, punishable by death, were adultery and blasphemy against the cross.

A prisoner once told some rebel Maya not to confuse the cross with God. He was summarily executed. Once a week at midnight, the senior officers of the rebellion were summoned for the orders of the cross. They were seated in back near the cross. Other rebel villagers were seated behind a drawn curtain. The doors were closed. The candles extinguished. The cross now spoke through the son of Tata Naz. The pronouncements were heralded by the sounding of a bugle. Then there came a noise like the flapping of a large bird. The foreheads of the congregation smashed into the dirt floor. The assembled beat their breasts and said, "We believe in the Santa Cruz who will talk to us." Then the cross spoke in a loud whistling voice. It began by saying, "I have just returned from a long excursion in the capital and principal military guarded town of Yucatan." In this way, the military strategy of the rebels was formulated. For instance, it is known an attack on Valladolid was devised in this manner.

That attack was a bust. But others were incredibly successful, such as one against Tekax just north of the Puuc Hills in central Yucatan, somewhat closer to Merida than to Santa Cruz. Thanks to political machinations, most of the Yucatecan troops had been called away. They were sent to Campeche, which Merida was again feuding with. The remaining soldiers were mostly Campechanos. When a force marched into town wearing Campeche ribbons in their hats, the soldiers assumed they were fellow Campechanos. The newcomers called to the men in ranks to desert. Many did despite the pleas of their officers. When the now unarmed soldiers had joined their supposed comrades, the newcomers turned on them. They shot and hacked them like animals. Then the turn of the pueblo came. Doors were battered down. Stores were looted, homes were sacked, women raped. A small detachment of government troops kept firing at the rebels from the second story of a building. The rebels started a slow fire. They watched the veranda burn and fall away, while strumming their guitars and enjoying the terror of the soldiers trapped by the flames.

A similar action occurred at Tinkas. This village was situated almost exactly halfway on a straight line between Valladolid and Merida. It was a long way from Santa Cruz. The area by almost any stretch of the imagination should be secure. Yet one September day in 1861, three columns of men were seen marching toward it on the road from Merida. They showed no haste, nor any sign of hostility as they stomped into the plaza. The commander of the first wing saluted those he knew by name. Like a maneuver staged for a western movie, the men disarmed the militia in its barracks without incident and blocked avenues of escape. Immediately, they began rounding up the entire population, more than 700 souls. The citizens were locked up in public buildings and their houses were systematically looted. Having secured the plunder, the 700 were liberated from their temporary prison and marched to Santa Cruz. Those who couldn't keep up were macheted. Once they arrived in the rebel capital, the vecinos, or whites, were killed, the others were set to toil as slaves on the plantations of the various commanders.

The leader in both military and civil matters at Santa Cruz at this juncture may have been Venancio Puc. Some of his partisans had nested on the British Honduras border for a time, making several incursions below it and harassing "pacified" Indians. The British superintendent wrote him a letter on behalf of Queen Victoria. A reply was demanded within one month. Two lieutenants were detailed to await the response. The Santa Cruz commander (and the cross) found the tone of the letter insulting. Plumridge and Twigge, the officers, were disarmed and shut up in a shed without food or water until midnight.

At this time a bugle sounded. The British were called from their shed. They were taken to the church, now a stone building. Pushed forward to the sacristy, they were made to kneel. A small voice told them in Yucatec Mayan the letter was insulting. It said those Maya who had crossed into British territory had already been punished. The English were free to send thousands of troops if they liked, the cross said. The rebels would defeat them. At this point, the interpreter jumped in and disavowed the letter. He claimed the reason for the officers' visit was trade. They were not there, he fibbed, to fuss about past problems. The next morning Governor Puc called the British officers. He was already drunk. He forced Lt. Twigge to swallow a tablespoon of habanero pepper and wash it down with a tumbler of anise seed liquor. By now Puc was falling down drunk, but that didn't keep him from kissing and hugging the officers, slapping them around, making them dance and sing. He wandered the streets in this stage of public inebriation, an assistant carrying his bottle to quench his frequent thirsts. The British would be let go, they were told, after the cross spoke next. By a strange coincidence, the cross never spoke when Puc was drunk.

According to Robert Sharer and Charles Golden, the Classic-era Maya monarchs ruled by dint of the moral authority of their office (Sharer and Golden 2004). Correct behavior was expected of the king and everyone else in the society. The moral code of the ancient Maya was considerably different from any the modern reader is likely to be familiar with. In part, one's morality was destined by one's birthdate and other imponderables. Nevertheless, it is difficult to imagine drunken behavior of the sort Venancio Puc displayed as acceptable to the Classic Maya. Or as a matter of fact, to the pious campesinos who were the foot soldiers of the revolution.

By now slightly more than ten years after the start of the rebellion, the population of Campeche, far to the west and more or less out of harm's way, had dropped by 12 percent. The area covered by the state of Yucatan lost more than 40 percent of its people, going from 422,000 at the beginning of rebellion to less than a quarter million. Some emigrated, others were killed. The rebel area suffered the worst losses. From an estimated population of about 95,000 at the beginning of hostilities, it fell 62 percent to 35,500 in 12 years or so. By 1870, the population of rebels had dropped to less than 12,000 with about 3,000 men at arms, no doubt thanks to the excesses of the leadership.

Not surprisingly, drunken leaders like Venancio Puc were frequently assassinated. Perhaps just as predictable, talking crosses turned up at Tulum — and at least one other center. During the Preclassic and Classic period, a framework had evolved over centuries that kept the state on track. But neither the recent experiences of the Maya nor Spanish governance had provided a model for a system of government that could persist in the modern world. So the last Maya state wobbled and careened along, its continuing independence owing less to its resilience than the incompetence and lack of interest by the formal states of the peninsula.

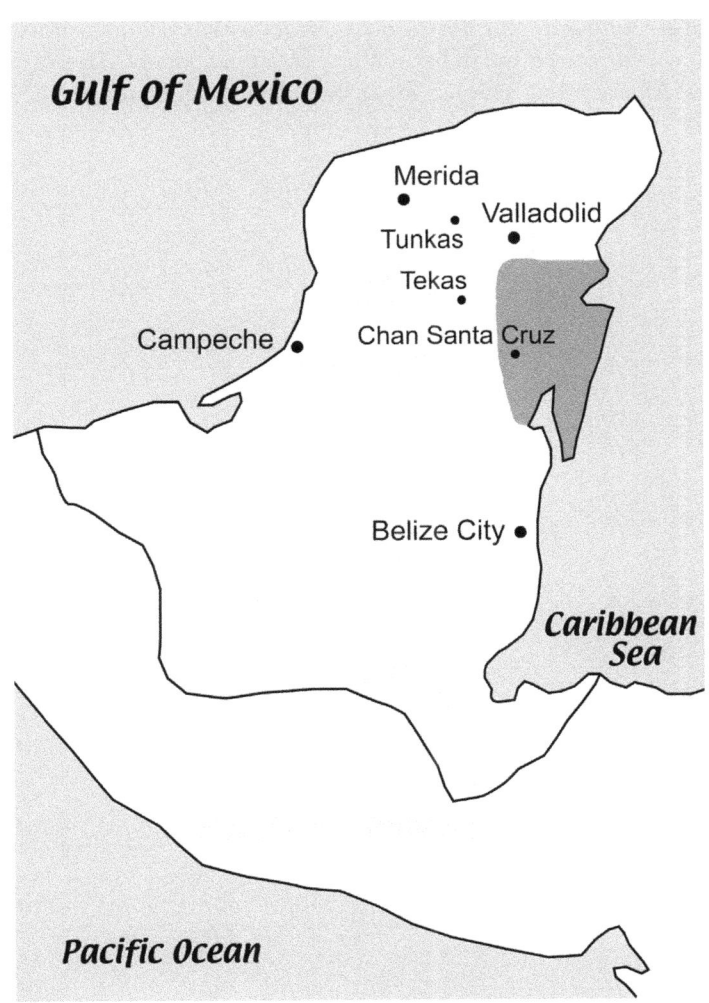

Shaded area shows the territory of the bravo forces during much of the late 19th century.

It was not until the turn of the 20th century when President Dias of Mexico and the British came to an agreement that numbered the days of the Maya republic. But the grandiose successes and the large populations of early days by that time were long in the past. The rebel Maya were just hanging on. The Mexicans claimed total control of rebel lands in 1903. The name of Chan Santa Cruz, also variously known as Noh Cah Santa Cruz or Santa Cruz de Brazo, was changed to Felipe Carrillo Puerto; and a territory consisting of much of the former rebel territory was cut out of the state of Yucatan. It was called Quintano Roo. Rather than formerly surrendering, many of the so-called Maya bravos just fanned out into the brush where travelers, whether official or no, armed or no, rarely strayed until many decades into the 20th century.

By then, many of the markers of Maya high culture had long since passed into oblivion. The Long Count calendar had last been used a millennium earlier (although revived lately by end-of-the-world New Agers). Maya hieroglyphic writing had been destroyed by the Spanish. The independent political system, backed up by Maya religion, was tottering (or had collapsed) before the Spanish Conquest. But Maya folk culture, which retains many elements of the high civilization, is practiced today by millions of contemporary Maya in lower Mexico and upper Central America, just as it has for at least the past three thousand years.

References

Abrams, Elliot
    1998 "Structures as Sites: The Construction Process and Maya Architecture." In *Function and Meaning in Classic Maya Architecture*, edited by Stephen D. Houston. Washington, DC: Dumbarton Oaks Research Library and Collection. http://www.doaks.org/publications/doaks_online_publications/ClassicMaya/maya03.pdf.

Adam, Thomas (editor)
    2005 "Bernoulli, Carl Gustav." In *Germany and the Americas: Culture, Politics and History*. Santa Barbara, CA: ABC-CLIO.

Ambrosino, James N., Traci Ardren, and Travis W. Stanton
    2003 "The History of Warfare at Yaxuna." In *Ancient Mesoamerican Warfare*, edited by M. Kathryn Brown and Travis W. Stanton. Walnut Creek, CA: Altamira.

Anaya Hernández, Armando
    1996 "La noción de Casa como modelo explicativo del sistema de parentesco del Clásico Maya" In *Cultura y Comunicación: Edmund Leach in Memoriam*. J.J. Jaureguí, A.M. Olivarria, V. Franco (eds.). Universidad Autónoma Metropolitana, CIESAS, México, 129–154.
    2001 *Site Interaction and Political Geography in the Upper Usumacinta Region During the Late Classic: A GIS Approach*. Hadrian Books, BAR International Series 994. Oxford.

Anaya Hernández, Armando, Stanley Guenter, and Marc Zender
    2003 "Sak Tz'i,' a Classic Maya Center: A Locational Model Based on GIS, and Epigraphy." *Latin American Antiquity* 14(2), 2003. En coautoría con Stanley Guenter y Marc Zender, 179–191.

Anaya Hernández, Armando and Stanley Guenter
    2008 Calakmul y el Reino de Kan: Su Historia y Desarrollo a través de las Inscripciones. En, *Los Investigadores de la Cultura Maya Vol. 16 Tomo II*. Universidad Autónoma de Campeche, pp. 492–503.

Andrews, Anthony P.
    1995 "An Ancient Maya Seaport at Isla Cerritos, Yucatan." *LORE* (June).

Andrews, Anthony P., and Shirley B. Mock
    2002 "New Perspectives on the Salt Trade." In *Ancient Maya Political Economies*, edited by Marilyn A. Masson and David A. Freidel. Walnut Creek, CA: Altamira, 307–334.

Arnold, Dean E., Jason R. Branden, Patrick Ryan Williams, Gary M. Feinman, and J. P. Brown
    2008 "The First Direct Evidence for the Production of Maya Blue." *Antiquity* 82 (March): 315.

Aveni, Anthony
    2008 "Bringing the Sky Down to Earth." *History Today* 58.6 (June).

Beach, Timothy, Sheryl Luzzadder-Beach, Nicholas Dunning, Jon Hageman, and Jon Lohse
    2002 "Upland Agriculture in the Maya Lowlands: Ancient Maya Soil Conservation in Northwestern Belize." *Geographical Review* 92.3, Social Science Module: 372.

Berryman, Carrie Ann
    2007 "Captive Sacrifice and Trophy Taking among the Ancient Maya: An Evaluation of the Bioarchaeological Evidence and Its Sociological Implications." In *The Taking and Displaying of Human Body Parts by Amerindians*, edited by Richard Chacon and David Dyes. Philadelphia: Springer Science and Business Media, 377–399.

Blom, Frans, and Oliver La Farge
    1926 *Tribes and Temples: A Record of the Expedition to Middle America Conducted by the Tulane University of Louisiana in 1925*, vol. 1. New Orleans.

Boynton, Robert S.
    1980 *Chemistry Technology of Lime and Limestone*. New York: John Wiley & Sons. Quoted in Schreiner 1994.

Braswell, Geoffrey E., Joel D. Gunn, Maria del Rosario Dominguez Carrasco, William J. Folan, Laraine A. Fletcher, Abel Morales Lopez, and Michael D. Glascock
    2004 "Defining the Terminal Classic at Calakmul, Campeche, in Perspective." In *The Terminal Classic in the Maya Lowlands: Collapse, Transition, and Transformation*, edited by Arthur A. Demarest, Prudence M. Rice, and Don S. Rice. Boulder: University of Colorado Press.

Brown, Kathryn M., and James F. Garber
    2003 "Evidence of Conflict During the Middle Formative in the Maya Lowlands: A View from Blackman Eddy." In *Ancient Mesoamerican War-*

fare, edited by M. Kathryn Brown and Travis W. Stanton. Walnut Creek, CA: Altamira.

Brunhouse, Robert L.
  1973 *In Search of the Maya: The First Archaeologists.* Repr., New York: Ballantine Books, 1990.
  1975 *Pursuit of the Ancient Maya: Some Archaeologists of Yesterday.* Albuquerque: University of New Mexico Press.
  1976 *Frans Blom.* Albuquerque: University of New Mexico Press.

Bunch, Roland
  1995 "An Odyssey of Discovery: Principles of Agriculture for the Humid Tropics." *ILEIA Newsletter* 11.3: 18.

Caballero-Briones, F., A. Iribarren, and J. L. Pena
  2000 "Recent Advances on the Understanding of the Nixtamalization Process." *Superficies y Vacío* 10: 20–24.

Carmean, Kelli, Nicholas Dunning, and Jeff Karl Kowalski
  2004 "High Times in the Hill Country: A Perspective from the Terminal Classic Puuc Region." In *The Terminal Classic in the Maya Lowlands: Collapse, Transition, and Transformation,* edited by Arthur A. Demarest, Prudence M. Rice, and Don S. Rice. Boulder: University of Colorado Press.

Castaneda, Carlos
  1968/1998 *The Teachings of Don Juan: A Yaqui Way of Knowledge.* Repr., Berkeley: University of California Press.

Chase, Arlen F., and Diane Z. Chase
  2004 "Terminal Classic Status Linked Ceramics and the Maya 'Collapse': De Facto Refuse at Caracol, Belize." In *The Terminal Classic in the Maya Lowlands: Collapse, Transition, and Transformation,* edited by Arthur A. Demarest, Prudence M. Rice, and Don S. Rice. Boulder: University of Colorado Press.

Chase, Diane Z., and Arlen F. Chase
  1998 "The Architectural Context of Caches, Burials, and Other Ritual Activities for the Classic Period Maya (as Reflected at Caracol, Belize.)" In *Function and Meaning in Classic Maya Architecture,* edited by Stephen D. Houston. Washington, DC: Dumbarton Oaks Research Library and Collection. www.doaks.org/etexts.html.
  2003 "Texts and Contexts in Maya Warfare: A Brief Consideration of Epigraphy and Archaeology at Caracol, Belize." In *Ancient Mesoamerican Warfare,* edited by M. Kathryn Brown and Travis W. Stanton. Walnut Creek, CA: Altamira.

Clark, John E.
  1997 "The Arts of Government in Early Mesoamerica." *Annual Review of Anthropology* 26, Social Science Module: 211.

Clark, John E., and Michael Blake
  1996 "The power of prestige: Competitive Generosity and the Emergence of Rank Societies in Lowland Mesoamerica." In *Contemporary Archaeology: A Reader,* edited by Robert W. Preucel and Ian Hodder. Malden, MA: Blackwell.

Clark, John E., and Richard D. Hansen
  2001 "The Architecture of Early Kingship: Comparative Perspectives on the Origin of the Maya Royal Court." In *Royal Courts of the Ancient Maya,* vol. 2, edited by Takeshi Inomata and Stephen Houston. Boulder, CO: Westview.

Cobos Palma, Rafael
  2004 "Chichen Itza: Settlement and Hegemony During the Terminal Classic Period." In *The Terminal Classic in the Maya Lowlands: Collapse, Transition, and Transformation,* edited by Arthur A. Demarest, Prudence M. Rice, and Don S. Rice. Boulder: University of Colorado Press.
  2006 "The Relationship Between Tula and Chichen Itza." In *Lifeways in the Northern Maya Lowlands: New Approaches to Archaeology in the Yucatan Peninsula,* edited by Jennifer P. Mathews and Bethany A. Morrison. Tucson: University of Arizona Press, 173–186.

Coe, Michael D.
  1968 *America's First Civilization.* New York: American Heritage Publishing.
  1986 "Preface." *The Blood of Kings: Dynasty and Ritual in Maya Art* by Linda Schele and Mary Ellen Miller. New York: Thames and Hudson.
  1992 *Breaking the Maya Code.* New York: Thames and Hudson.
  2005 *The Maya.* 7th ed. New York: Thames and Hudson.

Colas, Pierre R., and Alexander Voss
  2009/2001 "A Game of Life and Death—the Maya Ball Game." In *Maya: Divine Kings of the Rain Forest,* edited by Nikolai Grube assisted by Eva Eggebrecht and Matthias Seidel. Cologne, Ger: Ullmann.

Cowgill, George L.
  1997 "State and Society at Teotihuacan, Mexico." *Annual Review of Anthropology* 26:129–161.

Curtis, Jason A.
  1997 "Climatic Variation in the CircumCaribbean During the Holocene." PhD Diss., Gainsville: University of Florida.

Cyphers, Ann
  1999 "From Stone to Symbols: Olmec Art in Social Context at San Lorenzo Tenochitlan." In *Social Patterns in Pre-Classic Mesoamerica: A Symposium at Dumbarton Oaks 9 and 10 October 1993,* edited by David C. Grove and Rosemary A. Joyce. Washington, DC: Dumbarton Oaks Research Library and Collection.

Cyphers, Ann, Belem Zuniga and Anna Di Castro
  2005 "Another Look at Bufo Marinus and the San Lorenzo Olmec." *Current Anthropology* 46: 129–133.

Cyphers, Ann, and Ferdinand Botas
  1994 "An Olmec Feline Sculpture from El Azuzul, Southern Veracruz." *Proceedings of the American Philosophical Society* 138.2: 273–283.

Demarest, Arthur A.
  2004a "After the Maelstrom: Collapse of the Classic Maya Kingdoms and the Terminal Classic in Western Peten in Perspective." In *The Terminal Classic in the Maya Lowlands: Collapse, Transition, and Transformation,* edited by Arthur A. Demarest, Prudence M. Rice, and Don S. Rice. Boulder: University of Colorado Press.
  2004b "Ancient Maya: The Rise and Fall of a Rainforest Civilization." Cambridge: Cambridge University Press.

Desmond, Lawrence, and Phyllis Messenger
  1988 *A Dream of Maya: Augustus and Alice Le Plongeon in Nineteenth Century Yucatan*. Albuquerque, NM: University of New Mexico Press. http://maya.csuhayward.edu/archaeoplanet/LgdPage/Dream/Start.htm.
Dias, Bernal
  1963/1632 *The Conquest of New Spain*, translated by J. M. Cohen. London, UK: Penguin Books.
Diehl, Richard A.
  2004 *The Olmecs: America's First Civilization*. London, UK: Thames and Hudson.
  2005 "Patterns of Cultural Primacy." *Science* 307. 5712: 1055.
Diehl, Richard A., and Michael D. Coe
  1995 "Olmec Archaeology." In *The Olmec World: Ritual and Rulership*. New Jersey: Art Museum, Princeton University.
Dorfman, John, and Andrew L. Slayman
  1997 "Maverick Mayanist." *Archaeology Magazine* 50.5.
Drucker, Philip
  1981 "On the Nature of Olmec Polity." In *The Olmec and Their Neighbors: In Memory of Matthew W. Stirling*, edited by Elizabeth P. Benson. Washington, DC: Dumbarton Oaks Research Library and Collection.
Dumond, Don E.
  1997 *The Machete and the Cross, Campesino Rebellion in Yucatan*. Lincoln: University of Nebraska.
Empire State Building Official Site
  2009 http://www.esbnyc.com/tourism/tourism_history.cfm?CFID=35363683&CFTOKEN=43403917.
Evans, R. Tripp
  2004 *Romancing the Maya: Mexican Antiquity in the American Imagination, 1820–1915*. Austin: University of Texas Press.
Fash, William L., E. Wyllys Andrews, and T. Kam Manahan
  2004 "Political Decentralization, Dynastic Collapse, and the Early Postclassic in the Urban Center of Copán, Honduras." In *The Terminal Classic in the Maya Lowlands: Collapse, Transition, and Transformation*, edited by Arthur A. Demarest, Prudence M. Rice, and Don S. Rice. Boulder: University of Colorado Press.
Fash, William L., and Ricardo Agurcia Fasquelle
  2005 "Contributions and Controversies in the Archaeology and History of Copán." In *Copán: The History of an Ancient Maya Kingdom*. Santa Fe, NM: School of American Research Press, 3–32.
Flannery, K. V., and A. K. Balkansky, G. M. Feinman, D. C. Grove, J. Marcus, E. M. Redmond, R. G. Reynolds, R.J. Sharer, C.S. Spencer, and J. Yaeger
  2005 "Implications of New Petrographic Analysis for the Olmec 'Mother Culture' Model." *Proceedings National Academy of Sciences* 102:11219–11223.
Foias, Antonia
  2002 "At the Crossroads: The Economic Basis of Political Power in the Petexbatun Region, Southwest Peten, Guatemala." In *Ancient Maya Political Economies*, edited by M. Masson and D. Freidel. Walnut Creek, CA: Altamira, 223–248.

Folan, William
  1992 "Calakmul, Campeche: A Centralized Urban Administrative Center in the Northern Peten." *World Archaeology* 24.1. *Humid Tropics*. Rutledge.
  2007 Personal interview with Steve Glassman. July.
Folan, William, Ellen R. Kintz, Laraine A Fletcher, and Burma H. Hyde
  1982 "An Examination of Settlement Patterns at Coba, Quintana Roo, Mexico, and Tikal, Guatemala: A Reply to Arnold and Ford." *American Antiquity* 47.2: 430–436.
Folan, William, Joel D. Gunn, and Maria del Rosario Dominguez Carrasco
  2001 "Triadic Temples, Central Plazas and Dynastic Palaces: A Diachronic analysis of the Royal Court Complex, Calakmul, Campeche, Mexico." In *Royal Courts of the Ancient Maya*. Vol. 2, edited by Takeshi Inomata and Stephen Houston. Boulder, CO: Westview, 223–265.
Folan, William J., Betty Faust, Wolfgang Lutz, and Joel D. Gunn
  2000 "Social and Environmental Factors in the Classic Maya Collapse." In *Population, Development, and Environment on the Yucatan Peninsula: From Ancient Maya to 2030*, edited by Wolfgang Lutz and Leonel Prieto. Laxenburg, Aus: International Institute for Applied Systems Analysis.
Folan, William J., Joyce Marcus, Sophia Pincemin, Maria del Rosario Dominguez Carrasco, Laraine Fletcher and Abel Morales Lopez
  1995 "Calakmul: New Data from an Ancient Maya Capital in Campeche, Mexico." *Latin American Antiquity*, 6.4: 310, 334.
Foster, Lynn V.
  2002 *Handbook to Life in the Ancient Maya World*. New York: Oxford University Press.
Fox, John Gerard
  1996 "Playing with Power: Ballcourts and Political Ritual in Southern Mesoamerica." *Current Anthropology* 37.3: 483–509.
Freidel, David A.
  2008 "Maya Divine Kingship." In *Religion and Power: Divine Kingship and the Ancient World and Beyond*, edited by Nichole Brisch. IL: Oriental Institute of the University of Chicago.
Freidel, David A., Barbara MacLeod, and Charles K. Suhler
  2003 "Early Classic Maya Conquests in Words and Deeds." In *Ancient Mesoamerican Warfare*, edited by M. Kathryn Brown and Travis W. Stanton. Walnut Creek, CA: Altamira.
Freidel, David A., Kathryn Reese-Taylor, and David Mora-Maran
  2002 "The Origins of Maya Civilization: The Old Shell Game, Commodity, Treasure and Kingship." In *Ancient Maya Political Economies*, edited by Marilyn Masson and David Freidel. Walnut Creek, CA: Altamira, 41–86.
Freidel, David A., and Linda Schele
  1988 "Kingship in the Late Preclassic Maya Lowlands: The Instruments and Places of Ritual Power." *American Anthropologist* 90.3: 547.
Freidel, David A., Linda Schele, and Joy Parker
  1995 *Maya Cosmos: Three Thousand Years on the Shaman's Path*. New York: William Morrow.

Furst, Peter T.
 1968 "The Olmec Were — Jaguar Motif in the Light of Ethnographic Reality." *Dumbarton Oaks Conference on the Olmec. October 28 and October 29, 1967*, edited by Elizabeth Benson. Washington, DC: Dumbarton Oaks Research Library and Collection Trustees for Harvard University.
 1995 "Shamanism, Transformation, and Olmec Art." In *The Olmec World: Ritual and Rulership.* New Jersey: The Art Museum, Princeton University.

Gillespie, Susan
 2007 "Toltecs, Tula, and Chichen Itza: The Development of an Archeological Myth." In *Twin Tollans: Chichen Itza, Tula and the Epiclassic to the Early Postclassic Mesoamerican World.* Washington, DC: Dumbarton Oaks, 85–128.

Graham, Ian
 1963 "Across the Peten to the Ruins of Machaquila." *Expedition* 5.4: 2–10.
 1967 *Archaeological Explorations in El Petén, Guatemala.* New Orleans: Tulane University, Middle American Research Institute, pub. 33.

Grove, David
 1987 *Ancient Chalcatzingo.* Austin: University of Texas Press.
 1997 "Olmec Archaeology: A Half Century of Research and Its Accomplishments." *Journal of World Prehistory* 11.1.
 1999 "Public Monuments and Sacred Mountains: Observations on Three Formative Period Sacred Landscapes." In *Social Patterns in Pre-Classic Mesoamerica,* edited by David C. Grove and Rosemary A. Joyce. Washington, DC: Dumbarton Oaks Research Library and Collection.

Grube, Nikolai
 2000 "The City States of the Maya." In *A Contemporary Study of Thirty City-States,* edited by Mogens Herman Hansen. Copenhagen: The Royal Danish Academy of Sciences and Letters, 547–566.
 2008a/2001 "Cacao — the Beverage of the Gods." In *Maya: Divine Kings of the Rain Forest,* edited by Nikolai Grube assisted by Eva Eggebrecht and Matthias Seidel. Cologne, Ger: Ullmann.
 2008b/2001 "The Insignia of Power." In *Maya: Divine Kings of the Rain Forest,* edited by Nikolai Grube assisted by Eva Eggebrecht and Matthias Seidel. Cologne, Ger: Ullmann.
 2008c/2001 "Tortillas and Tamales — the Food of the Maize People and their Gods." In *Maya: Divine Kings of the Rain Forest,* edited by Nikolai Grube assisted by Eva Eggebrecht and Matthias Seidel. Cologne, Ger: Ullmann.

Grube, Nikolai, and Ruth J. Krochock
 2007 "Reading between the Lines: Hieroglyphic Texts from Chichen Itza and Its Neighbors." In *Twin Tollans: Chichen Itza, Tula and the Epiclassic to the Early Postclassic Mesoamerican World.* Washington D.C.: Dumbarton Oaks, 205–250.

Grube, Nikolai, and Simon Martin
 2008/2000 "The Dynastic History of the Maya." In *Maya: Divine Kings of the Rain Forest,* edited by Nikolai Grube assisted by Eva Eggebrecht and Matthias Seidel. Cologne, Ger: Ullmann.

Guenter, Stanley
 n.d. "El Mirador." *Mesoweb Resources* at http://www.mesoweb.com/encyc/view.asp?act=viewdata&i=0&s=kan&ext=n&sit=8&id=0&expert=y&sAND=preclassic&sANDNOT=
 2000 "Death of a Tikal Queen." *The PARI Journal* 1.2: 22–24.
 2005 "La Corona Find Sheds Light on Site Q Mystery." *The PARI Journal* 6.2: 16–18.

Hammond, Norman
 1992 "Preclassic Maya Civilization." In *New Theories on the Ancient Maya,* edited by Elin C. Danien and William Sharer. Philadelphia: University Museum Symposium Series, vol. 3, 137–144.
 2008/2001 "The Origins of Maya Civilization — the Beginnings of Village Life." In *Maya: Divine Kings of the Rain Forest,* edited by Nikolai Grube assisted by Eva Eggebrecht and Matthias Seidel. Cologne, Ger: Ullmann.

Hammond, Norman, Jeremy R. Bauer, and Jody Morris
 2002 "Squaring off: Late Middle Preclassic Architectural Innovation at Cuello, Belize." *Antiquity* 76.292:327.

Hammond, Norman, Jeremy R. Bauer, and Sophie Hay
 2000 "Preclassic Maya architectural ritual at Cuello, Belize." *Antiquity* 74.284: 265.

Hammond, Norman, Julie Mather Saul, and Frank P. Saul
 2002 "Ancestral Faces: A Preclassic Maya Skull-Mask from Cuello, Belize." *Antiquity* 76.294: 951.

Hansen, Eric Floyd
 2000 "Ancient Maya Burnt Lime Technology: Cultural Implications of Technological Styles." PhD Diss., University of California, Los Angeles.

Hansen, Richard Duane
 1992 "The Archaeology of Ideology: A Study of Maya Preclassic Archaeological Sculpture at Nakbe, Peten, Guatemala." PhD Diss., University of California, Los Angeles.
 1998 "Continuity and Disjunction: The Preclassic Antecedents of Classic Architecture." In *Function and Meaning in Classic Maya Architecture,* edited by S. Houston. Washington, DC: Dumbarton Oaks, 49–122.
 2001a "Marvels of the Ancient Maya, Guatemala: The Past Engages the Future." *Archaeology,* (September/October), 51–58.
 2001b "The First Cities — The Beginnings of Urbanization and State Formation in the Maya Lowlands." In *Maya: Divine Kings of the Rain Forest,* edited by Nikolai Grube. Verlag, Ger.: Konemann, 50–65.
 2008/2001 "The First Cities — The Beginnings of Urbanization and State Formation in the Maya Lowlands. In *Maya: Divine Kings of the Rain Forest,* edited by Nikolai Grube assisted by Eva Eggebrecht and Matthias Seidel. Cologne, Ger: Ullmann.
 2009 Richard Hansen, PhD, biography at http://www.miradorbasin.com/About/hansen.htm.

Hansen, Richard D., and Stanley P. Guenter
 2005 "Early Social Complexity and Kingship in the Mirador Basin." In *Lords of Creation: The Origins*

of Sacred Maya Kingship, edited by Virginia M. Fields and Dorie Reents-Budet. Los Angeles County Museum of Art, Scala Publishers, 60–61.

Hansen, Richard D., Steven Bozarth, John Jacob, David Wahl, and Thomas Schreiner
2002 "Climatic and Environmental Variability in the Rise of Maya Civilization: A Preliminary Perspective from Northern Peten." *Ancient Mesoamerica* 13: 273–295.

Harris, Charles H., III, and Louis R. Sadler
2003 *The Archaeologist Was a Spy*. Albuquerque: University of New Mexico Press.

Harrison, Peter D.
1999 *The Lords of Tikal: Rulers of an Ancient Maya City*. London, UK: Thames and Hudson.
2008/2001 "Maya Agriculture." In *Maya: Divine Kings of the Rain Forest*, edited by Nikolai Grube assisted by Eva Eggebrecht and Matthias Seidel. Cologne, Ger: Ullmann.

Hassig, Ross
1992 *War and Society in Ancient Mesoamerica*. Berkeley: University of California Press.

Hatch, Marion Popenoe de, Erick Ponciano, Tomás Barrientos Q., Mark Brenner and Charles Ortloff
2002 "Climate and Technological Innovation at Kaminaljuyu, Guatemala." *Ancient Mesoamerica* 13: 103–114.

Hather, Jon G., and Norman Hammond
1994 "Ancient Maya Subsistence Diversity: Root and Tuber Remains from Cuello, Belize." *Antiquity* 68.259: 330–335.

Haug, Gerald H., Detlef Gunther, Larry C. Peterson, and Daniel M. Sigman
2003 "Climate and the Collapse of Maya Civilization." *Science* 299.5613.

Haviland, William A.
1992 "From Double Bird to Ah Cacao: Dynastic Troubles and the Cycle of Katuns at Tikal, Guatemala. In *New Theories on the Ancient Maya*, edited by Elin C. Danien and William Sharer. Philadelphia: University Museum Symposium Series, vol. 3, 71–80.
2003 "Settlement, Society, and Demography at Tikal. In *Tikal: Dynasties, Foreigners, & Affairs of State: Advancing Maya Archaeology*, edited by Jeremy Sabloff. Santa Fe, NM: School of American Research Press.

Haviland, William A., and H. Moholy-Nagy
2000 "Distinguishing the High And Mighty From the Hoi Polloi at Tikal, Guatemala." In *The Ancient Civilizations of Mesoamerica: A Reader*, edited by Michael E. Smith and Marilyn Masson. Malden, MA: Blackwell, 39–48.

Hayden, Brian,
1996 "Feasting in Prehistoric and Traditional Societies." In *Food and the Status Quest: An Interdisciplinary Study*, edited by Polly Wiessner and Wulf Shiefenhovel. Providence, RI: Berghahn, 127–148.

Haynes, William
1946 *Southern Horizons*. New York: D. Van Nostrand, 208.

Hendon, Julia A.
1999 "The Pre-Classic Maya Compound as the Focus of Social Identity Social Patterns." In *Pre-Classic Mesoamerica*, edited by David C. Grove and Rosemary A. Joyce. Washington, DC: Dumbarton Oaks Research Library and Collection.

Hodell, D. A., J. H. Curtis, and M. Brenner
1995 "Possible Role of Climate in the Collapse of Classic Maya Civilization." *Nature* 375:391–394.

Hodell, D. A., M. Brenner, and J. H. Curtis
2007 "Climate and Cultural History of the Northeastern Yucatan Peninsula, Quintana Roo, Mexico." *Climatic Change* 83: 215–240. DOI 10.1007/s10584-006-9177-4.

Holden, Constance
1999 "Urban Decay in Old Mexico." *Science* 283. 5398: 31.

Houston, Stephen, and David Stuart
1996 "Of Gods, Glyphs and Kings: Divinity and Rulership Among the Classic Maya." *Antiquity* 70.268: 289–312.

Hurst, Jeffrey W., Stanley M. Tarka Jr., Terry G. Powis, Fred Valdez Jr., and Thomas Hester
2002 "Cacao Usage by the Earliest Maya Civilization: Foaming Chocolate Prepared in Spouted Vessels Made a Delectable Preclassic Drink." *Nature* 418 (July): 289–290.

Hutson, Scott R., Aline Magnoni, Daniel E. Mazeau, and Travis W. Stanton
2001 "The Archaeology of Urban Houselots at Chunchucmil." In *Lifeways in the Northern Maya Lowlands: New Approaches to Archaeology in the Yucatan Peninsula*, edited by Jennifer P. Mathews and Bethany A. Morrison. Tucson: University of Arizona Press.

Inomata, Takeshi
1995 "Archaeological Investigations at the Fortified Center of Aguateca, Peten, Guatemala: Implications for the Study of the Ancient Maya Collapse." PhD Diss., Nashville, TN: Vanderbilt University.

Jones, Grant D.
1998 *The Conquest of the Last Maya Kingdom*. CA: Stanford University Press.

Jose, Juan A.
2009 "Lindbergh in Mexico." At *Charles Lindbergh, an American Aviator*. http://www.charleslindbergh.com/history/mexico.asp.

Joyce, Rosemary A., Richard Edging, Karl Lorenz, and Susan D. Gillespie
1986 "Olmec Bloodletting: An Iconographic Study." In *Sixth Palenque Round Table, 1986*, edited by Virginia M. Fields. Norman: University of Oklahoma Press. http://www.mesoweb.com/pari/publications/rt08/RT06_00.html.

Kaufman, Terrence, and John Justeson
2008 "Epi-Olmec." In *The Ancient Languages of the Americas and Asia*, edited by Roger D. Woodward. Cambridge: Cambridge University Press, 193.

Kerr, Justin
1992 "The Myth of the Popul Vuh as an Instrument of Power." In *New Theories on the Ancient Maya*, edited by Elin C. Danien and William Sharer. Philadelphia: University Museum Symposium Series, vol. 3, 109–122.

Kidder, A. V.
1930 "Colonel and Mrs. Lindbergh Aid Archaeologists." *Masterkey* 3.6: 5–17.

Kowalski, Jeff K.
    1989 "Who Am I Among the Itza? Links Between Northern Yucatán and the Western Maya Lowlands and Highlands." In *Mesoamerica After the Decline of Teotihuacán*, edited by Richard A. Diehl and Janet C. Berlo. Washington, DC: Dumbarton Oaks, 173–186.
Kowalski, Jeff K., Alfredo Barrera Rubio, Heber Ojeda Mas, and Jose Huchim Herrera
    1996 "Archaeological Excavations of a Round Temple at Uxmal: Summary Discussion and Implications for Northern Maya Culture History." In *Eighth Palenque Round Table, 1993*, edited by Merle Greene Robertson, Martha J. Macri, and Jan McHargue. San Francisco, CA: The Pre-Columbian Art Institute Research Institute, 286–291.
Kowalski, Jeff K. and Cynthia Kristan-Graham
    2007 "Chichen Itza, Tula and Tollan: Changing Perspectives on a Recurring Problem in Mesoamerican Archeology and Art History." In *Twin Tollans: Chichen Itza, Tula and the Epiclassic to the Early Postclassic Mesoamerican World*. Washington, DC: Dumbarton Oaks.
Landa, Diego de
    1941 *Relación de las Cosas de Yucatán*. Ed. A. M. Tozzer. Cambridge: Harvard University Press.
Landon, Charles
    1935 "The Chewing Gum Industry." *Economic Geography* 11.2: 183–190.
Lara, Jorge Perez de
    2008 "A Brief History of the Rediscovery of Tikal and Archaeological Work at the Site." http://www.mesoweb.com/tikal/features/history/history.html.
Lawler, Andrew
    2007 "Beyond the Family Feud." *Archaeology* 60.2 (March/April): 20–25.
Lentz, David L., and Brian Hockaday
    2009 "Tikal Timbers and Temples: Ancient Maya Agroforestry and the End of Time." *Journal of Archaeological Science* 36: 1342–1353.
Leyden, Barbara W.
    1984 "Guatemalan Forest Synthesis After Pleistocene Aridity." *Proceedings of the National Academy of Sciences* 81: 4856–4859.
Li, Long, Shu-Min Li, Jian-Hao Sun, Li-Li Zhau, Xing-Guo Bao, Hong-Gang Zhang, and Fu-Suo Zhang
    2007 "Chinese Scientists Show That Intercropping Maize with Faba Beans Increases Yield." *Proceedings of the National Academy of Science* 104.27 (July 3): 11192–11196.
Lipscomb, Barney
    1995 "Cyrus Longworth Lundell, 1907–1993." *HerbalGram* 34:67.
Lucero, Lisa J.
    1999 "Water Control and Maya Politics in the Southern Maya Lowlands." *Archeological Papers of the American Anthropological Association* 9.1: 35–49.
Lundell, Cyrus
    1933 Archaeological Discoveries in the Maya Area. *Proceedings of the American Philosophical Society* 72.3: 147–179.
    1937 *The Vegetation of Peten, with an Appendix Studies of Mexican and Central American Plants*. Washington, DC: Carnegie Institution of Washington.
Madeira, Percy C., Jr.
    1931 "An Aerial Expedition to Central America." *University of Pennsylvania Museum Journal* 22.3: 95–153.
Marcus, Joyce
    1987 *The Inscriptions of Calakmul: Royal Marriage at a Maya City in Campeche, Mexico*. Technical Report 21, The Museum of Anthropology. Ann Arbor: University of Michigan.
    1992 *Mesoamerican Writing Systems: Propoganda, Myth and History in Four Ancient Civilizations*. New Jersey: Princeton University Press.
    1999 "Social Dimensions of Pre-Classic Burials." In *Social Patterns Pre-Classic Mesoamerica*, edited by David C. Grove and Rosemary A. Joyce. Washington, DC: Dumbarton Oaks Research Library and Collection.
Martin, Simon
    2001 "Unmasking 'Double Bird,' Ruler of Tikal." *The PARI Journal*. www.mesoweb.com/pari/publications/journal/201/DoubleBird.pdf.
    2005a "Caracol Altar 21 Revisited: More Data on Double Bird and Tikal's Wars of the Mid-Sixth Century." *The PARI Journal* 6.1. www.mesoweb.com/pari/publications/journal/601/Altar21.pdf.
    2005b "Of Snakes and Bats: Shifting Identities at Calakmul." *The PARI Journal* 6.2: 5–15. www.mesoweb.com/pari/publications/journal/602/SnakesBats_e.pdf.
    2008a/2001 "Power in the West—the Maya and Teotihuacan." In *Maya: Divine Kings of the Rain Forest*, edited by Nikolai Grube assisted by Eva Eggebrecht and Matthias Seidel. Cologne, Ger: Ullmann.
    2008b/2001 "Under a Deadly Star—Warfare among the Classic Maya." In *Maya: Divine Kings of the Rain Forest*, edited by Nikolai Grube assisted by Eva Eggebrecht and Matthias Seidel. Cologne, Ger: Ullmann.
Martin, Simon, and Nikolai Grube
    2000 *Chronicle of the Maya Kings and Queens: Deciphering the Dynasties of the Ancient Maya*. London, UK: Thames and Hudson.
Matheny, Ray T.
    1980 "El Mirador, Peten, Guatemala." Papers of the New World Archaeological Foundation, Salt Lake City.
McAnany, Patricia A.
    2000 "Living with the Ancestors: Kinship and Kingship in Ancient Maya Society." In *The Ancient Civilizations of Mesoamerica: A Reader*, edited by Michael E. Smith and Marilyn Masson. Malden, MA: Blackwell, 483–487.
McKillop, Heather
    2004 *The Ancient Maya: New Perspectives*. New York: W. W. Norton.
    2005 *In Search of Maya Sea Traders*. College Station: Texas A&M University Press.
McNeil, Cameron L., W. Jeffrey Hurst, and Robert J. Sharer
    2006 "Use and Representation of Cacoa During the Classic Period at Copan, Honduras." *Chocolate*

in Mesoamerica: A Cultural History of Cacao. Gainesville: University of Florida Press.

Meggers, Betty, and Jeffrey Blomster
2005 "The Origins of Olmec Civilization/Response." Science 309.5734.

Milanich, Jarald T.
1996. The Timucua. Oxford, UK: Blackwell.

Milbrath, Susan
1999 Star Gods of the Maya: Astronomy in Art, Folklore, and Calendars. Austin: University of Texas Press.
2005 "Last Great Capital of the Maya." Archaeology Magazine 58.2: 26–29.

Milbrath, Susan, and Carlos Peraza Lope
2003 "Revisiting Mayapan: Mexico's Last Maya Capital." Ancient Mesoamerica 14: 1–46.

Milbrath, Susan, James Aimers, Carlos Peraza Lope, and Lynda Florey Folan
2007 "Effigy Censers of the Chen Mul Modeled Ceramic System and Their Implications for Late Postclassic Maya Interregional Interaction." www.famsi.org/reports/05025/Chen_Mul_final.pdf.

Miller, Mary Ellen
1999 Maya Art and Architecture. London, UK: Thames and Hudson.
2001 "The Maya Ballgame: Rebirth in the Court of Life and Death." In The Sport of Life and Death: the Mesoamerican Ballgame, edited by E. Michael Whittington. New York: Thames and Hudson, 78–87.
2009 "How Painted Bodies, flattened Foreheads, and Filed Teeth Made the Maya Beautiful." Archaeology Magazine 62.1: 36–42.

Miller, Mary, and Karl Taube
1993 An Illustrated Dictionary of the Gods and Symbols of Ancient Mexico and the Maya. London, UK: Thames and Hudson.

Morley, Sylvanus
1933 "The Calakmul Expedition." The Scientific Monthly (September).
2001 "Diary." The PARI Journal 2.1.

Morrison, Bethany A.
2006 "From Swidden to Swamps: The Study of Ancient Maya Agriculture." In Lifeways in the Northern Maya Lowlands: New Approaches to Archaeology in the Yucatan Peninsula, edited by Jennifer P. Mathews and Bethany A. Morrison. Tucson: University of Arizona Press.

Nadal, Laura Filloy
2001 Rubber and Rubber Balls in Mesoamerica in the Sport of Life and Death: The Mesoamerican Ballgame. Edited by E. Michael Whittington. New York: Thames and Hudson, 21–31.

Neff, Hector
2003 "Park Profile — Guatemala Cerro Cahuí Protected Biotope." http://www.parkswatch.org/parkprofiles/pdf/ccpb_eng.pdf.
2006 "The Olmec and the Origins of Mesoamerican Civilization." Antiquity 80.309: 714.

Pagliaro, Jonathan B., James F. Garber, and Travis W. Stanton
2003 "Evaluating the Archaeological Signatures of Maya Ritual and Conflict." In Ancient Mesoamerican Warfare, edited by M. Kathryn Brown and Travis W. Stanton. Walnut Creek, CA: Altamira.

Paris, Elizabeth H.
2008 "Metallurgy, Mayapan, and the Postclassic Mesoamerican World System." Ancient Mesoamerica 19.1: 43–66.

Peraza Lope, Carlos, Marilyn A. Masson, Timothy Hare, and Pedro Candelario Delgado Ku
2006 "The Chronology of Mayapan: New Radiocarbon Evidence." Ancient Mesoamerica 17.2:153–175.

Pohl, Mary E. D., Kevin O. Pope, Christopher von Nagy
2002 "Olmec Origins of Mesoamerican Writing." Science 298.5600: 1984–1988.

Pool, Christopher
2007 Olmec Archaeology and Early Mesoamerica. Cambridge: Cambridge University Press.

Powis, Terry, Norbert Stanchly, Christine D. White, Paul F. Healy, Jaimie Awe, and Fred Longstaffe
1999 "A Reconstruction of Middle Preclassic Maya Subsistence Economy at Cahal Pech." Antiquity 73.280: 364.

Pugh, Marian Stirling
1981 "An Intimate View of Archaeological Exploration." In The Olmec and Their Neighbors: In Memory of Matthew W. Stirling, edited by Elizabeth P. Benson. Washington, DC: Dumbarton Oaks.

Pugh, Timothy W.
2001 "Flood Reptiles, Serpent Temples, and the Quadripartite Universe." Ancient Mesoamerica 12.2: 247–258.
2003 "The Exemplary Center of the Late Postclassic Kowoj Maya." Latin American Antiquity 14.4: 408–430.

Puleston, Dennis
1978 "Terracing, Raised Fields, and Tree Cropping in the Maya Lowlands: A New Perspective on the Geography." In Pre-Hispanic Maya Agriculture, edited by P. D. Harrison and B. L. Turner. Albuquerque: University of New Mexico Press, 225–245.

Reilly, F. Kent, III
1995 "Art, Ritual, and Rulership in the Olmec World." In The Olmec World: Ritual and Rulership. New Jersey: The Art Museum, Princeton University.

Rice, Prudence M., Arthur A. Demarest, and Don S. Rice, eds.
2004 "The Terminal Classic and the 'Classic Maya Collapse' in Perspective." In The Terminal Classic in the Maya Lowlands: Collapse, Transition, and Transformation. Boulder: University of Colorado Press.

Rice, Prudence M., and Don S. Rice
2004 "The Late Classic to Postclassic Transformation in the Peten Lakes Region, Guatemala." In The Terminal Classic in the Maya Lowlands: Collapse, Transition, and Transformation, edited by Arthur A. Demarest, Prudence M. Rice, and Don S. Rice. Boulder: University of Colorado Press.

Ricketson, Oliver, and A. V. Kidder
1930 "An Archaeological Reconnaissance by Air in Central America." Geographical Review 20:177–206.

Ricketson, Oliver, and Edith B. Ricketson

1937 *Uaxactun, Guatemala, Group E, 1926–1937*. Carnegie Institution of Washington, Publication 477.

Ringle, William
1999 *Pre-Classic Cityscapes: Ritual Politics among the Early Lowland Maya in Social Patterns in Pre-Classic Mesoamerica*. Edited by David C. Grove and Rosemary A. Joyce. Washington, DC: Dumbarton Oaks Research Library and Collection.

Ringle, William, George J. Bey III, Tara Bond Freeman, Craig A. Hanson, Charles W. Houck, and J. Gregory Smith
2004 "The Decline of the East: The Classic to Postclassic Transition at Ek Balam, Yucatan." In *The Terminal Classic in the Maya Lowlands: Collapse, Transition, and Transformation*, edited by Arthur A. Demarest, Prudence M. Rice, and Don S. Rice. Boulder: University of Colorado Press.

Ruppert, Karl, and John Denison
1943 *Archaeological Reconnaissance in Campeche, Quintana Roo and Peten*. Carnegie Institution of Washington, Publication 543.

Rust, William
1992 "New Ceremonial and Settlement Evidence at LaVenta and its Relation to Preclassic Maya Cultures." In *New Theories on the Ancient Maya*, edited by Elin C. Danien and William Sharer. Philadelphia: University Museum Symposium Series, vol. 3, 123–131.

Sabloff, Jeremy
2007 "It Depends on How We Look at Things: New Perspectives on the Postclassic Period in the Northern Maya Lowlands." *Proceedings of the American Philosophical Society* 151.1, Humanities Module: 11.

Saturno, William A., David Stuart, and Boris Beltran
2006 "Early Maya Writing at San Bartolo, Guatemala." *Science* 311.1281.

Scarborough, Vernon L.
1991 "Courting the Southern Maya Lowlands: A Study in Prehispanic Ballgame Architecture." In *The Mesoamerican Ballgame*, edited by Vernon L Scarborough and David Wilcox. Tucson: University of Arizona Press, 129–144.

Schele, Linda, and David A. Freidel
1990 *A Forest of Kings: The Untold Story of the Ancient Maya*. New York: William Morrow.
1991 "The Courts of Creation: Ballcourts, Ballgames, and Portals to the Maya Otherworld." In *The Mesoamerican Ballgame*, edited by Vernon L Scarborough and David Wilcox. Tucson: University of Arizona Press, 289–316.

Schele, Linda, and Mary Ellen Miller
1986 The Blood of Kings: Dynasty and Ritual in Maya Art. New York and London: Thames and Hudson.

Schele, Linda, and Peter Mathews
1998 *The Code of Kings: The Language of Seven Sacred Maya Temples and Tombs*. New York: Scribner.

Seitz, R. G., E. Harlow, V. B. Sisson and K. A. Taube
2001 "Olmec Blue and Formative Jade Sources: New Discoveries in Guatemala." *Antiquity* 75: 687–688.

Shafer, Harry J., and Thomas R. Hester
2000 "Lithic Craft Specialization and Product Distribution at the Maya Site of Colha, Belize." In *The Ancient Civilizations of Mesoamerica: A Reader*, edited by Michael E. Smith and Marilyn Masson. Malden, MA: Blackwell, 144–157.

Sharer, Robert
1992 "The Preclassic Origins of Lowland Maya States." In *New Theories on the Ancient Maya*, edited by Elin C. Danien and William Sharer. Philadelphia: University Museum Symposium Series, vol. 3, 131–136.
1994 *The Ancient Maya*. 5th ed. CA: Stanford University Press.
2003 "Tikal and the Copan Dynastic Founding." In *Tikal: Dynasties, Foreigners, & Affairs of State: Advancing Maya Archaeology*, edited by Jeremy Sabloff. Santa Fe, NM: School of American Research Press, 319–355.
2007 "Early Formative Pottery Trade and the Evolution of Mesoamerican Civilization." *Antiquity* 81.311: 201.

Sharer, Robert, and Charles Golden
2004 "Kingship and Polity: Conceptualizing the Body Politic." In *Continuities and Change in Maya Archaeology: Perspectives at the Millennium*, edited by Charles Golden and Greg Borgstede. New York: Routledge, 23–50.

Sharer, Robert, and Loa P. Traxler
2006 *The Ancient Maya*. California: Stanford University Press.

Sheets, Payson
2003 "Warfare in Ancient Mesoamerica: A Summary View." In *Ancient Mesoamerican Warfare*, edited by M. Kathryn Brown and Travis W. Stanton. Walnut Creek, CA: Altamira.

Shreiner, Thomas Paul
1994 "Traditional Maya Lime Production: The Environmental and Cultural Implications of a Native American Technology." PhD Diss., University of California, Berkeley.

Smith, Gregory J., William M. Ringle, and Tara M. Bond-Freeman
2006 "Ichmul de Morley and Northern Maya Political Dynamics." In *Lifeways in the Northern Maya Lowlands: New Approaches to Archaeology in the Yucatan Peninsula*, edited by Jennifer P. Mathews and Bethany A. Morrison. Tucson: University of Arizona Press.

Steinbrenner, Larry
2006 "Cacao in Gretter Nicoya: Ethnohistory and a Unique Tradition." In *Chocolate in Mesoamerica: A Cultural History of Cacao*, edited by Cameron L. McNeil. Gainesville: University of Florida Press.

Stephens, John Lloyd
1969/1841 *Incidents of Travel in Central America, Chiapas, and Yucatan*. Vols. 1–2. New York: Dover.

Stirling, Matthew W.
1940 "Great Stone Faces of the Mexican Jungle." *National Geographic* 78.3, (September): 309–334.
1943 "Stone Monuments of Southern Mexico." *Smithsonian Institute*.
1968 "Early History of the Olmec Problem." *Dumbarton Oaks Conference on the Olmec. October 28 and October 29, 1967*, edited by Elizabeth Benson.

Washington, DC: Dumbarton Oaks Research Library and Collection Trustees for Harvard University.

Stoltman, James B., Joyce Marcus, Kent V. Flannery, James H. Burton, and Robert G. Moyle
  2005 "Petrographic Evidence Shows That Pottery Exchange Between the Olmec and Their Neighbors Was Two-Way." In *Proceedings of the National Academy of Sciences*, 102.32 (August 9): 1213–11218.

Stuart, David
  1996 "The Shaman's Stance: Integration of Body, Spirit and Cosmos in Olmec Sculpture." *Eighth Palenque Round Table*.
  1998 "The Arrival of Strangers: Teotihuacan and Tollan in Classic Maya History." Extract of a paper presented at Princeton University, October 1996. *PARI Online Publications*. http://www.mesoweb.com/pari/publications/news_archive/25/strangers/strangers.html.
  1999 "Patrons of Shamanic Power: La Venta's Supernatural Entities in Light of Mixed Beliefs." *Ancient Mesoamerica* 10: 160–188.
  2008 "The Colossal Fetuses of La Venta and Mesoamerica's First Creation Story." In *Imagining the Fetus: The Unborn in Myth, Religion, and Culture*, edited by Vanessa R. Sassoon and Jane Marie Law. United Kingdom: University of Oxford Press.

Suhler, Charles, Traci Arden, David Freidel, and Dave Johnstone
  2004 "The Rise and Fall of Terminal Classic Yaxuna, Yucatan, Mexico." In *The Terminal Classic in the Maya Lowlands: Collapse, Transition, and Transformation*, edited by Arthur A. Demarest, Prudence M. Rice, and Don S. Rice. Boulder: University of Colorado Press.

Taube, Karl
  1985 "The Classic Maya Maize God: A Reappraisal." *Fifth Palenque Round Table*.
  1998 "The Jade Hearth: Centrality, Rulership, and the Classic Maya Temple." In *Function and Meaning in Classic Maya Architecture*, edited by Stephen D. Houston. Washington, DC: Dumbarton Oaks Research Library and Collection, 427–478.

Tedlock, Dennis, trans.
  1985 *Popul Vuh: The Mayan Book of the Dawn of Life*. New York: Simon & Schuster.

Tokovinine, Alexandre
  2002 "Divine Patrons of the Maya Ballgame." www.mesoweb.com/features/tokovinine/ballgame.pdf.

Tourtellot, Gair, and Jason J. Gonzalez
  2004 "The Last Hurrah: Continuity and Transformation at Seibal in Perspective." In *The Terminal Classic in the Maya Lowlands: Collapse, Transition, and Transformation*, edited by Arthur A. Demarest, Prudence M. Rice, and Don S. Rice. Boulder: University of Colorado Press.

Tuefel, Stefanie
  2008/2001 "Marriage Diplomacy: Women at the Royal Court." In *Maya: Divine Kings of the Rain Forest*, edited by Nikolai Grube assisted by Eva Eggebrecht and Matthias Seidel. Cologne, Ger: Ullmann.

Turner, B. L., and Peter D. Harrison
  2000/1983 *Pultrouser Swamp: Ancient Maya Habitat, Agriculture and Settlement in Northern Belize*. Salt Lake City: University of Utah Press.

Valdes, Juan Antonio, and Federico Fahsen
  2004 "Disaster in Sight: The Terminal Classic at Tikal and Uaxactun in Perspective." In *The Terminal Classic in the Maya Lowlands: Collapse, Transition, and Transformation*, edited by Arthur A. Demarest, Prudence M. Rice, and Don S. Rice. Boulder: University of Colorado Press.

Villagutierre Soto-Mayor, Juan de
  1983 *History of the Conquest of the Province of the Itza: Subjugation and Events of the Lacandon and Other Nations of Uncivilized Indians in the Lands from the Kingdom of Guatemala to the Provinces of Yucatan in North America*, translated by Robert D. Wood. Culver City, CA: Labyrinthos.

von Hagen, Victor Wolfgang
  1990/1947 *Maya Explorer: John Lloyd Stephens and the Lost Cities of Central America and Yucatan*. San Francisco, CA: Chronicle Books.

Wagner, Elizabeth
  2008/2001 "Jade—the Green Gold of the Maya." In *Maya: Divine Kings of the Rain Forest*, edited by Nikolai Grube assisted by Eva Eggebrecht and Matthias Seidel. Cologne, Ger: Ullmann.

Wahl, David Brent
  2005 "Climate Change and Human Impacts in the Southern Maya Lowlands: A Paleoenvironmental Perspective from Northern Peten, Guatemala." PhD Diss., University of California, Los Angeles.

Wahl, David, Roger Byrne, Thomas Schreiner, and Richard Hansen
  2006 "Holocene Vegetation Change in the Northern Peten and Its Implications for Maya Prehistory." *Quaternary Research* 65 (University of Washington): 380–389.
  2007 "Palaeolimnological Evidence of Late-Holocene Settlement and Abandonment in the Mirador Basin, Peten, Guatemala." *The Holocene* 17.6: 813–820.

Webster, David
  2000 "The Not So Peaceful Maya: A Review of Maya Warfare." *Journal of World Prehistory* 14.1: 65–118.
  2001 *The Fall of the Ancient Maya: Solving the Mystery of the Maya Collapse*. London, UK: Thames and Hudson.

White, Christine D.
  2001 "Isotopic Evidence for Maya Patterns of Deer and Dog Use at Preclassic Colha." *Journal of Archaeological Science* 28.1: 89–107.

White, Christine D., Michael W. Spence, Fred Longstaffe, and Kimberley R. Law
  2000 "Testing the Nature of Teotihuacan Imperialism at Kaminaljuyuu Sing Phosphate Oxygen-Isotope Ratios." *Journal of Anthropological Research* 56: 535–558.

Wilk, Richard
  2004 "Miss Universe, the Olmec, and the Valley of Oaxaca." *Journal of Social Anthropology* 4.1: 81–98.

Wilkes, Garrison
  1978 "Review of Corn and Corn Improvement." *Science* 200.4337: 41–42.
  2004 "Corn, Strange and Marvelous: But Is a Defin-

itive Origin Known?" In *Corn: Origin, History, Technology, and Production,* edited by C. Wayne Smith. Hoboken, NJ: John Wiley & Sons.

Wright, Lori E.
2005 "In Search of Yax Nuun Ayiin I: Revisiting the Tikal Project's Burial 10." *Ancient Mesoamerica* 16.1: 89–100.

Zender, Marc
2004 Sport, Spectacle and Political Theater: New Views of the Classic Maya Ballgame. *PARI Online Publications* 4.4: 10–12. http://www.mesoweb.com/pari/publications/journal/404/sport.pdf.

Index

Abrams, Elliot 48
Access Calakmul 98
Acosta, Jose 160, 169
adelantado 187, 204
Aeolus 60
Agnew, F.V. 35
aguada 112
Aguateca 149, 150, 151
Aguilar, Alvarez 115
Agurcias, Ricardo 135
Aj Bolon 153
allspice 40, 71
alm 211
Alta Vista 169
Altar 4 15, 16, 17, 23, 134
Altar Q 124, 125, 126, 127, 130, 135, 136
Alvarado, conquistador 53
Ambrosino, James N. 180, 184
Anaya Hernández, Armando 3, 7, 27, 223
Arbenz regime 69
Ardren, Traci 180, 184
aristocrats 49, 74, 81, 82, 93
Arroyo de Piedra 149
atlantean figures 159
atlatl 91, 158, 162, 168, 178, 179
attapulgite clay 182
Avenue of the Dead 92
avocado 20
Awe, Jaimie 7, 47
axe or axed 49, 73, 150, 181
Aztec 7, 13, 21, 28, 93, 158, 159, 160, 161, 186, 188, 189, 190, 196, 201

Bacalar 205–206, 217
bajo 30, 46, 61, 182
Bajo de Santa Fe 70
Balaj Chan Kawiil 149
Ball Court of Chichen Itza 168
ball courts 62, 168
ball game 6–7, 21, 53–54, 58, 62, 80–81, 87
Balsas River valley 44
Barbachano, Miguel 216

Barouss, Fr. Raphael 2
Barrera, Jose Marie 218–219
Barrera Rubio, Alfredo 179
Bat dynasty 116, 146, 148
Batres, Leopoldo 159
Beach, Timothy 46
beans 20, 41, 44, 46, 48, 72, 73, 82, 122, 201, 203
Beat Generation 36
Becan 46, 90
Belize 7, 11, 30, 31, 32, 35, 45, 47, 48, 49, 55, 70, 71, 72, 82, 90, 96, 98, 116, 117, 122, 130, 136, 139, 141, 145, 148, 150, 154, 164, 196, 203, 204, 205, 206, 217
Belize City 32
Belize River 47, 70, 116–117, 145
bells 201–202
Bernoulli, Carl Gustav 68
Bey, George 174, 200
big bluestem 43
big man 62–63
Blom, Franz 10–15, 19, 28, 64, 76, 157
blood sacrifice 5, 54–56, 61, 170
Bonampak 104–105
botan palm 51
Bourbon 212
Bowditch, Charles 101
Brainerd, George 161
Brasseur de Braumbourg 157
Braswell, Geoffrey E. 146
Brown, Kathryn M. 75
Brunhouse, Robert L. 12, 122, 155, 157, 158
bufotenin 24
Bureau of American Ethnology 14
burin-spall drill 49

C-shaped buildings 174, 179, 180
Caballero-Briones, F.A. 50
cacao 44, 48, 71–73, 81–82, 85, 132, 164, 192, 203
Cadiz 212

Cahal Pech 47–48, 234
Calakmul 4, 5, 35, 69, 98–103, 106–120, 125, 130, 132, 134–153, 160, 163, 165, 180, 184, 191, 208
Calakmul Biosphere 98
calcium carbonate 50–51
Campeche 3, 30, 34, 46, 100, 103, 113, 160–162, 172, 192, 196, 200–201, 204–209, 213–216, 220–221
campesino 8, 31, 211, 218
Cancun 3, 30–31, 98–100, 162, 213–214
Candelaria 34–35, 191
Canul 200
Caracol 32, 96, 97, 116–119, 136, 139, 141, 145–146, 148–149, 152, 165, 183–184, 197
Carassco, Ramon 120
Cardenas regime 157
Caribbean 5, 30, 32, 34, 47, 55, 70, 98, 100, 102, 116, 151, 164, 186, 188, 194, 203, 205
Carnegie Institution 10–11, 31–38, 68, 101, 103, 160, 195, 197
Castaneda, Carlos 4, 22–23
Castillo 45, 161, 166–168, 195, 197, 198, 199, 201–202, 210
catfish 20, 42, 47
Catherwood, Frederick 2, 105, 121–123, 125, 131, 155, 158, 175
censers 202
Central America 2, 7, 20, 36, 39, 43, 67, 101, 122–123, 155, 190, 193, 222
Central Buenfil 100
Central Plaza 109, 113, 115
Central Valley of Mexico 80
Centralists 214
Ceren 73
Cerros 25, 54–56, 58, 61, 63, 75
Chac 178, 203
chacmool 157–159, 162, 164, 167
Chakanputun 201, 203–204
Champoton 100, 201, 203

233

Index

Chan, F. 218
Chan Santa Cruz 186, 211, 222
Charnay, Desiree 9, 158–160
Chase, Arlen F. 73, 96, 139, 152
Chase, Diane Z. 73, 96, 139, 152
Chen Mul 183, 197, 202–204; effigy censer 202–203
Chenes 146, 165, 171–172, 176
chert 41, 49, 64, 71, 112, 182
Chetumal 32, 98, 205
chewing gum 99, 107
Chiapas 3, 4, 12, 49, 62, 104–105, 122–123, 155
Chichen Itza 1, 3–4, 34, 45, 68, 99, 101, 104, 157–174, 176, 178–180, 185, 193–197, 199, 202, 204–208
chicle 99, 100, 101, 107
chicleros 99, 100, 107
Chiik Naab 134
Chilam Balam of Mani 202, 207–208
chili peppers 44
Cholula 189
Chuc 170
chultun 47, 95
Chunchucmil 163
CIA 69
Civil War (U.S.) 2, 8, 116
Clark, John E. 26, 62, 224
Classic 1, 4, 22, 31, 34–35, 45, 48, 52, 55, 58, 59, 63–69, 71–78, 80, 83, 90, 95–98, 106, 108–109, 111–113, 115, 119, 127, 135, 145, 148, 150, 152, 153, 154, 155, 160, 163–165, 169, 172, 176, 180, 182, 189, 193–194, 196, 208, 209, 221
Clovis point 39
Coatzacoalcos 10, 18, 27, 187, 191, 192
Coba 3, 31, 104, 112, 163, 172, 181, 182, 183, 184, 185, 196, 218
Cobos Palma, Rafael 169–170, 224
Cocom 184, 200, 204, 206, 207
Coe, Michael D. 7, 9, 12, 18, 19, 20, 26, 54, 55, 101, 105, 107, 157
Colas, Pierre R. 225
The Conquest 2, 11, 27–28, 51, 59, 127, 183
Conservatives 35, 105, 215
copal 85, 88, 203
Copan 4, 106, 107, 121–123, 125–130, 132, 134–137, 143–145, 159, 164, 167
copper 51, 164, 202
corbelled arch 77–78, 113, 165
corbelled vault 178
corn 5–6, 19–23, 25, 37, 39–52, 54, 58–61, 63–65, 73–75, 81, 83, 85, 88, 112, 119, 122, 132, 137, 141, 150, 151, 153, 165, 168, 170, 172, 178–179, 186–187, 192, 193, 194, 203, 208, 211, 213, 217, 219
Corn Belt 6
La Corona 107–108
corozo palm 20
Cortes, Hernan 1, 186–194, 204, 205, 206, 207–208, 213
corvee labor 152, 183
Cosmic Ceiba 105
cosmogram 52, 55, 138–139, 178, 199, 208
Costa Rica 12
Cowgill, George L. 91, 93, 94, 225
Cozumel 34, 164, 172, 186, 190, 196, 216
creation myth 4, 50, 52, 53–55, 70, 74–75, 181, 197–198
Cuba 34, 186, 188–190, 216
Cyphers, Ann 20, 24, 27

Dahlin, Bruce 38
Danta Pyramid 29, 30, 35, 61–62, 100, 112
Dark Sky 147
Dark Sun 146
de Avendano, Fr. Andres 209
de Landa, Diego 59, 157, 184, 194, 200
Delgado, Fr. 206
Demarest, Arthur A. 150–152
democracy 26
Denison, John 103
de Oli, Cristobal 190
Dias, Bernal 186, 187, 190, 192, 193
dibble stick 41
Diehl, Richard A. 7, 19
dire wolves 39
divine kings 74, 76, 95, 110, 135, 151–154, 160, 164, 196
divine kingship 4, 79, 147, 150, 152, 154, 164, 169, 174, 184, 193
Diving Eagle 190–194
Dixon, Alice 156
dogs 47–48, 189
Dominguez Carrasco, Maria del Rosario 104
Donna Marina 186–189, 190
Dorfman, John 36, 226
Dos Pilas 108, 119, 138–141, 143, 145, 148, 149–151
Double Bird 96, 136
drought 65–66, 80, 96, 135, 146–147, 151–154, 174, 184
Drucker, Philip 9, 24–26, 184, 226
Dumond, Don E. 211, 217, 218
dwarfs 84
dyes 41, 197
Dzibanche 107, 116
Dzibilchaltun 104, 163, 176

E-Group 62, 64, 74, 77, 109, 184
Early Preclassic 14, 201
Egypt 105, 121, 148, 175

Ehecatl 165, 179
18 Rabbit 4, 130, 131, 132, 134, 135, 136, 143, 145
Ek Balam 163, 170–174, 176, 179, 181, 185
El Chorro 150
El Duende 149, 151
El Mirador 1, 4, 29–32, 35, 37, 38, 54, 56, 60–62, 64, 65, 68, 71, 74, 80, 87, 97, 100, 112–113, 116, 135, 151–152, 163, 180, 191
Emal 163, 171
Empire State Building 29–30, 226
Epi-Olmec 28, 77
Escarcega 98, 100
ethnohistories 158–161, 176, 200–201, 208
eugenia 41
Europe 1, 6, 45, 116, 118, 121, 156, 212–213
European knights 2

Fash, William L. 135
feasts 63–64, 72, 207, 215
feather serpent balustrade 166
feathered serpent pyramids 92
Felipe Carrillo Puerto 218, 222
Fiery Claw 120, 132, 140–141, 145, 149
Fire Is Born 90–91, 94–95, 125, 127, 141, 180–181
First Crocodile 90–91, 94, 116, 146, 179, 181
First Quetzal Motmot 125, 129
flame brows 58
Flannery, K.V. 226, 238
flint 5, 41, 49, 75, 88–89, 108, 120, 132, 176, 203
Foias, Antonia 71–73, 226
Folan, William 104, 108, 112–113, 115, 146, 151, 182–183
Foliated Ahaw 127
Foster, Lynn V. 163, 167, 171, 227
foundation house 125, 135, 160
Fox, John Gerard 227
Freidel, David, A. 55, 74, 75, 79, 94, 97, 180–181
French Revolution 212, 217
frijoles 73
Fuensalida, Fr. 206
Furst, Peter 24

galeota 210–211
Galindo, Juan 121–123, 125
Garber, James 7, 75
Gates, William E. 11–12
Genesis (Bible) 50, 53
Gifford, Dr. John 39
Gijalva River 191
Gillespie, Susan 162
glyptodon 39
gold 1, 72, 156–157, 164, 167, 188, 193, 196, 202, 204, 208
Goodman, Joseph 106

Graham, Ian 36–38, 60, 77, 113, 159, 161, 170
Great Britain 122, 217
Great Jaguar Paw 79–82, 85, 87, 90, 94–95, 141
Great Plaza 70, 109, 123, 130–131, 138–139, 141–142, 144, 147
Great Sun Jaguar 119
Great Terrace 166, 168
Grove, David 7
Grube, Nicholae 74, 77, 94–96, 106, 109, 116, 119, 126–127, 129, 134–135, 137, 139, 141, 143, 145–147, 149, 150, 153, 169–170, 172
Guantanamo Bay 2
Guatemala 1–2, 11, 28–29, 37, 47, 49, 53, 56, 67–69, 71–72, 82, 90–91, 99–100, 107, 122–123, 164, 173, 191, 193, 194, 207–210
Gulf Coast 14, 57, 98, 161–162, 171, 189, 204
Gulf of Mexico 67, 192, 203
gumbo limbo 40, 52

Halakal 173
Hansen, Richard D. 51, 57–59, 61–64, 66
Harrison, Peter 45, 67–70, 138–139, 141, 143
Harvard University 10, 38, 68, 101
Hasaw Chan 4, 138
Hattie, Hurricane 37
Hawk Skull 85, 88
Heavenly Standard Bearer 4, 132, 134, 138–145, 148–149
hematite 19, 30, 83
Hero Twins 4, 50, 52–56, 58–59, 61–64, 74–75, 80, 86, 128, 132, 168, 171, 174
hieroglyphs 4, 53, 55, 68–69, 77, 80, 90–91, 100–101, 106, 108, 115, 125–126, 134, 141, 143, 146, 156–157, 162
High Priest's Temple 165–167, 197
Hodel, D.A. 151
Honduras 11–12, 35, 99, 106–107, 122, 125, 130, 190, 193, 196, 200, 202, 217–219, 221
House of the Governors 177, 179
Hueyapan Hacienda 8, 14
Hueyapan Head 9–10, 26–28
human sacrifice 19, 23, 75, 104, 179, 181, 196
Hun Hun-Ahaw 55, 58, 59, 74–75, 81
Hun Pik Tok 173–174
hunal 58, 63, 74–75, 88, 127, 180–181
Hunal Temple 127–129
hunchbacks 84

Ichmul de Morley 173
idea-ist 75
Iman, Santiago 213
INAH 10, 98, 109–110, 115
Incidents of Travel in Central America, Chiapas and Yucatan 123
indigo 88, 182, 196, 197
Inomata, Takeshi 149–151
intensive agriculture 45–46
intercropping 46
Isla Cerritos 163, 171, 223
isotopic analysis 42, 127, 129
Itza 158, 161–165, 167–174, 176, 184, 193, 196–197, 200–201, 204, 205–210
Itzamna 56, 59, 74, 203

jade 11, 16–17, 19–20, 25–26, 49, 71–75, 79, 81, 83, 85, 88, 95, 105, 115, 120, 125, 129, 132, 134, 143, 151, 164, 180–181
Jade Sky 35
jaguar 12, 71, 159, 168
jaguar-snake-bird images 159
Jasaw Chan 4
Jawbone 170, 176
Jefferson, Thomas 2
jester-god 127
Jimenez Moreno, Wigberto 160
Jones, Grant D. 190–193, 204, 207
Jose, Juan A. 31
Jupiter 80
Justeson, John 28

Kabah 161, 176, 179
Kachichel 53
Kak Tiliw 132, 134–135
Kaku Pacal 170, 176, 185
kaloomte 90–91, 127, 132, 134, 150, 180–181
Kaloomte Balam 95–96
Kaminaljuyu 80, 85, 90–91
Kan 4, 81, 87, 94, 96–97, 116, 145, 172–173, 180, 184, 193, 206–207, 209–210
Kan Ek 193, 206, 208–211
Kanasayab 100
katun 14, 27, 76, 96, 103, 135, 141, 147, 150, 153, 161, 201, 203
Kaufman, Terrence 28
Kejache 193, 207
Khrushchev, Nikita 44
Kidder, A.V. 31–32
killing alley 172, 174
Knickerbockers 121
Komchen 71
Kowalski, Jeff 159, 161, 164, 168–170, 176, 178–179
Kowoj 209–211
Kukulkan 161, 165, 170, 197

El Laberinto 112
Lacandon 12, 192

Lady Kayim 170, 176
Lady of Tikal 96
Lady 12 Macaw 42–143
Ladyville, Belize 39
Laguna Puerto Arturo 41
Lake Coba 182
lake district of Peten 32
Lake Peten Itza 193, 208, 209
Lake Petexbatun 148, 153
Lake Yaxha 35
Lamanai 204
land reform 68
Landon, Charles 99
LaPorte, Juan P. 69
Las Casas, Francisco de 190
Late Classic 73
Late Preclassic 57, 65
Lawler, Andrew 42
Le Plongeon, Augustus 156–158, 167
Leyden, Barbara 41, 154
liberals 213–215
lime 20, 49–52, 54–56, 61, 65, 93, 112, 138, 182, 208
Lindbergh, Charles 4, 31–35, 38, 45, 154
Lipscomb, Barney 99
logwood 41
Long Count 7, 14–15, 28, 38, 42, 77, 80, 103, 106, 115, 161, 172, 222
Lord Chac 176–179, 200
Lord Palmerston 122
Los Higos 135
Lost Generation 36
Lost World Pyramid 70, 74, 77, 82, 86, 87–88, 90
Lucero, Lisa J. 232
Lundell, Cyrus 99, 100–104, 113, 115–116, 120, 146, 182, 208

Macanxoc 182
MacArthur Foundation 38
macaws 71
Machaquila 36
The Machete and the Cross 217
Madiera, Percy C., Jr. 34–35, 37
maize 6, 21, 43, 44–45, 54, 84
Maize God 42, 56, 58–59, 63, 74–75, 86, 132, 134, 143, 168, 171, 203
Maler, Teobert 68
Malinche 187
Mam Maya 53
mamey 20
manioc 20, 48
mantles 71–72, 82, 156
Marcus, Joyce 7, 106, 108, 146
Martin, Simon 10–12, 74, 77, 94–96, 109, 119, 126–127, 129, 134–139, 141, 143, 145–149, 153, 209
Masaal 95, 139
masewalob 218, 219
Master of Fire 150

Matheny, Ray T. 38
Mathews, Peter 22, 34, 55, 107–108, 127, 131–132, 163, 167, 169, 176, 178–179, 201
Maudslay, Lord Alfred 68
may cycle 27, 200, 201
Maya blue 196, 197
Maya clay 65
Maya Mountains 49, 136, 151, 193
Mayapan 186, 194–197, 198–204, 207, 208
McAnany, Patricia A. 154
McKillop, Heather 53
McNeil, Cameron I. 129
megafauna 39
Melgar, J. M. 9, 28
Mendez, Col. Modesto 68
Mercado 168–169
Merida 32, 34–35, 104, 157, 176, 197, 210, 213–216, 220
Mesoamerica 2, 4, 5, 7, 8, 10, 11, 14–15, 19, 21–23, 28, 43–44, 75, 91–92, 94, 104, 108, 125, 157–159, 164–165, 168, 185, 197, 201, 203
Mexico 1–3, 7, 10–13, 15, 17, 20, 22, 27, 31, 32, 34, 36, 39, 43, 44, 46, 67, 69, 70, 80–82, 87, 90–91, 93–94, 98, 100, 104–105, 107, 117, 119, 122, 127, 141, 146, 155–156, 158–159, 161–165, 168–169, 171, 173, 178, 179, 185–192, 196, 203, 209, 212–217, 222
Mexico City 2–3, 11, 30, 32, 37, 67, 69, 76, 80, 90, 91, 96, 105, 108, 123, 155, 159, 189–190, 204, 211, 216
Mico Mountains 123, 145
Mid Classic Hiatus 97, 152
middens 20, 72, 184, 203
Middle Preclassic 14, 47
Mije-Sokean 28
Milbrath, Susan 197, 200, 202, 203
Miller, Mary Ellen 54, 162–163, 165, 167, 174, 185
milpa 39, 46, 212, 216
Minatitlan 10, 18
mining 36, 155, 182
Mirador Basin 29–31, 37, 39, 41, 43–47, 55–56, 59–61, 64–66, 79, 90, 139, 152, 181
Mixtec 7
Moctezuma II 15, 189–190
Monjas 161, 165, 174
Monos 29–30
Montejo, Francisco de 204
monumental architecture 7–8, 163, 174
Moral 107, 119
Morley, Frances 102
Morley, Sylvanus 10–12, 14, 36, 68, 101–105, 107, 160–161, 173

Morrow, Anne 31, 38
Motagua 72, 79, 125, 135–136, 164
mother culture 1, 7, 11, 159
motmot 127
Motul de San Jose 150, 153
Mt. Orizaba 190
Museum of Natural History 13
Mutal 68, 120

Naachtun 30
Nadal, Laura Filloy 234
Nahuatal 187, 196, 200
Nakbe 1, 4, 30, 35, 37, 38, 45, 56–59, 61–63, 65, 113
Napoleonic Wars 212
Naranjo 96, 116–120, 136, 139, 141, 144–146, 148, 152
National Autonomous University of Mexico 27
National Geographic Society 14, 61
Nazario Nah 219
necropolis 138
Neff, Hector 234
New Empire 99, 102, 160–161
New Orleans 11–12, 117, 158
Nicaragua 72
Night Sky 143–146
Nim Li Punit 130
nixtamalization 50
Noh Cah Santa Cruz 222
Nojpeten 193, 204, 205–208, 209, 210
North Acropolis 70, 74, 85, 91, 95, 138, 148, 180
Northern Lowlands 91
Nunnery 177–179

obsidian 5, 23, 49, 62, 71, 82, 93, 97, 164, 173, 180
Old Empire 68, 99, 102–103, 160
Olman 13, 20, 27–28
Olmec 1, 4, 7–28, 38, 42, 48, 52, 55–58, 62, 64, 75, 77, 79, 88, 184, 191, 197, 201
Orbita, Father 206
origins of corn 43
ostrocods 151
Ox-te-tun 08, 113
Oxkintok 91, 127, 180–181, 184

Pacal 105, 137, 170, 173, 176, 184
pacificos 218
Pagliaro, Jonathan B. 75, 234
Palenque 55, 77, 105–106, 117, 119, 122, 137, 143, 155–156, 165
palisades 146
Pan American Airways 31–32, 56
papaya 20
Paris, Elizabeth H. 155–156, 201–202
parrots 71
Pasion River 36, 70, 119, 148, 153
Pat, Jacinto 218

Peabody Museum 38, 68, 101
Pec, V. 218
Pecos, New Mexico 32
pellagra 50
Peraza Lope, Carlos 234
El Peru 81, 87, 90, 94, 107–108, 117, 119–120, 141, 145, 146
Peten 2, 11, 29–30, 32, 36–37, 39, 56, 67–69, 71–72, 74, 80–82, 87, 90–91, 94–96, 99, 101, 107, 113, 116, 118, 122, 126–128, 130, 132, 134–135, 137, 138, 141, 143, 146, 150, 152, 154, 163–164, 180, 182, 193, 203, 205, 207–212
Petexbatun 148–151, 153
Petra 121
Piedras Negras 34, 106, 165
Place of Reeds 160
Planet of the Apes 31
Platform of the Eagles 168
plazuela 48
Pohl, Mary E.D. 234
polychrome 77, 95
Pool, Christopher 234
Popol Hol 127–130
Poptun 36
Popul Vuh 53–54, 232, 238
Postclassic 4, 16, 27, 34, 154, 192–196, 201–204
power animals 22–23
Powis, Terry G. 230
Pratt and Whitney Wasp 32
Preclassic 1, 4, 14, 16, 31, 38, 44–45, 47–49, 52, 54, 55, 56–57, 60, 64–65, 71, 74–75, 77, 79, 112–113, 152, 154, 162, 166, 172, 180–181, 199, 201, 203–204, 221
Pretender Tikal 148
Principal Bird Diety 56, 58–59, 74, 128, 203
Proskouriakoff, Tatiana 106
Proyecto Calakmul 103
Puc, Venancio 220
Pueblo 189
Puerto Rico 2
Pugh, Marian Stirling 14
Pugh, Timothy W. 197, 199, 200
Puleston, Dennis 45
Punta de Chimino 149–151
Pusilha 130
Pustunich 100
Puuc 161, 163, 165–166, 171–178, 184, 195, 197, 204, 205, 216, 220
Pyramid of the Magician 156
Pyramid of the Sun 29, 92

La Quemada 169
quetzal 71, 75, 81, 88, 95, 145
Quetzalcoatl 159, 161–162, 165, 170–171, 174, 179, 185, 197, 202
Quiche 53

Quintana Roo 4, 30–31, 107, 222
Quirigua 107, 125–128, 130, 132, 134–136, 145, 164

radial temple 77
Rafinesque, Constantine 106
Rainey, Froelich 68
ramon (breadnut) 37, 40
Red House 161, 165, 171
Relacion of Bishop Landa 194
remote sensing 4, 31, 33
Revolutionary War (American) 211
Ricketson, Oliver 30, 31, 32, 38, 45
Ringle, William 170, 172, 174, 200
Rio Bec 146
Rio Dulce 191, 194, 206
Rio Lagartos 171
Room 22 174
Roys, Lawrence 196, 208
Roys, Ralph 207
Ruler 4 150
Ruler of Aguateca 150
Ruler 1 149
Ruler 28 146
Ruler 2 143, 149
Ruppert, Karl 36, 103

saber-tooth cats 39
Sabloff, Jeremy 195–196
sacbe 61, 112, 183–184, 218
sacred cenote 167, 205, 219
sacrificial victims 96, 182, 197, 199
sajal 82, 86–90
salt 21, 25, 37, 52, 62, 71–72, 79, 82, 85, 118, 163–164, 171, 182, 196
San Antonio Cayo 150
San Cristobal de las Casas 12
San Lorenzo 7, 10, 17–21, 24–28, 191, 201
San Martin Pajapan 10, 11, 12
San Pedro Martyr River 145
San Pedro Sula 190
San Salvador 12
Santa Anna, General 213
Santa Cruz 156, 219–221
Santa Cruz de Brazo 222
Santa Cruz Maya 156
sapodilla 20, 99–100
sascab 182
saw-grass marshes 41, 66
Schele, Linda 22, 54–55, 74–75, 127, 131, 163, 167, 169, 176, 178–179, 201
Schliemann, Heinrich 1, 3
Schreiner, Thomas 54
Scroll Serpent 119
Scrollhead 145
seasonally dry tropical forest 40
Seibal 70, 149–150, 153–154, 164

Seler, Eduard 9
serpent balustrades 197
serpent temples 197, 198, 199
Seven Macaw 53, 58–59, 128, 130
Shafer, Harry J. 49
shamanism 22–24
Sharer, Robert 69, 125, 127, 129, 162, 164, 176, 190–192, 200, 209, 221
Sheets, Payson 73, 132
shell beads 72–73, 85, 201
Shield Skull 119, 136–139, 148–149
short-faced bears 39
Shreiner, Thomas 50, 51, 65
Sikorsky pontoon aircraft 33
Sinai 121
Sirius 183
sister culture 1, 7
Site Q 107–108
Skull Rack 161, 168
Sky Witness 117–119
Sky X 134–135
slash and burn 21, 24, 31, 41, 46, 64, 70, 102
slaves 5, 72, 81, 93–94, 153, 183, 186–187, 221
Smith, Gregory J. 173
Smithsonian 14, 31
Smoke Imix 129–130
Snake 87, 97, 116–117, 145
Snakehead 81, 94, 96–98, 107–108, 116–117, 120, 145–146
Snakeheads 108, 116–117
Sokean 28
Southern Lowlands 1, 4, 69, 71, 154, 164, 169–170, 172, 178, 182, 193–194
Spain 188, 193, 204, 206, 212–213, 217
Spanish-American War 2
Spearthrower Owl 91, 94, 179, 181
Spinden, Herbert 159
squash 41, 44, 46, 48, 85
Steinbrenner, Larry 72
Stela C 14, 132
Stephens, John Lloyd 2–3, 67, 105, 121–125, 131, 136, 155, 157, 158–159, 175, 193
Stirling, Matthew 14–19, 24, 77, 157
Stone Hand Jaguar 116–117
strangler fig 40
strip mining 182
Structure 1 56–62, 145
Structure 7 99, 109, 113
Structure 2 5, 109–113, 115, 120, 140, 145–146
Stuart, David 68, 108
Superintendant of British Honduras 218–219
sweet peppers 44
swidden 41, 45–46

Tabasco 11, 15, 107, 162, 176, 186, 191, 196, 200, 204, 214
Tajin 185
talking cross 219, 221
Tamarindito 149, 150
Tata Naz 219
Tate, Carolyn 24
Taube, Karl 54, 58, 165
Tayasal 186, 193, 204, 205–208, 210, 211
Tedlock, Dennis 52
Tekax 220
Temple B at Tula 169
Temple of the Hieroglyphic Jambs 169
Temple of the Magician 178
Temple of the Three Lintels 165
Temple of the Warriors 161, 168–169
Temple I 85, 86, 142, 143, 144, 167
Temple VI 146
Temple 33 138, 139
Temple 22 138
Temple II 85, 138, 142
teosinte 43–44
Teotihuacan 29, 80–83, 85, 87, 90, 91, 93, 94, 96, 97, 125–128, 141, 159, 179–181, 183, 197
Terminal Classic 4, 155, 169, 180, 183, 196
terracing 46
terrigenous input 64–65
Thompson, Edward 157
Thompson, J. Eric 16, 59, 105, 196
Three Stone Place 107–108, 113
Thunder Horse 206, 210
Tigre 29–30, 35, 62–64, 172, 191
Tikal 2, 4, 11, 32, 38, 67–74, 76, 77, 80–83, 85–87, 90–91, 94–97, 103, 106, 108, 109, 113, 116–120, 122, 125–127, 130, 132, 134, 136–141, 143–154, 163, 167, 173, 176, 179–181, 184, 193–194, 209
Tinkas 220
Tintal 30, 65
Tipu 205–206
Tlahuizcalpantecuhtli 203
Tlaloc 92, 203
Tlazolteotl 203
Tollan 127, 159–160
Toltec 159–163
Tonina 95
Torres, Armijo 115
Totonac 7
Tozzer, Alfred 161–162, 232
trade 25–26, 32, 47, 49, 71–72, 79–80, 82, 87, 93, 107, 125, 130, 145–146, 150, 163–164, 171, 180, 196, 202–203, 218, 221
Traxler, Loa P. 69, 162, 164, 176, 190–191, 200, 209

Tres Zapotes 14–15, 18, 25, 28, 77
tribute 73–74, 93, 96, 130, 134, 141–142, 145–146, 165, 168, 174, 178, 180, 184, 186, 200, 202, 206, 209, 212, 213
Trippe, Juan 31
tripsicum 43
Troy 1, 3, 191, 207
Tula 127, 158–162, 168–169, 171, 185
Tula Chico 169
Tulane University 11
Tulum 3, 34, 99, 196, 221
tumbaga 202
tun 76, 108, 109, 113
turquoise 169
Tut, Ambrosio 68
Tutul Xius 176, 200
Tuxpena 100
Tuxtla 10, 15, 24
Twigge, Lt. 220
two-headed jaguar throne 157
Two Pyramid Place 145
Tzib, Fernando 150
Tzimin 213
Tzompantli 168

U Kit Kan Lek 172, 173
Uaxactun 11, 32, 64, 68, 91, 94–95, 127, 180
Ucanal 141, 153, 164
United Fruit Company 68
United States 4, 53, 99, 102, 106–107, 117, 122, 148, 158, 175, 211, 216
University of Pennsylvania Museum 33, 106, 191

Ursua, Martin de 208, 209, 210, 211
Usumacinta 3, 30, 70, 95, 106, 107, 117, 119, 145, 149, 164, 176, 191
Uxmal 1, 4, 5, 143, 156–157, 159, 161, 174, 176, 178, 179, 185, 194, 200, 204

vague year 76
Vaillant, George 12
Valladolid 213–215, 217–219
Valley of Mexico 190
vecinos 212, 213, 217, 221
Velasquez, Gov. 187–189, 190
La Venta 1, 7, 11–12, 15–21, 24–25, 28, 57, 62, 76, 79, 134
Venus 54–56, 61, 63, 80–81, 96, 132, 165, 170, 179, 199, 203
Veracruz 8, 10, 14, 18, 24, 28, 187

Wagner, Elizabeth 125
Wahl, David Brent 41
Waldeck, "Count" 105, 155, 156
Wallace, Henry 44
War Horse 206
War of the Castes 156, 211, 213
Waxaklahun-Ubah-K'awil 4
Waxaklajuun Ub'aah K'awiil 130
Webster, Daniel 123
were-jaguar 14, 16–17, 19, 24–25, 74
White, Christine D. 47–48, 106, 196
wild coffee 40
Wilkes, Garrison 42–44
Woman Cooking 101
World War I 102

Wright, Frank Lloyd 1, 91, 106, 174, 175, 177

Xibalba 52, 55, 110, 134, 143
Xipe 203
Xiu 176, 200, 202, 204, 207, 210
Xukpi 106, 125

yajaw 91
Yax Ehb Shock 74–76, 80, 82, 95, 138, 141
Yax K'uk Mo' 126–127, 129, 130
Yax Pasaj 125, 135–136
YaxBalam 55, 74
Yaxchilan 34, 95, 104, 117–118, 150
Yaxha 35, 68, 149
Yaxuna 112, 163, 180–181, 184, 185
Yucatan 1–2, 4, 30, 32, 34, 38–39, 48, 55–56, 59, 61, 65, 67–68, 70, 71, 79, 90, 99, 100–102, 104, 107, 123, 127, 143, 145, 154, 155–159, 161–165, 169–174, 176, 180, 181–182, 186, 187, 190–197, 200–201, 203–214, 215–222
Yucatec 2, 51, 56, 67, 101, 156, 161–162, 186, 193, 208, 219, 221
Yuknoom 119, 120, 137, 138, 139, 140, 145, 149
Yuknoom Head 119
Yuknoom the Great 119, 137–140, 145, 149

Zea mayas 41
Zemurray, Samuel 11
Zoomorph P 134

www.ingramcontent.com/pod-product-compliance
Ingram Content Group UK Ltd.
Pitfield, Milton Keynes, MK11 3LW, UK
UKHW050533150426
5217IPUK00026B/1924